The Rise of the Chinese Empire

*Frontier, Immigration, and Empire in Han China,
130 B.C.–A.D. 157*

漢代之邊疆與帝國

張春樹

The Rise of the Chinese Empire

Volume Two

FRONTIER, IMMIGRATION,

& EMPIRE *in* HAN CHINA,

130 B.C.–A.D. 157

Chun-shu Chang

THE UNIVERSITY OF MICHIGAN PRESS • ANN ARBOR

Copyright © by the University of Michigan 2007
All rights reserved
Published in the United States of America by
The University of Michigan Press
Manufactured in the United States of America
♾ Printed on acid-free paper

2010   2009   2008   2007   4   3   2   1

No part of this publication may be reproduced, stored
in a retrieval system, or transmitted in any form
or by any means, electronic, mechanical, or otherwise,
without the written permission of the publisher.

A CIP catalog record for this book is available from the British Library.

Library of Congress Cataloging-in-Publication Data

Chang, Chun-shu, 1934–
   The rise of the Chinese Empire / Chun-shu Chang.
     2 v.
   Includes bibliographical references and index.
   Contents: v. 1. Nation, State, and Imperialism in Early China, ca.
1600 B.C.–A.D. 8. — v. 2. Frontier, Immigration, and Empire in Han
China, 130 B.C.–A.D. 157.
    ISBN-13: 978-0-472-11533-4 (v. 1; cloth : alk. paper)
    ISBN-10: 0-472-11533-2 (v. 1; cloth : alk. paper)
    ISBN-13: 978-0-472-11534-1 (v. 2; cloth)
    ISBN-10: 0-472-11534-0 (v. 2; cloth)
   1. China—History—To 221 B.C.   2. China—History—Qin dynasty,
221–207 B.C.   3. China—History—Han dynasty, 202 B.C.–220 A.D.
I. Title.

DS741.5.C41616   2006
931—dc22   2006010072

This book is dedicated to the memory of five great teachers:
Professors Li Chi, Kao Ch'ü-hsun, & Ruey Yifu of Academia Sinica;
Professors Lien-sheng Yang & John K. Fairbank of Harvard University

Acknowledgments

THIS BOOK HAS BEEN a long time in the making, and I have benefited in the process from the assistance of many individuals, institutions, and organizations. I wish to acknowledge my profound indebtedness to them.

The writing of this book started in 1964 as a revision of my dissertation, completed at Harvard in 1963, entitled "The Colonization of the Ho-hsi Region: A Study of the Han Frontier System." In 1966, a chapter was published as "The Han Colonists and Their Settlements on the Chü-yen Frontier," and in 1977 another chapter was published as a long article on the Han and Hsiung-nu conflicts in early Han times. While the writing of this book continued, I also worked on a book on the Sung dynasty in the twelfth century and two books on the Ming-Ch'ing period, 1600–1700. These books were published in 1981, 1992, and 1998, respectively. The completion of this book was postponed until 1998 (with some critical additions and revisions made between 1999 and 2002), although the first draft was finished in the spring of 1982. The present version has a larger scope than and a different approach from the original project. It has four parts. The first treats the evolution of the state in early China up to the founding of the first centralized bureaucratic empire, the Ch'in (221–207 B.C.). The second treats the reformation of the Chinese empire under the Former (also called the Western) Han dynasty (202 B.C.–8 A.D.) through military expansion and a complex frontier system. The third treats the Han colonization of modern Central Asia, northern Korea, northern Vietnam, South Asia, and southeastern and southwestern China. The final part outlines how this grand expansion reshaped the political culture of the Chinese empire in its socioeconomic structure, national consciousness, concept of empire and state, and worldview.

In March 1982, without having placed the manuscript for publication, I accepted an invitation from Lanchou (Lanzhou) University to teach Han era wooden and bamboo documents (*Han-chien*), the basic source (about twelve thousand documents discovered between 1900 and 1944) of my dissertation and the main part of the new book. I left for China for six months, and the work of publication was postponed. However, during my stay in China a new and unusual research opportunity opened. I was able to see key documents recorded on some of the 22,500 Han era wooden and bamboo slips discovered in the Chü-yen and Tun-huang regions and other places in Kansu from 1972 to 1979. In addition, I was able to start my investigation of Han dynasty sites in Kansu and Sinkiang in the summer of 1982. That opened the door for continued archaeological fieldwork in 1983, 1985, and 1990. As a result, I explored almost all the major Han sites from central Kansu west to Shu-lei and Kashgar at the foot of the Pamirs in Sinkiang. Consequently I significantly revised and expanded the second and third parts of my book from 1982 to the mid-1990s. The book then went through several revisions until 1998, and the title was changed to *Frontier and Empire in Former Han China*. In 1999–2001, a few new bibliographical items were added and some revisions and additions were made. In early 2002, upon the suggestion of an anonymous reader for the University of Michigan Press, the book was changed to the current two-volume format by moving the third part of the original long manuscript to form the main body of the second volume while other parts (1, 2, and 4) constitute the first volume. Some critical changes in both volumes were also made accordingly. The new book then assumes the current title, *The Rise of the Chinese Empire*, and the two volumes are also titled individually as *Nation, State, and Imperialism in Early China* and *Frontier, Immigration, and Empire in Han China*. The book as it stands is up-to-date only to 2001 and in some special cases to the first half of 2002.

In my research for this book throughout the years, I am indebted to a number of libraries in this country and abroad, which have provided rare materials essential to my study. Space allows me to list only a few of them here: the Harvard-Yenching Library at Harvard University, the Chinese and Korean Section of the Library of Congress, the Far Eastern Library of the University of Chicago, the East Asiatic Library of the University of California at Berkeley, the East Asian Library of Columbia University, the Yale University Library, the Indiana University Library, the Fu Ssu-nien Library of Academia Sinica in Taipei, and the National Central Library in Taipei. I am grateful to the staff members of the Interlibrary Loan Department of the Harlan Hatcher Graduate Library of the University of Michigan, who arranged numerous loans from the libraries acknowledged here. For their kindness in allowing me to use some rare materials unavailable elsewhere, I wish to thank the senior staff members of Peking Library, Shanghai Library, Nanking University Library, Lanchou University Library, Chungshan University Library, T'ien-shui Culture Museum, Min-hsien Culture Museum, Wei-yuan Culture Museum, Wu-wei Culture Museum,

Chang-yeh Culture Museum, Chiu-ch'üan Culture Museum, Chia-yü Kuan Museum, Tun-huang Culture Museum, Sinkiang Provincial Museum (Archaeology and Culture), Fu-k'ang Culture Museum, Chi-mu sa-erh Culture Museum, Ch'i-t'ai Culture Museum, and Kashi (Kashgar) Museum. I owe much to my friends Wan Wei-ying and Ma Wei-yi and members of the staff of the Asia Library at the University of Michigan, who have gathered a remarkable Chinese collection that has been tremendously convenient for me, and to Miss Naomi Fukuda and Mr. Masaei Saito of the Asia Library at Michigan, who secured important Japanese books and periodicals for the library's Japanese collection.

Preparation of this book was greatly aided by generous research grants from Harvard University, the Harvard-Yenching Institute at Harvard University, and the Rackham School of Graduate Studies and the Center for Chinese Studies, both of the University of Michigan, as well as from the Chinese University of Hong Kong. My special appreciation goes to these institutions. I wish to express my special gratitude to the University of Michigan for its valuable research support through sabbatical leaves and the award of the Richard Hudson Professorship. I am most grateful to the Social Science Research Council and the American Council of Learned Societies for financial assistance for research on this project.

This book could not have been written without the profound instruction and inspiring guidance of my teachers in archaeology, ethnography, early Chinese history, sinological-historical methodology, and Ch'in-Han studies: Professors Li Chi, Kao Ch'ü-hsun, Ruey Yifu, Ch'en P'an, Ch'ü Wan-li, Lao Kan, Yang Hsi-mei, Li Tsung-t'ung, and Yao Ts'ung-wu, all of National Taiwan University and Academia Sinica; and Professors Lien-sheng Yang, William Hung, John K. Fairbank, and Benjamin Schwartz, all of Harvard University. I am forever indebted to them, and their example has forever guided me in my teaching career. I wish to express my profound gratitude to several senior scholars who through the years have encouraged and enriched me in my discussions with them on ancient and early Imperial Chinese history: Professors T'ao Hsi-sheng, Ch'ien Mu, Yang Hsiang-k'ui (Yang Xiangkui), Shih Nien-hai (Shih Nianhai), Wang Yü-ch'üan (Wang Yüquan), Teng Kuang-ming (Deng Guangming), Ho Ping-ti, Yen Keng-wang, Chow Tse-tsung, Chao T'ieh-han, Jachid Sechin (Cha-chi Ssu-ch'in), Kaizuka Shigeki, Hiraoka Takeo, and Muramatsu Yuji. I am most grateful to many friends who have benefited me by their works and discussions on some aspects of this study: T'ien Yü-ch'ing (Tian Yuqing), Ch'en Ch'iao-i (Chen Qiaoyi), Kwang-chih Chang, Cho-yun Hsu, Ying-shih Yü, Hao Yen-p'ing, Lo Jung-pang, David N. Keightley, Joseph F. Fletcher, Thomas Metzger, Timoteus Pokora, Han Fu-chih, Ma Hsien-hsing, Liu Kuang-hua (Liu Guanghua), Hsueh Ying-ch'ün (Xue Yingqun), Ch'u Shih-pin (Chu Shibin),

Wu Jen-hsiang (Wu Renxiang), Tu Ching-kuo (Du Jingguo), Mu Shun-ying (Mu Shunying), Wang Ping-hua (Wang Binghua), Wang Ming-che (Wang Mingzhe), Li Cheng (Li Zheng), Wu Chiu-lung (Wu Jiulong), Nunome Chōfō, Hibino Takeo, Fujieda Akira, Ōba Osamu, and Nagata Hedemasa. My former graduate students in ancient and early Imperial Chinese history benefited me enormously during the research and writing of their dissertations and theses under my direction: Barry Blakeley, P. Vijai Pillai, Karen Turner, Ellis Tinios, Charles Holcombe, Andrew Chittick, Charles Benn, Jonathan Skaff, Keith W. Taylor, Insun Yu, William Mills, Robert Haisen, and Kenneth Cochran, all in the United States; and Wang Ta-chih, Lai Ming-chiu (Li Ming-chao), Mu Fan, Yuan Lin, and Lo Ch'u-nan (Luo Chunan), all in China, Hong Kong, or Taiwan. Their searching questions about the structure of the Chinese empire, early Chinese society, and the variety and nature of primary sources have inspired me to rethink these issues, and I thank them for having given me such a challenging undertaking. Hou Ts'an (Hou Can) of Sinkiang (Xinjiang) and Shao Hung (Shao Hong) of Kiangsi (Jiangsi) attended my special class in Han-chien studies in Lanchou (Lanzhou) in 1985, wrote and published very important papers, and raised questions about the deciphering of the newly discovered Lou-lan (Lop-nor) documents and interpretations of certain old documents that made me reexamine these issues; I thank them for that.

My long stay in China and archaeological travels and explorations in Kansu (Gansu), Sinkiang, and Tsinghai (Qinghai) were made possible by the following: Presidents Liu Ping (Liu Bing), Nieh Ta-chiang (Nie Dajiang), Lu Jun-lin (Lu Runlin), and Hu Chih-teh (Hu Zhide) and Director Chang Ying-huai (Zhang Yinghaui), all of Lanzhou University; and the government authorities of Xinjiang Autonomous Region, T'ien-shui (Tianshui), Wei-yuan, Min-hsien, Yü-chung, Yung-teng, Wu-wei, Chang-yeh, Chiu-ch'üan, Tun-huang, T'u-lu-fan (Turfan), Yen-ch'i (Yenqi, Karashahr), K'u-erh-lei (Kurla), Lun-t'ai, K'u-ch'e (Kucha), Pai-ch'eng, Aksu, Kashi (Kashgar), and Hsi-ning (Sining) of Tsinghai. To all of them goes my deepest gratitude.

At Michigan, in the long course of preparation of the present study, I have benefited from discussions of some issues in the book with many scholars of various disciplines: David Bien, Juan Cole, John Eadie (now at Michigan State University), Geoffrey Eley, Albert Feuerwerker, John Fine, the late Charles Gibson, Victor Lieberman, Rudi Lindner, Shaw Livermore, Rudolf Mrazek, Brian Porter, Jack Price, Ronald Suny (now at the University of Chicago), the late Chester Starr, Roman Szporluk (now at Harvard University), Ray Van Dam, the late Sylvia Thrupp, Charles Tilly (now at Columbia University), Thomas Trautmann, Maris Vinovskis, Gerhard L. Weinberg (now at the University of North Carolina), Ernest Young, the late James I. Crump, Kenneth DeWoskin, and the late Alexander Eckstein. Al Feuerwerker and Alex Eckstein also gave me special encouragement in the early stages of this project. To all of them goes my profound appreciation for their help as friends and inspiration as colleagues.

Parts of the book have been presented at various meetings and before both popular and scholarly groups at numerous associations, academic institutions, and international conferences in the United States, Canada, Mexico, Europe, Japan, China, Hong Kong, and Taiwan. There numerous colleagues offered words of encouragement and constructive suggestions, and they all have my heartfelt thanks.

I should like to express my special thanks to the three anonymous readers for the press for their extremely beneficial suggestions, one of which led to the present structure of the manuscript in two volumes.

With a few exceptions, the Chü-yen documents discovered by the Sino-Swedish Scientific Expedition are at the Institute of History and Philology, Academia Sinica, in Taipei. The new Chü-yen documents, unearthed in the 1970s, and the Hsuan-ch'üan documents are at the Institute of Archaeology of Kansu Province in Lanzhou. I am extremely grateful to Dr. Li Chi for full access to the earlier Chü-yen documents and indebted to scholars at the Institute of Archaeology for the exchange of ideas and use of some documents. All *Han-chien* illustrations are based on the Chü-yen documents at the Institute of History and Philology in Academia (*Chü-yen Han-chien; Lai-tzu pi-lo yü huang-ch'üan*). The one Hsuan-ch'üan slip is from the collection in the Institute of Archaeology in Lanchou, Kansu (Lanzhou, Gansu; Tun-huang Hsuan-ch'üan Han-chien). All the other illustrations are photographs I took during my several archaeological trips to Kansu and Sinkiang from 1982 to 1990.

This book would never have been completed without the care, love, assistance, and encouragement of my family. Jean, Deborah, and Victor have lived with this book all their lives. Their activities and curiosity in their childhood and youth challenged my patience and inspired me to complete the book; their creativity and assistance in their adulthood helped me to consider its completion a hopeful possibility. David Giandomenico, Edward Feigen, and Susan Lord helped me set up a good working environment. Jean, Debbie, and Edward have also assisted me with moving books and cataloging files, two of the most essential tasks in this endless undertaking. David also used his unusual computer skills to redraw all but two of my original hand-drawn maps and important figures and charts, which has given me the comfort of knowing that the book has indeed reached its final stage. To all of them go my special appreciation and long-lasting affection. But my deepest feelings of appreciation go to the most important person in my adult life, Shelley Hsueh-lun Loh. Since the day we became a family, she has enriched me as a life partner and challenged me as a diaspora intellectual. She was with me when the first words of this book were written, she helped me when the final manuscript volumes were carried to the press, and she helped me in many other ways in between. To her goes my immeasurable gratitude and deepest devotion.

My special thanks go to Beni, Janet Fisk, Jeanette Diuble, Connie Hamlin, Lorna Altstetter, Susan Silagi, Marguerite Schaible, Janet Opdyke, Dawn L. Shewach, and Gordon J. Shewach, who typed patiently and artistically the many drafts of the various versions of the manuscript at different stages of its development. It was Jeanette Diuble's miraculous typing and organizational skills that made possible the completion of the last three drafts and the rearrangement of the completed manuscript. She has my profound appreciation and everlasting gratitude.

I wish to thank Janet Fisk for making my research environment most enjoyable. My profound gratitude goes to Dorothy Marschke and the late Jean Jones for their thoughtful assistance in the critical years 2000–2002, without which I would not have been able to complete the final step in this long, hard endeavor.

At the University of Michigan Press, Philip Pochoda and Mary Erwin have made this publication possible, Chris Hebert and Julia Goldstein bravely pushed and organized the large volumes into the actual process of production, and Chris Milton, Andrea Olson, and Janet Opdyke edited and polished the final product. To all of them goes my profound gratitude.

Contents

List of Tables and Illustrations   xv

A Note about Romanization   xix

Chronology: Han Rulers and Reigns,
221 B.C.–A.D. 220   xxi

Equivalents of Weights and Measures   xxiii

Basic Sources, Conventions, and Style of Citing Han
Wooden and Bamboo Documents   xxv

General Abbreviations and Translations of Technical Terms   xxxi

Preface   xxxiii

Introduction: Virgin Land, National Security, and
Agricultural Colonization   1

1. The Han Frontier System: Origins, Theories, and
   Structural-Functional Patterns   15

2. The Han Colonists in Chü-yen: The Organization,
   Composition, and Character of the Han Frontiersmen   23

3. The Han Settlements in Chü-yen: Structure, Pattern,
   and Function   79

4. Population on the Han Frontier: Numbers, Distribution,
   and Characteristics   107

5. The Making of a Han Frontier Region: Control and
   Communication in Chü-yen   129

Conclusion: Frontier, Colonization, and Empire   173

Major Dynasties and Periods of China   179
Notes   181
Glossary   223
Han-chien Terms   233
Selected Bibliography   239
Index   293
About the Author   301

Tables and Illustrations

TABLES

1. Expansion of Borders in the Historical and Developmental Stages 22
2. Command Structure of the Han Garrison Establishment 27
3. Command Structure of the *T'un-t'ien* Organization in Chü-yen 28
4. Rank and Pay Structure of Han Garrison Personnel in Chü-yen (Former Han period) 30
5. Local Administrative Divisions and Channels of Authority in the Chü-yen Region 31
6. Command Structure of the *Hsien* Administration and the Garrison Establishment in Chü-yen 33
7. Stature of Han Chinese Adults 50
8. Height Differentials between Interior and Ho-hsi Chinese 51
9. Regional Background of Han Settlers and Garrison Personnel in Chü-yen 54
10. Population Density and Natural and Human Calamities in Han China, 104 B.C.–A.D. 9 56
11. Distribution of Aristocratic Ranks among Han Settlers and Garrison Personnel in Chü-yen 60
12. Young Aristocratic Rank Holders Recorded in the Chü-yen Documents 64
13. Han Social Stratification, 103 B.C.–A.D. 9 69
14. Age Distribution of the Han Colonists in Chü-yen 72
15. Regional Background of the *Ch'i-shih* in Chü-yen 74
16. Han Garrison Settlements in Chü-yen: Major Units and Their Modern Locations 81

17. Major Garrison Settlements in Chü-yen   85
18. Numbered Watch Stations in Chü-yen   87
19. Residential Wards in Chü-yen District   90
20. Common *Li* Names between Chü-yen and Other Regions: Frontier Development and the Migration of Place Names   91
21. Density of Han Settlement in Chü-yen   102
22. Distribution of Soldiers among the Watch Stations   108
23. Han Family Size as Recorded in the Chü-yen Documents   120
24. Selected Demographic Characteristics of the Population of Chü-yen   126
25. Han Family Types as Seen in the Chü-yen Documents   128
26. Geographical Origins of Carts in Chü-yen   145
27. Organization of Carts in Chü-yen   146
28. Privately Owned Horses in the Garrisons   149
29. Characteristics of Horses on the Chü-yen Frontier   150
30. Provisions for Horses in Chü-yen   151
31. Characteristics of Oxen on the Chü-yen Frontier   153
32. Time Divisions in Han Times   167
33. Time Limits for Transmission of Han Correspondence as Seen in the Chü-yen Documents   169
34. Speed of Postal Transmission in Chü-yen   170

PLATES

Plates follow page 120

1. Headquarters of the chief commandant of Yü-men Pass
2. Remains of a Han oven in Yü-men Pass
3. Ruins of the "River Granary City"
4. Ruins of a Han beacon tower and watch station
5. Register of station carts dated 23 B.C.
6. Imperial decree dated 61 B.C.
7. Three-piece staff report on an official's leave
8. Three Han documents from Chü-yen
9. Register of weapons and related items dated A.D. 93–95
10. Two Han documents found in Chü-yen
11. Part of the headquarters of the Chia-ch'ü commandant (P'o-ch'eng *tzu*)
12. Han silk document found in P'o-ch'eng *tzu*

FIGURES

1. Plans of garrison settlements in Chü-yen: city, fortress, and watch stations   95
2. Reconstruction of three probable plans for a Han *li*   97
3. Reconstruction of a Han *li* without an outer enclosure   97
4. Spatial pattern of the Han settlement network in Chü-yen (Chü-yen *tu-wei*)   104
5. Dominance in the Han settlement network in Chü-yen   105
6. Plan of the Chin Pass establishment   136
7. Communications routes in northern Chü-yen   155

MAPS

1. The Han Colonial Empire in the First Century B.C.   2
2. The Ho-hsi Region during the Han Dynasty   7
3. Major Han Garrison Settlements in the Chü-yen Region   82
4. The Han Road Network on the Northwestern Frontier   159

A Note about Romanization

I HAVE FOLLOWED THE Wade-Giles system in my romanization of Chinese characters. But I have also made some necessary modifications, such as leaving out the umlauts in the words *yuan* (instead of *yüan*), *lueh* (instead of *lüeh*), *hsu* (instead of *hsü*), and *hsueh* (instead of *hsüeh*), when such changes do not affect the basic phonetic structure of a word. For place-names, I have generally employed the *Postal Atlas of China*, thus Peking for Wade-Giles's Pei-ching, Nanking for Nan-ching, Kiangsu for Chiang-su, Kansu for Kan-su, Sinkiang for Hsin-chiang, Tsinghai for Ch'ing-hai, Lanchow (or Lanchou) for Lan-chou, and so on. In certain special cases, in order to make the context clear to the reader, I have added a word romanized in the more recent pinyin system after the Wade-Giles romanization, for example, Lanzhou after Lanchou, Gansu after Kansu, Xinjiang after Sinkiang, Qinghai after Tsinghai, Zhang after Chang, Ju after Chü, Xia after Hsia, Run after Jun, and Deng after Teng.

Chronology: Han Rulers and Reigns, 221 B.C.–A.D. 220

The Han dynasty, 202 B.C.–A.D. 220
    The Former (Earlier, Western) Han
        Emperor Kao (Kao-ti, Kao-tsu, Liu Pang*), 202–195 B.C.
        Emperor Hui (Hui-ti), 195†/194/††–188 B.C.
        Empress Lü, 187–180 B.C.
        Emperor Wen (Wen-ti), 180/179/–157 B.C.
        Emperor Ching (Ching-ti), 157/156/–141 B.C.
        Emperor Wu (Wu-ti), 141/140/–87 B.C.
        Emperor Chao (Chao-ti), 87/86/–74 B.C.
        Emperor Hsuan (Hsuan-ti), 74/73/–49 B.C.
        Emperor Yuan (Yuan-ti), 48–33 B.C.
        Emperor Ch'eng (Ch'eng-ti), 33/32/–7 B.C.
        Emperor Ai (Ai-ti), 7/6/–1 B.C.
        Emperor P'ing (P'ing-ti), A.D. 1–5
        Ju-tzu Ying, A.D. 5/6/–8
The Hsin dynasty
        Wang Mang,* A.D. 9–23
    The Latter (Later, Eastern) Han
        Emperor Kuang-wu (Kuang-wu-ti, Liu Hsiu*), A.D. 25–57
        Emperor Ming (Ming-ti), A.D. 57/58/–75
        Emperor Chang (Chang-ti), A.D. 75/76/–88
        Emperor Ho (Ho-ti), A.D. 88/89/–105

*Founder's name (surname first).
†The year in which a new ruler was enthroned.
††The year in which a ruler's reign officially began.

Emperor Shang (Shang-ti), A.D. 106
Emperor An (An-ti), A.D. 106/107/–144
Emperor Ch'ung (Ch'ung-ti), A.D. 145
Emperor Chih (Chih-ti), A.D. 146
Emperor Huan (Huan-ti), A.D. 146/147/–167
Emperor Ling (Ling-ti), A.D. 168–188
Emperor Shao (Shao-ti), A.D. 189
Emperor Hsien (Hsien-ti), A.D. 189–220

Equivalents of Weights and Measures

THE HAN PERIOD

1 *liang* = 24 *shu* = 15.25 grams
1 *hsiao-shih* = 3/5 (0.6) *ta-shih*
1 *shih* (*hsiao-shih*) or *hu* = 10 *tou* = 100 *sheng* = 0.565 U.S. bushel = 19.9682 liters
1 *chung* = 6 *hu* 4 *tou* = 3.616+ U.S. bushels
1 *ch'ih* (foot) = 0.232 meter = 9.134 inches
1 *pu* (full pace) = 6 *ch'ih* = 1.392 meters
1 *chang* = 10 *ch'ih* = 2.32 meters = 7 feet 7.3403 inches
1 *p'i* (bolt) = 4 *chang* = 9.28 meters = 30 feet 5.3536 inches
1 *li* (mile) = 300 *pu* = 1,800 *ch'ih* = 1368.1+ English feet = 417 meters = 0.259 mile
1 *mou* or *mu* (acre) = 0.11391+ English acre
1 *ch'ing* = 100 *mou* = 11.391+ English acres
1 *chin* (catty) = 16 *liang* = 244 grams = 0.538 pounds
1 *chün* = 30 catties = 7.32 kilograms
1 *chin* of actual gold = 244 grams = 10,000 *ch'ien* (cash, copper coins)

These weights and measures represent the standard system of Han times. Changes and regional variations in the Han dynasty and other periods are noted where applicable. The Ch'in system was different in some respects and will be so noted.

Basic Sources, Conventions, and Style of Citing Han Wooden and Bamboo Documents

BASIC SOURCES FOR HAN WOODEN
AND BAMBOO DOCUMENTS

Chang Chia-shan	*Chang Chia-shan Han-mu chu-chien "Erh-ssu-ch'i hao Mu"* (Han Bamboo Documents from Tomb 247 at Chang Chia-shan in Chiang-ling, Hupei), ed. Cheng-li hsiao-tsu. Beijing: Wen-wu ch'u-pan she, 2001.
Chang Feng	*Han-Chin hsi-ch'ui mu-chien hui-pien* (A Collection of the Wooden Documents of the Han and Chin Periods Discovered in Western China). Shanghai: Yu-cheng shu-chü, 1931.
Chavannes, Édouard 1913	*Les documents chinois découverts par Aurel Stein dans les sables du Turkestan Oriental.* Oxford: Oxford University Press, 1913.
Chia-pien (Cp)	*Chü-yen Han-chien chia-pien* (The Han Wooden and Bamboo Documents from Chü-yen, Pt. 1), ed. Institute of Archaeology, Chinese Academy of Sciences. Peking: K'o-hsueh ch'u-pan she, 1959.
Chü-yen I	*Wen-wu* (Cultural Relics) no. 1 (1978): 1–43.
Chü-yen II	*K'ao-ku* (Archaeology) no. 2 (1979): 174–80.
Chü-yen (*Chia-i pien*)	*Chü-yen Han-chien chia-i pien* (The Han Wooden and Bamboo Documents from Chü-yen, Pts. 1 and 2), ed. Institute of Archaeology, Chinese Academy of Sciences. 2 vols. Peking: Chung-hua shu-chü, 1980 [1981]. Pt. 1: plates; pt. 2: text.

Chü-yen Han-chien pu-pien	(The Han Wooden and Bamboo Documents from Chü-yen, Supplement), ed. Chien-tu cheng-li hsiao-tsu, Institute of History and Philology, Academia Sinica. Taipei: Chung-yang yen-chiu yuan, 1998.
Chü-yen hsin-chien (1990)	*Chü-yen hsin-chien: Chia-ch'ü Hou-kuan yü ti-ssu Sui* (The New Han Wooden and Bamboo Documents from Chü-yen: Chia-ch'ü *Hou-kuan* and Fourth *Sui*), comp. Kansu sheng wen-wu k'ao-ku yen-chiu so et al. One vol. in simplified characters. Peking: Wen-wu ch'u-pan she, 1990.
Chü-yen hsin-chien	*Chü-yen hsin-chien: Chia-ch'ü Hou-kuan* (The New Han Wooden and Bamboo Documents from Chü-yen: Chia-ch'ü *Hou-kuan*), comp. Kansu sheng wen-wu k'ao-ku yen-chiu so et al. Two vols. in regular characters. Vol. 1: text; vol. 2: plates. Peking: Chung-hua shu-chü, 1994.
Conrady, August	*Die chinesischen Handschriften-und sonstigen Kleinfunde Sven Hedins in Lou-lan*. Stockholm: Generalstatens Litografiska Anstalt, 1920.
HCHC	*Hsuan-ch'üan Han-chien* (The Deciphered Text of the Hsuan-ch'üan Han Wooden and Bamboo Documents). Manuscript containing the deciphered text of 17,867 documents.
Ho-chiao (CYC)	*Chü-yen Han-chien Shih-wen ho-chiao* (Collected Collations of Old Deciphered Texts of the Han Wooden and Bamboo Documents from Chü-yen), ed. Li Chün-ming et al. 2 vols. Peking: Wen-wu ch'u-pan she, 1987.
Hsia Nai 1948	"Hsin-huo chih Tun-huang Han-chien" (Newly Discovered Han Wooden and Bamboo Documents in the Tun-huang Region). CYYY 19 (1948): 235–65.
Hsuan-ch'üan Han-chien	"Tun-huang Hsuan-ch'üan Han-chien" (Archaeological Report of the Discovery of Han Wooden and Bamboo Documents at Hsuan-ch'üan in the Tun-huang Region) and "Tun-huang Hsuan-ch'üan Han-chien shih-wen" (The Deciphered Text of the Hsuan-ch'üan Han Wooden and Bamboo Documents: Selections), by Kansu wen-wu k'ao-ku yen-chiu-so. *Wen-wu* 5 (2000): 21–46.
Lao Kan 1943–44	*Chü-yen Han-chien k'ao-shih* (The Deciphered Text with Special Studies of the Han Wooden and Bamboo Documents from Chü-yen), ed. Lao Kan. Li Chuang:

	Chung-yang yen-chiu-yuan li-shih yü-yen yen-chiu so (Shih-yü so), 1943–44.
Lao Kan 1949	*Chü-yen Han-chien k'ao-shih,* ed. Lao Kan. 2 vols. Shanghai: Shang-wu yin-shu kuan, 1949.
Lao Kan 1960a	*Chü-yen Han-chien k'ao-shih chih-pu* (The Han Wooden and Bamboo Documents from Chü-yen: Deciphered Texts and Studies), ed. by Lao Kan. Taipei: Chung-yang yen-chiu yuan shih yü so, 1960.
Lao Kan 1957	*Chü-yen Han-chien t'u-pan chih-pu* (The Han Wooden and Bamboo Documents from Chü-yen: Plates), ed. by Lao Kan. Taipei: Chung-yang yen-chiu yuan shih-yü so, 1957. 3 vols.
Lao Kan 1985	*Han-Chin Hsi-ch'ui mu-chien hsin-k'ao* (New Studies of the Wooden and Bamboo Documents of the Han and Chin Periods Discovered in Western China). Taipei: Chung-yang yen-chiu yuan shih-yü so, 1985.
Lin Mei-ts'un	*Shu-lo ho liu-yü ch'u-t'u Han-chien* (The Han Wooden and Bamboo Documents Discovered along the Su-lo River [in Western Kansu]). Peking: Wen-wu ch'u-pan she, 1984.
Lou-lan Ni-ya	*Lou-lan Ni-ya ch'u-t'u wen-shu* (Documents Discovered in Lou-lan and Ni-ya [in Sinkiang]), ed. Lin Mei-ts'un. Peking: Wen-wu ch'u-pan she, 1985.
LPCR	*Lo-pu nao-erh k'ao-ku chi* (Archaeological Explorations and Excavations in the Lop-nor Region [in Sinkiang]), by Huang Wen-pi. Peking: Chung-kuo k'o-hsueh k'ao-ch'a t'uan, 1948.
LSCC	*Liu-sha chui-chien fu pu-i* (Documents on Wood and Bamboo in the Desert of Western China, with Supplements), ed., with notes, Wang Kuo-wei and Lo Chen-yü. 4 vols. Chen-han lou, 1914.
Ma Hsien-hsing	*Chü-yen Han-chien hsin-pien* (A New Edition of the Han Wooden and Bamboo Documents from Chü-yen), ed. Ma Hsien-hsing et al. Taipei: Chien-tu hsueh-hui, 1981.
Maspero, Henri 1953	*Les documents chinois de la Troisième Expédition de Sir Aurel Stein en Asie Central.* London: British Museum, 1953.
Meng Fan-jen	*Lou-lan Shan-shan chien-tu nien-tai hsueh yen-chiu* (A Study and Chronology of the Documents on Wood and Bamboo from Lou-lan and Shan-shan [in Sinkiang]),

	by Meng Fan-jen. Ürümqi, Sinkiang [Xinjiang]: Jen-min ch'u-pan she, 1995.
Photos	Photos of all Chü-yen *Han-chien* in the Institute of History and Philology, Academia Sinica (Chung-yang yen-chiu yuan shih-yü so). Photographs taken in the 1960s (large size).
San-chien	*San-chien chien-tu ho-chi* (A Collection of Documents on Wood and Bamboo Not Found in Major Collections), ed. Li Chün-ming and Ho Shuan-ch'üan. Peking: Wen-wu ch'u-pan she, 1990.
She-lan pen	*She-lan pen Han-chien shih-wen* (Manuscript Copy of the Deciphered Text of the Han Wooden and Bamboo Documents from Chü-yen), by Lao Kan. Peiping, manuscript.
Shih-ts'ui	*Chü-yen hsin-chien shih-ts'ui* (Decipherings and Studies of Selected New Han Wooden and Bamboo Documents from Chü-yen), by Hsueh Ying-ch'ün et al. Lanchou, Kansu: Lanchou ta-hsueh ch'u-pan she, 1988.
Shui-hu-ti	*Shui-hu-ti Ch'in-mu Chu-chien* (The Ch'in Documents on Bamboo from Shui-hu-ti [in Yun-meng, Hupeh]). Peking: Wen-wu ch'u-pan she, 1978.
THHCW (1949)	*Tun-huang Han-chien chiao-wen* (A Corrected Version of the Han Wooden and Bamboo Documents from Tun-huang), by Lao Kan, in Lao Kan 1949.
THHCW (1960)	*Tun-huang Han-chien chiao-wen* (A Corrected Version of the Han Wooden and Bamboo Documents from Tun-huang), by Lao Kan, in Lao Kan 1960a.
Tun-huang Han-chien	*Tun-huang Han-chien* (The Han Wooden and Bamboo Documents from Tun-huang), comp. Kansu sheng wen-wu k'ao-ku yen-chiu so et al. 2 vols. Peking: Chung-hua shu-chü, 1991–92. Vol. 1: text; vol. 2: plates.
Tun-huang Han-chien shih-wen	*Tun-huang Han-chien shih-wen* (The Deciphered Text of the Han Wooden and Bamboo Documents from Tun-huang), comp. Wu Jen-hsiang, Li Yung-liang, and Ma Chien-hua. Lanchou, Kansu: Jen-min ch'u-pan she, 1991. Includes Chavannes, Maspero, and Hsia Nai.
Wu-wei (1964)	*Wu-wei Han-chien* (The Han Wooden and Bamboo Documents from Wu-wei [in Kansu]), ed. Kansu sheng po-wu kuan and Chung-kuo k'o-hsueh yuan k'ao-ku yen-chiu so. Peking: Wen-wu ch'u-pan she, 1964.

CITING HAN WOODEN AND BAMBOO DOCUMENTS • XXIX

Wu-wei (1975)	Wu-wei Han-tai i-chien (The Han Wooden and Bamboo Documents on Medicine from Wu-wei), ed. Kansu sheng po-wu kuan and Wu-wei hsien wen-hua kuan. Peking: Wen-wu ch'u-pan she, 1975.
Yin-ch'üeh shan	Yin-ch'üeh shan Han-chien shih-wen (The Han Wooden and Bamboo Documents from Yin-ch'üeh Shan [in Lin-i, Shantung]), comp. Wu Chiu-lung. Peking: Wen-wu ch'u-pan she, 1985.
Yin-wan	Yin-wan Han-mu chien-tu (The Han Wooden and Bamboo Documents from Yin-wan [in Lien-yun-kang, Kiangsu]), comp. Lien-yun-kang shih po-wu kuan et al. Peking: Wen-wu ch'u-pan she, 1996–97.

CONVENTIONS

The following conventions for citing wooden and bamboo documents are used.

a. For a document from the *Chü-yen Han-chien k'ao-shih chih-pu* (Taipei, 1960), the plain document number is given. For example, 2781 means the document numbered this way in Lao Kan 1960a.
b. For a document from the *Chü-yen Han-chien k'ao-shih* (Shanghai, 1949), the number of the document followed by its page number in parentheses is given. For example, 140.5 (87) means document 140.5 on page 87 in Lao Kan 1949.
c. For a document from the *Chü-yen Han-chien chia-pien* (Peking, 1959), the document number prefixed by the abbreviation of this work, Cp, is given. For example, Cp 1102 means the document numbered 1102 in the *Chia-pien*.
d. Occasionally, the plate number of a document is given at its end, mostly following the regular document number(s). This number is prefixed by the abbreviation pl. (plate). If no additional abbreviation is attached, the reference is to a plate in Lao Kan 1957 (i.e., *Chü-yen Han-chien t'u-pan chih-pu*). If it is further followed by Cp, the reference is to a plate in the *Chia-pien*.
e. For a document from other collections, the document number is prefixed by the abbreviation of the work, for example, *Chü-yen hsin-chien* EPT–59: 582.
f. Wooden documents in other collections are cited with both the titles of the collections, or their abbreviations, and the document numbers.

XXX • CITING HAN WOODEN AND BAMBOO DOCUMENTS

STYLE

In citing and translating the Han wooden and bamboo documents, the following symbols are used.

1. In Translation
   (x) ....   The upper part of a strip broken off.
   .... (x)   The lower part of a strip broken off.
   ... (?)   Two or more undecipherable characters in the original Han era Chinese document.
   (?)   An undecipherable character in the original Chinese document.
   ...   An omission in the English translation.
   [?]   A tentative English translation.

2. Original Chinese Documents
   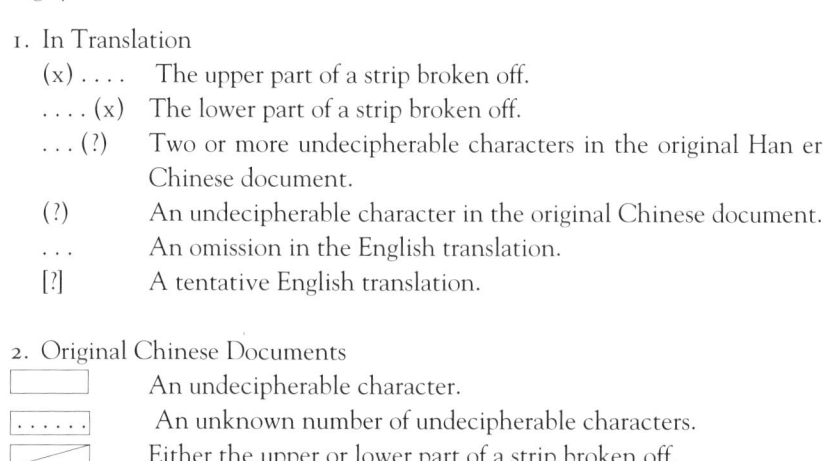
   An undecipherable character.
   An unknown number of undecipherable characters.
   Either the upper or lower part of a strip broken off.
   ......   An omission in the citation.
   (?)   Tentative deciphering suggested in my citation.

General Abbreviations and Translations of Technical Terms

app.	appendix	fig.	figure
b.	born	ibid.	in the same place
ca.	circa	no.	number
cf.	compare	p.	page
chap.	chapter	pl.	plate
comp.	compiled, compiler	pt.	part
d.	died	r.	reigned
diss.	dissertation	rev.	revised
doc.	document	sec.	section
ed.	editor, edited, edition	ser.	series
esp.	especially	suppl.	supplement
et al.	and others	trad.	traditional dating
ff.	and following	trans.	translated, translator
fl.	flourished	vol.	volume

ch'ien	cash, a round copper coin with a square hole in the middle
chüan	chapter, volume
chün	prefecture, province, or commandery, depending on the historical context and time (mostly Ch'in and Han); in general, "commandery" is the most appropriate translation before 180 B.C., "province" for 180–90 B.C., and "prefecture" after 90 B.C.
hsiang	county (Ch'in and Han)
hsien	district (Ch'in and Han)
kuo	(feudal) kingdom
li	ward
nien	age, aged
sui	age (Chinese system counting age)

Preface

IN BROAD TERMS, this study traces the origins and evolution of the state in ancient and early Imperial China from the seventeenth century B.C. to the first century A.D. In more specific terms, it examines the critical role that the frontiers or peripheral zones played in shaping the course of Chinese history. The main body of the text, however, focuses on the territorial expansion and colonization of the frontier regions and the growth of the state and the empire in early Imperial China and how all that changed the worldview, the self-perception, and the conceptualization of a Chinese nation in the Chinese empire during its first four hundred years. In its thematic dimension, the work consists of five sections in two volumes: the larger issues about the evolution and models of the state, nation formation, and empire building; the origins and processes of military and territorial expansion; and the detailed organization and operational mechanics of the huge colonial and frontier systems. That being the case, I will give a special introduction to the question of how these themes and issues were interconnected in the history of the period under discussion and hence how this study is constructed and structured as a coherent whole.

The Ch'in (221–207 B.C.) and Han (202 B.C.–A.D. 8, 25–220) were the first two major dynasties of Imperial China. Not only did they lay down the institutional foundations of the political system of a centralized bureaucratic Chinese empire, but they also defined the main territorial dimensions of that empire. Although the Ch'in regime, founded by the First Emperor (Shih huang-ti; Ying Cheng, 260/259–210 B.C., r. 221–210 B.C.), was short-lived, it initiated both structures. The Han, founded by Kao-ti (Liu Pang, 247–195 B.C., r. 202–195 B.C.), developed both to their maturity. But it took a long time for the Han to reach that stage. When the Han dynasty began in 202 B.C., it inherited an empire that was torn apart by six years of war and destruction between contending independent states after the collapse of the Ch'in in 207 B.C. For its first seventy years, the Han empire was plagued by both internal political instability and external foreign challenge. For the latter, the most threatening was the continuing Hsiung-nu attack on the northern and northwestern borders. The Hsiung-nu forces even marched twice to the vicinity of the imperial capital at Ch'ang-an and even made the survival of the Han empire doubtful for a period of time. But for a variety of reasons the Han was unable to make an effective counterattack, not until the reign of Han Wu-ti (Liu Ch'e, 156–87 B.C., r. 141–87 B.C.).

In Wu-ti's time, the Han initiated a massive attack on the Hsiung-nu and its allies, aiming to eliminate the threat once and for all. The Han forces then marched far into the Hsiung-nu strongholds in the north, in modern Inner and Outer Mongolia, and regained the territories lost to the Hsiung-nu during the six years of the Ch'in-Han transition, 208–202 B.C. In the northwest, the Han troops crossed the former westernmost boundary by the Yellow River under the Ch'in and advanced all the way to the western border of modern Kansu to gain control over all of the region of Ho-hsi (west of the Yellow River) and part of the western Ch'iang territory in the Huang river valley in modern Tsinghai and modern southern Ninghsia (now part of Inner Mongolia). And then they moved to modern Sinkiang, then called Hsi-yü (the Western Regions), and established colonies to command the thirty-eight (traditionally thirty-six) native states in the region. In 104–101 B.C., Han Wu-ti's army of over 70,000 soldiers, 100,000 oxen, and 30,000 horses marched over the Pamirs into Central Asia and reached as far as Ta-yuan (capital in Ferghana) and K'ang-chü (Sogdiana, capital in Maracanda [Samarkand]) in modern Uzbekistan. The Han military conquest in the west reached its zenith, and it secured the safety of the eastern section of the route of communication between Han China and Ta-Ch'in (the Roman Empire), later called the Silk Route, which extended for over 6,000 miles (4,200 miles in straight distance) from the Han capital in Ch'ang-an to Tyre (in Lebanon) on the eastern shore of the Mediterranean Sea. In the many campaigns in these western regions (Ho-hsi, Ch'iang, and Hsi-yü) and the Hsiung-nu land, the Han sent a total force of over 1.2 million cavalrymen, 800,000 foot soldiers, and 10.5 million men in support and logistic roles. The total area of land seized in Ho-hsi alone was 426,700 square kilometers. In developing this region, the Han spent 100 billion in cash per year, compared to the regular annual government revenue of 12 billion. In the process, the Han government moved from the interior over 1 million people to populate and develop the Ho-hsi region. Thus, the Han conquest of the land west of the Yellow River was the greatest expansion in Chinese history, and the Han development of the Ho-hsi region was the grandest scheme of colonization in the annals of Imperial China.[1]

The main focus of the present study is on the history, process, operational mechanics, administrative organization, physical structure, and far-reaching impact of the colonization of the Ho-hsi region and the Western Regions in Former Han times (202 B.C.–A.D. 8). It also examines the origins, causes, processes, and consequences of the Han westward expansion movement under Wu-ti, which influenced not only the Han empire itself but also the later course of Chinese history. It also traces the historical origins and theoretical framework of the Han frontier system, the structural base of the blueprint for the Han colonization of the Ho-hsi region. Finally, it looks into the question of how the Han employed their experience of frontier development in Ho-hsi to establish colonies in the Hsi-yü region in modern Sinkiang and other new frontier territories on the Han borders. The Han used its frontier structures as a critical component of empire building. The military expansion resulted in the acquisition of new land, but the complex frontier systems consolidated the new territories and turned them into permanent parts of the empire.

The Han expansion originated in its defense against the Hsiung-nu attacks, but in the end it turned the Han into a powerful imperial power. It also transformed the structure of the Chinese state. Therefore, the evolution of the Chinese state from its origins to Han Wu-ti's time must be reexamined to understand that transformation in its long historical context. In the same light, the far-reaching implications of Han Wu-ti's new empire and state for later dynasties, and even the modern era, are analyzed in both political and historical terms.

Although the westward expansion was an important event in Han history, except for a few of its most important military operations, it received scarcely any systematic or detailed treatment in the literary records of the Han period. The structural details and operational mechanics of the development of the Ho-hsi region, Hsi-yü, and the Western Ch'iang territory find almost no mention at all. A page of critical importance in Chinese history was missing, and the historians of later dynasties were left with little knowledge with which to fill in this significant gap in the history of Imperial China. Only with the discovery of over sixty thousand decipherable Han era documents on wood and bamboo in the old Han Ho-hsi, Hsi-yü, and Western Ch'iang regions in the last one hundred years has that lost page of Han history come to light. These are the daily records of the Han colonists and frontiersmen in these regions. They were written in Han script and cursive style on wood and bamboo strips of varying size, with a considerable number of them measuring about 22.1–24.8 cm long and about 3.0–4.5 cm wide. They date mostly from the late Wu-ti reign (141–87 B.C.) to the reign of Emperor Kuang-wu (A.D. 25–57) of the Latter or Eastern Han (A.D. 25–220), and a few are even as late as the mid–second century. The largest amount originated in the period of emperors Chao (87–74 B.C.) and Hsuan (74–49 B.C.). These documents, generally referred to as Han-chien, of varying forms and styles and both public and private in nature, contain much information about the frontier regions, including the structure of different frontier settlements, organization and construction of various military garrisons, geographical distribution of Han forces (military personnel), living conditions of both soldiers and civilians, local government administration, communication between local and central governments, the land system, population figures, local products and market prices, physical characteristics of servicemen and local inhabitants, family systems, slavery, aristocratic ranks, crimes and convicts, records of amnesties, imperial decrees, laws and statutes, household goods, local education, religious life, calendars, illness and medicine, official registers for various functions, physical and economic geography, and cultural activities.[2] Thus, they are in fact the archives of life on the Han frontier, and with them historians can examine in detail almost every aspect of the Han frontier system and the daily lives of the colonists and frontiersmen. The present study is such an attempt, a reconstitution of the Han frontier system and people's lives within it.

First, we must take a close look at the geographical distribution and dating of these Han wooden and bamboo documents.

1. The Chü-yen documents: Chü-yen is a region located in the northern part of the Ho-hsi region in modern northern Kansu and southern Ninghsia (now part of Inner Mongolia). In 1930–31, Folke Bergman of the Sino-Swedish Scientific Expedition discovered 10,529 documents of the Han period written on wood and bamboo. A large number of these slips range in date from 102 B.C. to A.D. 31, and a complete book roll of 78 slips is even dated as late as A.D. 93–95. From 1972 to 1976, the Chü-yen Archaeological Team organized by the Kansu Provincial Museum in Lanchou unearthed over 23,000 slips, of which 19,965 have decipherable writings and 1,222 have specific dates ranging from 102 B.C. to A.D. 31.[3]

2. The Tun-huang documents: The Tun-huang region is located on the western edge of the Han Ho-hsi region in modern western Kansu. In his three Central Asian expeditions of 1900–1901, 1906–8, and 1913–16, Aurel Stein found over 3,000 documents on wood and bamboo, of which 2,000 are decipherable, with half of them dated to the Han dynasty, from 98 B.C. to A.D. 153. In 1940, Hsia Nai of Northwest Scientific Expedition discovered 48 Han era slips. In 1979, the Kansu Provincial Museum unearthed 1,217 slips in the western part of the region, ranging in date from 71 B.C. to A.D. 23. In 1981, the Tun-huang Culture Department found 76 Han documents on wood ranging from 80 B.C. to A.D. 23.[4]

3. The Chiu-ch'üan documents: Chiu-ch'üan is a region on the east of Tun-huang also in the western part of the Han Ho-hsi region in modern western

Kansu. In 1977, the Institute of Cultural Relics of Chia-yü Kuan discovered 91 Han slips in the central part of Chiu-ch'üan, dating to the reigns of emperors Wu, Chao, and Hsuan.[5]

4. The Lop-nor documents: The Lop-nor area, called Yen-tse (Salt Lake) and P'u-ch'ang hai (Lake P'u-ch'ang) in Han times, is in modern eastern Sinkiang. In 1930 and 1934, Huang Wen-pi of the Sino-Swedish Expedition discovered 71 wooden documents of the Former Han period on the northern bank of the Lop-nor lake (also spelled Lob-nor or Lop Nor).[6]

5. The Ta-t'ung documents: Ta-t'ung is located in eastern Tsinghai; it was part of the western Ch'iang territory acquired by the Han forces. In 1978, the Archaeological Team of the Tsinghai Provincial Museum unearthed 400 documents, most of which date to the period of Emperor Hsuan.[7]

6. The Hsuan-ch'üan documents: Hsuan-ch'üan is in Wu-tung County of Tun-huang in western Kansu; it was known as Hsuan-ch'üan Station (Chih) in Hsiao-ku District in Tun-huang in Han times. From October 1990 to December 1992, the Excavation Team of the Institute of Archaeology of Kansu Province excavated the site and discovered over 35,000 Han era wooden and bamboo documents; 23,000 of them contain writing, of which 17,864 have been deciphered. The dating of these documents ranges from 111 B.C. to A.D. 107. While they provide information on almost all aspects of the lives of Han soldiers and colonists, the garrison structure, and governmental operations in the area and the Ho-si region, they contain special information about geopolitical organization and the garrison network, including the distance between major Han garrison settlements throughout the Ho-hsi region, and about Han operations in the Western Regions. The last three groups of documents make these new materials especially valuable.[8]

Han wooden and bamboo documents have been discovered in other parts of the Ho-hsi region in modern Kansu, such as Wu-wei, T'ien-shui, and Yung-teng (Ling-chü in Han times), but they bear almost no significant reference to our study of Han frontier development. They will be used for our study of Han life and society in general and for comparative purposes. In the same light, the ten thousand Han wooden and bamboo documents found outside western China and in the old Han territory in modern Korea (such as Lolang) will also be consulted.[9]

A tremendous amount of archaeological work on Ch'in and Han China has been done since 1950.[10] The new archaeological finds have become necessary sources for any study of the Ch'in and Han period. It was these extensive excavations and surveys that led to the discovery of more than fifty-three thousand new wooden and bamboo documents of the Han period in the old Han Ho-hsi and Hsi-yü regions. The archaeological records and fieldwork reports of the Han frontier settlements and other sites in these regions are a significant part of our primary sources for this study.

The third group of primary sources for this work is the literary records of the Han period that have survived to modern times, the most important of which are the *Shih-chi* (Historical Records) by Ssu-ma Ch'ien (145–86 B.C.); the *Han-shu* (History of the [Former] Han Dynasty) by Pan Ku (A.D. 32–92) and others; the *Yen-t'ieh lun* (Discourses on Salt and Iron) by Huan K'uan (fl. mid- to late first century B.C.); various encyclopedias, treatises, and reference works by Han scholars; collected writings and fragments by Han authors; and philosophical works by various Han thinkers and writers. Written works of later dynasties on the Han period are also considered primary sources in this monograph. Some of the most important writings in this category are the *Hou-Han shu* (History of the Latter Han Dynasty) by Fan Yeh (A.D. 398–446) and others; *Pu Han ping-chih* (Treatise on the Military of the Han Dynasty) by Ch'ien Wen-tzu (Sung); *Han-chih k'ao* (On Han Institutions) by Wang Ying-lin (1223–96); and *Tzu-chih t'ung-chien* (A Comprehensive Mirror for Aid in Government) by Ssu-ma Kuang (1019–86).

These three large groups of primary sources form the main source materials for our analysis and interpretation in the present study. These and other materials used in this work, however, are not devoid of contradictions and inconsistencies. All such issues will be compared in this study, and our preference for one version over the others will be explained. The many secondary studies by later and modern scholars sometimes compound the confusion that surrounds this era due to their different interpretations of some key readings.[11] All such problems will be examined.

This book is the first study in any language on the history, structure, operational mechanics, and influence of a frontier region in Han China, although there have been numerous studies of some aspects of the Han frontier and the wooden and bamboo documents in Chü-yen and other frontier regions. In fact, it is the first such study of a new frontier region in any period in Chinese history. (Although there are numerous studies of the frontier regions of the Chinese empire, these territories had been acquired by previous dynasties.) As such, this work follows a "comprehensive history" approach—a composite of many methodological and intellectual approaches, including political and military history, frontier studies, diplomatic history, demography, social and economic history, and anthropological and cultural analysis. Its discourse covers both humanistic and social-science approaches, but due to the nature of this work it places more weight on the latter. In its main thematic inquiry, this study addresses four questions. What motivated Han westward expansion under Wu-ti and his heirs? What was the course of action? What was achieved? And how did the expansion affect the Han dynasty and the later course of Chinese history? The core issue of this study is the development of frontier regions and colonies under the complex Han system and the transformation of such newly acquired territories into permanent Chinese lands under the regular Han administrative system. That is the question of how Han military expansion resulted in the acquisition of new land, how the development of the new land led to empire building and nation formation, and how the new Han empire changed the course of the Han dynasty and Chinese history.

The discourse of this work mainly follows the critical connecting threads of these themes. The textual presentation goes through a narrative course in five sections. The first section, in one chapter (Prologue), introduces this study by relating it to the development of the state, the formation of the Chinese nation, and the evolution of empire building from high antiquity to the founding of the first centralized empire in 221 B.C. The second section, in three chapters, examines the origins, foundations, and processes of Han expansion and frontier development. The third section, in two chapters, treats the large issue of Han territorial expansion in Ho-hsi (in modern Kansu [Gansu], Tsinghai [Qinghai], and Suiyuan [western Inner Mongolia]), Hsi-yü (in modern Sinkiang [Xinjiang] and eastern Central Asia), and other areas and how that expansion transformed the Han empire into the largest imperialist power in Asia. The fourth section, in five chapters, analyzes the history, structure, and operation of the Han frontier system in Ho-hsi and Hsi-yü in general and Chü-yen (in northern Ho-hsi) in particular as a case study. The fifth section, in one chapter (Conclusion), reviews the results of the Ch'in and Han expansion movements from 221 B.C. to A.D. 8; examines their political, economic, social, military, intellectual, and cultural consequences; and relates this study to the enduring question of the interaction between the frontier challenge and the pattern of empire building in Chinese history.

In its physical structure, this study, entitled *The Rise of the Chinese Empire*, is divided into two volumes. While sections 1, 2, 3, and 5 are in the first volume, subtitled *Nation, State, and Imperialism in Early China, ca. 1600 B.C.–A.D. 8*, section 4 constitutes the second volume, subtitled *Frontier, Immigration, and Empire in Han China, 130 B.C.–A.D. 157*. For the sake of coherence and the reader's convenience, parts of the first volume dealing with the acquisition, development, and historical significance of Ho-hsi and Hsi-yü in general and the Chü-yen region in particular are summarized in volume 2, though without the notes, in the introductory and concluding sections. Thus, although the two volumes can be read as one larger book, each volume can stand on its own and serve as a separate book for a separate readership.

The appendixes in volume 1 cover topics that are either too textually technical or too historically broad to be included in the main text but are necessary in making clear or understandable certain key issues and vital arguments in the main text, which, as required by the flow of the narrative stream, can only be presented in summary or passing fashion. Thus, they serve certain key roles in explicating the subject matter to which they are appended and need be viewed as such.

The sections on the sources used in this book consist of three parts: "Basic Sources" consists of the Han documents on wood and bamboo (Han-chien); "Abbreviations" includes some frequently cited materials; and the "Selected Bibliography" lists the main primary and secondary sources in Western, Japanese, and Chinese languages. With just three exceptions, the three groups do not duplicate each other. Because of their obvious difference in scholarly coverage and purposes as outlined above, volume 2 has all three sets of listings, while volume 1 has only "Basic Sources" and "Abbreviations." In all cases, the "Selected Bibliography" is up to date only to the end of 2001 and in a few cases to the middle of 2002.

Introduction

Virgin Land, National Security, and Agricultural Colonization

THE HAN EXPANSION during Wu-ti's reign (141–87 B.C.) carried the Chinese far beyond their old borders and gave them a systematic, complex, and effective method of colonizing newly acquired territories. These territories had greatly increased the size of the Chinese empire and to some extent changed its whole physical makeup (see map 1). The colonization of the Ho-hsi region is a good example of this development. Its acquisition extended the borders of the Han empire from the banks of the Yellow River to the eastern part of modern Sinkiang. But, important as this expansion was, details of the colonization of these areas can scarcely be found in the Han literature. Taking Ho-hsi as an example, only a few lines in the *Shih-chi* (Historical Records), by Ssu-ma Ch'ien (145–86 B.C.), the *Han-shu* (History of the [Former] Han Dynasty), by Pan Ku (A.D. 32–92), and other sources refer to the process of colonization in that area. Fortunately, recently discovered wood and bamboo records in that region have proved very revealing. It is quite possible that the colonization of Ho-hsi represents a fairly common pattern used by the Han in developing newly acquired border areas such as the eastern Sinkiang region. This book aims to reconstitute this process, using the Ho-hsi records as the basis for a case study in the broad pattern of the Han frontier system. Since the Chü-yen region has produced the largest decipherable Han documents on wood and bamboo (over thirty-two thousand documents), it will be the core of this study. It is hoped that the large structural frame, the organizational apparatus, and the operational mechanics of

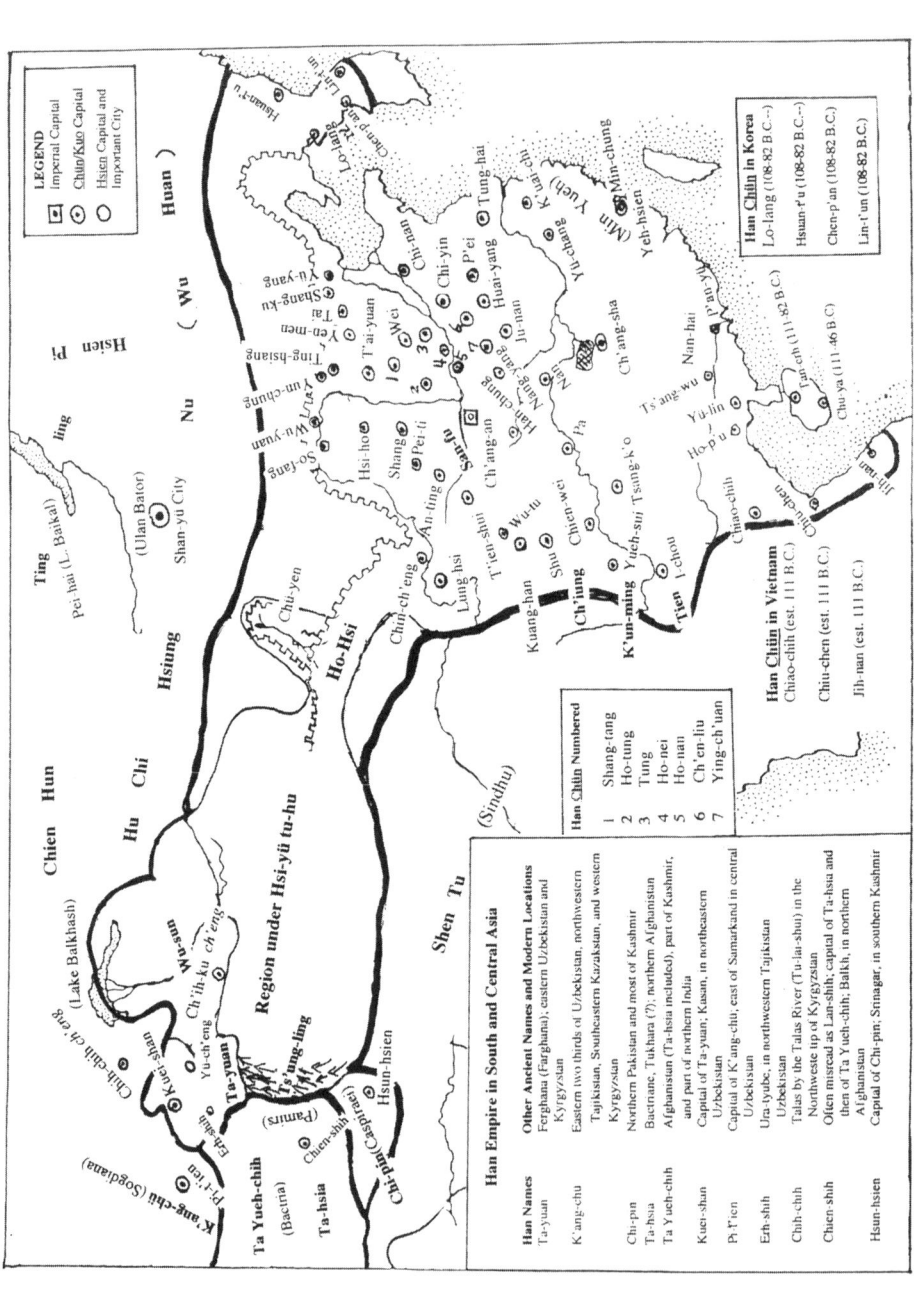

Map 1. The Han Colonial Empire in the First Century B.C.

the Han frontier system at Chü-yen can serve as a template for the Han frontier system in general.

HO-HSI BEFORE 121 B.C.

The Ho-hsi region, consisting of four *chün* (prefectures in this case) in Han times—Wu-wei, Chang-yeh (Chang-i), Chiu-ch'üan, and Tun-huang—is located west of the Yellow River and extends westward to the eastern part of the modern province of Sinkiang (see map 2). It corresponds approximately to the modern province of Kansu plus the southern part of Ninghsia, a small part of eastern Sinkiang, and at one time a small part of northwestern Tsinghai. On the southern edge of the region lies the Nan-shan mountain range, which extends roughly east-southeast to west-northwest and penetrates as far north as latitude 48° north at longitude 98° west. On the northern side of the region, there are two lower mountain ranges, the North Mountains (Pei-shan) in the west and the Ho-li Mountains in the east. Both ranges run parallel to the Nan-shan Range. Between the parallel mountain chains lies the narrowest part of the province of Kansu, the so-called Ho-hsi or Kansu Corridor, which is now 80 to 100 kilometers wide. In this corridor, the mountain streams flow down the slopes of the Nan-shan Range in a northwesterly direction. In the middle part of the region, most of these streams gradually unite with the Pei-ta (or Lin) River in the west and the Kan-chou (or Jo) River in the east. On the north flank of the depression, the two rivers encounter the foothills of the North and Ho-li Mountains, and are forced together through a gorge between these ranges. The newly merged river, called the Edsen-gol, runs in a northeasterly direction to its terminal lakes. After having covered about three-eighths of its course, the Edsen-gol reaches the easternmost offshoots of the North Mountains near latitude 40 north, where it divides; the new branch is called the Moren-gol. Farther north the Edsen-gol divides again into two main branches, the Narin-gol in the west and the Ikhen-gol in the east, the latter being a direct continuation of the Edsen-gol.

In the western part of the Ho-hsi region, we find the Shu-le (or So-lo) River (also called the Bulungir River), which originates on Mount Ch'i-lien and runs in a northwesterly direction. After passing the modern city of An-hsi, it is joined by the Tang River coming from the city of Tun-huang. From there the Shu-le River continues to flow westward and finally merges into the Khara-nor (also called Hala Lake or Hsi-hai-tzu).

In the eastern part of the Ho-hsi region is the Po-t'ing River, which also comes down from the Nan-shan range. It runs in a northeasterly direction and merges into Po-t'ing Lake.

As for the nature of the land, the section between the Pei-ta and the Kan-chou Rivers, or roughly between the modern cities of Chiu-ch'üan and Chang-yeh, has the most fertile soil. Numerous small branches of the main rivers make irrigation in this area quite workable. Though the land is suitable for pasturage as well as farming, the area near the North and Ho-li Ranges is especially good for grazing.

Our knowledge of the ancient history of Ho-hsi is only fragmentary, but relying on the limited information available a general picture of this region before its acquisition by the Han in 121 B.C. can be tentatively reconstructed. When the Ch'in empire collapsed in 207 B.C., three groups of nomads lived in this region, the Yueh-chih, Wu-sun, and Ch'iang. The Yueh-chih (which may also be read as Jou-chih), with a population of over 400,000, were at one time the ruling group; even the Hsiung-nu sent a prince to their court as a hostage. Later the Yueh-chih were defeated by the Hsiung-nu, which had a population estimated at 1.0 to 1.3 million at the time. After that defeat, most of the Yueh-chih moved westward, first to the territory of the Sai, or Sakās (in the modern I-li area of Sinkiang and west to Lake Balkhash), and finally to Ta-hsia (Bactria) in modern northern Afghanistan in the basin of the Oxus River in Central Asia. A small group moved southward to the Ch'iang's region of the Nan-shan Range and were henceforth called the Minor (Little) Yueh-chih. The less powerful Ch'iang occupied the southern mountain regions. The Wu-sun, the third group in the area, were relatively weaker and smaller in number, with a population of around 105,000 at the time. They were defeated by the westward-moving Yueh-chih, and their king, Nan-tou-mi, was killed, but his infant son, La-chiao-mi (referred to later by his title, *k'un-mo*, in Han texts), survived and was reared by the *shan-yü* of the Hsiung-nu. After having grown to manhood, K'un-mo La-chiao-mi gathered his people, who had lived leaderless under the *shan-yü*'s rule since Nan-tou-mi's death, led them to new homes in the Hsi-ch'eng area, and imposed a program of strict military training. Consequently, the Wu-sun developed formidable power under La-chiao-mi, though they still accepted the *shan-yü*'s rule. Later, with the consent of the *shan-yü*, K'un-mo La-chiao-mi led his army to attack the Yueh-chih in the Sai territory; he avenged his father's death by defeating the Yueh-chih and killing their king. As the Yueh-chih moved farther west into Ta-hsia, the *k'un-mo* and his people settled in the Sai territory and established a new kingdom under the old name of Wu-sun. Independence from Hsiung-nu rule was also declared. Thus, the Hsiung-nu became the sole master of the land of Ho-hsi.

The major stages in the history of Ho-hsi before its acquisition by the Han in 121 B.C. can be outlined as follows.

Year (B.C.)   *Major Events*
204–203   First Hsiung-nu war with the Yueh-chih in northeastern Wu-wei. Beginning of Yueh-chih westward retreat.

INTRODUCTION • 5

177–176   Yueh-chih migration to the Sai territory after suffering a severe Hsiung-nu attack between the Chü-yen River and the Ch'i-lien Mountains. Formation of the Minor Yueh-chih. Defeat of Wu-sun by Yueh-chih between Ch'i-lien and Tun-huang. Control of Ho-hsi by Hsiung-nu.

161–160   K'un-mo La-chiao-mi's defeat of Yueh-chih in the Sai territory and restoration of the old Wu-sun state there. Yueh-chih migration to Ta-hsia. Hsiung-nu become sole inhabitants of Ho-hsi except for Ch'iang in the southern mountainous regions.

After the Hsiung-nu conquest, the Ho-hsi region was under the jurisdiction of the Worthy King of the Right (*Yu hsien-wang*), the commander of the western wing of the Hsiung-nu. But actual supervision was carried out by two lesser kings, Hun-yeh and Hsiu-ch'u, and their subordinates. The total Hsiung-nu population in Ho-hsi was about one hundred thousand at this time. According to the *Treatise on Geography* (*Ti-li chih*) in the *Han-shu*, Hun-yeh's territory was to the west of Hsiu-ch'u's. This matter has raised needless controversy. Considering that a nomadic people such as the Hsiung-nu had to move from place to place in search of water and pasture, there probably existed no fixed lines of demarcation between the territories of the two kings.

During the Hsiung-nu rule of Ho-hsi, the Yellow River became the border between the Han empire and the Hsiung-nu kingdom. From 177 B.C. onward, the Hsiung-nu made frequent raids on the Chinese border regions of Lung-hsi (in middle and southern Kansu) and Pei-ti (in northeastern Kansu and southeastern Ninghsia) and on the area later designated Chin-ch'eng *chün* (in northeastern Tsinghai and southwestern Kansu). As a result, the Han government maintained heavy defenses along the Yellow River, stationing a large number of garrisons there.

THE ACQUISITION AND DEVELOPMENT OF HO-HSI

Emperor Wu of the Han resolved to eliminate the Hsiung-nu problem once and for all and opened a new era in the Hsiung-nu campaign by introducing large-scale military operations and swift cavalry. Ho-hsi naturally became one of the primary targets of Han attack. In 121 B.C., two major Ho-hsi expeditions were launched, both commanded by General Huo Ch'ü-ping, who had ample opportunity to demonstrate his military genius. In each campaign, he led a force of over ten thousand cavalrymen, penetrating deep into Hsiung-nu territory as far as the middle of the Ch'i-lien Mountains. The total number of Hsiung-nu captured or killed by Huo's forces is said to have amounted to well over forty-thousand, about one-third to one-half of the total Hsiung-nu forces in Ho-hsi. The Hsiung-nu *shan-yü* was so distressed at this loss that he wanted to execute the two kings in charge of the Ho-hsi defenses, but King Hun-yeh and King Hsiu-ch'u were in league and decided to surrender their remaining forces to the Han. However, en route to meet with the Han troops dispatched by General Huo, King Hsiu-ch'u suddenly changed his mind, and instead of proceeding he led a group of dissenters out of the main force. His actions came too late, for Huo's men immediately rushed to the scene and they, together with King Hun-yeh's loyalists, killed Hsiu-ch'u and eight thousand of his followers. Finally, King Hun-yeh surrendered his force of about forty thousand men to General Huo, thereby ending the Hsiung-nu rule in Ho-hsi. The Ho-hsi region thereafter became a part of the Han empire.

Following the surrender of King Hun-yeh, the western border regions, such as Lung-hsi, Pei-ti, and Shang (northern Shensi), were no longer the westernmost frontiers of the Han empire and were troubled far less by the Hsiung-nu. The government therefore moved about 725,000 indigents from the Kuan-tung area (east of the pass, mainly the central and eastern Yellow river valleys) to populate the region south of the bend of the Yellow River known as Hsin-Ch'in-chung. In 119 B.C., as successful expeditions led by Generals Wei Ch'ing and Huo Ch'ü-ping forced the Hsiung-nu to retreat even farther from the Chinese borders, the Han sent about 60,000 farming officials and soldiers to the western side of the Yellow River to construct irrigation works in the area extending from So-fang (central-western Suiyuan) to Ling-chü (modern P'ing-fan in central Kansu). These events suggest that after 121 B.C. the Han government concentrated its efforts on developing its western border regions through immigration and farming.

Immediately after the acquisition of Ho-hsi the Han set up *t'ing sui* (watch stations) in the eastern part of the region. It appears likely that in the course of populating the western border regions the Han constructed a strong fort at Ling-chü to direct development of the surrounding area. The Han Court, however, did not have plans to proceed immediately with colonization of the entire Ho-hsi region, for the cost of systematically developing such a vast expanse would have been too great for the economy, which was already overburdened from financing the large-scale military operations and the establishment of the western border regions. It was the Hsiung-nu on the northern borders of this territory who, by threatening to retake the region, forced the Han government into immediate action to consolidate its control over Ho-hsi. The Han first sought to induce the Wu-sun to reenter the western part of the region so that a Han–Wu-sun alliance could be formed to block any further Hsiung-nu movement southward. The veteran diplomat Chang Ch'ien (ca. 165–115 B.C.) was

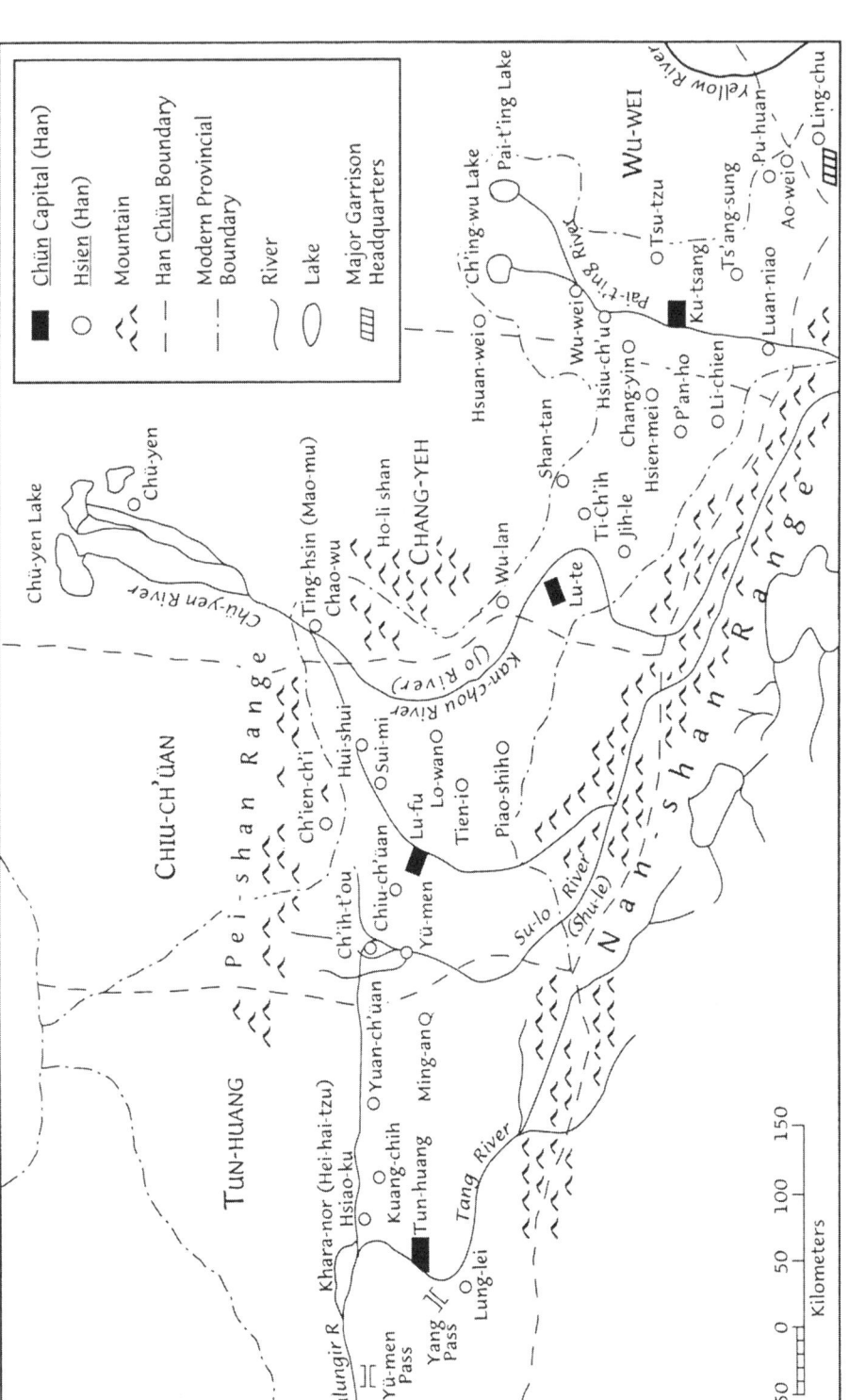

Map 2. The Ho-hsi Region during the Han Dynasty

called upon to carry out this mission in about 116 B.C., but he found only that the Wu-sun under K'un-mo La-chiao-mi had no intention of going back to their former homeland. This left the Han no choice but to develop the Ho-hsi region at once and on their own. In 115 B.C., Ling-chü was again expanded into a *sai* (large barrier or command post) to direct the Ho-hsi colonization project. In 114 B.C., criminal exiles were sent as far west as Tun-huang (in western Kansu) to engage in land cultivation.

At this time, an alliance was formed between the Hsiung-nu in the north and the Ch'iang in the south to squeeze the Han out of Ho-hsi. In 112 B.C., the Ch'iang, whose population is estimated to have exceeded fifty thousand at this time, attacked the neighboring regions of Ling-chü, and the Hsiung-nu raided on the northwestern border. The security of the Ho-hsi Corridor was thus at stake. In 111 B.C., the Han government sent a counterattack force of over one hundred thousand foot soldiers and cavalrymen to campaign against the Ch'iang and at the same time dispatched twenty-five thousand cavalrymen under the command of General Kung-sun Ho and General Chao P'o-nu to attack the Hsiung-nu. Kung-sun's forces marched from Chiu-yuan (in west-central Suiyuan near the Yellow River bend), and Chao's marched from Ling-chü; both were reported to have been victorious. The Han government then sent six hundred thousand garrison soldiers, together with a number of farming officials, to Ho-hsi and some neighboring regions for garrison duty and land cultivation. It is clear that the Han Court at this time had resolved not only to develop Ho-hsi as rapidly and completely as possible but also to reinforce the various western border regions, upon whose stability and strength the future of Ho-hsi depended. In addition, two *chün*, Chang-yeh and Chiu-ch'üan (in central and western Kansu), were established in Ho-hsi at this time to administer its full colonization. With the establishment of these two jurisdictions, the history of Ho-hsi entered a new stage. Based in these well-developed *chün*, the Han forces gradually moved westward to colonize the Tun-huang area (in westernmost Kansu) and northward along the Chü-yen River to occupy the Chü-yen region (in northwestern Kansu and southwestern Ninghsia). Tun-huang *chün* was established in about 98 B.C. and Wu-wei *chün* (eastern Kansu) in about 72. Thus, the entire Ho-hsi region was completely colonized by 72 B.C.

The development of Ho-hsi was the result of migrations of people from the interior and the establishment of civil and military agricultural colonies, a process known as *t'un-t'ien* (military-agricultural colonization). But the actual process of colonization and the various administrative measures that the Han employed in consolidating their control of the area are not clearly indicated in Han documents. Only in the light of recent archaeological discoveries can we understand some aspects of their complex methods. Based on these new documents, in the first volume of this study we conducted a detailed analysis of the colonization of three parts of Ho-hsi—Tun-huang, Lung-le (in westernmost Kansu), and Chü-yen—as case studies, tracing their development in an attempt to reconstruct the general pattern of the Han colonization process in Ho-hsi and other newly acquired regions.

THE GENERAL PATTERN OF HAN COLONIZATION

These studies on the development of three areas in Ho-hsi have clearly suggested patterns in the Han colonization process. The first step was to establish watch stations and/or a fortress in a region slated for development. In addition to the examples given earlier, further evidence can be drawn from the development of two other areas: the western part of Chiu-ch'üan *chün*, that is, from the city of Chiu-ch'üan to the old Yü-men (Jade Gate) Pass, which was located east of modern Tun-huang city; and the establishment of watch stations and large fortresses in the long expanse between the Wu-yuan barrier (Yü-lin barrier of Wu-yuan *chün*) and Lu-Chü (in modern Outer Mongolia near Arbi Khere), a distance of more than 1,000 *li*. The *Memoir of the Western Ch'iang* in Fan Yeh's (A.D. 398–445) *Hou-Han-shu* (History of the Latter Han Dynasty) clearly refers to the expansion movement of Emperor Wu's reign as the establishment of barriers, fortresses, and watch stations on the frontiers. In a proposal for the development of Lun-t'ai in the Western Regions submitted to Emperor Wu by Sang Hung-yang (also known as Sang Hung-hsiang, 152–80 B.C.) and others in 89 B.C., and in the imperial edict responding to this proposal, the opening of a new frontier area was also referred to as the establishment of watch stations (*ch'i t'ing sui*). The selection of an appropriate spot depended on four factors: (1) strategic importance; (2) availability of water sources; (3) convenience of communication with adjacent commanding headquarters; and (4) arability of the land in the surrounding area. The development of such an area was under the command of a military officer, but civilians who went to the area as migrants or hired laborers of the government also stayed in these watch stations and fortresses. While the military guarded the area, the civilians tilled the land outside to make the area self-supporting. If all conditions worked out favorably for further development, the government would transfer more people to the area to construct more watch stations and fortresses and open more arable land. As expansion progressed, the control and administration of such areas became more complicated and a chief commandant (*tu-wei*) would be appointed as supervisor. The appointment of a chief commandant to an emerging area also marked the beginning of a more advanced stage of colonization.

The area under the command of a chief commandant usually consisted of many fortress units and their related organizations, with each such unit being under a single commandant (*hou* or *hou-kuan*), who also commanded a series of subordinate units. In general, the various units in an area under a chief commandant formed the following hierarchy.

tu-wei
↓
hou-kuan
↓
hou
↓
t'ing, sui

Each of these units was also headed by a military officer: the whole region by a *tu-wei*, the *hou-kuan* by a *hou-kuan* or *hou* (commandant), the *hou* by a *hou-cheng* (subcommandant), and the *t'ing* or *sui* by a *t'ing-chang* or *sui-chang* (commander). Since each of these units had jurisdiction over a specified area, a *tu-wei* unit over the whole territory and a *t'ing* or *sui* unit over the smallest area, they can be designated as follows.

chief commandant area
↓
commandant area
↓
subcommandant area
↓
commander area

Han dynasty documents on wood and bamboo discovered in the old Ho-hsi region have revealed some details of the organization of chief commandant areas. For example, in the Yü-men chief commandant area (Yü-men *tu-wei*) there were two commandant areas, Yü-men and Ta-Chien, four subcommandant areas, and fifteen commander areas.

Yü-men *tu-wei*:
I. Yü-men *hou-kuan*
   1. Pei-pu *hou*
   2. Yü-men *hou*
      a. Kuan *sui*
      b. Tang-ku *sui*
      c. Kuang-hsin *sui*
      d. Hsien-ming *sui*

3. Hu-meng *hou*
    a. Hu-meng *sui*
    b. I-ch'iu *sui*
    c. Yung-kan *sui*
    d. Ta-fu *sui*
II. Ta-chien-tu *hou-kuan*
  1. Hsi-pu *hou*
    a. Fu-ch'ang *sui*
    b. Kuang-wu *sui*
    c. Pu-ch'ang *sui*
    d. Ling-hu *sui*
    e. Ya-hu *sui*
    f. Kuang-ch'ang *sui*
    g. Ta-chien-tu *sui*

The organization of the Chü-yen chief commandant area was even more complex: As will be discussed in the next few chapters, at its peak of development the Chü-yen region had at least 7 *hou-kuan,* over 40 *hou* (*pu*), and about 260 *t'ing* or *sui*. The area covered by these units of garrison and administration extended over 250 kilometers from south to north and 12 to 50 kilometers from east to west.

The commander areas under the various subcommandant areas are too numerous to be listed here. In general, there were five to six commander areas under a subcommandant area. In a chief commandant area the chief commandant resided in a city, the commandants in *chang* or fortresses, and the subcommandants and commanders in watch stations. Civilian migrants engaging in land cultivation and other pursuits also stayed in special sections within the headquarters of various levels. These sections were known as *li,* or "wards," when they were within a city and as *t'ing-pu* or *pi* (alternately *wu* or *wu-pi*) when they were outside a city or within fortresses and watch stations. While the region was directed either by the office of a governor (*t'ai-shou*) of a *chün* or by the central government, the chief commandant had sole jurisdiction over both military and civil affairs in his region, this being the unique characteristic of chief commandant areas. Such an area could expand rapidly given favorable external or internal conditions. Its continued growth naturally extended and complicated the dimensions of local civil government. This led to the establishment of a *hsien* type of administration over the region in which the magistrate assumed command of civil affairs and the duties of the chief commandant became more strictly military but civil matters relating to the military establishment remained under the chief commandant's authority.

The establishment of a *hsien* government marked, in general, the end of military rule in a region and the completion of the colonization. If the region was on the border of an existing *chün* and had already been developed under the supervision of a *chün* government, the new *hsien* would be incorporated into the regular *hsien* system of that *chün*; it might be split up to form a new *chün* with adjacent *hsien* and special areas. Tun-huang is an example of the latter case. Tun-huang *hsien* was established in about 98 B.C., and at approximately the same time Tun-huang *chün* was formed over Tun-huang *hsien*, along with its adjacent districts and newly developed areas to the west (such as Lung-le *hsien*), which up to this point had belonged to Chiu-ch'üan *chün*. On the other hand, if a region had originally been developed under the direction of the central government the new *hsien* was incorporated into an adjacent *chün*. Chü-yen's being annexed to Chang-yeh is an example. In 72 B.C., Chang-yeh was too large to be administered as a single *chün*, so its eastern and northeastern parts were split, forming a new *chün* named Wu-wei. The western part still carried its old name, Chang-yeh, but it was enlarged to include the Chü-yen region to the north, over which a *hsien* government was probably established at the same time. These jurisdictional changes in developing areas represent the final stage in the progression toward regular Han governance. In all the cases here discussed, the *tu-wei* still remained functional, although it eventually became one of the regular *tu-wei* in a *chün* and its name was sometimes changed to *chün-wei*.

The foregoing discussions have made clear the pattern of colonization that prevailed in certain parts in Ho-hsi. Further evidence, however, also shows that the opening and colonization of the entire Ho-hsi region most likely also followed this path. The *Biography of Li Kuang-li* in the *Han-shu* tells us that at the time of the construction of Chü-yen city during the Ta-yuan Expedition (104–101 B.C.) the city of Hsiu-ch'u was also built to prevent the Hsiung-nu from marching southward. The context clearly indicates that Hsiu-ch'u city was on the border of the Han establishments in Ho-hsi. Since the capital of Wu-wei *hsien* (north of modern Min-ch'in *hsien* in central Kansu) was in Han times still farther north of Hsiu-ch'u city, which was between modern Wu-wei city and Chen-fan city (slightly south of Wu-wei), the area of Wu-wei *hsien* was evidently not well colonized until the last years of Wu-ti's T'ai-ch'u period (104–101 B.C.) or later. Therefore, the systematic development of the region of Ho-hsi north of Chang-yeh *hsien* did not take place until during and after the Ta-yuan Expedition. Li Tao-yuan's (A.D. 467–527) suggestion in his *Shui-ching chu* (Commentary on the Water Classic) that Wu-wei *hsien* was established in 101 B.C. is probably not far from fact. Although details of the colonization of this region are not known, the fact that, like Chü-yen, Hsiu-ch'u city was later under the command of a *tu-wei* suggests that sections of this region also went through the chief commandant area stage. The existence of *t'ing* and *chang* in these areas strongly supports this point.

As for the development of the other parts of Ho-hsi, it is quite clear that from 108 to 101 B.C. the line of systematically maintained Han watch stations gradually extended westward from Chiu-ch'üan city, first to the old Yü-men Pass (modern Chia-ku Pass in western Kansu) and then to the Salt Lake (Lop-nor) area. The northern expansion that began at Chang-yeh followed the same path. Based in the Mao-mu (Ting-hsin) area in modern central Kansu, the Han line of watch stations extended gradually northward along the Edsen-gol. By 103 B.C., the area of modern Khara-Khoto became the headquarters of a cluster of Han watch stations, and by 90 B.C. the Han forces had already developed quite fully the northernmost part of the Chü-yen region, T'ien-pei in the modern Wayen-torei area. Thus, the northern and western parts of Ho-hsi had been opened and were being colonized no later than 90 B.C.

Of the entire Ho-hsi region, the area whose stages of development are least clear is that part covered by the Chang-yeh and Chiu-ch'üan *chün* in about 111 B.C., the oldest Han establishment in Ho-hsi. We know only that the colonization of this area started with the building of watch stations. But, even though no information is available regarding its further development up to the founding of those two *chün*, on the basis of the facts just related and the pattern of development shown in parts of Ho-hsi it seems reasonable to assume that this area, or its oldest key sections, went through the same stages before *hsien* governments were instituted. Consequently, one may conclude that the opening and colonization of the Ho-hsi region on the whole followed the pattern under consideration. But it must be noted that the Han establishments in Ho-hsi were constructed gradually and consolidated over the course of about thirty years, from the earliest settlements in 119 B.C. to the development of T'ien-pei in the far north of the Chü-yen region in 90 B.C. or earlier. During this period, Han colonization in Ho-hsi was accomplished through westward- and northward-moving fronts of systematic settlements. Obviously, the Han pattern of colonization under consideration was practical and typical only for the development of settlements in regions on these fronts. For regions in the interior, such measures were unnecessary. As such fronts moved outward, the boundary lines of the old establishments would expand, and the old administrative system would also have to undergo changes. New *hsien* governments were established, and at times new *chün* governments were also instituted by splitting the old. As just mentioned, the founding of the Chang-yeh and Chiu-ch'üan *chün* in about 111 B.C. was a result of such a process, as was that of the Tun-huang and Wu-wei *chün* in about 98 and 72 B.C., respectively, Tun-huang being the result of first-stage development in Ho-hsi and Wu-wei the result of further expansion. While each was a landmark in the course of Ho-hsi colonization, the formation of Wu-wei *chün* marked the completion of the formal process of colonization.

In the chapters that follow, we will examine closely the blueprint and operational mechanics of the Han frontier system at work in Chü-yen. This analysis will serve to reveal the origins, nature, power, and impact of the Han system in acquiring, developing, and consolidating the empire's frontier regions.

I

THE HAN FRONTIER SYSTEM

*Origins, Theories, and
Structural-Functional Patterns*

THE COLONIZATION OF THE Ho-hsi region by the Han empire followed a well-structured model of frontier development. That model was a long time in the making. Its origins can be traced back to the late Shang and early Chou period from the thirteenth to the tenth century B.C., its formative stage to the Ch'un-ch'iu (Spring and Autumn) and Chan-kuo (Warring States) periods from the seventh to the third century, its most elaborate development to the Ch'in dynasty (221–207 B.C.), and its theoretical construction to early Han times from 202 to 141 B.C. After the Han emperor Wu-ti (r. 141–87 B.C.) put that long-developed model of frontier development into practice in colonizing the newly acquired territory in the Ho-hsi region, it gained further structural refinement and functional improvement. Later it was applied to develop other Han territorial acquisitions beyond Han borders during and after the reign of Wu-ti.

The model consists of eight essential components: (1) forced and voluntary migration of people to the new regions, (2) full government support of new immigrants, (3) military protection of regions under development, (4) land cultivation by civilians or military or both, (5) free land for immigrants, (6) organization of immigrants under the military system in the initial stage and under the regular local administrative system at the developing stage, (7) strict military control of frontier regions, and (8) immigrants forbidden to leave their assigned locations without government permission.[1] These components did not develop together, and some of them evolved in times and places quite far apart, but they share some common features. The first and most common was the development and defense of frontier territories and border regions. The second was political control and security through forced population migration. The third was economic development of sparsely populated regions.

ORIGINS, DEVELOPMENT, AND THEORIES

In guarding against the various nomadic peoples on its northern and northwest borders, the Shang government stationed troops in these areas and used them to till the land to support themselves.[2] This was the origin of the institution of "land cultivation by troops stationed" (*chün-shih t'un-t'ien* or simply *chün-t'un*). The system was followed by the Chou, who imported their own people to occupy and develop the Shang land in the east and relocated the defeated Shang people to new locations under Chou control. These Shang-Chou practices were followed in later dynasties. In the Ch'un-ch'iu and Chan-kuo periods, the many powerful states became independent after the collapse of the Chou feudal order, and some of them, such as Ch'i, Yen, Wei, Chin, and Ch'in, removed civilians to their border regions and assigned them land for cultivation with the aim of making them permanent settlers. This was the origin of the institution of "land cultivation by migrant civilians" (*min-shih t'un-t'ien* or simply *min-t'un*). The system of forced population migration was developed during the Shang-Chou transition period in the mid-eleventh century B.C., and it was used as a means of political control. For example, many times the victorious Chou removed the defeated Shang royal and noble families from their homeland to regions under Chou control or regions where they would be unable to fight the Chou.[3] It was during the Ch'un-ch'iu and Chan-kuo periods that forced migration was employed to populate and develop border areas and newly conquered territories by such states as Ch'i, Yen, Ch'in, Ch'u, Wu, Yueh, Chao, and Wei. This was a period of continued fighting and territorial annexation among states and between Chinese and non-Chinese, and the measure of forced migration came to be a regular institution of territorial acquisition and consolidation.[4] In the process, its operational mechanics and support system were gradually but significantly improved and expanded. The state of Ch'in is a good case for the understanding of this development. The earliest known forced migration in Ch'in history occurred in 639 B.C., when the empire transferred the Jung people of Kua-chou (modern northern Shensi) to I-ch'uan (in modern western Honan) and seized their land.[5] From 359 to 223 B.C., sixteen such forced migrations were undertaken by the Ch'in. The most important characteristics of these migrations are as follows.[6]

1. Purpose of population removal: consolidation of political and military control, territorial expansion, development of virgin land and land not fully cultivated, and implementation of new laws.
2. Type of migration: removal of natives (non-Ch'in) from their homeland and transfer of Ch'in people to a specific place for various reasons.
3. Location: newly acquired land in the border regions.
4. Categories of migrants: newly conquered non-Chinese people; people of neighboring states; and Ch'in criminals and hooligans, rebels, commoners, merchants, and powerful families.
5. Enticement for migration of Ch'in people: pardon or parole for convicts, bestowal of aristocratic ranks, and exemption from taxation and service.
6. Number of people in each migration: from a few clans and tribes to over 100,000 families, that is, about 500,000 people.

In 221 B.C., the Ch'in state unified China and established the Ch'in dynasty. The dynasty lasted until 207 B.C. In that period of fourteen years, the Ch'in conducted eleven forced migrations. New characteristics emerged during these migrations. Their purpose was expanded to include the consolidation of political control by removing powerful and rich magnates from local regions to the national capital in Hsien-yang (in 221 B.C., 120,000 such families were transferred), the celebration of certain events, and populating cities where imperial mausoleums were located. To the categories of migrants were added corrupt officials, men who married out to their wives' families and changed their surnames to their wives', and unmarried women.[7] Other significant new developments can be best illustrated by the following migrations.

214 B.C.   Men who were once criminals, men who married out to their wives' families and changed their surnames to their wives', and men who were merchants were drafted as soldiers and sent to conquer the huge region of Luliang in Nan-yueh, where the Kueiling, Hsiang, and Nan-hai *chün* (commanderies) were established. Five hundred thousand people were sent to garrison these regions and live together with the Yueh (Viet) people. Fifteen thousand unmarried women were also sent to Yueh along with many other groups of people.[8]

214 B.C.   General Meng T'ien drove the Hsiung-nu from the northwest and established forty-four new districts (*hsien*) extending from Yü-chung (in modern southern Suiyuan) to the land east of the Yellow River as far as the Yin Mountains. Barriers and walls were constructed along the Yellow River.

Meng T'ien and his army also crossed the Yellow River and captured Kao-ch'üeh, Yang-shan, and Pei-chia-chung. There they built fortresses and watchtowers to guard against the Jung people. Convicts were brought in to populate the newly established districts in these regions.[9]

214 B.C. The First Emperor (r. 221–210 B.C.) removed the Ch'iung people from a region 200 *li* (83 kilometers) southwest of Lin-ch'iung (in modern central Szechwan) to Shang *chün* (in northern Shensi) in the northwest and transferred Ch'in people to populate the region the Ch'iung had vacated.[10]

The basic structure of the Han model of developing new frontier regions was formed under the Ch'in state and particularly the Ch'in dynasty. All the critical components and operational mechanics of the Han system can be traced to the Ch'in.

The Han inherited the Ch'in territory and faced the severe challenge from the Hsiung-nu, which threatened the very existence of the Han regime in its first seventy years following Emperor Kao-tsu's defeat in P'ing-ch'eng (east of Tatung in northern Shansi) in 200 B.C. But for various reasons the Han were unable to launch an effective counterattack, and the policy of appeasement, *ho-ch'in*, devised by Liu Ching (Lou Ching, fl. 202–198 B.C.) did not work at all. Therefore, the question of how to strengthen the defenses of the northern and northwestern border regions emerged as one of the most urgent issues in the young and still unstable Han empire. Different proposals were made to the court. None was as comprehensive and systematic as the one made by Ch'ao Ts'o (200–154 B.C.) in 169 to Emperor Wen (r. 180–157 B.C.). Its full text, entitled *Shou-pien pei-sai* (Guard the Frontiers and Protect the Borders) reveals the rationale and intellectual logic for border migration as the most effective means of defense, the details of its operational mechanics, the comprehensive blueprint of frontier establishments, and the long-range benefits of such an undertaking. In essence, it includes the following in its presentation to the emperor.[11]

Policy Advantage
1. It is necessary to settle permanent residents in border regions since expeditionary soldiers from other parts of the empire do not understand the character and capacities of the Hsiung-nu.

Structure of Frontier Establishments
2. The government will provide houses and land for the immigrants.
3. For the immigrants in such border areas, the government will construct walled cities, well protected by high walls, deep moats, catapults, and thorns. Each city, along strategic points and thoroughfares, will be designed to hold no fewer than one thousand households.

4. Each city will have an inner wall and an outer wall 150 paces (about 209 meters) apart. Each residential area in the outer-wall area is to be surrounded by "sandy fields" (*t'ien-t'ien*, "heavenly fields") to detect the intrusion of enemies in the night (intruders will leave footprints in the fields).

Government Support of Immigrants
5. The government will construct houses and provide farming tools before the arrival of the migrants. It will also provide winter and summer clothing and food to the migrants until they become self-supporting.
6. The government will buy mates for those migrants without husbands or wives, for without a mate a migrant will not remain contented on the frontier.

Rewards
7. The government will reward anyone who stops a Hsiung-nu raid and will award him half of what he recovers from the enemy.

Recruitment of Migrants
8. First enlist ordinary and pardoned convicts, then slaves given by their masters to purchase aristocratic ranks, and then all those commoners who desire to go. The government will reward them with ranks, and their families will be exempt from taxation and service requirements.

Frontier Communities
9. The government will build frontier communities that are rooted locally, tightly connected, mutually assisted, and militarily united against the "barbarians." This system will be much more efficacious than reliance on garrison soldiers from the interior.

Early historical records indicate that Emperor Wen acted on Ch'ao Ts'o's proposal immediately and enlisted people for removal to the northern frontier regions.[12] Ch'ao Ts'o later added some new components to his proposal to augment the structure of his plan, which included the following.[13]

1. Frontier cities will be located close to water resources and an abundance of good arable land.
2. Houses will each have two bedrooms and one living room and be fully furnished with furniture and necessary appliances. Trees will be planted in the living area.

3. The government will hire doctors and shamans for each new frontier settlement to take care of the immigrants' medical and religious needs.
4. In organization, five families will comprise a *wu*, to be headed by a *wu-chang* (head of a five-family unit); ten *wu* will comprise a *li* (ward), to be headed by a *chia-shih* (ward head); four *li* comprise a *lien* (company), to be headed by a *chia wu-pai* (head of five hundred); ten *lien* comprise an *i* (city), to be headed by a *chia-hou* (magistrate). Each leader will be selected from among the migrants who are most talented, able, and familiar with local conditions and who best understand the minds of the people.
5. All able men will receive military training in peacetime under their local unit leaders and will fight as groups under these leaders.
6. All migrants will be forbidden to leave their localities without government permission.

These suggestions in Ch'ao Ts'o's second memorial were also acted on by Emperor Wen. The two proposals were the earliest, most comprehensive blueprint for developing frontier and border regions in Chinese history.[14] They were conceived from the Ch'in theoretical framework and composed from the Ch'in practice of such measures. But Ch'ao Ts'o added new elements to expand the Ch'in model to fit Han needs. The Ch'in plan was designed to develop newly conquered territories that were already under the firm control of the Ch'in, but the Han model placed emphasis on the defense of border regions that frequently came under enemy attack.

THE NEW FRONTIERS

Ch'ao Ts'o's plan for the development of frontier regions was a result of the Hsiung-nu challenge from the north and northwest. The Han frontiers were essentially a defense line on the empire's northern and northwestern borders. Four decades later, the situation changed. Under Wu-ti, the Han empire launched the greatest expansion movement in Chinese history. Its armed forces marched in different directions and seized huge territories everywhere. In the north and northwest, they captured modern western Kansu beyond the Yellow River and key regions in modern Sinkiang, Tsinghai, Inner Mongolia, and Ninghsia. In the south and southwest, they seized new land and consolidated old Ch'in territory lost to natives after its fall. In the northeast, they captured modern northern Korea and established four new *chün*. As a result, the nature of the Han frontiers changed. The Han frontiers now were in five categories.[15]

1. Territories newly acquired beyond the old Han borders (e.g., the Ho-hsi region)
2. Expanded Han lines of defense against non-Han peoples (e.g., the Han-Ch'iang borders in modern Ninghsia)
3. Han colonies far from Han borders (e.g., the Hsi-yü region in modern Sinkiang)
4. New Han administrative regions in neighboring countries and independent tribal territories (e.g., the four *chün* in Ch'ao-hsien [Korea] and middle Vietnam)
5. Undeveloped regions in old border areas (e.g., Han territories in modern Inner Mongolia)

The development and control of these frontier regions required different policies and plans. Ch'ao Ts'o's model worked only for categories 1 and 5, while the other three needed different measures or a much modified Ch'ao Ts'o model. Category 4 was a matter of administrative structure and the transfer of people to settle among the natives, all under the regular Han governing apparatus, the *chün-hsien* (province/prefecture-district) system. For category 2 frontiers, the Han assigned both defensive and farming duties to regular troops. This was a more elaborate system of *chün-t'un* (land cultivation by troops) than that discussed earlier. At war, the soldiers fought to defend their territory; in peacetime, they worked on the farm and did food-producing chores to support themselves. Thus, the frontier armies could be economically self-sufficient. For frontiers in category 3, the Han stationed two kinds of soldiers: *shu-tsu* (regular garrison soldiers) for military duties and *t'ien-tsu* (farming soldiers) for land cultivation. But sometimes the Han sent only farming soldiers to distant regions for both agricultural and military duties. In both categories 2 and 3, no migration of civilians was involved; that usually took place after the frontiers and colonies reached greater military security and consolidation.

Under Wu-ti, the Han generally developed category 1 frontiers by first using the *chün-t'un* model, then adding farming soldiers, and finally bringing in civilian migrants following the Ch'ao Ts'o plan. The development of the huge Ho-hsi region is a good example of this practice. The Ho-hsi region eventually came under the regular *chün-hsien* system and became a permanent part of the Chinese empire. Then the Han frontier line continued to push westward far beyond the Ho-hsi region into modern Sinkiang.

FRONTIER AND EMPIRE

The Han frontier structure was the result of two major facets of the fabric of the Chinese empire from its earliest stage: border defense and military expansion.

As a fixed institution, the former had its origin in the Shang dynasty and the latter in the Ch'in, though elements of both were developed by different states and regimes in different areas and periods long before the birth of Imperial China in 221 B.C. as a unified, centralized, bureaucratic empire. Border defense was an essential element in any sovereign state. In the case of the Chinese, the border conflicts were between an agricultural empire and neighboring nomadic peoples and between two different cultures and ways of life. And that was a moving force in the development of Chinese history and civilization. In fact, it was one of the most important factors leading to the expansion of the Chinese empire. Great expansion movements, beginning with the Ch'in and the Han, almost always started with the defense of borders against nomadic attacks in the north and northwest. As victories were won, the defense turned into offense with the pretext of *yung-ch'u hou-huan*, "solving the trouble once and for all." In the end, the territories of the Chinese empire greatly expanded through new land acquisitions. Its borders extended far into the nomadic lands, and new frontier regions became either Chinese colonies or new border settlements through population migration. The Chinese frontier was a moving line, following in the victorious footsteps of the empire's expeditionary forces. As a result, new borders formed. This process is summarized in table 1.

Chinese frontier regions have served as bases for both defense and offense in Imperial China since the Ch'in and Han dynasties. The frontier structure that developed in Han times after a long process of evolution was a comprehensive design for both defensive and offensive strategic functions. Although sometimes the non-Chinese were able to push these borders inward by recapturing some of their lost land when the Chinese empire was in crisis during some period of transition, in the long run the empire made permanent territorial gains and steadily extended its borders. The Han frontier structure therefore served as one of the most critical and moving forces in the growth of the Chinese empire. The development of the Ho-hsi region in the present study is a good illustration of that frontier structure at work. The chapters that follow will provide a full picture of its organization and operation.

TABLE 1. Expansion of Borders in the Historical and Developmental Stages

Stages	Causes	Results
1	Border defense ↓	New territorial acquisitions ↓
2	Military expeditions ↓	New frontiers ↓
3	Victory led to expansion ↓	Immigration and development ↓
4	Distant military campaigns	New borders

2

THE HAN COLONISTS
IN CHÜ-YEN

*The Organization, Composition, and Character
of the Han Frontiersmen*

THE HSIUNG-NU IN THE Ho-hsi region surrendered to the Han empire in the fall of 121 B.C., but the Han did not set up garrison outposts in the Chü-yen region until 119. At this time, they established watch stations in the modern Mao-mu area, the southern tip of the later Han garrison establishment in Chü-yen. It was only in the mid-Yuan-feng period (110–105 B.C.) of Emperor Wu's reign that the Han began their systematic development of the Chü-yen region by gradually expanding their garrison establishments northward along the Edsen-gol. Specifically, in 103 B.C. the Han forces fortified the area later called Khara-Khoto and established a walled headquarters called Chü-yen city (Chü-yen *ch'eng*). In 102 B.C., General Lu Po-te (fl. 119–89 B.C.), then chief commandant of crossbowmen, was sent to direct the establishment of its fortifications and garrison. Lu established his headquarters at the Che-lu Fortress beside the city of Chü-yen and stayed in the region until his death. The Han settlements in Chü-yen were gradually organized and enlarged under Lu's supervision.

The Chü-yen region, in its early period of development, was an independent administrative unit under Lu Po-te and after Lu's death under the Office of the Chü-yen Tu-wei (Chief Commandant), being directly controlled by the central government.[1] It continued to be so until about 72 B.C., when a *hsien* (district) administration was instituted over the region to direct local civil affairs and related matters. But even after the establishment of the *hsien* administration, the Office of the Chü-yen Chief Commandant still functioned as the sole authority over military affairs, matters related to *t'un-t'ien*, the families of servicemen of various statuses, and all the civilians residing at or being attached to the garrison. For in a frontier region such as Chü-yen military matters were always of primary concern, and only a limited number of affairs of civil concern were left to the *hsien* government. This explains the fact that the Office of Chü-yen Chief Commandant not only overshadowed the local district governments but was superior to that of the other chief commandant in the region, the Chien-shui *tu-wei*. It is most likely that the Chü-yen chief commandant had the whole region under his command for a considerable period.

The main goal of this chapter is to examine the organization, composition, and geographic and socioeconomic background of the Han colonists who consolidated and developed the Chü-yen region during the course of its colonization. It is hoped that such a study will reveal the characteristic organizational structure of Han colonial frontier communities, the general pattern of Han frontier emigration, and a detailed profile of Han frontiersmen. This study will also show the close political, economic, social, and military links and interactions between Han frontier establishments and the interior society. This last aspect, in turn, sheds new light on the inner workings of the Han governmental institutions both on the frontier and in the interior.

ORGANIZATIONAL STRUCTURE OF THE HAN FRONTIER COLONIES

The Chü-yen region was a Hsiung-nu territory before the Han conquest. The Han people had moved to Chü-yen, by government order or voluntarily, for one purpose: colonization of the new land. Therefore, the development of Chü-yen by the Han followed two clearly defined stages: first, consolidation of military control; and then economic and political development. The pattern of the organizational structure of Han establishments in Chü-yen was determined by this primary consideration.

The Han colonists in the Chü-yen region were governed by two organizational hierarchies: the garrison system and the *hsien* government. As garrisoning and related matters commanded the most local attention, the garrison system was far more complicated than the *hsien* government. We will discuss the garrison establishment first.

The Garrison System in Chü-yen: The Tu-wei System

The main organizational hierarchy of the Han garrison command in Chü-yen has been reconstructed through the study of the Chü-yen wooden documents as follows.[2]

    tu-wei (chief commandant)
    ↓
    hou-kuan or *hou* (commandant)
    ↓
    hou-chang (subcommandant)
    ↓
    sui-chang or *t'ing-chang* (commander)

Such a system is not found in the extant written literature of the Han period. Wang Kuo-wei holds, however, that it was developed from the Han military system. The *Treatise on Officials* (*Pai-kuan chih*) of the *Hou-Han-shu* has a passage on Han military organization.[3]

> The grand general commands five *pu*; each *pu* is headed by a colonel [who is ranked] equal to 2,000 *shih* [of grain]. Under the *pu*, there are the *ch'ü*, commanded by the *chün-hou* [who is ranked] equal to 600 *shih* [of grain]. The *t'un* are under the *ch'ü* and commanded by a *t'un-chang* [who is ranked] equal to 200 *shih* [of grain].

Following this system, Wang contends that the position of the chief commandant of the garrison on the frontier is comparable to the position of a colonel under a general, the commandant is comparable to the *chün-hou*, and the subcommandant and commander are comparable to the *t'un-chang*.[4] He has, however, overlooked the difference between a subcommandant and a commander. The commanders were in fact subject to the subcommandants.[5] There are other points of doubt in Wang's analogy. First, a *pu* in Chü-yen, as will be illustrated later, was not headed by a chief commandant but by a subcommandant. Second, while the analogy between the chief commandant and the colonel, and the commandant and the *chün-hou*, is correct from the viewpoint of rank and pay scale, the authority and power of the chief commandant were higher than those of an ordinary colonel in the army and the responsibility was wider. From these facts, it seems clear that the garrison system was instituted—or gradually developed from the existing military system—for the colonization of frontier regions; the system as a whole was unique among the Han institutions.

Some contemporary scholars have equated these Han frontier garrison units with modern military organizations, considering a "company" comparable to a *hou-kuan*, a "platoon" comparable to a *hou*, and a "section" comparable to a *sui*.[6] This is also impractical, for the two systems do not have corresponding numbers of soldiers. For instance, a platoon in the modern system has a strength of forty-five to sixty soldiers, but a *hou* on the Han frontier commanded generally fifteen to eighteen and at the most thirty soldiers. In addition, the basic structure of the two systems is fundamentally different.[7]

The headquarters of these head officers in the frontier garrison system were termed *tu-wei fu*, *hou-kuan*, *hou*, and *sui* (or *t'ing*), respectively. These garrison units, as was discussed previously, were both military and administrative organizations: military because they commanded and directed all the garrison forces and military operations within their jurisdictions and administrative because they oversaw all civil affairs (including land cultivation) within their domains. Therefore, each of these units was a military unit on one hand and an administrative unit, with a specified domain, on the other.

Because these garrison units had so many complex duties, their organization was also complex. In the routine garrison system, the principal command and staff structure, as seen in the Chü-yen documents, is briefly sketched in table 2 in descending hierarchical and rank order.[8]

In the Chü-yen region, as will be detailed later, there were 2 *tu-wei* commands, 7 *hou-kuan* units, over 40 *hou*, and about 260 *sui* and *t'ing*. It is clear that under each of the major commanding officers in the garrison system there were a number of subordinate officers and administrative staffers.[9] But the main forces of all the garrison units were the soldiers of various classifications. It was they who carried out the daily defensive and offensive military operations, guard and mess duties, routine labor, and specially assigned tasks.

The main garrison organizations were supported by units with special functions such as *t'un-t'ien* (military farming), logistics, security, and communications. The number of soldiers in such units varied considerably. The *t'un-t'ien* organization, the largest of these special units, directed and supervised all the farming and related activities in the garrison establishments. It was headed by a *hu-t'ien chiao-wei* (colonel of military farming) or *nung tu-wei* (agricultural chief commandant) after about 72 B.C.; his subordinates and staff included *t'ien-kuan* (farming directors), *ch'eng-kuan* (or *ch'eng*) or *chang-kuan* (farming commanders), *nung-ling* (agricultural prefects), *pieh-t'ien ling-shih* (foreman clerks of land cultivation), *chien-ch'ü tso-shih* (accessory clerks of canal supervision), and so on.[10] The command structure of the *t'un-t'ien* organization in Chü-yen is sketched in table 3. In the *t'un-t'ien* organization, a large number of farming soldiers (*t'ien-tsu*), irrigation soldiers (*ho-ch'ü tsu*), and cowherds (*mu-shih*) carried out the work of land cultivation. At times, garrison soldiers (*shu-tsu*) also were

TABLE 2. Command Structure of the Han Garrison Establishment

Garrison Units (headquarters)	Commanding Officers	Subordinate Officers (A) and Staff (B)
TU-WEI (Tu-wei fu)	Tu-wei →	**A** Ch'eng (assistant chief commandant) Wei or ch'eng-wei (headquarters commandant) Ssu-ma (marshal) Ch'i ssu-ma (cavalry marshal) Chia ssu-ma (deputy marshal) Ch'ien-jen (chiliarch) Wu-pai (chief of five hundred) **B** Yuan (head clerks) Shu (assistant clerks) Tsu-shih (operations clerks) Shu-tso or tso with various functions (clerical assistants) Shih (clerks)
HOU-KUAN (Hou-kuan)	Hou-kuan → Hou	**A** Hou-ch'eng (assistant commandant) Sai-wei, Chang-wei, Hou-ch'eng-wei (fort commandant) Shih-li (operations officers) **B** Ling-shih (foreman clerks) Wei-ts'ung-shih (adjutant to the commandant) Wei-shih (assistant to the commandant)
HOU (Hou)	Hou-chang →	Hou-shih (hou clerks) Ling-shih
SUI, T'ING (Sui, t'ing)	Sui-chang T'ing-chang →	Chu-li (assistants)

Sources: Based on my own research and works such as Lao Kan 1960a, p. 38; Akira Fujieda 1954, pp. 637–50; Ma Heng 1957, p. 107; L. Carrington Goodrich 1956, pp. 209–10; Ch'en Meng-chia 1964, esp. pp. 84–85; Itō Michihara 1953; and Yoneda Kenjirō 1955.

Note: Special and temporary commissions such as commander or leader of a dispatch unit or a group on special assignment are not included.

assigned, often en masse, to work the land and so were criminals who had been pardoned so they could undertake farming duties.

The logistical units were responsible for supporting and providing services to the garrison forces and civilian colonists under the jurisdiction of the garrison authorities. Their main functions were the acquisition, transportation, distribution, storage, and maintenance of all military and nonmilitary supplies. The two main logistical organizations were the granary and treasury system and the transportation system. The former consisted of a series of granaries and treasuries (storehouses) for the garrison units of various levels. Under the direct command of the *tu-wei*, the granary (*ts'ang*) was headed by the granary chief (*ts'ang-chang*) and the treasury (*k'u*) by the treasury director (*k'u-ling* or *k'u-chang*). These head officers were assisted by minor officers and staff. Under the granary chief were foremen clerks, clerks (*shih*), and clerical assistants; under the treasury director were foremen clerks and clerks. In both the granaries and the treasuries, specially assigned troops called granary soldiers (*ts'ang-tsu*) and treasury soldiers (*k'u-tsu*) carried out the routine assignments. A similar organizational structure is found in the major garrison commands at lower levels and the special system of *tai-t'ien* granaries (granaries for the rotation-of-furrows fields). But the chief administrator of the *tai-t'ien* granaries was the granary chief (*ts'ang-chang*) before 87 B.C. and thereafter the granary supervisor (*ts'ang-chien*) or granary head (*chu-ts'ang*). The *tu-ch'eng* (assistant chief, assistant supervisor, or assistant head) was second in command in the *tai-t'ien* granaries. This officer was unique to the *tai-t'ien* granaries and is not found in other granary organizations in the garrison establishment.

The transportation system was responsible for the management and operation of the transport facilities, which included vehicles, horses, oxen, elephants, and other sources, as well as the garages for vehicles and stables for horses and

TABLE 3. Command Structure of the *T'un-t'ien* Organization in Chü-yen

hu-t'ien chiao-wei
nung tu-wei
↓
t'ien-kuan
↓
ch'eng-kuan
chang-kuan
nung-ling
↓
pieh-t'ien ling-shih
chien-ch'ü tso-shih
etc.

oxen. The vehicles were under the command of cart commanders (*chü-chang*), and the stables were managed by stable directors (*chiu se-fu*) or the like. These head officers were assisted by *ling-shih* and comparable clerical workers. These units also employed specially trained soldiers to man the vehicles and care for the draft animals.[11]

Besides routine military security measures, the Chü-yen region, like all Han frontier regions, had a special security system comprised of a series of passes and control points established along the gateways to the Chü-yen region and between large garrison units within the region. These units were commanded by the *kuan se-fu* (director of the pass) assisted by the *kuan-tso* (pass assistants). The *kuan-tsu* (pass soldiers) guarded and were stationed at the passes.[12]

The communications system consisted of two closely connected organizational structures, the regular postal stations (*i* or *so*) and the garrison establishments. The latter were part of the garrison command structure and will be discussed here. The postal stations were under the direction of post station clerks (*i hsiao-shih*). Under their supervision were the post soldiers (*i-tsu* or *yu-tsu*), who carried out the actual postal work.[13]

The *t'un-t'ien*, logistical, security, communications, and other related organizations were all under the direction of the main garrison command units, of which the highest was the Chü-yen *tu-wei*. This was particularly true in the early stage of the development of the Chü-yen region because there were no civil authorities. It seems plausible to assume that part of the *t'u-t'ien* organization was transferred to the civil *hsien* administration after the *hsien* government was instituted in about 72 B.C. But the process of this transfer is not recorded in the extant written literature, nor is it revealed in the Chü-yen documents.

The garrison personnel, from the highest officer (*tu-wei*) to the soldiers at bottom, were paid according to an established scale. The pay scale, as sketched in table 4, was basically in accordance with the general rank and pay structure of the Western Han government, and it clearly reflects the hierarchical structure of the garrison establishment in Chü-yen.[14]

The Civil Administration in Chü-yen: The Hsien Government

In contrast to the garrison establishment, the *tu-wei* system, the civil administration, and the *hsien* (district) government was small scale. The main reasons for this were threefold. First, a frontier region such as Chü-yen took military affairs as its major concern because they were directly linked to the consolidation, development, and security of the region. Under the circumstances, civil affairs in Chü-yen were naturally relatively scarce. Second, the *hsien* administration was a later establishment; as was discussed earlier, after its institution the civilians who were settled in the original garrison establishments were still under the control and administration of the garrison authorities because they still conducted their business under the protection of the garrison units. This again reduced the responsibilities of the civil government in the region. Third, the *hsien* government probably ruled over only the major cities (such as Chü-yen and Chien-shui) and their immediate environs in the period of our investigation because the transfer from military to civil administration in a frontier region usually took a long time to complete, a fact that information in wooden documents from Tun-huang and Chü-yen clearly supports. Hence, it simply was

TABLE 4. Rank and Pay Structure of Han Garrison Personnel in Chü-yen (Former Han period)

Position	Salary Rank (Annual)	Monthly Grain Provisions[a] (in *shih*)	Monthly Pay in Cash (coins)	Dates
Tu-wei	Equal to 2,000 *shih*	60.000	10,850 (?)	
Ch'eng (tu-wei fu)	600 *shih*	30.000	6,000	
Ssu-ma	600 *shih*	30.000	6,000	
Hou-kuan hou	Equal to 600 *shih*	—	3,000	
Sai-wei wei	200 *shih*	—	2,000	
Hou-chang	Equal to 200 *shih*	3.333	1,200	53 B.C.
			1,600	
			1,800	
Shih-li	Equal to 200 *shih*	3.333	1,200	27 B.C.
Tsu-shih	100 *shih*	—	—	
Kuan se-fu	100 *shih*	—	720	53 B.C.
Wei-shih	*Tou-shih*[b]	3.333	600	
			900	
Ling-shih	*Tou-shih*[b]	3.333	900	
Se-fu	*Tou-shih*[b]	—	900	
Sui-chang	*Tso-shih*[b]	3.333	600	71–60 B.C.
			900	
T'ing-chang	*Tso-shih*[b]	3.333	600	
Hou-shih	*Tso-shih*[b]	3.333	570	68 B.C.
			700	53 B.C.
Ling-shih (lower class)	Unranked	3.333	500	
			480	
Ling-shih (*hou*)	Unranked	3.333	480	81 B.C.
Kuan-tso	Unranked	—	480	
Shu-tso	Unranked	—	360	81 B.C.
Shih	Unranked	—	360	78 B.C.
Tsu	Unranked	3.333[c]	300	
		3.223[c]		

Sources: Chang Chun-shu 1963, pp. 316–37; Chü-yen I, pl. 6; Ch'eng Shu-te, pp. 76–77; Lao Kan 1951b; Ch'en Meng-chia 1963a.

[a]Unhusked grain (millet, barley, etc.); *shih* refers to *hsiao-shih*.

[b]The equivalent of *shih* on an annual basis for this category in the Former Han salary system cannot be positively ascertained, but it must have been less than 100 *shih*.

[c]The rate of 3.333 was for a thirty-day month whereas the rate of 3.223 was for a twenty-nine day month.

more convenient for the *hsien* government to leave the administration of civil affairs in areas far from the major centers of civil administration in the hands of the garrison authorities.

The *hsien* government of Chü-yen was headed by a *ling* (magistrate). His major subordinate officials and staff included a *ch'eng* (assistant magistrate), a *wei* (police chief), *yüan* (head clerks), *ling-shih* (foremen clerks), *tso* (clerical assistants), and a host of minor staff officers. Under the *hsien* government were the smaller administrative units called *hsiang* (counties). The *hsiang* officials (*hsiang-kuan*) included the *san-lao* (county education official), the *yu-chih* (county administrator of taxes and justice with rank for larger counties), the *se-fu* (county administrator of taxes and justice for ordinary counties), and the *yu-chiao* (county security officer). The county officials were probably assisted by the clerks called *hsiang-tso*. The *li* (wards) were the units under the *hsiang*. They were overseen by the *li-cheng* (ward headmen). The administrative hierarchy and pay structure of these local officials are summarized in table 5.[15]

As will be discussed later, there were two *hsien* governments, Chien-shui and Chü-yen, in the Chü-yen region for a short period, but for most of the time

TABLE 5. Local Administrative Divisions and Channels of Authority in the Chü-yen Region

Administrative Division	Officials	Estimated Salary Rank (annual)
HSIEN	Hsien-ling	600 *shih*
	Hsien-ch'eng	400 *shih*
	Hsien-wei	200 *shih*
	Yüan	100 *shih*
	Ling-shih	*Tou-shih*
	Tso	Unranked
HSIANG	San-lao	100 *shih*
	Yu-chih	100 *shih*
	Se-fu	100 *shih*
	Yu-chiao	100 *shih*
	Tso	*Tso-shih*
LI	Li-cheng	Unranked (?) (50 *shih* ?)

Sources: Chang Chun-shu 1963, pp. 113–14, 204 (nn. 42–44); Chü-yen I, pl. 6; Chang Chun-shu 1965b; Chang Chun-shu 1966, pp. 159, 224; Lao Kan 1960a, pp. 16–17; Lao Kan 1939; Lao Kan 1954; Akira Fujieda 1954, pp. 655–57; Tseng Tzu-sheng, vol. 2, pp. 244–50; T'ao Hsi-sheng and Shen Chü-ch'en, pp. 187–92; Yen Keng-wang 1961, pp. 216–51; Wang Chia-wu, esp. pp. 29–59, 150–57.

Note: The actual monthly grain provisions for *hsien-ling*, *hsien-ch'eng*, and *hsien-wei* (left and right) were 30, 20, and 15 *shih*, respectively. Provisions for other officials are not known, nor can they be intelligently estimated.

there was only one *hsien* government, Chü-yen. Three *hsiang* and thirty-three *li* were probably under Chü-yen *hsien* for an extended period of time.

The *hsien* government was supported by a series of granaries and treasuries. They were referred to as the *hsien-ts'ang* (district granary) and *hsien-k'u* (district treasury) and were located in the two district cities, Chü-yen and Chien-shui. The granaries were headed by the *ts'ang-chang* (granary chiefs) and the *k'u* by the *k'u se-fu* (treasury directors). These head officials were assisted by the *ling-shih* (foremen clerks) and some lower staff officers such as the *tso* (clerical assistants).[16]

Thus, the *hsien* government in the Chü-yen region was basically comparable to the *hsien* government in the interior, but it was smaller in size and jurisdiction.

As was discussed earlier, the Chü-yen region became a *hsien* of Chang-yeh *chün* in about 72 B.C.; a civil *hsien* administration was established over the region, and the Office of the Chü-yen Tu-wei, which took orders directly from the central government, then became the Office of the Chü-yen Tu-wei of Chang-yeh *chün*. The chain of command of the Chü-yen garrisons and civil administration is sketched in table 6.

HAN FRONTIERSMEN AND COLONISTS

We have outlined the leadership organizations of both the military establishment and the civil administration in the Chü-yen region. It was under the command and direction of the officials of these military and civil offices that the multitude of the Han frontiersmen and colonists, with some assistance from surrendered Hsiung-nu natives who were settled in the region by the Han Court, had gradually developed Chü-yen into a militarily secure and economically inhabitable region that was eventually to become a permanent component of the Chinese empire. It is true that the garrison officers and *hsien* officials commanded and directed the consolidation and development of the Chü-yen region, but they accounted for only a very small number of the Han settlers in Chü-yen. The transformation of Chü-yen from an undeveloped new land into first a well-developed frontier region, and then a *hsien*, was in practice achieved by the multitude of common Han settlers of various social and economic classes who moved to Chü-yen under different circumstances. For this reason, we will devote this section to examining the Han settlers in Chü-yen, both permanent and temporary, and to analyzing the major contribution of these settlers to the colonization of Chü-yen.

It should be pointed out, however, that because Chü-yen was a developing frontier community dominated primarily by military concerns, the Han colonists, about whom the Chü-yen documents have revealed a good deal of information, were mostly military personnel and civilians who were associated

THE HAN COLONISTS IN CHÜ-YEN • 33

in various fashions with the garrison establishment. But information about the latter group and the ordinary civilians still reveals certain significant aspects of life in the Han frontier society.

Civilians

The civilians in this region came from the interior of the empire and other parts of the prefecture of Chang-yeh. They were emigrants. While a small number of them came at their own expense, the majority were settled there at government expense. As was discussed earlier, it was a common Han practice for the government not only to bring people from the interior to develop a newly acquired territory but to support them on the frontier for a reasonable period until they became self-sufficient. Records in the Chü-yen documents provide abundant information about the immigration of people from the interior regions to Chü-yen.

TABLE 6. Command Structure of the *Hsien* Administration and the Garrison Establishment in Chü-yen

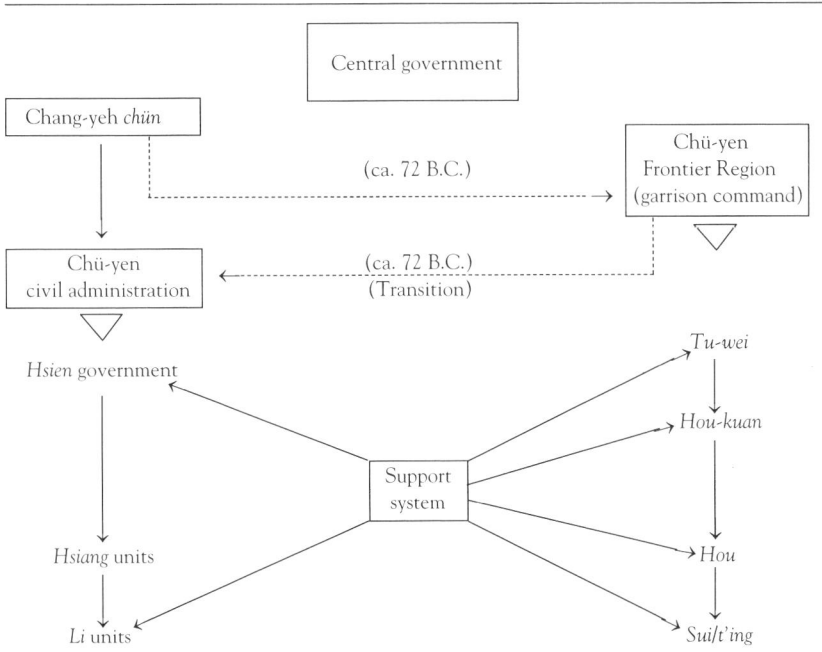

Sources: Chang Chun-shu 1963, pp. 113–14, 204 (nn. 42–44); Chü-yen I, pl. 6; Chang Chun-shu 1965b; Chang Chun-shu 1966, pp. 159, 224; Lao Kan 1960a, pp. 16–17; Lao Kan 1939; Lan Kan 1954; Akira Fujieda 1954, pp. 655–57; Tseng Tzu-sheng, vol. 2, pp. 244–50; T'ao Hsi-sheng and Shen Chü-ch'en, pp. 187–92; Yen Keng-wang 1961, pp. 216–51; Wang Chia-wu, esp. pp. 29–59, 150–57.

It is understandable that most of the civilians in this region were engaged in land cultivation, but such terms as *shang-jen* (merchants), *tzu-chia* (wealthy people), and *chiu-jen* or *yung-jen* (hired hands) also are frequently found in the wooden documents. This reflects the variety of occupations among the civilians in Chü-yen. More significantly, the Chü-yen documents show that the frontier society was unusually commercially active, though its main economic basis was still agrarian, and that wealthy merchants and landowners controlled a significant amount of economic power and financial resources.[17]

Servicemen

The military constituted the majority of the population of the region. Among them, the largest group was the garrison soldiers (*shu-tsu*). Farming soldiers (*t'ien-tsu*) constituted the second-largest group. Cavalrymen (*ch'i-shih*) were few. The last group was previously regarded by scholars as garrison soldiers assigned to agricultural duties. While this theory may be partly true, there are documents indicating that a number of the farming soldiers were recruited specifically to cultivate the land.[18]

Received thirty-nine farming soldiers of the prefecture of Ta-ho.   1746

Further evidence for this is that the clothing provision of the garrison soldiers differed from that of the farming soldiers; slips 542 and 7860 in Lao Kan 1960a clearly record that, although both Li Hsiu and Chao Lu were recruited from Huai-yang *chün*, their clothing provisions were different. A possible explanation for this is that Li was a farming soldier whereas Chao was a garrison soldier. Since the clothing provisions were supplied by the local governments, the distinction between a garrison soldier and a farming soldier would have been made at the time of recruitment. One may suggest that the difference in the clothing provisions lies in the fact that the two soldiers came from different districts. However, since all the government clothing provisions for the farming soldiers from Huai-yang Prefecture were the same, such an argument does not stand here.

The term *shu-t'ien-tsu* (garrison-farming soldier) appears in several documents; one slip records fifteen hundred *shu-t'ien-tsu* of the prefecture of Huai-yang who drained canals in the Hsin-ma farming region (*t'ien-kuan*) in 85 B.C.[19] Since the term *shu-t'ien-tsu* is always used to indicate a group of people and never precedes the name of an individual, I am inclined to interpret it as designating *shu-tsu* (garrison soldiers) who were assigned farming duties.

In addition to garrison and farming soldiers, *ho-ch'ü-tsu* (irrigation soldiers) appeared on regular registers.[20] Whether the irrigation soldiers were actually farming soldiers or garrison soldiers assigned to irrigation work is not clear. But since they had specific registers they were probably recruited specifically as irrigation soldiers.[21]

From the point of view of the garrison settlements where they were stationed and worked, the servicemen in the Chü-yen region can be classified as *sui-tsu* or *sui-shu-tsu* (soldiers stationed in a *sui*), *t'ing-tsu* or *t'ing-shu-tsu* (soldiers stationed in a *t'ing*), and *chang-tsu* or *shou-chang-tsu* or *chang-shu-tsu* (soldiers stationed in a fortress). Among the various titles of soldiers, the *sui-tsu* were the most common. In most cases, whenever a soldier was referred to, the *sui* where he was stationed preceded his name as an identification, for example, Shui-men *sui tsu* Su Tang-shih (Su Tang-shih, soldier of the Shui-men *sui*) or Ti-ssu *sui tsu* Yü Hu (Yü Hu, soldier of the fourth *sui*).[22] Sometimes the word *sui* was omitted, for example, Shui-men *tsu* T'ien-an, Ti-ssu *tsu* Li Pao.[23] Sometimes the word *shu* (garrison) was added before the word *tsu* (soldier), for example, Ch'eng-pei *sui shu-tsu* Meng Nu (Meng Nu, garrison soldier of the Ch'eng-pei *sui*) or Ti Shih-san *sui shu-tsu* Chang Ch'iu (Chang Ch'iu, garrison soldier of the thirteenth *sui*).[24]

In addition to the regular servicemen, there were a number of people in the garrison settlements who seem to have retired from the service. One group in this category was the *ku-li* (retired officials or former officers). According to the *Han-shu*, in the second year of the Shih-yuan period of Emperor Chao (85 B.C.) a number of retired officials were sent by the government to command farming soldiers in the prefecture of Chang-yeh.[25] The Chü-yen documents confirm this.

> (x) ... to Chü-yen for land cultivation, send retired official ... of Hsiao li, with the rank of *ta-fu* ... (x) 52.30(32)
>
> (x) ... The commander of the Second T'ing [of the T'ung-tse of T'ien-pei Commandant Area], [Wang] Shu, receives [grain] from retired official Chien, head of the Kan-hu Granary, and Assistant Head Yen-shou.[26] 148.3(321)
> 6234

The first document indicates that retired officers were in the *t'un-t'ien* organization. Since the Kan-hu Granary was one of the *tai-t'ien ts'ang* (granaries for the rotation-of-furrows fields),[27] retired official Chien in the second document was probably also in the *t'un-t'ien* organization.

The term *pa-tsu* is seen often in the Chü-yen documents. In the *Biography of Kuo K'uan-jao* in the *Han-shu*, one passage reads as follows.[28]

His Majesty arrives to give a feast to the *pa-wei-tsu*.

Commenting on the term *pa-wei-tsu*, Yen Shih-ku (A.D. 581–645) says:[29]

> The soldiers who are ready to leave for their homes after having completed their turn [as capital guards] and having their replacements [in place].

Thus, *pa-wei-tsu* can be translated as "retired capital guards." Similarly, the *pa-tsu*, also called *pa-shu-tsu*,[30] must have been soldiers who had completed the prescribed regular garrison service and retired. Certainly, most of the retired soldiers went back to their homes after the completion of their service in the Chü-yen region, as one strip indicates.

> Ying-chieh belongs [or . . . Ying, all belong] to the *ku-hsia*,[31] preparing the carriages for the retired soldiers . . .
> 19.33(82)

However, some of the retired soldiers remained in the garrison settlements, as is recorded in the following documents.

> Yang P'ing, the clerk of the tenth *hou* [reported]: retired soldier(s) arrived in the *pu* on the fourth day of the month . . .[32]
> Cp1533

> The commander of the Wan-shih *sui* [arrived]; he was appointed acting *ling-shih* in charge of commanding and protecting retired soldier(s) in the sixth month, *chia-tzu* . . .
> 15.2(451)

> The second year of the Shen-chüeh period [of Emperor Hsuan] (60 B.C.), the commandant of Chia-ch'ü: not enough clothing for the retired garrison soldier(s) . . . (x)
> 40.14(466)

In addition, one document records the presentation of arrows to retired soldiers who had stayed in the garrison settlements.[33] On the basis of these documents and the use of retired officials in the *t'un-t'ien* organization, one may suggest that a number of retired soldiers chose to stay in the garrison settlements for farming or other work. Whether to stay or return was probably a retired soldier's own decision.

Besides voluntary retirement, soldiers and officials could be forced to retire on account of disease or incapacity. Two documents indicate that handicapped soldiers were not allowed to remain with the garrison units.[34] If he was incapable of carrying out his assignments (*pu sheng-jen*), an official was to be deposed; the following is an example.[35]

> Subcommandants Wang Ch'iang [of Ping-t'ing][36] and Wang Pa [of ?] are charged with failing in *pan-hu* (carrying out assignments and protecting people). They are incapable of doing their duties and [are] hereby deposed. Their names are now reported to the Office of the Chief Commandant [of Chü-yen]. 5391

But the status of an official so dismissed is not clearly stated in the wooden documents.[37] As his name was removed from the list of officials, he would probably have been demoted to soldier status and expected to serve out his remaining term. Strip 198 in Lao Kan 1960a records the term *pa-fu*;[38] very likely it designates the official who was deposed but later reinstated.

The *mu-tsu* or *mu-ping* (hired soldiers) were employed in the various military campaigns during Emperor Wu's period.[39] In the reigns of later emperors, the hired soldiers became an important component of the Han military forces. For example, in the expedition against the Ch'iang tribes in 61 B.C. some of the forces commanded by General Chao Ch'ung-kuo (137–52 B.C.) were *ying-mu* (hired soldiers).[40] The *mu-tsu* were also recorded to have been employed in the garrison of the Chü-yen region.

> Hay provision of the sixteenth day [or sixteen days] of the fourth month for three horses was given to *wei* [commandant], hired soldier, and officer; each of the three owns one horse.[41] 290.12(272)

The status of the hired soldiers was equal to that of the regularly recruited garrison soldiers.[42] Of the hired soldiers, some came from the interior of the empire and others were hired from among the local residents. For the latter, one strip records that in the year 3 B.C. a subcommandant named Ch'ung reported to the Office of the Chief Commandant the names of the garrison soldiers whom he had hired on the order of the commandant.[43]

Along with the various servicemen, there were *fu-tsu*, *yang-tsu*, *sheng-tsu*, and *mu-shih*, which are classifications based on the soldiers' duties. The *fu-tsu* were the soldiers who had the responsibility of carrying things such as grain, hay, hemp, and the like,[44] and they had regular working schedules:

> Register of daily work of the *fu-tsu* of the seventeenth *pu* in the fifth month of the second year of the Chien-shih period [of Emperor Ch'eng (31 B.C.)]. 113.3(503)

The *yang-tsu* were the soldiers who served mess duties in the garrison settlements,[45] a fact that was pointed out by Édouard Chavannes and Wang Kuo-wei.[46]

Sheng-tsu is a rather strange term in the Chü-yen documents. Its interpretation has therefore long challenged both the historical knowledge and the imaginations of scholars.[47] By examining various related facts, however, a tentative sketch of its function and status can be given.[48]

    I. *Sheng-tsu* have separate registers in the garrison system.[49]
        1. In the fourth month, beginning on the day *ting-wei*, of the third year of the Wu-feng period [of Emperor Hsuan (55 B.C.)], on the day *hsin-wei*, Subcommandant Hsien respectfully reports:
           A register of *sheng-tsu* is respectfully submitted here.
                                                    159.21(57)
                                                        4522
    II. The families of *sheng-tsu* are listed separately.[50]
        2. The register of the families of *sheng-tsu*.   3859
    III. The work of *sheng-tsu* is mostly light and miscellaneous, not of the category of regular military duties.
        3. Three *sheng-tsu*: One of them guards the *ti* storehouse.
           One guards the *ko* storehouse.
           One tends horses.
           One guards the door.[51]
                                                               3955
                                                               pl. 207
        4. Twenty-two *sheng-tsu*: Two of them cook.
            Four pick leeks.
            Two . . . . (?)
            Two plaster walls with mud.[52]
            Two make bamboo brushes.
            Five smear [the *ngo* clay
            (gypsum?) over fagots (?)].
            (?) make mud.
                                                               629
                                                               pl. 31
        5. Account of *sheng-tsu* cutting hay.[53]   4464
    IV. While on duty or in process of transfer, the *sheng-tsu* are commanded by a garrison officer, and such activities are recorded in the offices concerned or the Office of the Chief Commandant.[54]
        6. Commander Ch'ang of the Ch'a-wei *sui* commands *sheng-tsu* to go to the headquarters of [Chia-ch'ü] *hou-kuan*; entered at dawn, the day *chia-hsü* of the eleventh month.
                                                        89.5(202)
                                                           9889

7. Scribe Tsung informs Subcommandant Jen of Ping-t'ing *hou* to dispatch *sheng-tsu*.

132.1
pl. 131

8. The third month, the day *jen-shen*: the commandant instructs Subcommandant Chiu of the fourth *hou* and others:
> In accordance with the instructions from the Office of [the Chü-yen] Chief Commandant, send an operations officer to command forty-two *sheng-tsu* . . . (x)[55]

Cp432

From these facts, the function and position of *sheng-tsu* become quite clear and understandable. But the reason for using this term to designate soldiers as such needs further clarification. It is evident that the understanding of the word *sheng* holds the key to the solution of the problem. And it is on this point that the views of scholars have been diverse.

In an article of 1963, Yü Hao-liang suggests that the word *sheng* in *sheng-tsu* and other related cases, such as in *sheng-tso*, designates a soldier's being reduced from such lower garrison units as *sui* and/or *hou* for miscellaneous and labor work at the higher command posts, *hou-kuan* or *tu-wei fu*.[56] He based his conclusion on similar usage in the *Annals of Emperor Hsüan* and the *Biography of Chao Ch'ung-kuo* in the *Han-shu*, where *sheng* means "to reduce [from]."[57] To a certain extent, Yü's theory is workable for the interpretation of the *sheng-tsu* documents. But it still encounters difficulties. For one thing, documents 3126 and 2620 indicate that *sheng-tsu* were not soldiers released from certain units. They were regular parts of garrison units. For another, the work of *sheng-tsu* was not restricted to the *hou-kuan* and the *tu-wei fu*; it was also performed in garrison units at the *hou* level. The following strip records an example.

9. (x) . . . Soldier Wu-ch'iu Shou patrolled from the day *chi-yu* to the day *ting-ch'ou* of the ninth month (inclusive), totaling twenty-nine days of patrol, during which period he found no person or horse [i.e., people, enemy forces, etc.] . . . (x)

The day *keng-hsü* of the ninth month: Soldier Tung-Fu worked at the headquarters at the Twenty-first *sui*.

The day *kuei-hai* of the ninth month: Soldier An-shih worked at the *hou* headquarters at the twenty-first *sui*.

145.33
3685
pl. 187

According to document 3612, the twenty-first *sui* was a *hou* headquarters, which thus proves the point.[58] These points suggest other ways of interpreting *sheng* on slips.

The word *sheng* is also clearly used as a noun in several documents, including *tang-wang-sheng* in document 2008 and T'o-t'o *sheng* in document 96.[59] The last example indicates that *sheng* designates a garrison office. From the fact that document 4942 describes the arrival at a *hou* office as *tao-sheng*,[60] it appears likely that *sheng* was the name of the office or headquarters of a *hou*. Looking into the documents in connection with *sheng-tsu*, this suggestion draws further support. First, as revealed in documents 3126, 3716, 4522, and Cp432, the *sheng-tsu* were all related to *hou* or *pu* (another name for *hou*) whenever their garrison units were given.[61] Second, the work of *sheng-tsu*, according to documents 2620 and 2685, was performed in the *hou* headquarters. Furthermore, if the above theory is correct, it also throws light on the study of the Han garrison organization in the Chü-yen region. As will be discussed later, each of the larger garrison units, such as *hou-kuan* and *tu-wei*, established its headquarters at a key locale to control, directly or through its subordinate units, the area under its jurisdiction. These headquarters, in the form of large fortresses and cities, were all specifically named: *fu* (command city) for *tu-wei*, and *chang* (fortress) for *hou-kuan*. The likeness between the works of *chang-tsu* (soldiers of a *chang*) and *sheng-tso*, which are, in fact, identical to a certain extent, and the parallel usages of *chang-tso* (work at *chang*) and *sheng-tso* (work at *sheng*) strongly suggest that *chang* and *sheng* were of the same category.[62] Thus, *sheng* and *hou*, which were also larger garrison units by virtue of the fact that they commanded several *sui*, may also be paired in the fashion of *chang* and *hou-kuan* and *fu* and *tu-wei*. The use of the term *hou-sheng* in strip 227.5 seems to prove this point.[63] Accordingly, like the terms *chang-tsu* and *fu-tsu*, the term *sheng-tsu* designated the place where soldiers worked.

As far as the interpretation of *sheng-tsu* documents is concerned, the meaning of *hou* headquarters for *sheng* raises no problems. But its application to documents with the single word *sheng* sometimes calls for caution. The following strip is one example.

10. *Yu tsu i-jen sheng kuan*
                                                                                                    254.18
                                                                                                    5030
                                                                                                   pl. 299

If the meaning of *hou* headquarters for *sheng* is to remain, the document may be understood as follows.

Listed on the right is a soldier of the *sheng* [of this *hou*], now, at the *hou-kuan*.[64]

But for such an expression, the original Chinese document should probably be written in the form of "Yu *sheng-tsu* i-jen *kuan*" instead. Furthermore, similar usage is not found elsewhere in the Chü-yen documents. Therefore, other interpretations for the word *sheng* in such cases should be considered. Lien-sheng Yang, who first discussed *sheng-tsu* in 1950, more recently suggested to this writer that the word *sheng* in *sheng-tsu* and other related cases might refer to an office higher than *sui* and that a soldier who was sent to such an office for certain services was called a *sheng-tsu*. To the same effect, a soldier who, in accordance with certain rules, was sent to an office higher than that of his current garrison unit was also called a *sheng-tsu*.[65] This procedure is quite similar to the expression *chih-sheng* (to be on duty at the headquarters) in the later periods. According to this theory, the document may be translated as follows.

> Listed on the right is a soldier at the headquarters of the *hou-kuan*.

The same meaning for *sheng* may also be applied to interpret most of the documents in connection with *sheng*.[66] But the evidence for establishing this theory to cover all the *sheng* documents is still not conclusive.

In this passage, several suggestions for the meaning of *sheng* in *sheng-tsu* and related cases have been briefly discussed.[67] It appears that *sheng* in *sheng-tsu* refers to the *hou* headquarters, but it may also mean a garrison office higher than a *sui*. Perhaps further studies together with new discoveries of material on this subject will be able to assert the validity of the two theories.

The last category of the military personnel in the Chü-yen region is *mu-shih*, who were herders of cattle.[68] Five documents record *mu-shih*; they are only a small part of a large group of about seventy documents dated from 90 to 81 B.C. and unearthed in the modern Wayen-torei area (of Ninghsia Province).[69] In this group of documents, there are records of the *tai-t'ien* granary and work schedules of farming soldiers. According to the *Treatise on Food and Money* (*Shih-huo chih*) in the *Han-shu*, oxen were used in the *tai-t'ien* method of cultivation, and Chü-yen was one of the areas where this method was employed.[70] Further, the *Annals of Emperor Chao* (*Chao-ti-chi*) in the *Han-shu* also says that the frontier prefectures received oxen in the reigns of Emperors Wu and Chao. In commenting on this record, Ying Shao (ca. A.D. 140–206) wrote:[71]

> Emperor Wu first opened the three borders and transported people to colonize them through the frontier garrison system. They were all given oxen for plowing.

In view of these facts, Chü-yen was certainly among the areas that received oxen for plowing in the course of colonization. One wooden slip proves this point.

... After receiving this instruction, inspect and grade the oxen. The registers [or reports] of the grades of the oxen should be submitted to Minister of Finance [Fei] Tiao.[72]

238.36(42)

On the basis of the foregoing discussion, the *mu-shih* were probably the herders of oxen that were assigned by the government to Chü-yen for the purpose of land cultivation. Since these *mu-shih* documents were unearthed in the T'ien-pei area, and some of them record the *tai-t'ien* granaries, perhaps T'ien-pei was then a *tai-t'ien* center in Chü-yen.

An examination of the *mu-shih* documents shows that there were thirteen *mu-shih* in the T'ien-pei area: seven from Ch'ang-i *kuo*, and six from the prefecture of Chien-wei. Since herders of cattle received the same amount of monthly grain provisions as the *li-tsu* (officers and soldiers) did, they may have had the same status as ordinary soldiers.[73]

Family Members of Servicemen

Some of the residents in the Chü-yen region were servicemen's families. Most of them lived in the *shu* (*hou* and *sui* headquarters),[74] as is recorded in the following slips.

Register of soldiers' family members who reside in the *shu*.

185.13(495)

On [the] right is the register of the soldiers' family members who now reside in the *shu*.[75]

94.13(497)

It seems that only the family members of the soldiers and officers who were not natives of Chü-yen lived in the garrison settlements.[76] This group included the parents, wives, children, brothers, and sisters of the servicemen.[77] The following are the examples.

	Wife, *ta-nü*, [named] Chih, age thirty-five
THE FAMILY OF HSÜ I,	Daughter, *shih-nü*, Shih, age nine
SOLDIER OF THE FIFTH *SUI*:	Son, *wei-shih-nan*, Yu, age three
	2752 pl. 133
	Father, *ta-nan*, Wen, age fifty-two
	Mother, *ta-nü*, Ching-ch'ing,
THE FAMILY OF NING KAI-I,	age forty-nine

SOLDIER OF THE SIXTH *SUI:*   Wife, *ta-nü*, *Nü-tsu*, age twenty-one
3282
pl. 161

The terms *ta-nü*, *ta-nan*, and so forth represent age groups. In fact, the registers of the families of servicemen provide sufficient information to reconstruct the age groups of the Han period.[78]

1. *Wei-shih-nan* and *wei-shih-nü*, "preservice male and female"—six years and under
2. *Shih-nan* and *shih-nü*, "serviceable male and female"—seven to fourteen years.
3. *Hsiao-nan* and *hsiao-nü*, "underage male and female"—fourteen and under (i.e., 1 or 2)
4. *Ta-nan* and *ta-nü*, "adult male and female"—fifteen and over

Semi-independent People and Volunteers

This category includes the personal attendants or private followers called *ssu-ts'ung*, *ts'ung-che*, or *i-ts'ung*.[79] The followers were probably of two sorts: the private followers of an officer, called *li ssu-ts'ung-che*;[80] and the volunteers in the army, called *i-ts'ung* or *ts'ung-tsu*.[81] With regard to the latter, there was a technical term, *fu-ma ssu-ts'ung*, designating them as soldiers with their own horses.[82] One wooden document records this practice.

Doing patrol duty with a private horse.   Cp1191

There is even a record of a rich person who wanted to be in the garrison service with his own saddle, horse, and bow on the condition that he be appointed a *hou* clerk.

(x) . . . twenty-eight years old, is rich enough to possess saddle, horse, bow, and crossbow; [with all of these he] wants to be appointed a *hou* clerk.[83]
214.57(477)

The position of the personal attendants cannot be compared to that of the volunteers. In the interior of the empire, private followers were actually servants and did the same work as slaves.[84] However, judging from their monthly grain provisions and register form, the position of the followers in the garrison settlements was quite different and much higher.[85] Some of the followers and volunteers came from the interior of the empire, but the majority were from Chü-yen or nearby districts.[86]

Convicts and Slaves

The people in this category had no freedom; they were either owned by the government or by individuals. Regarding the convicts, the Chü-yen documents record the *t'u* and *ch'ih-hsing*. *T'u* was the general term for convicts or prisoners doing hard labor.[87] New convicts were called *hsin-t'u*.[88] Among the various types of *t'u*, the Chü-yen documents record *wan-ch'eng-tan* (convicts serving four-year terms), *k'un-ch'ien ch'eng-tan* (shaved and collared convicts serving five-year terms), *ssu-k'ou* (convicts serving two-year terms),[89] and *fu-tso*.[90] The traditional interpretations of the term *fu-tso* are diverse, but all scholars except Wei Hung (fl. 25–57) and Li Ch'i (fl. 200 A.D.)[91] agree that the *fu-tso* had their punishments relaxed. The central point of controversy is whether they still held the status of convicts.[92] After having examined the various theories, A. F. P. Hulsewé concluded: "On the occasion of an amnesty, felons condemned to hard labor were removed from the status of convicts, but they were still obliged to finish the term of their sentence by performing work for the government."[93] However, document 726, or Cp2333AB, records the usage of *t'u fu-tso*. This fact, judging from a similar use of *t'u k'un-ch'ien ch'eng-tan* on the same strip, asserts the convict status of the *fu-tso*. The following strip further clarifies this point.

> (x) ... now we have 370 *fu-tso* convicts; [of these] 60 were given to the Chien-shui *pu*, [and] the [said] *pu* sends officer(s) to receive them.
>
> 34.8(231)

In view of this discussion, one can conclude that the convict status of the *fu-tso* was not removed even though the punishment had been reduced. And most likely this is what distinguishes the *fu-tso* from the *ch'ih-hsing*.

The *ch'ih-hsing* are not called *t'u* (convicts)[94] but *shih* (*t'ien-shih*) or *t'un-shih* (*t'un-t'ien shih*) in the Chü-yen documents.[95] They are also recorded as regularly receiving monthly grain provisions, as the soldiers did, but in a lesser amount.[96] Furthermore, their register forms and types of work were the same as those of the regular soldiers.[97] One strip even records that the *ch'ih-hsing* had the same duties as the *chiang-chü* (cart drivers).

> It was on the day *kuei-wei* of the fifth month of the second year of the Yuan-k'ang period [of Emperor Hsuan (64 B.C.)], ... Wei-ch'eng She was sent to command fifty *ch'ih-hsing* with carts managed by them.[98]
>
> 118.17
> Cp678

On the basis of these facts, one can conclude that the *ch'ih-hsing* were criminals whose punishment had been relaxed and whose commoner status had been restored but who were still working out the period of their original sentences in the army or the garrison settlements.[99] In an account of agricultural garrisons in Ch'ü-li in the Western Regions (in 68 B.C. and 64 B.C.) in the *Han-shu,* the *shih* and *t'un-shih* are also special terms used to describe criminals whose punishment had been relaxed, whose status as convicts had been removed, and who were being used in military campaigns and garrison settlements primarily for farming.[100] From this definition, the difference between a *ch'ih-hsing* and a *fu-tso* lies in the fact that the convict status of the former was removed and that of the latter was not. An examination of the register forms of the *t'u, fu-tso,* and *ch'ih-hsing* also supports this point. The forms of the first two groups are the same, but they are different from that of the third, which is the same as that of the common people.[101] This affirms not only the convict status of the *fu-tso* but also the basic distinction between the *fu-tso* and the *ch'ih-hsing*.

The information concerning the geographical origins of the *t'u* and the *ch'ih-hsing* in the Chü-yen documents shows that they came from both local districts and the interior of the empire.[102] The total number of the convicts and *ch'ih-hsing* in the garrison settlements must have been much less than that of the garrison and farming soldiers, though they did provide a considerable supply of manpower.

The slaves recorded in the Chü-yen documents are of various types and ages. They included male and female slaves owned by the government (*kuan nu-p'ei*) and individuals (*ssu nu-p'ei*).[103] They were classified by age as *ta-nu* and *ta-p'ei* (adult male and female slaves) and *hsiao-nu* and *hsiao-p'ei* (underage male and female slaves).[104] In the Chü-yen documents, there is no record of the total number of slaves in the region. The slaves were obviously in the market for sale; two wooden slips record this fact.[105] The price for an adult female slave was twenty thousand in cash and that for an underage male slave fifteen thousand.[106]

Temporary Visitors

This category of residents in the Chü-yen region included merchants, fugitives, *k'o-tzu*, and *k'o-min*. Most of the merchants or travelers were from nearby districts (such as Lu-te) or the prefecture of Tun-huang.[107] Some, however, came from as far away as Ch'ang-an (of Ching-chao-yin), Mao-ling (of Yu-fu-feng), and other such places.[108] In the Chü-yen documents, there are a number of records of orders and actions to arrest fugitives (*wang-jen*).[109] In one case, the government even offered a reward of one hundred thousand in cash for the arrest or killing of an escaped criminal named Yen Chiu-chün;[110] in another case, twenty-six soldiers and officers were sent to search for desperadoes who were thought to be hiding in a certain place in a subcommandant area.[111] Those wanted included counterfeiters, murderers, and escaped slaves. The places where the crimes were committed or whence the slaves had fled included various places in the interior of the empire, such as the prefecture of Yu-fu-feng, as well as Chü-yen.[112] Since Chü-yen was distant from the interior of the empire, a number of desperadoes must have fled there from the interior or other places in the Ho-hsi region, and some probably even settled in Chü-yen.

The third group of temporary visitors in Chü-yen were the *k'o-tzu*. The interpretation of this term presents difficulties. The term *k'o-tzu* appears in two wooden documents.

> *Ch'i-shih* [cavalryman] Li Tsung from Kuang-tu *li* of Chü-yen District was convicted of killing *k'o-tzu* Yang Ch'ung; he fled in the fourth year of the Yuan-feng period [of Emperor Chao (March 7, 77 B.C.)], the first month, [the day] *ting-yu*.
>
> Cp524

> Chang An-shang, a *k'o-tzu* from An-ping *li* of Lu District of the prefecture of Yü-yang. He has two horses and two small carriages with him.
>
> Cp: Supp. 40

These documents indicate that the *k'o-tzu* were from the interior of the empire and were neither poor nor dependent people. But the exact status of the *k'o-tzu* is still not fully understood. One wooden strip seems to shed light on this problem.

> (x) . . . Ching T'an, from Huai *li* of P'u-yang District [of Tung Prefecture], *k'o-chü* [resided as a guest, or temporarily resided] in the fifth *pi* . . . (?). He sold on credit a sword at the price of seven hundred in cash to Hsün Ch'eng of Lu-te District . . . (x)[113]
>
> 271.1(509)
> 3445
> pl. 171

The context of the term *k'o-chü* in this document seems clear enough for us to interpret it as "reside as a guest" or "temporarily reside."[114] In this light, and on the basis of the linguistic connection between the expressions *k'o-chü* and *k'o-tzu*—both with the root word *k'o* ("guest, visitor")—I am inclined to interpret *k'o-tzu* as a term referring to those who *k'o-chü* in some place other than their native localities. That is, the *k'o-tzu* were either temporary visitors or new migrant workers who had not yet been settled in a new region. Thus, *k'o-tzu* is likely a synonym of *k'o-min* (guest resident) which is seen in both the *Hou-Han shu* and the Chü-yen documents, one of which is translated here.

> (x) . . . The case of *k'o-min* [guest resident] Wang Feng, of the subcommandant area:
>
>> Commander Hsüeh Li-ping of the Yao-lu
>> commandant area ordered [or was ordered to become] the
>> Acting Operation Officer.[115]
>
> 308.38
> pl. 437

A wooden document unearthed in 1974 at P'o-ch'eng-tzu, the headquarters of the Chia-ch'ü *hou-kuan* in Han times, also records the term *k'o-min*. In this document, which is part of a thirty-six-strip legal testimony, a person named K'ou En was referred to as *k'o-min* because he was from K'un-yang *hsien* of Ying-ch'uan *chün* and resided in Chia-ch'ü. Similar usage of *k'o-min* is found in the *Hou-Han shu*, where the people who resided in a different *chün*, such as those of Chin-ch'eng residing in Wu-wei, are referred to as *k'o-min*.[116] Accordingly, *k'o-min* were unsettled emigrants. In view of these discussions, one may conclude that the *k'o-tzu* or *k'o-min* in Chü-yen was a person from the interior who resided as a guest in the *pi* or other garrison headquarters. On the basis of the evidence in the wooden documents, it seems reasonable to assume that *k'o-tzu* refers to visitors or unsettled emigrants residing in the civilian establishments and probably with a higher social status and *k'o-min* refers to those residing in the garrison establishments and generally with a lower social status.

Non-Chinese

The preceding discussion of the six categories of the Chü-yen population has roughly covered the Chinese in this region. At this point, it is interesting to note that non-Chinese also participated in the colonization and development of Chü-yen. One wooden strip supplies the following information.

> On the day *chi-wen*, the eighth month beginning on the day *wu-hsü*, the third year of the Cheng-ho period [October 3, 90 B.C.] [Wang] Shu, commander of the second *t'ing* gave 43 *shih* and 2 *tou* of red millet to the *chiliarch* (chief of the thousand) and centurion (chief of the hundred) of the Dependent States (*shu-kuo*) . . . (x)   148.1(332)

The *shu-kuo* (Dependent States) were organizational units that the Han established for the administration of surrendered barbarians settled on the frontier regions. A *shu-kuo* was headed by a Chinese chief commandant (*shu-kuo tu-wei*), and the *chiliarch* and centurion were among his major subordinate officers.[117] The second *t'ing* in this document was under the T'ung-tse *hou* of the T'ien-pei *hou-kuan*, north of Chü-yen city. Therefore, as early as 90 B.C. there were non-Chinese people, presumably Hsiung-nu, of a Dependent State in the northern part of the Chü-yen region. Since the colonization of northern Chü-yen began only in 103 B.C., it is apparent that non-Chinese took part in the colonization of Chü-yen at its earliest stage. In addition, some Hsiung-nu probably surrendered themselves to the Han in the Chü-yen region. Among the names of the numerous watch stations in Chü-yen one finds *shou-hsiang*, meaning literally "to receive the surrendered."[118] This was likely a commemoration of an actual event.[119]

The total number of non-Chinese in the Chü-yen region at any given time during the period in question is not recorded in the wooden documents or other Han historical sources, and there is no way to make a sensible estimate.

THE LINK BETWEEN FRONTIER AND EMPIRE

The preceding section gave a brief account of the Chü-yen residents in seven main categories. The records of and about these residents in the wooden documents have revealed many of their characteristics as individuals and functioning groups. These characteristics manifest the most notable character and spirit of the Han frontiersmen and colonists in Chü-yen, which mirrors in a large measure the larger Ho-hsi region; more importantly, they evince the process and the links between the frontier and the empire and the workings of the Han system of government and society in developing the frontier.

The main sources for this study in the wooden documents are the numerous personal registers, records of passes and checkpoints, passports of various types, and records of day-to-day operations of the garrison system and its related establishments.[120] Specifically, these documents supply details about both personal and institutional characteristics. For instance, for the former they provide such information on the Han colonists as specific military status, geographical origin, age, height, skin color, and order or aristocratic rank. Thus, on the basis of these documents certain significant personal, military, geopolitical, and socioeconomic aspects of the Han frontier system can be examined.

Physical Characteristics of the Han Colonists

The large number of documents in this category register two interesting features of the Han colonists: height and skin color.[121]

> Wan Shang-shan: Clerical assistant in the Office of the Chief Commandant of Chü-yen; from Shih-chih *li* of Chü-yen [*hsien* (District)];

age thirty-four; 7 *ch'ih* 5 *ts'un* in height; [of] black [skin color].

43.2
2863

Shih Hsiao: From Pei-chung *li* of Ho-nan *hsien* [District] of Ho-nan *chün* [Prefecture]; with the rank of *kung-ch'eng*; age thirty-two; 7 *ch'ih* 2 *ts'un* in height; [of] black [skin color].

43.7
2872

Issued on the day *chi-yu* of the first month of the fourth year of the Yung-kuang period [of Emperor Yüan; March 4, 40 B.C.]. The travel pass (*fu*) of Chang P'eng-tsu, commander of the Yen-shou watch station of the T'o-t'o *hou-kuan*:

> Wife, *ta-nu* [adult female], from Wan-sui *li* of Chao-wu [*hsien* of Chang-yeh *chün*], named ... (?), age forty-two.
> Son, *ta-nan* [adult male], named Fu, age nineteen.
> Son, *hsiao-nan* [underage male], named Kuang-tsung, age twelve.
> Daughter, *hsiao-nü* [underage female], named Nü-tsu, age nine.
> [Daughter-in-law] Fu's wife, named Nan-lai, age fifteen.
> They are all black [in skin color].

29.2
Cp218

The words *hei-se* (black) in the original documents are of great interest to both historians and anthropologists. It appears likely that they describe the subject's hair color. But a phrase such as *hei-se fei ta-t'ou shao-fa* (black color, fat, big head with little hair) rules out this possibility.[122] According to document 193 (or Cp1590), persons who are no longer with the garrison units must be reported to superior offices on a fixed form, which in part reads, in this order, *shu* (office), *chün* (prefecture), *hsien* (district), *li* (ward), *ming* (first name), *hsing* (family name), *nien* (age), *ch'ang* (height), *wu-se* (complexion), and so forth. This is the exact form of the first two documents cited. Therefore, the words *hei-se* in these and similar documents describe the complexion of the persons being registered.

On the basis of all the information available in the Chü-yen documents, I have conducted a detailed analysis of the height and skin color of the Han Chinese.[123] A summary of this study is presented in the following pages.

Height is discussed first. In the forty-five cases I examined, the following figures were revealed.[124]

Height (in Han *ch'ih*)	Number of Persons
6.0	1
6.3	1

7.0	2
7 plus (?)	2
7.1	3
7.2	18
7.3	8
7.4	1
7.5	8
7.6	1
7.7	1

The average stature is 7.28 *ch'ih* or 168.89 centimeters. However, the person only 6 *ch'ih* tall was only twelve years old, and the one 6.2 *ch'ih* tall was sixteen. Accordingly, they should be excluded from statistics of this nature. By excluding these cases and others in which the age of a person is not known, the average stature of a Han Chinese age eighteen and over is 7.31 *ch'ih* or 169.59 centimeters (see table 7). This average should be considered more representative of the average Han Chinese stature than the previous one. Interestingly, this average is also very close to the average stature of 168.5 centimeters among the modern inhabitants of North China, from which all of the geographically identified Han colonists in our table came. The average stature of 169.59 centimeters belongs to the supermedium class (168.0 to 172.0 centimeters) in the modern classification of human stature commonly used by physical anthropologists; it is higher than the general average stature, medium class (161.2 to 167.6 centimeters), among modern Chinese as a whole.[125]

The colonists in Chü-yen were from almost every corner of the Han empire. Some of the strips used in this study give the geographical origins of the persons concerned. It is interesting to note that differences in height have been found between people of Ho-hsi and people of the interior prefectures. Table 8, excluding persons under eighteen, illustrates this observation. Table 8 indicates that the Ho-hsi people were slightly taller than the people of the interior in

TABLE 7. Stature of Han Chinese Adults

Height (*ch'ih*)	Number of Persons
7.1	1
7.2	15
7.3	5
7.4	1
7.5	7
7.6	1
7.7	1

Note: Average height is 7.31 *ch'ih*.

Han times. But, since only eighteen cases are available, it is hard to judge the validity of this observation.

A problem equally interesting is the relationship between height and officeholding. An examination of all relevant documents gives the following picture.

Status	Height
Garrison soldier	7.1
Farming soldier	7.2
Cart attendant	7.2
Clerical assistant (three examples)	7.3, 7.4, 7.5
Commander (three examples)	7.2, 7.3, 7.5
Subcommandant	7.6
Marshal	7.2

If these results are not coincidental, there existed a close correlation between a person's height and his status in the garrison units. Not only were the officers taller than the soldiers, but all except two were above 7.2 *ch'ih*. It appears very likely that a certain standard of height was among the physical qualifications required of a garrison officer. Considering the nature of the assignments of an officer on the frontier, this would be understandable.

Of all the physical characteristics of the Han Chinese revealed by the Chü-yen documents, the most puzzling is skin color, for it paints a strange picture, indeed. In the fifty-five cases I have checked, the range of skin color reported is as follows.

Color	Number of Persons
Black (*hei*)	53
Jet black (*ch'ing-hei*)	1
Tawny (*huang-hei*)	1

TABLE 8. Height Differentials between Interior and Ho-hsi Chinese

Height (*ch'ih*)	Number of Persons	
	Interior	Ho-hsi
7.1	1 (From Ju-nan)	—
7.2	2 (Wei, Ho-nan, Ju-nan)	6
7.3	3 (Tung, Ho-tung)	2
7.4	—	1
7.5	—	5
Average	7.25 *ch'ih*	7.33 *ch'ih*

Note: Persons under eighteen years of age are excluded.

Contrary to general expectations, not a single person in the Chü-yen documents, except for one doubtful case, is listed as being *huang* (yellow), which has been the color of the Chinese for ages.

The fact that about 98 percent of the people listed, or about 96 percent if the doubtful yellow case is included, were classified as black is astonishing. Looking into the various facts about these people, I have found that the peculiarity of their skin color can by no means be related to a particular social status, occupation, region, or race. Sixteen of the fifty-four "black" and "jet black" persons held aristocratic rank ranging from the first order to the eighth.

Order of Rank	*Number of Persons*
Kung-shih	1
Shang-tso	3
Pu-keng	1
Ta-fu	5
Kung-ta-fu	1
Kung-ch'eng	5

Also included in this group are five officers, two soldiers, and three fugitives. These facts certainly indicate a wide variety of social status and occupations among these people. In addition, the geographical distribution of twenty-five persons in this group reveals that while seventeen were natives of Ho-hsi eight came from the interior of the Han empire: three from Ho-nan, two from Tung, and one each from Yu-fu-feng, Wei, and Ho-nei.[126] Apparently, characteristics of skin color cannot be explained in geographical terms. From all these angles, there can be little doubt that the fifty-five people under discussion are common Han Chinese.

But why, then, unlike the modern Chinese, did a majority as large as 98 or 96 percent of the Han Chinese known from the Chü-yen documents have such a physical appearance? There is as yet no clue. It might be suspected that there is a difference between the Han and later Chinese meaning of the word *hei*. This is not the case, for this same word, along with *pai* (white) and *huang*, was used to describe the color of cows and horses in the Chü-yen documents. Perhaps, indeed, a considerable portion of the Han population was dark-skinned. It seems, as I have analyzed elsewhere, that the dark-skinned people belonged to a special racial group and were so identified in ancient China before the Ch'in. But by Han times they had been socially and politically integrated into the fabric of Chinese society. This explains why such information is missing in Han era historical writings. Skin color became an issue in the wooden documents because the forms of Han documentary writings such as registers, passports, and certain routine reports and circulars in the frontier garrisons were inherited from pre-Ch'in China, where skin color was a noticeable issue and a requisite item on such documents.[127] Thus, interestingly, the continuity of the documentary style from ancient China to the Han accidentally preserved a very important page in ancient Chinese social and racial history.[128]

This investigation leads us to conclude that the Han frontiersmen and garrison personnel in Chü-yen were not of any particular social or racial segment of the Han empire. They rather represent a general cross section of the Han population, and, as the next section will show, they also came to Chü-yen from the various corners of the Han empire.

Region, Economy, and Frontier

The Han frontiersmen and colonists in Chü-yen came from different regions of the empire. A large number of wooden documents record the regional origins of them and hence provide a clear picture of how the various regions were involved in colonizing Chü-yen. Table 9 is a tabulation of such information. It is primarily based on the numerous records and registers of individuals in all documents discovered in Chü-yen and Tun-huang and other connected regions. When a general account of the number of individuals from a certain region—that is, an account without specifying the names of individuals—is used, a special effort is made to eliminate any possible duplication of the entries already recorded in another category. In the same vein, cases of uncertain geographical identification are excluded. The *ch'i-shih* (cavalrymen), totaling over fifty, are excluded from this table because they will be discussed later.[129]

The data in table 9 reflect several important points regarding the regional origins of the Han frontiersmen and colonists in Chü-yen. First, the implications of the pattern of geographic distribution with respect to regional participation in the development of Chü-yen as a frontier colony will be discussed. For the benefit of the nonspecialist, I shall analyze some of the issues in this regard in terms of modern administrative geography. As the table shows, the Kansu area registers the largest number, a total of 236 or about 39 percent of the grand total of 602. Then comes Honan with over 160 or over 27 percent. Shantung runs a close third with about 70 or about 9 percent. That Kansu supplied the largest number is understandable because Chü-yen was part of Chang-yeh Prefecture. But Honan is distant from the Chü-yen region, and Shantung is even farther away. The fact that these areas supply the largest totals seems to be related to the emigration policy of the Han government, which was based on demographic and economic conditions in the Han empire. A combined total of over 250 persons, or nearly 42 percent, came from the so-called Central Plain region (Chung-yüan) or the loosely termed Han-time Kuan-tung region, which included Honan, western Shantung, southern Shansi, southern Hopei, north-

TABLE 9. Regional Background of Han Settlers and Garrison Personnel in Chü-yen

Modern Provinces and Regions	Han Prefectures and Kingdoms	Garrison Soldiers[a]	Farming Soldiers[a]	Officers	Civilians	Classification Unknown	Total
Kansu	Wu-wei	—	—	1	2	—	3
	Chang-yeh	77	1	74	68	8	228
	Chiu-chüan	—	—	—	2	—	2
	Tun-huang	—	—	1	1	—	2
Subtotal		77	1	76	73	8	235
Northeastern Kansu, Southeastern Ninghsia	Pei-ti	—	—	—	1	—	1
Subtotal							
Shensi	Ching-chao-yin	—	—	—	1	—	1
	Yu-fu-feng	1	—	1	8	—	8
	Tso-p'ing-i	1	—	—	3	—	5
	Han-chung	—	—	—	3	—	4
Subtotal		—	—	1	7	1	9
Southwestern Shansi	Ho-tung	2	1	2	21	1	26
	Shang-tang	7	—	1	5	—	14
Subtotal		1	—	—	1	—	2
Southwestern Hopei	Chao (kuo)	8	1	1	6	1	16
	Chü-lu	4	—	—	1	1	6
	P'ing-kan (kuo)	2	—	—	—	—	2
Subtotal		2	—	—	1	2	3
Southeastern Hopei, Eastern Shantung	Tung	8	—	—	1	—	11
		7	2	—	1	—	10
Subtotal							
Honan	Ho-nei	7	2	—	1	—	10
	Hung-nung	—	—	—	5	—	5
	Ho-nan	19	—	—	1	—	1
	Huai-yang	7	1	1	7	4	32
	Huai-yang (kuo)	1	20	—	—	—	27
	Ying-ch'uan	6	1	1	2	—	4
	Ch'ien-liu	6	—	—	3	—	10
			—	—	2	—	8

Region	Subregion						Total
Subtotal		39	22	2	20	4	87
Northeastern Honan, Southern Hopei	Wei	51	3	—	8	—	62
Subtotal		51	3	—	8	—	62
Eastern Honan, Western Shantung	Ch'ang-i (*kuo*)	6	19	—	5	5	35
Subtotal		6	19	—	5	5	35
Eastern Honan, Northwestern Kiangsu	Liang (*kuo*)	6	1	—	—	—	7
Subtotal		6	1	—	—	—	7
Southeastern Honan, Northwestern Anhui	Ju-nan	4	7	—	—	—	11
Subtotal		4	7	—	—	—	11
Southwestern Honan, Northwestern Hupei	Nan-yang	15	—	1	1	—	17
Subtotal		15	—	1	1	—	17
Southwestern Shantung	Chi-yin	6	1	1	5	1	14
	Chi-yin (*kuo*)	—	1	—	—	—	1
	Tung-p'ing (*kuo*)	—	—	1	—	—	1
	Ta-ho	8	39	—	1	—	48
Subtotal		14	41	2	6	1	64
Southeastern Anhui, Southwestern Kiangsu, Northwestern Chekiang	Tan-yang	—	—	—	1	—	1
	Pei	1	—	—	—	—	1
Subtotal		1	—	—	1	—	2
Hupei	Nan	2	—	—	—	—	2
Subtotal		2	—	—	—	—	2
Szechwan	Shu	—	6	—	—	—	6
	Chien-wei	—	2	—	—	—	2
Subtotal		—	8	—	—	—	8
Uncertain		—	1	1	1	6	9
Subtotal		—	1	1	1	6	9
Total (28 prefectures, 7 kingdoms)		241	105	84	145	27	602

Sources: All the documents listed in "Basic Sources, Conventions and Style of Citing Han Wooden and Bamboo Documents."

[a] All categories of *shu-tsu* and *t'ien-tsu* are included.

western Kiangsu, and northwestern Anhui. This region was then the most populated in the Han empire, but it was also frequently plagued by natural calamities and human catastrophes. As table 10 shows, it had a population density almost two times the national average and four times the combined average of all the other regions included in table 9. The contrast is even sharper when we compare the national average with the main part of the Central Plain region, Honan and western Shantung, which had an average population density of 110.3 and 208.2 persons per square kilometer, respectively. The number of major natural calamities and human catastrophes in the Central Plain region during the period in question amounted to 60 percent of the national total, while the other regions in table 10 accounted for only 17.5 percent. These facts clearly suggest a correlation between Han immigration into Chü-yen from an interior region and the overpopulation and high frequency of natural calamities and human catastrophes in that region. This is consonant with the previously discussed Han policy of using migration to frontier regions as a means of lessening population pressure and settling dislocated people during times of disaster.

The modern Honan and Shantung areas were the richest in Han times. They had the most advanced agricultural economy and highly developed light and heavy industries, such as textiles, clothing, salt, bronze, iron, mining, transportation, and handicrafts. As was discussed previously, the imperial government in Ch'ang-an was dependent on these areas for grain and industrial supplies and services. Together with overpopulation, the prosperous economy with its attendant advanced commerce brought about a high level of urbanization, with an average population of 61,539 per district in the Central Plain region (compared to an overall national average of 44,275 per district), which in turn resulted in a crime rate higher than that of the other regions. As it was a long established Han policy to use criminals to colonize and develop frontier regions, the Central Plain sent more pardoned criminals to the Chü-yen frontier than did the other regions, and this is probably one of the reasons for the higher rep-

TABLE 10. Population Density and Natural and Human Calamities in Han China, 104 B.C.–A.D. 9

Region	Density of Population (persons per square kilometer)[a]		Major Natural Calamities and Human Catastrophes	
	Average	Percentage	Total	Percentage
Empire	42.3	100	40	100
Central Plain	76.4	180.6	24	60
Other regions	17.8	42.1	7	17.5

Sources: Shi-chi; Han-shu; Lao Kan 1935c; Ch'en Kao-yung 1939, vol. 1, pp. 40–58.
Note: Calculations are my own.
[a]Late first century B.C. and early first century A.D.

resentation of the Central Plain in table 9. Ironically, but understandably, the advanced agricultural and industrial economy also contributed to this higher representation, for the agricultural and industrial technology of the Central Plain region became the essential means of development and consolidation in the frontier regions. That the Central Plain region supplies nearly 90 percent of the farming soldiers in table 9 readily testifies to this point. As will be detailed in a later chapter, this region also supplied all the carts and their specially trained drivers that are recorded in the Chü-yen documents and can be geographically identified. The same theory of the need for "development experts" in the frontier regions can explain the presence of the Szechwanese cowherds (*mu-shih*) in Chü-yen because the Szechwan Basin in Han times was a region with an agricultural economy that was highly advanced, probably next only to the Central Plain region.

The geographic origins of the Han garrison personnel also reveal certain significant characteristics of the Han institutions that are either new to historians or add critical information to correct existing knowledge that has been partly inaccurate. The regional origins of the garrison and farming soldiers in table 9 draws our special attention. Of the three capital *chün* (*San-fu*)—Ching-chao-yin, Yu-fu-feng, and T'so-p'ing-i—only two supplied soldiers with certainty, although there were civilians from these three *Chün*. This seems to indicate that the people of the three capital prefectures were mostly or generally not liable for garrison duties on the frontier in Han times. This is contrary to the long-prevailing theory that in fulfilling their military service requirement the eligible residents of draft age in these special prefectures were not treated differently than residents of other regions and that they performed both guard duties in the capital for one year and garrison duties on the frontier for another year.

In table 9, Chang-yeh *chün* registers the largest number of garrison soldiers; next come Wei, Ta-ho, Tung, Huai-yang, Nan-yang, Chi-yin, Ch'ang-i, and Liang. It is understandable that Chang-yeh is in such a position because it was the local prefecture.[130] The other eight regions were the most populous, with highly developed agricultural economies and an average population density of 108.7 persons per square kilometer. Thus, the same demographic and economic factors that were discussed earlier can be applied here. The table also shows that such western and northwestern border *chün* as Wu-wei, Chiu-ch'üan, Tun-huang, T'ien-shu, Chin-ch'eng, Lung-hsi, An-ting, and So-fang are not recorded to have supplied garrison or farming soldiers to Chü-yen.[131] This leads us to believe that the people in these border regions were probably required to remain in their native prefectures, which were also being consolidated and developed and needed a strong military. It seems to have been a general Han policy that the residents of border regions performed garrison duties only in their native prefectures.

The second major issue in the regional origins of the Han garrison personnel concerns whether the subjects of feudal kingdoms in Han times had to provide garrison service on the frontier. It was previously considered a general rule that in the Han period people of the feudal kingdoms were exempt.[132] But table 9 shows that there were thirty-eight soldiers from six feudal kingdoms: seventeen from Ch'ang-i, seven from Liang, six from Chi-yin, four from Chao, and two each from Huai-yang and P'ing-kan. This fact clearly disproves the prevailing theory, and it shows that in matters of military service and garrison obligations the policy of the Han Court was based more on practical considerations than the noble status of a region.

The third major issue relates to the geographic origins of minor officers. Of the eighty-four minor officers listed in table 9, seventy-four were from the local prefecture of Chang-yeh and only ten from other prefectures. The geographic distribution of the seventy-four minor officers from Chang-yeh is as follows.

Names of Districts	Number of Officers
Chang-yeh	1
Chao-wu	1
Chü-yen	37
Hsien-mei	1
Lu-te	30
Ti-ch'ih	3
Wu-lan	1

Here, next to Ch'ü-yen itself, Lu-te District supplied the largest number (about 41 percent) of the geographically identifiable minor officers in the Chü-yen region. Perhaps because Lu-te was then the capital district—the political, economic, military, and administrative center—of Chang-yeh it had more competent and experienced military officers than did the other districts.

It is considered by some scholars a general practice in the Han period for minor officers of a prefecture to be appointed from among the natives.[133] But our study shows that there were five minor officers from other prefectures in Chü-yen: one *ling-shih* from Han-chung, one *wei-shih* from Ho-nan, one *tsu-shih* from Ho-tung, one *ling-shih* from Chi-yin, and one *sui-chang* from Wu-wei. Most likely, this practice was not strictly observed in the Chü-yen region.

Through a study of the geographic origins of the Han frontiersmen and garrison personnel, we have seen the regional demographic, economic, technological, and geographic links between the frontier and the empire. In addition, we have learned about certain new characteristics of the Han governmental institutions, which seem to have been enormously flexible and practical in their approach to specific issues, of which the consolidation and development of frontier regions such as Chü-yen was one.

Class, Society, and the Frontier

The rich data for the preceding analysis of the regional origins of the Han settlers and garrison personnel also provide information about the aristocratic ranks (*chüeh*) held by these people. A careful examination of these data shows that eighty-five of the geographically identified people held aristocratic ranks, which ranged from the first order, *kung-shih*, to the eighth, *k'ung-ch'eng*.[134] Table 11 summarizes the distribution of aristocratic ranks among the various classes of people. Several interesting and significant points emerge from this table: (1) over 28 percent of the Han garrison personnel and settlers held an aristocratic rank; (2) officers have a higher percentage of rank holding (over 47.62 percent); (3) the Chü-yen documents record no one with an aristocratic rank higher than *kung-ch'eng* in the military service; and (4) among the servicemen, the farming soldiers have greater representation (31.42 percent), but the garrison soldiers have a higher percentage of high ranks, with about 81.48 percent of them being of the fifth or higher orders, compared to only 1 percent for the garrison soldiers. All of these issues are directly related to the political culture and social structure of the Former Han dynasty when they are examined in light of the larger sociopolitical context.

Central to the issues under consideration is the structure and function of the Han system of aristocratic rank. As was discussed in chapter 1 in volume 1, the founder of the Han dynasty, Kao-tsu, used the system of aristocratic ranks, which the Han inherited from the Ch'in, as the basis of social stratification and divided the society essentially into two classes: the holders of aristocratic rank as the ruling elite and those without noble rank as the ruled. At the beginning of the dynasty, rank holders enjoyed significant privileges: (1) exemption from poll taxes and labor and military service requirements for them and their families; (2) reduction of the penalty if they committed a crime; (3) selection priority for official appointments; (4) special treatment by high local officials for the holders of high ranks (*kao-chueh*, the seventh, or higher); and (5) receiving revenue from estates for the holders of high ranks. This made the rank holders a privileged class of prestige, wealth, influence, and power in Han society—very much like the gentry class of later periods, though it was created and sustained not by bureaucratic machinery but by arbitrary means.

The original group of rank holders at the beginning of the Han dynasty included only the soldiers, generals, and officers who had fought for the dynastic founders, his civilian followers, the wealthy commoners who supported his

TABLE 11. Distribution of Aristocratic Ranks among Han Settlers and Garrison Personnel in Chü-yen

Rank (Order) Class	Kung-shih (1st)	Shang-tsao (2d)	Tsan-niao (3d)	Pu-keng (4th)	Ta-fu (5th)	Kuan ta-fu (6th)	Kung ta-fu (7th)	Kung-ch'eng (8th)	Rank Holders Class Totals	Percentage of Class
Garrison soldiers (241)	2	2	1	—	15	—	—	7	27	11.20
Farming soldiers (105)	26	4	—	—	2	1	—	—	33	31.43
Officers (84)	—	8	—	—	11	3	3	15	40	47.62
Civilians (145)	—	2	—	2	4	—	—	59	67	46.21
Class unknown (27)	—	1	—	—	—	—	—	4	5	18.52
Totals (602)										
Rank totals	28	17	1	2	32	4	3	85	172	
Percentage of grand total	4.65	2.82	0.16	0.33	5.32	0.66	0.49	14.12		28.57

Note: Numbers in parentheses following each class indicate the total number of persons whose geographical origins are identified with certainty in the Chü-yen documents. Rank holders whose residence was not or could not be determined with certainty to have been in Chü-yen are excluded.

cause, and those who traced their ancestry to China's dynastic or legendary past. But with the passage of time, especially from the era of Han Wu-ti onward, the size of the group gradually expanded for a variety of reasons—such as the court's decision to broaden its ruling base, the sale of ranks for financial reasons and to open new opportunities to the wealthy and discontented, and the bestowal of ranks on special occasions (imperial accession, change of reign titles, natural portents, and so on). When this took place, practical considerations, such as reductions in state revenue and the pool of men available for labor and military service, forced the Han Court to restructure the privileges of the rank holders. First, exemption from poll taxes and labor and military service was limited to only those with the ninth or higher order or rank; second, the category of *kao-chueh* (high ranks) was changed to include only the ninth (*wu ta-fu*) or higher orders; and, third, bestowal of ranks by the court could go only as high as the eighth order, *kung-ch'eng*.[135] The tabulated data on aristocratic rank holding among the Chü-yen settlers and garrison personnel reflect all of these significant changes. No one with an aristocratic rank higher than the eighth order was recorded to have been in the military; the first order (*kung-shih*) and the eighth (*kung-ch'eng*) have the largest representations in the table, 6.68 and 8.48 percent, respectively. This was so probably because the *kung-shih* order was the first phase of rank purchase or bestowal and because the *kung-ch'eng* order was the highest that an accumulation of orders or ranks by purchase or bestowal could reach. The table shows that nearly 22 percent of the Han soldiers in the Chü-yen garrison establishment held aristocratic rank. Considering the fact that soldiers on the frontier were generally not from the privileged classes, this indicates that bestowal of aristocratic ranks by the court was frequent and the holding of noble ranks became widespread. By the same token, this can explain the unusually high percentage (over 21 percent) of rank holders among all the subjects in the table.

The last fact can be further explained by the Han policy of promoting frontier migration. As was discussed earlier, Ch'ao Ts'o (ca. 200–154 B.C.) suggested in 167 B.C. that the government bestow *kao-chueh* on people willing to move to the frontiers. Since the Han government used Ch'ao's proposals as a blueprint in its development of border regions and its colonization of newly acquired areas, and since bestowal of noble ranks on people who were moved to the borders by the government was recorded, the large percentage of rank holding among the Chü-yen population in our discussion can be considered to be due partly to the Han policy of frontier development.[136] But the fact that most of the aristocratic ranks of the Chü-yen colonists are of the lower orders suggests that the Han government in Wu-ti's time and later, the period of the Chü-yen documents, had modified Chao Ts'o's proposal. This is probably especially true for the farming soldiers, since 80 percent of them are recorded to have held a rank of the first order, *kung-shih*. This pattern of rank holding among the farming soldiers strongly suggests that a majority of them were specifically recruited or drafted for their farming expertise and were given aristocratic rank as a reward for moving to the frontier. This also explains the relatively higher percentage of rank holding for farming soldiers in comparison with garrison soldiers, who were stationed in Chü-yen simply for the fulfillment of their regular military obligation.

Table 11 shows that the officers have the largest percentage of rank holding, and all but one of them have noble rank higher than the fifth order, *ta-fu*. The explanation for this can again be found in the Han institutional structure. Recall that document 214.57 records that a rich person requested an appointment as a *hou* clerk because he was rich enough to supply his own horse, saddle, bow, and crossbow. This indicates that wealth could purchase an office even in the military. In fact, the earlier Former Han government functioned exactly this way. There was a property qualification for official appointment, the philosophical rationale for which was that wealthy officials were less vulnerable to corruption. At the beginning of the dynasty, the Han Court made total assessed taxable wealth of one hundred thousand coins (the average wealth of a "middle-class" family) the minimum property qualification for official appointment, but in 142 B.C. it lowered the requirement to forty thousand coins.[137] Beginning with Wu-ti's reign, this rule was no longer strictly enforced. But the Chü-yen document confirms its practice on the frontier, though probably in a modified fashion. The Chü-yen documents concerning the wealth and tax assessments of minor garrison officers indicate that a commander generally had assessed taxable wealth of over one hundred thousand coins.[138] This further supports the theory that property qualifications for office in frontier garrisons were common. Thus, it is apparent that the garrison officers were men of reasonable wealth. Since poor people generally could not be appointed to office and aristocratic ranks could be purchased, it comes as no surprise to see that garrison officers have the largest percentage of ranks.

Some specific technical issues with respect to the Han system of aristocratic ranks remain to be examined. The first is the process of the bestowal of noble ranks. The Chü-yen documents have a number of such records.[139] One is quoted here as an example.[140]

> On the day *chia-ch'en* of the second month of the second year of the Yung-kuan period [of Emperor Yüan's reign; March 10, 42 B.C.], an amnesty is granted; the imperial decree orders the bestowal of a single order [*kung-shih*] on the male commoners [*nan-tzu*].

Cp1216
8192
pl. 519

There are also many records of the bestowal of rank on individuals. The following is an example.[141]

(x) ... Tai T'ung, a soldier from Sung li of Yeh [District, Wei Prefecture], [with the rank of] *kung-ch'eng* [which is an accumulation of eight single orders of rank] was granted on the dates of *ting-wei* when he was a *hsiao-nan* [an underage male], *ting-wei, ping-ch'en, wu-yin, i-hai, kuei-ssu, kuei-yu,* and *ting-ssu* ... (x)

162.14(478)
8036
pl. 513

The dates denoted by the Chinese *kan-chih* (calendar signs, literally, "celestial stems and earthly branches")—*ting-wei, ping-ch'en,* and so forth—can be identified as follows.

Calendar Sign	Dates Denoted
Ting-wei	twenty-fifth day, sixth month, the fifth year of the Shih-yuan period of Emperor Chao (August 10, 82 B.C.)
Ting-wei	twenty-second day, first month, fourth year of the Yuan-feng period of Emperor Chao (March 17, 77 B.C.)
Ping-ch'en	twenty-sixth day, fifth month, first year of the Pen-shih period of Emperor Hsuan (July 2, 73 B.C.)
Wu-yin	twenty-fourth day, fifth month (intercalary month), second year of the Pen-shih period (July 19, 72 B.C.)
I-hai	first day, third month, first year of the Yuan-k'ang period of Emperor Hsuan (April 11, 65 B.C.)
Kuei-ssu	twenty-fourth day, third month, second year of Yuan-k'ang (April 23, 64 B.C.)
Kuei-yu	tenth day, second month, third year of Yuan-k'ang (April 1, 63 B.C.)
Ting-ssu	thirtieth day, third month, fourth year of Yuan-k'ang (May 7, 62 B.C.)

On each of these dates, the person in the document was granted a single order of rank; therefore, his ultimate rank was the eighth, *kung-ch'eng*.[142] Tai T'ung received the first order, *kung-shih*, when he was only a *hsiao-nan* (underage, a male under the age of fifteen) and was under the draft age; therefore, he was then still in his native Wei Prefecture.

The second major technical issue in the Han system of aristocratic ranks concerns the legal age of receiving and relinquishing the orders of the noble ranks. Document 162.14 records a person named Tai T'ung as having received a rank when he was only a *hsiao-nan*, that is, under the age of fifteen. Another wooden document records an even earlier age.[143]

> Ku Shou, [from] Luan-niao [district of Wu-wei], Hsien-chung *li*, [with the rank of] *shang-tsao*, age twelve . . .
>
> 2066
> pl. 100

According to these two documents, the bestowal of rank could begin at least at the *hsiao-nan* age. Twelve is the lowest age recorded for the bestowal of an aristocratic rank in the Chü-yen documents. The *Han-shu*, however, records that a person named Chang Pa was granted the rank of *kuan-nei hou* (marquis of the imperial domain) at the age of seven.[144] This is probably a special case. In the Chü-yen documents, as table 12 shows, only a few of the rank holders were at or under the age of twenty-one other than the two mentioned here.

The question of whether a rank holder relinquished his rank at a certain age has long been a puzzling one. Some scholars have suggested that at the age of fifty-six Han rank holders relinquished their aristocratic orders.[145] But the information in the Chü-yen documents proves this incorrect. For example, the following two strips record that men age sixty and over still held the aristocratic rank.

> . . . (?) Wang Fu, [with the rank of] *shang-tsao*, age sixty . . .
>
> 14.13(432)

> Ch'iu I, [from] Shan-chü li of Feng-ming [district of Ching-chao-yin], [with the rank of] *kung-ch'eng*, age sixty-nine . . .
>
> 53.15(422)

The *Shih-chi* also mentions that a person named Ch'ing Yang from Lin-tzu (in modern Shantung) still had the rank of *kung-ch'eng* when he was over seventy

TABLE 12. Young Aristocratic Rank Holders Recorded in the Chü-yen Documents

Name	Age	Rank	Nativity (district/prefecture)
Ku Shou	12	*Shang-tsao*	Luan-niao, Wu-wei
Tai T'ung	under 15	*Kung-shih*	Yeh, Wei
Li Yun	16	*Pu-keng*	Luan-niao, Chang-yeh
Sun Fu	18	*Kung-ch'eng*	?
?	18[a]	*Kung-shih*	?
Ssu-ma Feng-te	20	*Pu-keng*	?
Wang I	20	*Tsan-niao*	Lu-te, Chang-yeh

Sources: Docs. 2066, 8036, 51.5 (546), 334.1(443), 2170, 387.3(440), 183.6(445).
[a]In the 1949 edition of the *Shi-wen*, it reads *nien-pa* (twenty-eight) instead of *shih-pa* (eighteen). The photograph on p. 106 in Lao 1957 proves that eighteen is correct.

years old.[146] No wooden documents record the relinquishment of aristocratic ranks at a certain age. It thus seems reasonable to assume that such a regulation did not exist in the Han period.[147]

An equally interesting question regarding the Han system of aristocratic ranks is whether the low ranks were hereditary. The Chü-yen documents provide no direct answers to this question. But the noticeable absence of such records and the lack of any positive evidence in the Han written literature strongly suggest that the low orders of rank were not inherited.[148]

The third technical issue in the Han system of aristocratic ranks is the interpretation of certain key names of social classes. It is hoped that an examination of these terms will shed new light on the Han social structure, particularly the hierarchy of classes. The first term is *shih-wu*. This term appears in Han historical writings, where its interpretation by various scholars through the ages has resulted in both controversy and confusion.[149] Although contemporary views of the Former Han period seem to have clearly defined *shih-wu* as a designation of status for a person who had been deprived of his aristocratic rank because of misconduct or a crime, later commentators on Han historical works and scholars of Han institutions have been divided on their interpretations of the term.[150] Wei Hung (fl. A.D. 25–57), of the early Later Han period, suggested in his *Han chiu-i* (Han Old Observances) that a *shih-wei* was a former noble rank holder who still had some legal privileges.[151] Ju Shun (fl. 189–265) offered two differing views: on one occasion, he suggested that *shih-wu* was a designation of status for a person who had been deprived of his noble rank because of improper conduct or a crime; on another, he broadened his view, writing that *shih-wu* referred to a person who had been deprived of both his noble rank (*chueh*) and his official position or office (*kuan*) because of improper conduct or a crime. Both of his views were followed by the celebrated T'ang commentator Yen Shih-ku (581–645).[152] Li Ch'i (fl. 221–65), a contemporary of Ju Shun, however, held that *shih-wu* referred only to those who had been deprived of their noble ranks (*tuo-chueh*), and this view was shared by the famous Ch'ing scholar Wang Ming-sheng (1722–98).[153] But another Ch'ing scholar, Shen Ch'in-han (1775–1831) argued that a *shih-wu* had been deprived of both his noble rank and his official position.[154] Still some others, such as the Ming scholar Tung Yüeh (1620–86) and the Ch'ing legal scholar Shen Chia-pen (1840–1913), tended to interpret *shih-wu* as a term for a specific class of criminals.[155] To sum up, all sources and views agree that the term *shih-wu* referred to those whose aristocratic rank had been taken away because of misconduct or a crime. Three areas of disagreement remain: (1) the *shih-wu*'s eligibility for holding office; (2) retention of some legal privileges for the *shih-wu*; and (3) the question of the *shih-wu* having a criminal status. Traditional sources have been exhausted in the search for a solution, but they have produced only circular reasoning. The discovery of the Chü-yen documents has yielded new and critically important information on two of the three problems. Four of the documents are translated here for reference.

> P'eng Wu, farming soldier, [from] Ch'ang-i *kuo*, Hu-ling [District], Chih-ch'ang *li, shih-wu*, age twenty-four.[156]
>
> Cp1905
> 501.1(447)

> Chao An-shih, garrison soldier, [from] Chao *kuo*, Han-tan city, Yang-sui *li, shih-wu*, age thirty-five.[157]
>
> 50.15(453)
> 2449
> pl. 119

> Li . . . (?) farming soldier, [from] Huai-yang Prefecture, Ch'ang-p'ing [District], P'ing *li, shih-wu*.[158]
>
> 509.18(428B)
> 1481
> pl. 71

> Shun-yü Lung, [from] Ch'ang-i *kuo*, Huang [District], Yüan *li, shih-wu*, age thirty-four.[159]
>
> 517.1(445)
> 1407
> pl. 66

In the registers of garrison personnel, the position of the term *shih-wu* is the same as that of the aristocratic rank in other registers.[160] This seems to confirm the traditional interpretation that *shih-wu* describes a person who has been deprived of aristocratic rank. Since the age of the *shih-wu* in these registers ranges from twenty-four to thirty-five, the soldiers registered were all of the regular draft age and hence were regular garrison personnel. They were certainly not convicts, for if they were they would, as our earlier discussion made clear, be so indicated in the registers. Therefore, it may be safely concluded that *shih-wu* was not a term designating a specific class of convicts in Han times. As to the question of whether the term *shih-wu* indicates the deprivation of both rank and office, one wooden document clarifies the issue.

> Commander Li Kung of the twenty-seventh *sui* of the Chia-ch'ü Commandant Area of the Chü-yen Chief Commandant Area, *shih-wu* . . .
>
> 157.9(498)
> Cp908

Obviously, Li Kung was a *shih-wu* but at the same time an officer. This shows that the status of *shih-wu* was by no means related to one's being an officer. We have thus far established that the term *shih-wu* is used to denote only those who had been deprived of the aristocratic rank and no more than that.[161] But the question of whether a *shih-wu* still enjoyed some privileges, as Wei Hung suggested, remains to be resolved. The Chü-yen documents provide no clues to this particular problem, but they disclose significant information on a related key term in Han social classes, *nan-tzu*.[162] Three of these documents are partially translated here as examples.

> Wang . . . (?), [from] Hsia-hsing *li*, Ling-yang [District, Tan-yang Prefecture], *nan-tzu* . . . (x)   40.17(465)
> 4631
> pl. 267
>
> . . . Tu Kuang, [from] Ch'ang-kuan *li*, P'ing-ling [District of Yu-fu-feng], *nan-tzu* . . .   183.13(171–72)
> 1039
> pl. 74
>
> . . . Chang Tsung, [from] Ta-yung *li*, *nan-tzu* . . .   229.1(174–75)
> 7222
> pl. 443

The position of *nan-tzu* in these documents occupies the same spot as that of the aristocratic rank or *shih-wu* in corresponding registers. Therefore, it also denotes a type of status. Such an identification of social status (class) must have been a required item in registers and other official records. Both Han historical sources and modern scholarly studies have definitely established that the term *nan-tzu* referred to an ordinary male commoner.[163] The context in which the term *nan-tzu* appears in the Chü-yen documents only serves to affirm this interpretation. Therefore, we have two different terms for the designation of commoners, *nan-tzu* and *shih-wu*, and they were in use concurrently. Because there is no evidence that the two were interchangeable, there must be a distinction between a commoner who was classified as *nan-tzu* and a commoner who was classified as *shih-wu*. Wei Hung suggests, in his *Han-chiu-i*, that the distinction between the two statuses is as follows.[164]

> The Ch'in instituted the twenty orders of aristocratic rank. When *nan-tzu* received one order or more, they had their sentences reduced if they had committed a crime, and at the age of fifty-six they were exempted from punishment. When the rank holders were deprived of their rank, they were called *shih-wu* and were granted the privilege of exemption from mutilating punishment only when they reached the age of sixty and would receive no reduction in sentence if they had committed a crime.

This statement outlines the difference in legal privileges between a rank holder and a *shih-wu*. The specific focus is on the reduction in penal sentence and the privilege of receiving an exemption from mutilating punishment. It indicates that a *shih-wu* received no reduction in penal sentence but was exempted from mutilating punishment at the age of sixty. The fact that this last issue receives special notice indicates its distinction from the treatment that commoners (*nan-tzu*) received; otherwise it is meaningless because the last sentence of the statement—the *shih-wu* would not receive a reduction in penal sentence—would cover this aspect. This leads us to examine the treatment of the ordinary commoner in this respect in Han times.

In ancient China, as in modern times, old age was a source of great respect because the Chinese, then as now, regarded old age as a source of wisdom, on one hand, and were guided by the moral imperative of filial piety on the other. This ethical and social ideology was ingrained in the Chinese political culture. In Han times, not only was respect for the elderly mandated through legal instruments, but emperors frequently decreed that the elderly of the empire be given special treatment by government officials and be granted special privileges. Exemption from severe punishment was one such privilege. In 195 B.C., Emperor Hui issued an edict, ordering that commoners age seventy and over be declared exempt from mutilating punishment.[165] Several other emperors decreed that people age eighty and over were to be exempt even from severe interrogation and adjudication for crimes other than false accusation and murder.[166] But for all such special privileges granted to the elderly the lower age limit was always seventy.[167] Therefore, exemption from mutilating punishment at the age of sixty was still a privilege, one that marked the distinction between a *shih-wu* and an ordinary commoner.

We have thus far clarified the meaning of, and the distinction between, the statuses *nan-tzu* and *shih-wu*. In examining this and other issues in the Han system of aristocratic rank, we are impressed that in registers and other official records where identification was an essential concern the social status of a person, be it a commoner or a rank holder, was a required item of information. In such cases, everyone had to identify his social status along with such basic information as nativity and physical characteristics. Therefore, these status indicators were also class indicators, and they were required items in official documents concerning the individuals in question. Thus, in Han times class identification played an essential role not only in one's social life but in one's political and military endeavors. On the basis of such information in the Chü-yen documents and the various issues discussed here, we can divide Han society during and after Emperor Wu's reign into three classes: privileged rank holders, commoners, and slaves. But within each class significant differentials still existed. The details are presented in table 13.

As was discussed in an earlier chapter, the rank holders corresponded in many respects to the gentry class of the later period, except that those holding a high rank were more privileged and influential. The social stratification sketched in table 13 represents a transitional class structure between the Chou feudal system, which was based on birth and kinship, and the rising new system mainly based on landownership and education. In the Chou feudal system, the class structure was the society itself; in the later system, the class structure was first the creation of and then the basis for the political culture, particularly the bureaucratic system, which was based on the idea of meritocracy. The Former Han social stratification lies between the two in time and structure. In recruitment, mobility, institutional means of perpetuation, and political awareness and function, the Former Han ruling class represented a transition from the Chou feudal nobility to a landed class of literati-gentry.

The social class system on the Han frontier was no different from that of the interior society. The records of Han frontier society in Chü-yen in fact provide significant material for the clarification and understanding of some of the key aspects of the Former Han social structure that have heretofore been unclear. As the frontier society was a transplant of the interior society, the link between the two manifests itself clearly through the social origins of the Han settlers and garrison personnel in the Chü-yen region.

In the broader consideration of migration and social structure, the social changes that made military expansion under Emperor Wu possible were a major determinant of the Han migration to frontier regions, but it was not the only one. Factors such as natural and human calamities, as well as political and legal causes, also contributed to the Han migration to Chü-yen. Still, it was the expansion that resulted in the acquisition of Chü-yen, and it was the need for the colonization of Chü-yen that effected the population migration. In that sense, we may venture to state that early Han social and economic changes led to the Chü-yen migration. Regarding the question of how migration generated change in the social structure on the Han frontier, our study also provides a

TABLE 13. Han Social Stratification, 103 B.C.–A.D. 9

Class	Status
Rank Holders	
High ranks	High social, political, economic, and military privileges and influence. Exempt from public service.
Low ranks	Limited privileges and influence. Not exempt from public service.
Commoners	
Shih-wu	Some legal privileges. Liable for public service.
Nan-tzu	Liable for public service. No legal privileges.
Slaves	Dependent. No freedom.

mixed answer. It is true that to encourage frontier migration the Han government granted aristocratic ranks to migrants, which seems to have produced a high ratio of rank holders among the Han settlers and garrison personnel in Chü-yen. But none of the Han colonists whose records we have just analyzed held high ranks, the ranks that were the source of important social, political, economic, and legal privileges and hence placed their holders in the real ruling class. Migration to Chü-yen brought the migrants some limited benefits, but they were not significant enough to engender any important change in the social process. This is particularly true if one looks at the two major characteristics of frontier development: government-controlled migration with little free movement and economic opportunities, and allotment of land only by the government. Here again is the link between the empire and the frontier, the societal bond. The frontier society was merely a microcosm of the interior society with a strong military tinge.

Age and the Military Service

The Chü-yen documents contain much information about various facets of the Han military system and the functioning of that system on the frontier. An examination of such information not only broadens our knowledge of the Han military organization but increases our understanding of the changes that resulted from operations on the frontier. We will first look into the age composition of the Han military forces.

Information on the age of the Han garrison personnel and settlers is found mainly in the official registers of various functions in the Chü-yen documents. A careful analysis of such materials produces the data tabulated in table 14. While the data in this table indicate no special patterns about the civilians and those whose class is unknown, they show a very significant aspect of the age of Han servicemen. First, the age of the Han servicemen in Chü-yen ranges from only twenty to fifty—or to sixty-nine if the one case in the "unknown" category is included. Second, of the sixty-one soldiers and officers in the table, forty-one, over 67 percent, are in an age range from twenty-three to thirty. This strongly suggests that most of the Han servicemen were at or under the age of thirty. Third, the new information helps answer the question regarding the range of the Former Han draft age, a topic that has been under debate since the early Later Han times.[168] Modern studies, particularly the contributions of Hamaguchi Shigekuni and Yang Lien-sheng, have generally concluded that the draft age at the beginning of the Han period was probably twenty-three and that it was lowered to twenty after 155 B.C. But a question was raised about the possibility that it was raised to twenty-three again during Emperor Chao's reign (87–74 B.C.). Table 14 shows four soldiers under twenty-three, and since the majority of the Chü-yen documents belong to the period of Emperor Chao's reign and after it seems highly probable that the draft age did not always begin at twenty-three during that period. Furthermore, the table also shows four officers age twenty-three and under. Since some of the officers at the frontier were promoted from soldier status, and two of the four officers in the table can be dated to the period after Emperor Chao's reign, one to Emperor Hsuan's reign (74–49 B.C.) and one to Wang Mang's reign (A.D. 9–23), it may be reasonable to say that the draft age was lowered to twenty after the reign of Emperor Chao.[169]

Table 14 shows no serviceman under twenty. It is very likely that throughout the Han period the lowest regular draft age was twenty. Regarding the age of retirement from the military, the table provides no conclusive information. But no soldiers are indicated to have been over forty-four, and no officers are over fifty. Perhaps for this issue we can be content with the conclusions of modern studies that in the Han period a man was no longer liable for regular military or labor services at the age of fifty-five or fifty-six.

The second major issue about the military system on the frontier is length of service. Although by the established Han regulations of conscription and labor service the length of time a garrison soldier served on the frontier was only one year and that of a laboring soldier (*keng-tsu*) at home one month a year, the Chü-yen documents record a large number of servicemen who stayed on the frontier for a much longer period.[170] There were even many soldiers who remained in the service long enough to be promoted to the position of minor officer. For example, Ma Ping-chi, from the prefecture of Wei, was initially a soldier at a watch station in Chü-yen, but later he was promoted to the position of commander of the seventh *t'ing* of the T'ien-pei *hou-kuan*.[171] Similarly, Wang Ch'iang was originally a cavalryman from Chao-wu District in Chang-yeh. Later he was was appointed subcommandant of the Ping-t'ing *hou* of the Chia-ch'ü *hou-kuan*, and finally he was dismissed because of administrative faults.[172] There were also many minor officers who remained in the area long enough to receive several promotions and transfers. Fan Hung, a native of Lu-te in Chang-yeh, was first appointed assistant to the commandant in the office of the Chia-ch'ü *hou-kuan*, then was promoted to the position of foreman clerk in the same office, and finally was promoted to the position of chief clerk in charge of financial and grain matters for the whole Chia-ch'ü Commandant Area.[173] Similarly, Wang Ch'ung served first as commander of the Chü-ch'i *sui* of the Chia-ch'ü *hou-kuan* and then was promoted to the position of subcommandant of a certain *hou*.[174] Another officer, Yen-shou, began his career in the Chü-yen region as commander of the sixth *t'ing* of the T'ien-pei *hou-kuan* in 87 B.C. Later, in 85, he was appointed the assistant head of the Tai-t'ien Granary, and in 82 he was promoted to supervisor of the Tai-t'ien Granary.[175] Thus, he

TABLE 14. Age Distribution of the Han Colonists in Chü-yen

Age	Farming Soldiers	Garrison Soldiers and Laboring Soldiers	Officers	Civilians	Class Unknown	Total
11	—	—	—	1	—	1
12	—	—	—	1	—	1
13	—	—	—	2	—	2
16	—	—	—	1	—	1
17	—	—	—	2	—	2
18	—	—	—	2	1	3
19	—	—	—	2	—	2
20	—	2	1	1	—	4
21	1	—	3	—	1	4
22	5	1	1	1	—	2
23	5	1	1	1	1	9
24	2	2	—	—	—	7
25	—	1	1	3	—	7
26	3	2	2	2	1	6
27	1	1	—	—	1	5
28	—	—	1	2	—	4
29	4	4	5	1	1	2
30	—	—	5	1	1	14
32	1	—	1	1	1	3
34	—	1	—	—	—	2
35	1	—	1	—	2	3
36	—	—	1	—	—	2
37	2	—	—	—	—	1
39	—	—	—	1	—	2
40	—	1	—	1	—	1
42	—	—	—	—	—	1
44	—	—	1	1	—	1
46	—	—	1	2	—	3
47	—	—	—	—	—	1
50	—	—	—	1(?)	1	2
60	—	—	—	1(?)	—	1
69	—	—	—	—	—	
Total	25	16	20	30 (?)	9	100 (?)

spent at least six years on the frontier. In addition to these cases, there were minor officers who remained in their posts for quite long periods of time without being transferred or promoted. For example, the famous Commander Wang Shu of the second *t'ing* of the T'ien-pei *hou-kuan*, a native of Chü-yen, served in the same post for about nine years (90–82 B.C.).[176]

Clearly a number of soldiers served in the garrison settlements for a period much longer than the prescribed time of military service. If this was not a special case for a frontier region such as Chü-yen, certainly either the one-year regulation was not observed or these people were hired as professional soldiers. I am inclined to endorse the view that frontier regions such as Chü-yen were special cases whose development and security dictated some deviation from the established regulations. One might also suggest that such long terms of military service demonstrated their superiority and hence paved the way for the establishment of a professional army in early Later Han times.[177]

We have discussed two critical aspects of the Former Han military system as seen in the Chü-yen documents: age and length of service. For the former, the results present a clear age profile of the Han military forces on the Chü-yen frontier. It marks no significant deviation from the system understood through traditional sources but serves to clarify some of the unclear issues that have long been under debate. For the length of military service, the pattern of the Chü-yen garrison personnel shows a significant deviation from the established Han regulations of conscription and labor service. This deviation was a result of the interplay between two major factors: special conditions on the frontier and the need for stability and continuity within the military. The new pattern is assumed to have played a role in the eventual transformation of the Han military from a conscripted to a professional army. This was an important impact of frontier development on the Han empire.

Cavalrymen and Military Regionalism

The *ch'i-shih*, or cavalrymen, formed a unique category in the Han military. They had special quarters in the Chü-yen garrison establishment, they maintained a special organizational unit, and they were registered on special forms.[178] This reflects the special status of the *ch'i-shih*, a status that signified their importance and bespoke their unique role in Han military expansion and frontier development. In a larger sense, the importance of the *ch'i-shih* is related to military conditions, national priorities, and regionalism in the Han empire during the period under consideration.

The various documents that concern the *ch'i-shih* in the Chü-yen documents provide valuable information on some of these issues. We will first pose the same question about the *ch'i-shih* as we did for the other servicemen in the

Chü-yen garrison establishment. What were their regional distribution, ages, and aristocratic ranks?

Regarding their regional background, the available Chü-yen sources all indicate that the *ch'i-shih* in Chü-yen were from only one region, the local prefecture of Chang-yeh.[179] Table 15 shows the regional origins of those *ch'i-shih* whose nativity was recorded in the Chü-yen documents. They were from eight of the ten districts of Chang-yeh. But the districts of Ti-ch'ih and Lu-te supplied the largest numbers, seventeen (34.69 percent) and fifteen (30.61 percent), respectively. The reason for this is not readily understood. In the case of Lu-te, this might be due to the fact that it was then the capital of Chang-yeh and it communicated with Chü-yen more frequently.[180] This is similar to the fact that Lu-te supplied the largest number of garrison officers in the Chü-yen region. It may also be true that as a capital city Lu-te was a center for Chang-yeh's *ch'i-shih*, because they were the most elite military force in the frontier prefectures on the northwestern borders of the Han empire. In the case of Ti-ch'ih, distance should not be considered the reason that it supplied a higher percentage of *ch'i-shih* in Chü-yen because Chao-wu and Wu-lan were much closer. But Ti-ch'ih borders Lu-te on the west. Perhaps the two districts were the centers for Chang-yeh's cavalry forces in Han times.

No *ch'i-shih* in Chü-yen were from prefectures other than Chang-yeh. This suggests that the *ch'i-shih* did not serve in garrisons outside their native prefectures.

Regarding the ages of the *ch'i-shih*, the Chü-yen documents provide no positive information. No documents record the age of a *ch'i-shih*.[181] Scholars have generally assumed that while most of the *shu-tsu* (garrison soldiers) ranged in age from thirty to forty, the *ch'i-shih* were younger.[182] This assumption has found no definite proof in the Chü-yen documents. In the absence of any positive evi-

TABLE 15. Regional Background of the *Ch'i-shih* in Chü-yen

Districts in Chang-yeh	Number of *Ch'i-shih*	Percentage of Total[a]
Chao-wu	5	10.20
Chü-yen	7	14.28
Hsien-mai	1	2.04
Jih-le	1	2.04
Lu-te	15	30.61
P'an-ho	2	4.08
Ti-ch'ih	17	34.69
Wu-lan	1	2.04
Total	49	

[a]Figures have been rounded to two decimals.

dence for a different conclusion, we can only assume that there was no peculiar pattern of age for the *ch'i-shih*.

No *ch'i-shih* in Chü-yen is recorded to have received aristocratic rank in the Chü-yen documents. The reason for this is not understood. It is so strange a fact that one is led to speculate that at one time the title *ch'i-shih* was probably equivalent to an aristocratic rank or bestowed a special status in society.[183] But no positive evidence for this conjecture has been found. Instead, one wooden document indicates that the *ch'i-shih* may once have been considered an officer.

(x) . . . now is appointed (*ch'u*) *ch'i-shih* of Lu-te.[184]   510.3(432)
31
pl. 3

This document shows that the *ch'i-shih* were appointed, not conscripted, as were other soldiers, and that, because the word *ch'u* refers only to the appointment of officials, the *ch'i-shih*'s status was that of an officer, not a soldier.[185] Evidence for this can also be found in the *Han-shu*. In the *Biography of Kung-sun Ho*, the *Han-shu* has a passage that reads as follows.[186]

> In his earlier years [Kung-sun] Ho served as a *ch'i-shih*; he joined the expeditions and earned merit several times. . . . [Ho] says: "Your humble minister was originally a rustic in the border regions, and he first became an officer by virtue of his provision of saddle and horse and his skill at riding (*ch'i*) and shooting (*she*) . . ."

In the *Biography of Chao Ch'ung-kuo*, regarding the early life of General Chao, the *Han-shu* states:[187]

> Chao Ch'ung-kuo, styled Weng-sun, from Shang-kuei District of [the prefecture of] Lung-hsi, . . . At the beginning of his career, he was a *ch'i-shih*.

In these two cases, the *Han-shu* refers to the early careers of two eminent Han generals as "starting" (*shao-wei* or *shih-wei*) with the position of *ch'i-shih*. Obviously, the *ch'i-shih* status here is considered a step on the official ladder. Kung-sun Ho (fl. 133–91 B.C.) was a *ch'i-shih* in the last years of Emperor Ching (r. 157–141 B.C.), and Chao Ch'ung-kuo (137–52 B.C.) was a *ch'i-shih* in the early reign of Emperor Wu (141–87 B.C.). Therefore, most likely in the early years of Emperor Wu the term reflected this point. Furthermore, both the *Shih-ch'i* and the *Han-shu* indicate that as late as 119 B.C. the *ch'i-shih* were still included in the category of officials who were granted special tax exemptions.[188]

This, too, confirms the point that *ch'i-shih* was a status equal to that of the officer. In a commentary on the *Shih-chi*, Ju Shun says that the wealthy *ch'i-shih* of the northwestern border prefectures were indeed treated as officers (*kuan*).[189] This suggests a clear distinction between the well-equipped and expertly trained *ch'i-shih*, who grew up in the border regions and experienced mounted archery as a way of life, and the ordinary horsemen, regular foot soldiers trained as mounted archers who are simply referred to as *ch'i* or *ch'i-ping* in the accounts of military expeditions.[190] Perhaps the former also served as trainers for the latter in the government pastures that bred horses and trained mounted archers.[191]

The time when the officer status of the *ch'i-shih* was terminated is not known. But unless document 510.3 was brought to Chü-yen from somewhere else, something that, judging from the text of the document, seems improbable, this strip from Chü-yen indicates that the special institutional character of the *ch'i-shih* did not end earlier than 103 B.C., when Chü-yen was first developed by the Han forces.

Even if the *ch'i-shih* lost their special officer status at a later time, they remained a special military group under the Han empire. As late as Emperor Hsuan's reign, they still received orders directly from the central government; even the highest local authorities of the prefectures where they were stationed were prohibited from ordering or dispatching them without approval of the court.[192]

Why the *ch'i-shih* received such special treatment is an interesting question. It is an issue that goes beyond mere military considerations. It was really related to the major national concerns and priorities of the Han empire during the period in question. As was discussed earlier, the greatest threat to the national security of the Former Han empire from Kao-tsu to Wu-ti was the Hsiung-nu challenge on the northern and northwestern borders. As the sense of national humiliation resulting from Kao-tsu's defeat at P'ing-ch'eng and the danger to national security inflicted by continual Hsiung-nu border invasions and their successful march to the imperial capital at Ch'ang-an became the preoccupation of the Han Court, the Hsiung-nu problem and the search for its successful solution emerged to become the top national priority for the Han empire. The Han Court was determined to channel all of its resources and manpower into meeting the Hsiung-nu challenge, but it first had to build a large mobile cavalry force to match the military superiority of the Hsiung-nu nomadic horsemen. And here the *ch'i-shih* of the border prefectures in the north and northwest came to play a special role in Han dynastic history and probably in Chinese history as well. By virtue of their geographic and climatic conditions, the northern and northwestern border regions of the Han empire were arid steppe pastureland, and only there were skillful horse-breeding and mounted archery a natural way of life. Therefore, it was in this territory, which mainly consisted of those prefectures extending roughly from modern Kansu in the west to An-tung in Manchuria, that the Han Court established government pastures to undertake the mass breeding of horses and the training of hundreds of thousands of mounted archers, the key to the grand military campaigns against the Hsiung-nu and their allies in the Western Regions. In carrying this out, the Han Court must have been dependent on the expertise of the native *ch'i-shih* of these regions; they were the only such resource available in Han China, as the people of other regions lacked such skills. Therefore this was apparently the major reason for the *ch'i-shih* of these regions to have been given a special status. The northern and northwestern military campaigns resulted in a tremendous territorial expansion that had a lasting impact not only on the course of the Han dynasty but also on the course of Chinese history. Here the special role of the *ch'i-shih* is clearly manifested.

In examining the records of Han Wu-ti's Hsiung-nu and Western Regions campaigns, it becomes clear that, militarily speaking, the northern and northwestern border sections of the Han empire alone were responsible for making the campaigns a reality. The horses were bred in that region; massive numbers of horsemen were trained in, and were probably recruited mostly from, that region; the elite military *ch'i-shih*, who served as the trainers and leaders of the ordinary horsemen were from that region; and eighteen of the twenty commanding generals whose geographic origins are known came from that region.[193] Thus, all of the three basic elements of the military action—resources, manpower, and leadership—were from one region. In view of the dimensions and impact of Han Wu-ti's expansion, it may safely be reasoned that the border sections of the north and northwest shaped Chinese history through the various campaigns that produced the expansion. In the long history of China, each of its various geographic sections seems to have been associated with a particular historical or cultural mission. From our preceding observations, the historical mission of China's northern and northwestern border regions lies in their special contribution to the great Han expansion during the period of Emperor Wu.

Military regionalism also has some significant relevance to our discussion. In Han China, because of the differing geographic and economic conditions, each region was known for a peculiar military specialty. The region south of the Huai and Yangtze Rivers, known for its enormous rivers and lakes, extended seacoast, and marine climate, was famous for producing mariners (*lou-ch'uan*); the Szechwan Basin in the southwest, particularly such Han prefectures as Pa and Shu—marked by its endless hills and low mountains and its long agricultural tradition—was famous for producing skilled foot soldiers (*ts'ai-kuan*); the Central Plain region—particularly such Han prefectures as Ho-nei, Ho-tung, Ho-nan,

Ju-nan, Ying-ch'uan, Huai-yang and P'ei—marked by its generally dry, level terrain and its long agricultural tradition and cultural heritage, was famous for producing foot soldiers; and the northern and northwestern nomadic and mountainous pastureland just discussed—particularly such Han prefectures as Chin-ch'eng, T'ien-shui, Lung-hsi, An-ting, Pei-ti, Shang-tang, and Shang—was famous for producing skilled cavalrymen and ordinary horsemen.[194] Reviewing the acquisition and development of the Ho-hsi region and our preceding analysis of the various facets of the Han garrison personnel and frontiersmen in Chü-yen, this military regionalism is especially interlocked with the Han process of military expansion and colonial frontier development. It was the skilled cavalrymen and horsemen of the pastureland region that allowed and sustained the military expansion that resulted in the acquisition of the Ho-hsi region and more, but the consolidation of these regions through systematic garrison development was mainly achieved by the foot soldiers and émigrés from the Central Plain and Szechwan Basin regions. The skillful coordination and management of the different special military regions to achieve such goals may have been necessitated by the locational, economic, and military conditions of the Han empire at that time, but they also manifested clearly the exceptional vision and dimension of the managerial, organizational, and administrative minds of the Han leaders during this period of great expansion. For it was the leaders who put all the elements to work in a well-designed, grand scheme.

3

THE HAN SETTLEMENTS IN CHÜ-YEN

Structure, Pattern, and Function

THE SUCCESSFUL CONSOLIDATION and development of a frontier region such as Chü-yen depended not only on an efficient military and administrative organization, a practical and effective immigration scheme, and a close yet flexible link with the interior of the empire but also on a well-designed plan of colonization. This plan had to be based on local geographic conditions, local economic potential and needs, and military security; it also had to match perfectly the garrison organizational structure. The Han settlements in Chü-yen satisfied all of these requirements and can be regarded as a model plan in many respects. Being designed to fit the various local conditions and special needs, it was derived from both the administrative and the garrison organizational structures. Not only did it combine garrison and settlement into one, but it also made both civil administration and military establishments work together as one system on the frontier.

The main goal of this chapter is to examine the Han civilian and garrison settlements on the Chü-yen frontier. Specifically, it analyzes the structure, the physical plant, and the residential pattern of the numerous Han settlements of varying sizes and functions. It is hoped that this study will reveal the characteristic pattern of the Han frontier settlements not only in Chü-yen but also in the Ho-hsi region as a whole.

The Han settlements in the Chü-yen region consisted of garrison fortifications and buildings of different sizes and functions, as well as civilian and agricultural establishments. They formed the posts that the Han colonists inhabited and from which they developed and consolidated the region to make it a permanent part of the empire. In specific terms, the settlements were in the form of walled cities (*ch'eng*), fortresses (*chang*), and watch stations (*sui* or *t'ing*). In the Chü-yen region, the main nodes of settlement filled in an area extending along the Edsen-gol for 260 kilometers from south to north (for over 300 kilometers if the northernmost outposts are counted), and they ranged from 12 to 50 kilometers from east to west. All the Han settlements in the colonized area were organized into civil administrative and military garrison units. The civil administrative units followed the general structure of the Han local administrative system: *hsien* (district), *hsiang* (county), and *li* (ward). But the garrison units established a special system of frontier settlements. Although these units were named after those in the garrison organization, such as *tu-wei*, *hou-kuan*, *hou*, and *sui* or *t'ing*, they represented a hierarchy of settlement units and were much broader in scope than mere military organizational units. They were organizations that combined military and administrative responsibilities. As military units, they each commanded their respective military forces, carried out their assigned military duties, and were stationed in a headquarters. As administrative units, they controlled a well-defined territory and supervised all the civilian residents and civil affairs within their domains; they generally did so in the absence of civil authorities, but even where these did exist the garrison units were entrusted with civil power and authority. This was necessary in a region in which military concerns overshadowed civilian affairs and which was still in the process of development under military rule. For these reasons, I regard such garrison settlements as territorial units under a combined military and civil administration and call each of them an "area." So the hierarchy of garrison settlements is: chief commandant area for a *tu-wei* unit, commandant area for a *hou-kuan* unit, subcommandant area for a *hou* unit, and commander area for a *sui* or *t'ing* unit. The garrison settlements will be discussed first.

THE GARRISON SETTLEMENTS: *TU-WEI*, *HOU-KUAN*, *HOU*, AND *SUI* OR *T'ING*

The garrison settlements in Chü-yen had the same hierarchy as the garrisons themselves. The chain of command went from *tu-wei* unit to *hou-kuan* unit, then to *hou* unit, and finally to *sui* or *t'ing* unit.[1] There were two chief commandant areas in this region: the Chü-yen Chief Commandant Area (in the north), and the Chien-shui Chief Commandant Area (in the south). The former consisted of four commandant areas: Chü-yen, T'ien-pei, Chia-ch'ü, and Sa-ching;

the latter consisted of three commandant areas: T'o-t'o, Kuang-ti, and Chien-shui. The geographic distribution of these commandant areas in an approximately north-south order is outlined in table 16.[2] The headquarters of the Chü-yen chief commandant was in the city of Chü-yen and that of the Chien-shui chief commandant in the city of Chien-shui, which is Taralingin-durbeljin (Ta-wan), or A35, in Bo Sommarström's report. The commandant areas surrounded the two cities. The Chia-ch'ü Commandant Area was west and northwest of Chü-yen city; the T'ien-pei north and northeast; and the Sa-ching was southeast. The Chü-yen Commandant Area encompassed the city of Chü-yen and its hinterland.

In the Chien-shui Chief Commandant Area, the T'o-t'o Commandant Area was in the northernmost part, bordering the Chü-yen Chief Commandant Area in the north; the Chien-shui Commandant Area was between the T'o-t'o Commandant Area and Chien-shui city. The Kuang-ti Commandant Area was located south of the city of Chien-shui, bordering the Mao-mu area in the south, which is the point of entry to the whole Chü-yen region (see map 3).

The *hou* or subcommandant area was a subdivision of a commandant area. According to the Chü-yen documents, there are two types of *hou*: the *hou* with a literary name (e.g., Ping-t'ing *hou*), and the *hou* with a number as its name (e.g., the twenty-third *hou*). In addition, there are *pu*, which had the same organization as a *hou*. The relationship among the three has long puzzled scholars in the field; no constructive conclusion has heretofore been reached.[3] Here I wish to offer some tentative suggestions based on a fresh study of the Chü-yen documents. We shall start with the problem of the *pu*. One wooden document indicates clearly that the *pu* is superior to the *sui* or commandant area.[4]

TABLE 16. Han Garrison Settlements in Chü-yen: Major Units and Their Modern Locations

Hou-kuan (commandant areas)	Mongolian Names for the *Hou-kuan* Headquarters	Chinese Names	Corresponding Sites in Sommarström's Report
Chü-yen *tu-wei*			
T'ien-pei	Wayen-torei	Wa-yin-t'o-ni	A10
Chü-yen	Khara-khoto	Hei-ch'eng	K799
Chia-ch'ü	Mu-durbeljin	P'o-ch'eng-tzu	A8
Sa-ching	Boro-tsonch	Po-lo-sung-chih	P9
Chien-shui *tu-wei*			
T'o-t'o	Bagha-durbeljin	Hsiao-fang-ch'eng	A24
Chien-shui	Ulan-durbeljin	Ti-wan	A33
Kuang-ti	?	Man-Han-ch'eng in Shuang-ch'eng-tzu	A38

Sources: Chia-pien, p. 140, based on Lao Kan's studies and field observations; Bo Sommarström, 1956–58.

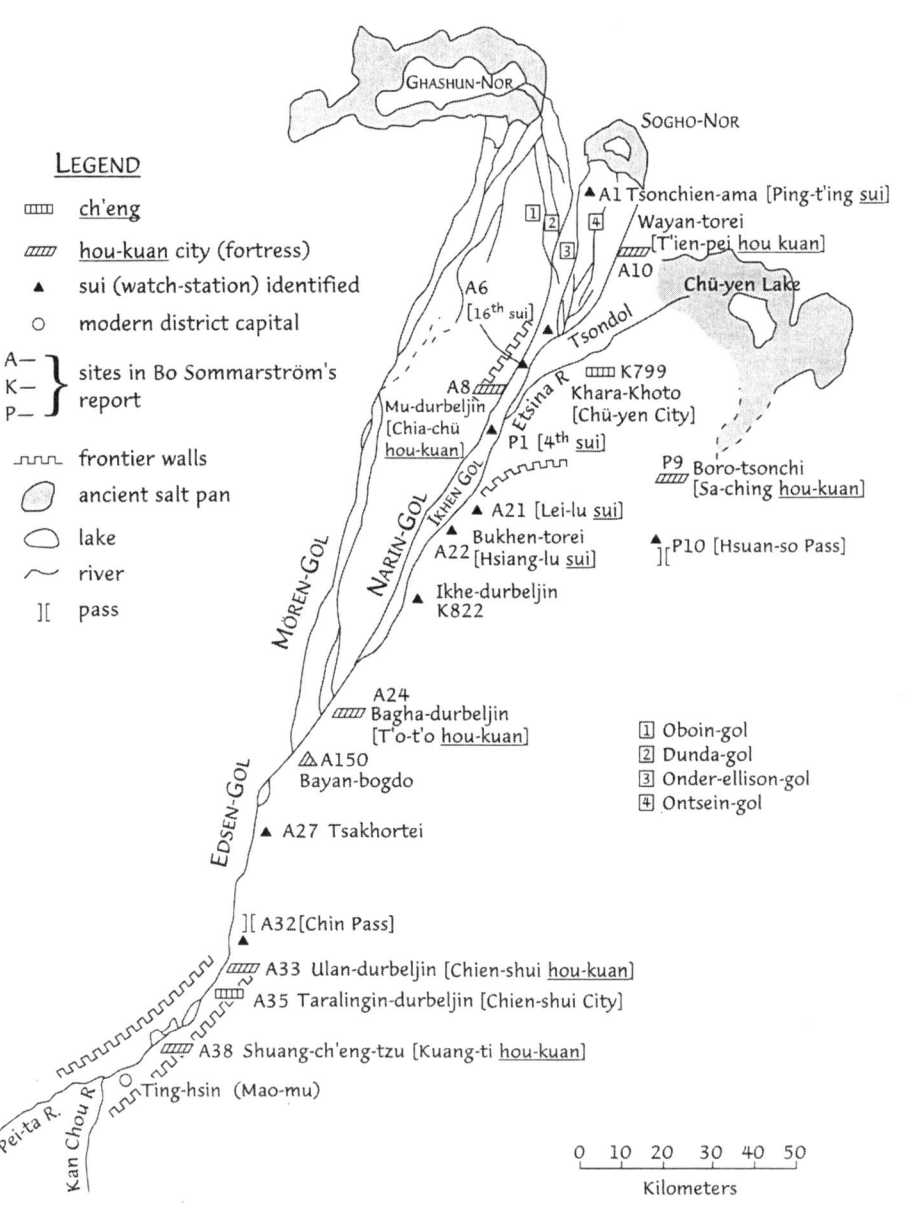

Map 3. Major Han Garrison Settlements in the Chü-yen Region

The T'un-yüan *pu*:
> [The payment of] *hou-shih li* (or *hou-shih* and *li*) has been collected.
> [The payment of] Commander Wei of the T'un-pei *sui* has been collected.
> [The payment of] the commander of the Wan-nien *sui* has been collected.
> Now [a] total [of] 3,600 cash has been collected. 112.29(288)
>   3889

Evidently, there were *sui* or commander areas under the *pu*. On the other hand, there was the *hou-kuan* or commandant area above the *pu*, as is recorded on the following wooden strip.

> The Chia-ch'ü Commandant Area [of the Chü-yen Chief Commandant Area]: The sixth month of the fourth year of the Chien-chao period [of Emperor Yüan (35 B.C.)], the *hou-chang* of the *pu* . . . 145.19(493)

Furthermore, this document indicates that the head of a *pu* was called a *hou-chang* (subcommandant). This is further evidenced by the following documents.

> . . . The *hou-chang* of the twenty-third *pu* . . .   157.29(80)
> . . . The *hou-chang* of the north *pu* . . .   232.18(368)
> . . . The *hou-chang* of the south *pu* . . .   232.33(361)
> . . . The *hou-chang* of the east *pu* . . .   Cp179A
> . . . The *hou-chang* of the tenth *pu* . . .   159.17(57)

From these examples one may conclude that the *pu* was identical to the *hou*. The earliest document that indicates the existence of the *pu* is dated the third year of the Yüan-feng period of Emperor Chao (78 B.C.). The dating of the twenty-third *pu* ranges from 77 B.C. to A.D. 25.[5] Indeed, the *pu* existed concurrently with the *hou*, and the two can be paired.[6]

Hou	Pu
The fourth *hou*	The fourth *pu*
The tenth *hou*	The tenth *pu*
The seventeenth *hou*	The seventeenth *pu*
The twenty-third *hou*	The twenty-third *pu*
Lin-mu *hou*	Lin-mu *pu*
Ping-t'ing *hou*	Ping-t'ing *pu*
Pu-ch'in *hou*	Pu-ch'in *pu*
T'un-yüan *hou*	T'un-yüan *pu*
Wan-sui *hou*	Wan-sui *pu*

As in the case of the *hou*, both literary names and numbered names were associated with the *pu*, and the relationship between the two is clearly indicated by document 45.15, which contains the expression *P'ing-t'ing ti nien-san pu*. Since Ping-t'ing is not a *hou-kuan* and several wooden documents record Ping-t'ing *pu* or Ping-t'ing *hou-chang*, this document proves that the Ping-t'ing *pu* and the twenty-third *pu* are identical.[7] In light of this understanding, the complete document 45.15 is translated here.[8]

> The register of sick soldiers of the Ping-t'ing (twenty-third) *pu* during the thirrd month of the fourth year of the Wu-feng period [of Emperor Hsüan (54 B.C.)].
>
> 45.15
> 2711
> pl. 131

Thus, this *pu* is clearly recorded as having both a literary name and a numbered name. Further, since the head of a *pu* is called a *hou-chang*, the establishment of this relation points to the conclusion that the Ping-t'ing *pu*, the Ping t'ing *hou*, the twenty-third *pu*, and the twenty-third *hou* are four names for the same subcommandant area. There are not enough documents to extend this relation to the other pairs of *hou* and *pu* listed earlier. But judging from this example it is quite possible that such a rule holds true for some other subcommandant areas in the same Chia-ch'ü Commandant Area.

On the basis of the preceding observations, other information, and the works of various scholars, I have worked out a list of the *hou* units in the Chü-yen region. These are listed in table 17.[9]

The smallest unit in the garrison settlement is the *sui* or *t'ing*, the commander area.[10] It is a subdivision of a subcommandant area. In the Chü-yen region, over 260 *sui* and *t'ing* are recorded on wooden strips, and 156 of them have already been archaeologically explored. These units stretch over 300 kilometers from Mao-mu northward to locations about 40 kilometers northwest of Tsonchien-ama (site Al in Bo Sommarström's report), and they spread from 12 to 50 kilometers east and west of this line. A subcommandant area is recorded to have generally consisted of five to eight commander areas, and the watchtowers in these fortifications were separated by average distances of 1,300 meters (for areas along the riverbanks) to 2,000 meters (for areas in the northeastern desert region).[11] Of the commander areas in the Chü-yen region, a great majority were called *sui*, but *t'ing* can also be found in all the commandant areas. Among the *t'ing* were several with names indicating their function, for example, the Ch'i-ping *t'ing* (Cavalrymen Commander Area) of the T'o-t'o Commandant Area and the Nung *t'ing* (Agricultural Commander Area) of the Chü-yen Commandant Area.[12] In addition, the names of certain *t'ing* indicated

TABLE 17. Major Garrison Settlements in Chü-yen

Hou-kuan (commandant areas)	Hou or Pu (subcommandant areas)	Document Numbers
T'ien-pei	T'ien-pei	30.4
	Ch'üeh-hu	273.9
	T'ung-tse	273.9
Chia-ch'ü	Pu-ch'in (hou, pu)	227.26, 55.10
	Ch'eng-pei (hou, pu)	265.11, 101.26
	Chia-ch'ü	202.1
	I-lu	303.18
	T'un-yüan (hou, pu)	203.28, 194.2
	Ping-t'ing (hou, pu)	
	Twenty-third (hou, pu)	
	Wan-sui (hou, pu)	82.39, 55.24
	Wu-shang	278.7
	Lin-mu (hou, pu)	137.4, 189.19
	Mi-ku	303.33
Chia-ch'ü	T'ui-mu	48.2
	Shou-lu	66.87
	An-chu	38.17
	Pu-ssu	35.8
	Kuo-tung pu	Cp 764
	Fourth (hou, pu)	154.54, Cp642A
	Seventh (hou, pu)	159.17 + 283.46; pl. 258; Cp492
	Tenth (hou, pu)	159.17, 123.24
	Seventeenth (hou, pu)	28.1, 214.78
Chü-yen	Chü-yen (hou, pu)	173.1, 89.43
	Tso-che-lu	145.32
Sa-ching	Che-yao	458.2
	Lei-lu	158.3
	Sa-ching	454.24
T'o-t'o	T'o-t'o	77.39
	Chung (hou, pu)	Cp574AB
Chien-shui	Chien-shui (hou, pu)	515.38, Cp178
	Yu-ch'ien	329.1
	Yu-hou	15.25
	Tso-ch'ien	10.34
	Tung (hou, pu)	314.26
	? Ts'ang-shih	433.32
	? Hsin-ma	Cp1317, Cp1992
Kuang-ti	Kuang-ti	562.9
	Pei (hou, pu)	177.14, 232.18
	Nan (hou, pu)	232.33, and pl. 413 in Lao Kan 1949
Unknown	An-lo	93.8, 332.14
	Ch'eng-pei	Cp437, Cp1227
	etc.	

Sources: Lao Kan 1957, vol. 1, pp. 9–11; Itō Michiharu 1953, pp. 48–49.

their size, for example, the Hsiao t'ing (Small t'ing).¹³ In the T'ien-pei Commandant Area, the t'ing were numbered; I have noticed the following numbered t'ing.

The second t'ing	275.21(335)
The fourth t'ing	273.9(319)
The sixth t'ing	275.21(335)
The seventh t'ing	275.20(335)

Since only a small number of t'ing are recorded in the Chü-yen documents, the relationship between these numbered t'ing and the literary t'ing cannot be traced.

Of the sui in the Chü-yen region, a large group were numbered, ranging from first to thirty-eighth. A complete list of these numbered sui is presented in table 18.

With these numbered sui, we again face the problem of whether they were just different names for sui with literary names. There is no evidence in the Chü-yen documents that supports the identification of the numbered with the literary sui. First of all, the register form of the provisions of the family members of the soldiers and minor officials in the numbered sui differs from that of the literary sui.¹⁴ Second, the soldiers in the numbered sui were identified by the number of their sui (e.g., soldier of the first sui), whereas the soldiers in the literary sui were identified by the name of their sui (e.g., soldier of Chü ch'i sui). Third, as far as the style of writing is concerned, the following document also seems to indicate that the numbers and the names were not two different designations for the same sui.

> [Commander] Wang Ch'ung of Chü-ch'i sui is now at I-ku.
> Commander Ma Kai-tsung of the twenty-second sui is at Yuan-ch'eng.
> Commander Wang Ch'ang-fu of the twenty-eighth sui is at Hsin-fu . . .
> 34.21(199)
> Cp241A

Here had the Chü-ch'i sui had a numbered name or had the twenty-second and the twenty-eighth sui had literary names they would have been used to create uniformity in the writing style. Similarly, the following strip gives further evidence to this point.

> From the thirtieth sui northward up to the northern boundary of the Ping-t'ing sui . . .
> 24.15(199)

TABLE 18. Numbered Watch Stations in Chü-yen

Sui	Document Numbers
1st	71.3
2nd	231.6
3rd	71.1
4th	154.29
5th	283.10
6th	176.30
7th	214.35
8th	227.56
9th	486.73
10th	154.27
11th	71.65
12th	72.57
13th	35.22
14th	143.15
15th	39.41
16th	231.106
17th	188.25
18th	281.33
19th	486.64
20th	231.50
21st	33.22
22nd	72.62
23rd	145.6
24th	283.38
25th	175.5
26th	317.16
27th	49.5
28th	78.17
29th	486.15
30th	33.22
31st	Cp19A
32nd	CpSupp. 12A
33rd	Cp19B
34th	214.15
35th	279.4
36th	Cp599
37th	180.32
38th	184.15

From these facts, one may conclude that there were probably both numbered and unnumbered *sui*.

Concerning the relative position of the numbered *sui*, one strip records:

From the southern boundary of the fourth *sui* northward up to the northern boundary of the ninth *sui* . . .

6.7(197)

According to this document, the numbers increase from south to north, the *sui* with a higher number being located to the north of the one with a lower number. Therefore, of the thirty-eight numbered *sui* the first one should be situated in the southernmost spot and the thirty-eighth in the northernmost. In the Chü-yen documents one strip reads:

> NOTICE: Commander Fu of the fifth *sui* of Chü-yen is transferred to the position of *ling-shih* of the Chü-yen *hou-kuan;* he should immediately be dispatched to the office of the [Chü-yen] *hou-kuan.* 40.21(145)

This document indicates clearly that the fifth *sui* belonged to the Chü-yen Commandant Area. Further, one strip records that the distance between the headquarters of two numbered *sui* was about 4.2 Han *li* or around 1,751 meters.

> The distance from the headquarters of the twenty-second *sui* southward to that of the seventeenth *sui* is 21 *li* [Han].[15] 188.25(208)

From this information, some of the lower numbered *sui*, at least up to the fifth *sui*, were in the Chü-yen Commandant Area or its neighboring commandant areas. If 4.2 *li* is generally the distance between the headquarters of two *sui*, the whole line of the numbered *sui* must stretch about 159.6 *li* (Han) or around 66.5 kilometers.[16] Since one document records that the Ping-t'ing *sui* was on the northern border of the numbered *sui*,[17] and another document, 28.1(52), records that the distance between the headquarters of Ping-t'ing *sui* and Chü-yen city (headquarters of the Chü-yen chief commandant) is 152 (Han) *li*, the above calculation is not far from being correct.

As for the relationship between the numbered *hou* and the numbered *sui*, some scholars have suggested that the numbered *sui* were the subdivisions of the numbered *hou*, as Mori Shikazō has summarized.[18]

Numbered *Hou*	Number of *Sui* Commanded
The fourth *hou*	The fourth to the ninth *sui*
The tenth *hou*	The tenth to the sixteenth *sui*
The seventeenth *hou*	The seventeenth to the twenty-second *sui*
The twenty-third *hou*	The twenty-third to the twenty-eighth *sui*

This theory encounters two difficulties: (1) it has left out the first three numbered *sui*; and (2) it has assigned sixteen *sui* to a single *hou*, the twenty-third, even though one wooden strip, Cp182, clearly shows that there were only about eight *sui* in the twenty-third *pu*. In several wooden strips, I have noticed that the numbered *sui* are listed side by side with the literary *sui*;[19] it is quite possible that the numbered and literary *sui* existed concurrently in the same *hou*. While the numbered *sui* formed a long line, roughly running from south to north, the literary *sui* were so situated as to flank this line.

THE CIVILIAN ESTABLISHMENT: HSIEN, HSIANG, AND LI

The administration of Chü-yen *hsien* (district) governed the civilian settlements of this region. Under it, there probably existed three *hsiang* (counties): Tu (Capital) County, Tung (East) County, and Hsi (West) County.[20] Capital County encompassed the seat of Chü-yen *hsien*, Chü-yen city, and its neighboring areas; East County the eastern portion of the district; and West County the western portion of the district. But the exact administrative geography of these counties is not recorded in the Chü-yen documents. Under these counties, there were a large number of *li* (wards or residential units), which were the basic units of local administration. Ninety-four to ninety-seven *li* are recorded in Chü-yen in all Chü-yen documents. It is doubtful that all of them existed at the same time in view of the gradual expansion and development of the Chü-yen region. Second, a large number of these *li* were under the jurisdiction of the Chü-yen chief commandant before Chü-yen *hsien* was established. Third, the economic environment simply could not support ninety-four to ninety-seven *li* in the Chü-yen region. I think one-third this number was the likely total at one time. By reviewing the dates and other specifics of the documents, I venture to suggest that the *li* listed in table 19 did exist concurrently. The exact locations of these *li* cannot be known for certain. It seems that most of them were inside the city of Chü-yen. By examining the *li* names, it is easy to see that, as in the garrison settlements, two systems of designation were in use: literary names and numbered names. The former were evidently a majority, and many of them are auspicious expressions such as *ch'ang-lo* (everlasting happiness), *wan-sui* (longevity), *yen-shou* (prolongation of life), *an-kuo* (pacifying the country), and so forth.

The ratio between *hsiang* and *li* in Han times has long been a topic of discussion among scholars. The range was widely spread between one hundred and just over ten *li* in a *hsiang*. According to the account just discussed, there were about eleven *li* under a *hsiang*, a fact that confirms a statement in Ying Shao's *Feng-su t'ung-i* (Comprehensive Meaning of Institutions and Customs) indicating that there were in general ten *li* under one *hsiang*.[21] This ratio probably was the norm in Chü-yen *hsien*.

Of the *li* in Chü-yen, some had names identical to *li* in certain interior prefectures and kingdoms and other districts of Chang-yeh. For example, Yang *li* could be found in both Chü-yen and the Che district of Huai-yang Prefecture. Table 20 lists seven such cases. Among the seven *li* names, *an-sui* and *an-kuo* are auspicious expressions, and *yang* and *shih-yang* are terms denoting direction or location. Accordingly, they were probably so commonly adopted as place names that they could be found almost anywhere. Very likely it was for this reason that both Chü-yen and other districts had them as *li* names. But P'ing and particularly Hsi-yeh and Kuang-ti cannot be included in this category. It appears cer-

TABLE 19. Residential Wards in Chü-yen District

Name of *Li*	Document Numbers
An-ku	340.39(456), 214.121(471)
An-kuo	224.28(477)
Ch'ang	38.13(464), 286.14(468)
	132.3(454)
Ch'ang-lo	CpSupp.29
Chien	482.11(478)
Chien-shui	465.4(35)
Chin-chi	136.2(476)
Chung-kuan	89.42(478)
Hsi-tao	77.33(450), 24.1(463)
Hsi-yeh	241.14(451)
K'ang	61.2(454)
Kuang-li	227.8(236), 486.64(468)
Kuang-ti	557.8(334)
Kuang-tu	88.5(174)
Le-shan	52.19(461)
Li-shang	231.109(482)
Lin-jen	45.12(35)
Lung-shan	188.32(469)
P'ing	206.28(388), 505.13(421)
P'ing-ming	55.6(464), 244.8(465)
Shih-chih	43.2(456), 77.16(450)
	58.2(462), 38.21(464)
Shih-yang	62.54(452)
Shou-yang (?)	173.22(466), 4686
Sun-shan	11.55(460)
Tang-i	133.9(463)
Tang-sui	188.15(469), 194.48(469)
Ti-chien	1232, 2272
Wan-sui	5125 and 6217
Yang	40.8(465)
Yen-shou	34.26(463)
Yu-tao	37.23(455)
First	211.17(168)
Second	287.13(515)

Note: In addition to these *li*, several others (e.g., Tsa [doc. 3927], and Tang-an and Fu-an [doc. 5853]) appear likely to have belonged to Chü-yen District, but due to lack of positive evidence they cannot be listed here.

tain that the emigrants transported these names from their old *li* to name their new settlements in Chü-yen. The fact that Huai-yang and Ch'ang-i *kuo* were not only among the first interior regions to send emigrants to Chü-yen but also two of three regions besides Chang-yeh that supplied the largest numbers of colonists to Chü-yen bolsters this observation. In fact, the transmigration of place names by emigrants later became a common practice in the Southern and Northern Dynasties period (A.D. 317–589), which then even included names of prefectures. It is interesting to note that if Shih-yang was also a transmigrated *li*, which in light of the existence of this practice in the region seems conceivable, it stopped over twice on its way to Chü-yen. It went first to Lu-te from Ch'ang-p'ing, then to Chao-wu, and finally to Chü-yen.

Documents concerning the Chien-shui *hsien* (district) are also found in the Chü-yen strips, but they do not provide enough evidence to reconstruct its organization.[22] This fact may be due to the short duration of the district; it is not even listed in the *Treatise on Geography* in the *Han-shu*.

CONSTRUCTION AND STRUCTURE OF THE HAN SETTLEMENTS

Ch'eng, Chang, *and* Sui

The *ch'eng* (walled district or city) was the largest type of construction in the region. There were two large cities, which were occupied by the chief commandants and district magistrates of the two respective areas: Chü-yen city and Chien-shui city. The city of Chü-yen was at modern Khara-Khoto and the city of Chien-shui at modern Taralingin-durbeljin. According to the archaeological

TABLE 20. Common *Li* Names between Chü-yen and Other Regions: Frontier Development and the Migration of Place Names

Name of *Li*	Regions with the Same *Li*		Document Numbers
	Prefecture or Kingdom	District	
An-kuo	Chang-yeh	Lu-te	287.24(242)
Hsi-yeh	Ch'ang-i *kuo*	Hsi-fang	510.29(445)
Huang-tu	Chang-yeh	Chang-yeh	220.12(468)
P'ing	Huai-yang	Ch'ang-p'ing	509.18(428B)
Shih-yang	Huai-yang	Ch'ang-p'ing	509.14(373)
	Chang-yeh	Lu-te	32.11(453)
	Chang-yeh	Chao-wu	560.27(437)
Wan-sui	Chang-yeh	Lu-te	77.7(448)
	Chang-yeh	Chao-wu	15.20(423)
Yang	Huai-yang	Che	491.3(434)
	Ju-nan	Chao-ling	212.104(481)
	Hung-nung	Lu-hun	170.2(453)

accounts, Chü-yen city was in the shape of a rectangle and covered an area of 171,000 square meters (380 × 450 meters). It was built of stamped clay bricks reinforced with inserted rafters. Chien-shui city occupied an area of 87,500 square meters (350 × 250 meters) and was also built of stamped clay bricks.[23]

The *chang*, or fortress, was also walled but considerably smaller. It served as the headquarters of a commandant area and was occupied by the commandant. For this reason, it was also called *hou-kuan ch'eng* or commandant city.[24] In the Chü-yen region, there were seven such commandant cities, whose locations and distribution were given earlier. The size of the fortresses was irregular. The fortress of Ulan-durbeljin, the headquarters of the Chien-shui Commandant Area, covers an area of 506.25 square meters (22.5 × 22.5 meters), but the fortress of Mu-durbeljin, the headquarters of the Chia-ch'ü Commandant Area, measures only 23.3 square meters, being one of the smallest of its kind in the Chü-yen region. The fortresses were also built of stamped clay bricks. All the fortresses were surrounded by large *wu* sections, each usually covering an area about one hundred times that of the fortress. For instance, the *wu* of Chia-ch'ü Fortress covered an area of over 2,161 square meters.[25]

The smallest unit of fortification in the Chü-yen region was probably the *t'ing* or *sui* (watch station). Its central construction was a watchtower (*feng-t'ai*) inside the circled *wu* (walls). Regarding its size, one wooden strip records the following information.

> Two garrison watchtowers of the Chien-shui Commandant Area: their bases are 2 *chang* and 8 *ch'ih* wide [about 6.5 meters]. 54.23(239)

Recent archaeological investigation reports that the bases of the watchtowers of the Chin Pass (site A32) and the fourth watch station (site P1) are 60.06 square meters (7.7 × 7.8 meters) and 61.6 square meters (7.7 × 8 meters), respectively.[26] Since the Chin Pass had a large organization and the fourth watch station was the headquarters of the Fourth Subcommandant Area, it may be said that the watchtowers of larger watch stations were generally larger than those of the regular watch stations, whose size is indicated in document 54.23.[27] The average height of the watchtowers was about 12 meters.

The watchtowers were chiefly built of stamped clay, but wood, hay, and other materials also may have been used.[28] A watch station consisted of both the watchtower and a solid enclosure, whose length usually measured three to four or even over five times the base of the tower. Watch stations were occupied by a commander or a subcommandant or both in some cases.[29] Perhaps the watch station occupied by a subcommandant was generally larger than that occupied only by a commander and it was also called *hou* (large watch station).

Names of Garrison Constructions

Each of the garrison constructions was specifically named at the Chü-yen frontier. The various names reflected not only the local geographic, military, and economic conditions but the aspirations, mental state, and activities of the Han colonists in Chü-yen. In broad categories, these names can be classified as follows.

1. Expression of geographic characteristics of the places (e.g., Chü-yen, named after the Chü-yen River; Lin-ching, the place close to wells; Ch'ü-ching, the place with canals and wells; Lin-mu, the place close to the woods; Kuang-t'ien, the place with a large field; and Ku-k'ou—the place at the outlet of a valley).
2. Expression of geographic location (e.g., Nan-*pu*, in the south; Pei-*pu*, in the north; Chung-*pu*, in the middle; Tung-*pu*, in the east; and Chieh-*t'ing*, at the border).
3. Expression of the function of the garrison settlements (e.g., Nung-*t'ing*, agricultural watch station; Ch'i-ping *t'ing*, watch station of cavalrymen; Ch'a-pei patrolling the north; and Wang-nan, patrolling the south).
4. Expression of good wishes and aspirations (e.g., Wan-sui, longevity; Wan-shih, everlasting; An-shih, peaceful world; Lo-tsai, happiness; and An-nung, agricultural prosperity).
5. Expression of hostility toward the barbarians, presumably the Hsiung-nu (e.g., T'ien-pei, to exterminate the people of the north; Chi-hu, to attack the barbarians; Mieh-hu, to exterminate the barbarians; T'un-hu, to swallow the barbarians; Fa-hu, to launch campaign against the barbarians; and Hsiang-hu, to suppress the barbarians).

The last category is particularly common among the place names. This reflects the mission of the Chü-yen settlers, attacking the enemy and guarding the territory.

Classification of Various Constructions

Wu, Wu-pi, or Pi

The *wu*, *wu-pi*, and *pi* were names for walls around a watch station or a fortress. If the walls wholly or partly circled a watch station, they were called its *wu* (*sui-wu*), for a larger watch station they were called *hou-pi*, and for a fortress they were called *chang-pi*.[30] The length of the walls was irregular, depending on the type of settlement of which they were a part. For the watch stations, some *wu* are only about 25 meters long; others range from about 72 to about 120 meters. The *wu* of the *hou-kuan* fortresses generally ran over 190 meters.[31] If the *wu* was too long or was discontinued at some point, the area in the inner circle was called the *nei-wu* (inner *wu*) and the area in the outer circle *wai-wu* (outer *wu*).[32] Usually residences were constructed along the walls, and the gate of these places could be opened toward either the outside or the inside of the walls. The former was called *wai-wu-hu* (outer *wu* gate) and the latter the *nei-wu-hu* (inner *wu* gate).[33] Figure 1 contains three illustrations of the construction of the *wu* together with other parts of a garrison settlement: the city of Chien-shui at Taralingin-durbeljin (Ta-wan, site A35), the fortress of Chia-ch'ü at Mu-durbeljin (P'o-ch'eng-tzu, site A8), and the fourth watch station at Pao-tu-ko (site P1). The plan of the Chin Pass is illustrated in figure 6 in a later chapter.

Li (ward or residential segment)

A *li* was both an administrative unit and a residential division in Han times. As an administrative unit, it was the link between the family and the *hsiang* (county) office. As a residential division, it generally consisted of a well-delimited zone with a defined number of families, normally fifty. Therefore, it was a physical unit and had a fixed structure. In the traditional understanding of the physical form of the *li*, it was surrounded with low walls, had two entrances (gates) called *lü* on its northern and southern sides, and was divided into two parts, north and south, by a partition wall, which had a passage gate called a *yen*.[34] The Chü-yen strips contain many documents about the *li* system, and some of them provide critical information about the structure of the *li* on the frontier. The following four are particularly important.

1. ... resides in the fifth door [house] in the *li*, entering from the east ... resides in Chü-yen ... [Surname] Chang-chün resides in Kuang-han *li* of Lu-te [District] ...[35]

    340.33
    pl. 145

2. ... resides in the second door [house] in the *li*, entering from the east. Hsü Kung-chün [or Mr. Hsü Kuang] of the same *li* is the witness.

    282.5
    pl. 263

3. ... resides in the third door [house] in the second *li* of ... entering from the east. Wen Shao-chi and Hsüeh Shao-ch'ing are the witnesses.

    287.13
    pl. 336

4. The fourth *li*, ... the third door [house], entering from the north.

    31.18
    pl. 543

I. Chia-ch'ü Fortress
(P'o-ch'eng-tzu)

II. Chien-shui City
(Ta-wan)

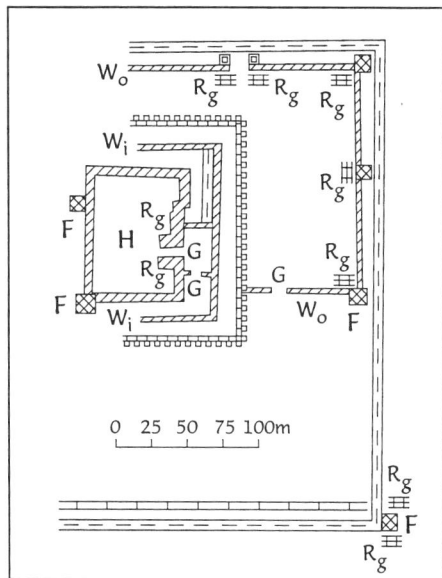

III. The Fourth Watch-Station
(Pao-tu-ko)

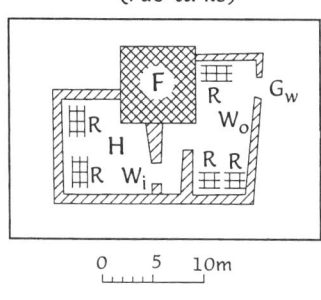

SYMBOLS

C — Chang
H — Headquarters
F — Watchtower
R — Room
W$_o$ — Outer wu
W$_i$ — Inner wu
G — Gate
G$_W$ — Wu gate
R$_g$ — Guardroom

▓▓▓ Wu
══ Regular wall
▂▂▂ Rampart
▧ Watchtower
▢ Lookout tower
▦ Rooms
═══ Moat

Fig. 1. Plans of garrison settlements in Chü-yen: city, fortress, and watch stations. (Reconstruction based on diagrams in Bo Sommarström 1956–58, p. 344; and Chü-yen I, pp. 3–4. The interpretation of the internal structure is my own.)

These documents reveal that the residential units, presumably houses, of a *li* were numbered and each was represented by its numbered door. Judging from their context and the traditional understanding of the physical plan of the *li*, the words *pei-ju* and *tung-ju* in the original Chinese documents likely meant "entering from the northern gate" and "entering from the eastern gate" of the respective *li*. If so, it is quite clear that in addition to the *li* with southern and northern gates there were *li* with eastern and western gates. Since a *li* is a residential unit, it is hardly possible that all the *li* so constructed had only southern and northern gates. There probably existed *li* with three or four gates and *li* without partitions of the outer walls if the situation so demanded. Thus, we can reconstruct several possible forms of the *li*, as in figure 2.

Archaeological field investigations of Chü-yen city (site K799) included the survey of a rectangular array of a series of ruined constructions in the interior of the city. The picture of this structure shows that it originally was composed of several square blocks, with each having an opening at the front.[36] This is probably a remnant of a Han *li*, with each block being a residential unit. If this was indeed the case, it was a *li* of a form different from the ones just sketched. It was not enclosed with a wall. Perhaps the *li* in the interior of the city were not surrounded by enclosures, unlike those located along the city walls or in special residential areas in a city. The Han open *li* can be sketched as in figure 3.

T'ien-she (farming house) and T'ien-sai (farming station)

The term *t'ien-she* appears in several wooden documents. The *Han-shu* indicates that *t'ien-she* is a farming house in the field where the agricultural laborers live during the season of cultivation.[37] However, the wooden documents of the *t'ien-she* indicate a different usage of the term.

> (x) . . . In the seventh month, again went without permission to the farming house of [the] Che-lu [Subcommandant Area] to sleep one night.[38]
>
> Cp717
>
> . . . went to the farming house of I-ku (?) without permission.
>
> Cp912
>
> Went to the farming house at Tang-tao (?) without permission . . . (x)[39]
>
> Cp1210

These documents show that the persons concerned were not allowed to go to the farming houses without permission. From this, it has been suggested that the farming houses were the residences of the family members of the farming soldiers.[40] It is equally possible that the farming soldiers were sent to work in distant fields during the season of cultivation and housed in watch stations close to these fields. Thus, they would not have been allowed to go back to their families without permission.

Four farming houses are recorded in the Chü-yen documents.

THE HAN SETTLEMENTS IN CHÜ-YEN • 97

Names of Farming Houses   Probable Location (commandant area)
Che-lu   Chü-yen
Chung-pu   Chia-chü (Cp765)
I-ku   Chia-ch'ü (?)
Tang-tao   Chia-ch'ü (?)

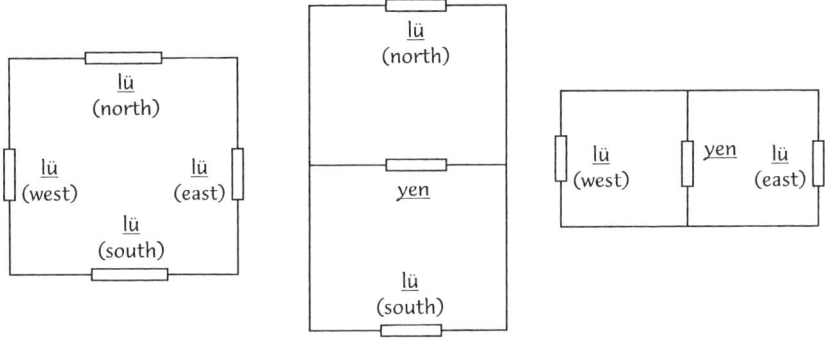

Fig. 2. Reconstruction of three probable plans for a Han *li*

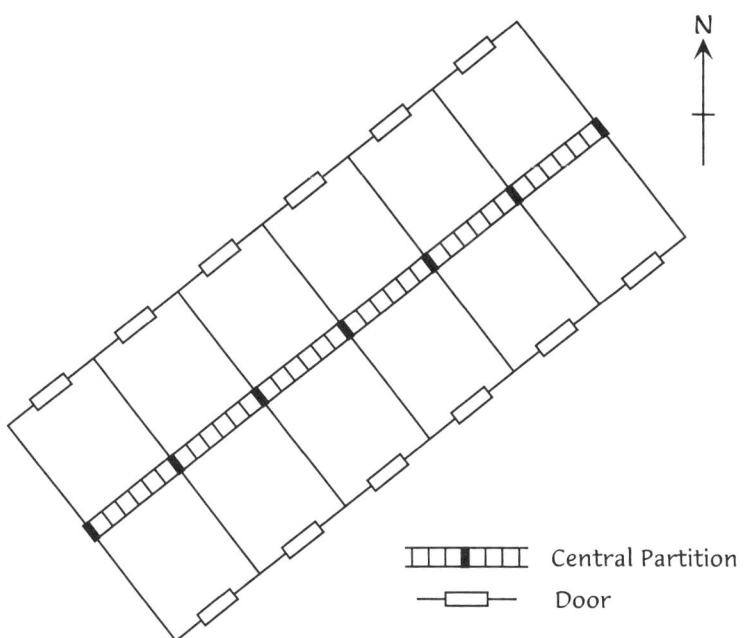

Fig. 3. Reconstruction of a Han *li* without an outer enclosure

In addition to the farming houses, there were *t'ien-sai,* or farming stations, under the command of a commandant or subcommandant.[41] It seems that all the farming stations were located in the Chia-ch'ü area. The function and construction of the farming stations are not recorded in the Chü-yen documents. They were probably the places where the farming soldiers were stationed and worked. But one strip renders the following information.

> Chao Yang-ling [?], salaried subcommandant of the farming station at the Chia-ch'ü Commandant Area of the Chü-yen Chief Commandant Area of [the prefecture of] Chang-yeh, from Ch'ang-ch'iu *li* of Lu-te [District], with the rank *kung-ch'eng,* age twenty-one (?), went to [the] *tai-t'ien* [field].
>
> 4218
> pl. 231

This document indicates that the *t'ien-sai* may have been connected with the *tai-t'ien* affairs.

Ti, Ko, and T'ing-pu

The *ti* was an ordinary storehouse for grain and other bulky but not particularly valuable materials. In his account of the fieldwork at Taralingin-durbeljin, Bo Sommarström reports the discovery of a layer of tightly packed millet 20 centimeters thick, together with a great number of wooden documents and an astonishingly large number of other finds, in a totally decayed house with two rooms.[42] This house was probably a *ti.* The *ko* was a tower.[43] The wooden strips record that coins and other valuable materials were stored in the *ko.*[44] Weapons were probably also stored there because it was relatively dry.

The term *t'ing-pu* appears in several wooden documents.[45]

> . . . male commoner Ch'iu Chang of Shan-chü *li* said that his family bought land from a guest resident and they have settled in the *t'ing-pu* of the Tu-t'ing.[46]
>
> Cp1982A

> . . . . 1,000 *shih* (of millet) are stored in the *t'ing-pu* of Kao-sha [watch station].
>
> 1,780 *shih* (of millet) are stored in the *t'ing-pu* of Hsien-chen [watch station].
>
> 1,687 *shih* (of millet) are stored in the *t'ing-pu* of Chi-shan [watch station].
>
> 4909
> pl. 288

> 1,600 ... (?) *shih* of hay are stored in the second room of the *t'ing-pu* of [Chi] Shan [watch station] ... (x)[47]
>
> 270.16(312)
> pl. 399

These documents indicate that the ordinary *t'ing-pu* were storehouses for grain and other materials at watch stations, but that the *t'ing-pu* of the Tu-t'ing was a residential area for farming settlers cultivating the land thereabouts. Since the Tu-t'ing was in general located outside the capital of a district,[48] in Chü-yen it should have been near the city of Chü-yen. In view of this point, the following document seems to shed light on the construction of the Tu-t'ing.

> Hsü Tzu-yü states that he lives in the fifth *pi* west of the city of Chü-yen and that he undertakes land cultivation thereabouts.
>
> 401.7(505)

From this document, it is clear that the farming settlers lived in the numbered *pi* around the city of Chü-yen. Certainly these *pi*, like the *li* (wards), were residential places. Judged from their location, they probably belonged to the Tu-t'ing. If so, the Tu-t'ing should have consisted of a series of numbered *pi*.

Garrison Offices

Due to their function and position as offices, the garrison constructions were classified in a different way in Chü-yen than in the interior of the empire. The offices of the chief commandants were called *fu*, such as the *fu* of the chief commandants at Chü-yen and Chien-shui.[49] The offices of the commandants were called *kuan*, or *hou-kuan*.[50] The offices of the subcommandants and commanders were called *hou* and *sui*, respectively.[51] These various offices also were probably generally called *ssu-she*.[52] Although the term *shu* was in general used to designate an office, in Chü-yen it was most likely used only to denote the offices of subcommandants and commanders. Of the nine documents on which the connection of the term *shu* with garrison offices is clearly recorded, seven indicate that *shu* was the term for the office of a commander and two identify *shu* as the office of a subcommandant.[53] Five in the former group refer to numbered watch stations such as the second watch station, the twelfth watch station, and so on.[54]

The nomenclature of the various garrison offices presents certain deviations from the system of office designation used in corresponding interior institutions. This demonstrates in part the uniqueness of the Han frontier system.

SETTLEMENT AND COLONIZATION

The distribution of the various settlement units discussed in the preceding sections displays an interesting pattern. They all were situated along the banks of rivers or the shores of lakes. From the Mao-mu area northward, the Han settlements were first located along the main course of the Edsen-gol. They then flanked its tributaries, the Mören-gol, Narin-gol, and Ikhen-gol, and finally they were placed among the tributaries of these small streams, the Oboin-gol, Dunda-gol, Onder-ellisin-gol, and Ontsein-gol as far as the shores of Sogho-nor (lake). In the northeastern section of the Chü-yen region, the shores of the old Chü-yen Lake were the locational preference for Han settlements. Map 3 provides a clear contour of this settlement pattern. Obviously there were several reasons for forming such a settlement system. First, the availability of water, both for ordinary consumption and for irrigation, was considered a primary condition for selecting settlement locations in the river and lake areas. Most of the Chü-yen region was, and still is, a desert, with summer temperatures ranging from forty to sixty degrees Celsius; it would have been hard for the settlements to survive if they had not been placed in oases along the rivers and lakes. Second, geographic conditions along the waterways provided favorable bases for constructing transportation corridors linking the settlements by convenient and efficient routes. Effective transportation and communications networks, as will be discussed later, were essential to the security and continuing development of frontier settlements. Third, the river and lake oases supplied the materials and resources needed for the construction of settlements and provisioning of garrisons. Fourth, militarily the rivers and lakes provided a natural defense against enemy attacks, a fact that is well illustrated by the Great Wall the Han forces built along the river and lake banks.[55]

The Han settlements were clustered in two fertile oasis areas, one in the south and one in the north. The southern cluster, covering an area of over 300 square kilometers, extended along the banks of the Edsen-gol from the vicinity of the Chin Pass (site A32) southward to just south of Chien-shui city (Ta-wan, site A35). It essentially covered the Chien-shui Commandant Area, with its headquarters at what is now Ti-wan (site A33), and the land under the direct supervision of the Chien-shui chief commandant. This was an area with an unusually high density of settlements. In the north, the triangle formed by T'ien-pei *hou-kuan* (Wa-yin t'o ni, site A10), Chü-yen *hou-kuan* (Hei-ch'eng, site K799), and Chia-ch'ü *hou-kuan* (P'o-ch'eng-tzu, site A8) contained a dense cluster of Han settlements. It covers an area of over 1,250 square kilometers around the Ikhen-gol and its tributaries. Chü-yen city (Hei-ch'eng), headquarters of the highest military and civil administrations in Chü-yen, was located in this settlement cluster.

The southern settlement cluster was established first. In 119 B.C., the first Han settlements were established in the northernmost part of this area, the Chin Pass.[56] When this area and its adjacent territories were fully colonized and developed, a *hsien* administration was probably instituted to govern them; it was called Chien-shui *hsien* and covered what was later the southern part of the Chü-yen region. The northern cluster of Han settlements was not developed until 103 B.C. But as the Han shifted their central interest in colonization in the Chü-yen region to the north, under the leadership of Lu Po-te, the northern area became more important, and more densely settled, than the southern area. This eventually led to the establishment of Chü-yen *hsien*, with its capital at Chü-yen city and with jurisdiction over both the south and the north; consequently, the older Chien-shui *hsien* was abolished.

The two settlement clusters were also the two major economic centers of the Chü-yen region. In the south, the headquarters of Chien-shui chief commandant was the command center of all economic and transportation activities. The land in the area was extensively farmed. Complex farming organizations were established to direct and supervise farming activities, among which were massive irrigation projects that sometimes employed a work force of over 1,500 soldiers in one farming unit. Oxen are recorded to have been quartered in this area for land tilling, and horses are recorded to have been used for the transport of farm products. These farming organizations seem to have been located in the same major settlements as were the garrison headquarters.[57] In the north, although Chü-yen city was the organizational center of all farming activities, separate agricultural settlements spread over the triangle of T'ien-pei, Chü-yen, and Chia-ch'ü in such varying forms as farming houses, stations, and *t'ing*, as well as *tai-t'ien* establishments. The north also stood out in the use of the *tai-t'ien* (annual rotation of furrows) method of farming, which was absent in the southern region.[58] These differences in structural and technological patterns of agricultural development between the south and the north were probably a result of the differences in geographic and economic conditions between the two subregions of Chü-yen. The south was close to the imperial highways that ran through the Ho-hsi Corridor to the Western Regions and had a lesser need for economic independence than did the north,[59] where self-sufficiency was the key to survival. Hence, the north had to experiment with the most advanced farming techniques and employ more organizational skills to increase its agricultural output. This fact clearly illustrates the importance of functional and locational specialization in the Han frontier system.

In the general spatial contour of the Han settlements in Chü-yen, we can examine the general distribution pattern of the entire region. As analyzed earlier, the Han settlements in Chü-yen can be divided into three size classes. The largest consisted of the *hsien* and *tu-wei* cities together with their surrounding residential areas, that is, Chü-yen and Chien-shui cities. The middle group was composed of the *hou-kuan* cities, of which 7 were clearly identified. The smallest settlement units were the watch stations, farming houses and stations, and similar or related constructions, of which over 270 were recorded and 166 have been archaeologically explored. For convenience, we shall refer to these three types of settlements as class 1, class 2, and class 3. Since the civilian settlements in Chü-yen, primarily *hsiang* and *li*, were part of the garrison settlements, they are not classified as separate units. As stated earlier, the Han settlements were located in a region extending about 300 kilometers from north to south and 15 to 50 kilometers from east to west. The average width of this strip of settlements is 31 kilometers. Thus, using this average width, we can estimate the total area of the Chü-yen region under Han control to have been 9,300 square kilometers. With reference to this, the density of each of the three classes of Han settlements in the Chü-yen region can be measured. Table 21 sums up the result. Thus, within the Chü-yen region there was, on average, a Han settlement in every 33.45 square kilometers if the recorded number of class 3 settlements are counted as the real number or in every 53.49 square kilometers if only the archaeologically explored class 3 settlements are counted. In either case, this density pattern probably reflects only the last three quarters of the first century B.C., during which Chü-yen was being fully developed and the number of Han settlements peaked.

Data for a detailed comparison with corresponding settlement units of all three classes in Chang-yeh are not available. But on the level of class 1 settlements, Chü-yen's density is three times higher than the average density of such settlements in the entire prefecture, which stood at 13,550 square kilometers for one class 1 settlement.[60] If this is any true indication of the general picture of the development of Chang-yeh at different levels, it shows that Chü-yen was more settled than comparable regions in Chang-yeh and attests to the degree of operational success of the Han frontier system in Chü-yen.

TABLE 21. Density of Han Settlement in Chü-yen

Settlement Class	Number	Average Area with One Settlement Unit (in kilometers)
1	2	4,660.00
2	6[a]	1,550.00
3 (a) Recorded	270	34.44
(b) Archaeologically explored	166	56.02
Total		
1, 2, 3 (a)	278	33.45
1, 2, 3 (b)	174	53.49

[a]Excluding Chü-yen *hou-kuan* in Chü-yen city.

The Han settlement units in Chü-yen formed a hierarchy. The units of the top two classes served as the major headquarters of high garrison and administrative units and hence were the centers of command and control. Under their direction and supervision were a large number of smaller (class 3) settlement units. Thus, the entire settlement system was in a pyramidal shape. In the garrison settlement, the *tu-wei* city was at the top of the chain of command, several *hou-kuan* cities followed, and finally there were the multitude of watch stations and similar or related units at the bottom. In the civilian establishment, the *hsien* seat was the central city, several *hsiang* headquarters followed, and finally there were a large number of *li* at the bottom of the pyramid. Within each of the two establishments, garrison and civilian, all units were closely and effectively linked by various systems of communication and transportation. Therefore, each of the settlements can be considered an administrative unit and a node of communication and transportation. The hierarchical nature of these nodes yields a dominant relationship among the units in the settlement network. In administrative order, the (highest) class 1 settlements dominated the (second-highest) class 2 settlements which in turn dominated the (lowest) class 3 settlements. In spatial contour, as discussed earlier and illustrated in map 3, the distance between class 1 settlements was longer than the distance between class 2 settlements, which in turn was longer than the distance between class 3 settlements. Figure 4 illustrates this observation. The relationship may be summed up by saying that the larger the settlement size the more space can be found between them. Thus, if we see the class 1 and class 2 settlements as the central nodes of administration, economy, transportation, and communication and the class 3 settlements as the peripheral nodes, the sparsely situated central nodes have a dominant relationship with the densely situated peripheral nodes. This finding is illustrated in figure 5. This, interestingly enough, fits the model of a central-place system in modern geographic-economic-settlement analysis.[61] This efficient settlement system, I believe, contributed critically to the success of the Han frontier operation.

As stated earlier, the civilian establishment followed the garrison establishment in the stages of frontier development. Or, in the larger pattern of frontier development, the civilian establishment was the result of the change from the stage of linked garrison settlements for security to linked civilian settlements for economic self-sufficiency and development. This settlement network placed a strong emphasis on military security and control through garrisons and communication and transportation efficiency. Even after both civilian and garrison establishments had been fully developed, the garrison system still overshadowed and dominated the civilian establishment.

The pyramidal hierarchy of the settlement network followed the basic pattern of the Han policy of planned and controlled frontier migration and settle-

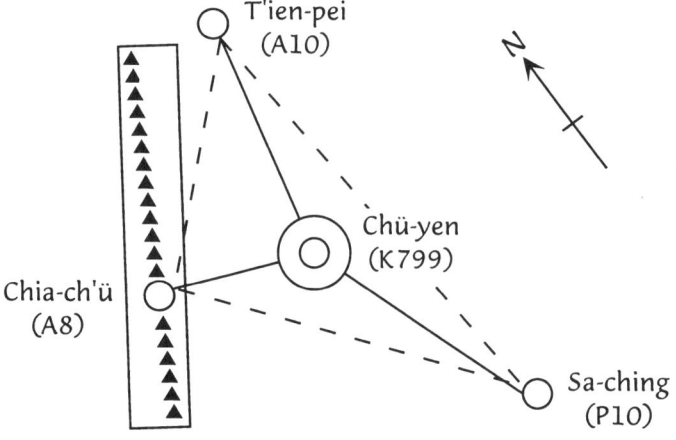

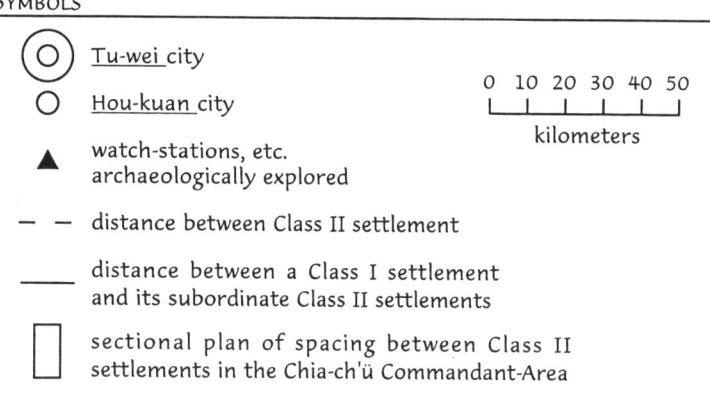

Fig. 4. Spatial pattern of the Han settlement network in Chü-yen (Chü-yen *tu-wei*)

ment.[62] Directives on matters of development and general order came down from the top, free opportunities generally did not exist, and individual initiative was not encouraged. Thus, the settlements of class 1, and to some extent class 2, served as the center of command and administration, and their orders were uniformly followed by lower settlement units. This system was highly efficient, and it generally achieved the goal of colonization and development with greater speed than did other systems. The Han success in its colonization of Chü-yen was a model example of this. However, the system did not allow the frontier

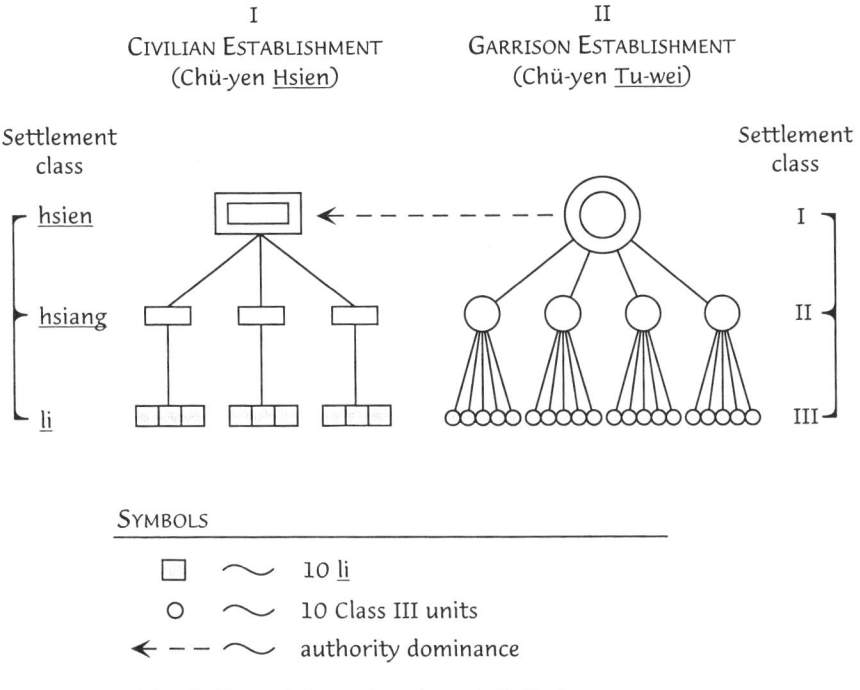

Fig. 5. Dominance in the Han settlement network in Chü-yen

society the opportunity to develop a character and spirit different from those of the mother society of the interior. The Han frontier society in Chü-yen was also a model example of this. Here we have seen the roots of the Han success with its frontier system and the essence of the weakness of that system both contained in its settlement policy and structure.

4

Population on the Han Frontier

Numbers, Distribution, and Characteristics

FROM ITS EARLIEST FORMULATION, the frontier policy of the Han empire consisted of two major components: the establishment of settlements by military and civilian means and the systematic peopling of these settlements. The first component led to the opening and consolidation of the frontier region; the second was designed not only to develop the frontier but also to perpetuate its control.

These two components interlock. Without the first, the second would not have been possible; without a solid development of the second, the frontier would never have become a permanent part of the empire. We analyzed the first component of the Han frontier system in the preceding chapters. We will examine the second phase in this and the next chapter. We will first look at the numbers and distribution of inhabitants in the garrison units and civilian settlements of Chü-yen *hsien*. Then we will examine the available data on the various population characteristics of Chü-yen and will attempt to create a demographic profile of the Han residents in this frontier colony. In a larger sense, this last aspect offers a study in miniature of the entire Han population during the period in question. Its results will provide a unique demographic look at Han age, sex, and marital status since similar data are not available elsewhere.

PEOPLING THE GARRISON SETTLEMENTS

The majority of residents in the garrison establishments were officers and servicemen. At the lowest level, the Chü-yen documents show an average of 3.36 soldiers in each watch station, as is evidenced in table 22. This table shows that most of the watch stations had four soldiers, some three, and some only two. The latter was designated a small watch station. Perhaps the small watch stations generally had two soldiers. The watch stations called *t'ing* seem to have normally had three soldiers, as one wooden document records.

> There are three persons in one *t'ing*.
>
> 511.26(238)
> Cp2099

But this was probably not applicable to the *t'ing* with special functions such as the cavalryman *t'ing*, the agricultural *t'ing*, and so forth. For instance, one cavalryman *t'ing* is recorded to have had from ten to nineteen cavalrymen.[1]

Table 22 does not include officers. In each watch station there was at least one, the commander, as is recorded on one slip.

> The Tz'u-t'ung *sui*
>   Commander Hsü Kuang.
>   Four soldiers: . . . .
>
> 57.15(275)

In the larger watch stations headed by a commander and a subcommandant, or the latter alone, there were certainly more officers. For example, under the sub-

TABLE 22. Distribution of Soldiers among the Watch Stations

Number of Soldiers	Watch Stations	Document Numbers
2	Hsiao-*t'ing*	557.5(334)
2	Lo-ch'ang	339.18(434)
3	Twenty-eighth	57.27(491)
3	Twenty-sixth	27.25(236)
3	Mo-shan	52.26(230)
3	An-ching	46.9(239)
4	First	2853
3	Fifteenth	4136
4	Thirty-first	82.24(235)
4	Kuang-t'ien	160.13(231)
4	K'uan-fan	512.27(336)
4	Chieh	132.40(229)
4	Wu-hsien	42.19(312)
4	Tz'u-t'un	57.15(275)

Note: The average number of soldiers is 3.36.

commandant there were the *hou-shih* and other minor officers.² One wooden document even records three *ling-shih* in one watch station.

> Three *ling-shih* reside in the second *sui*. 89.18(201)

Perhaps this is a special case. In general, there were two or more officers in a larger watch station.

Table 22 is based on documents that explicitly state the number of soldiers in the watch stations. Other documents supply such information indirectly. Most are records of soldiers' provisioning, which list, respectively, the soldiers from various watch stations, for example:

> List of Names of the Soldiers of the Twenty-third *pu* Who Received Grain Provisions in the twelfth month:
>
> 22 Soldiers:
> The 23rd Soldier   Li Yang
> The 23rd Soldier   Su Kuang
> The 23rd Soldier   Kuo Hai
> The 24th Soldier   Ch'eng Ting
> The 24th Soldier   Shih Chien
> The 24th Soldier   Chang Meng
> The 25th Soldier   Lu Chien
> The 25th Soldier   Han I
> The 25th Soldier   Chang Chien
> The 26th Soldier   Chang Chien
> The 26th Soldier   Shou An
> The 26th Soldier   Han Fei
> The 27th Soldier³ Chang Yüan
> The 27th Soldier   Shih Ssu
> The 28th Soldier   Hsiang Hsi
> The 28th Soldier   Yang Shih
> The 28th Soldier   Ma Kuang
> The 29th Soldier   Chang Chüan
> The 29th Soldier   Pao Kan
> The 29th Soldier   Tso Shih
> The 30th Soldier   Chung Ch'ang
> The 30th Soldier   Kao Kuan

As was discussed earlier, "The 23rd Soldier" in this document is a soldier from the twenty-third watch station, and the same holds for "The 24th Soldier" and the rest. Accordingly, one may add up the total number of soldiers from each of the watch stations so identified: three from the twenty-fourth watch station and so forth. The following distribution of soldiers among numbered watch stations is made according to documents of this sort.

Number of Soldiers	Watch Stations	Document Numbers
3	The 19th	5299
3	The 20th	5299
3	The 21st	5299
3	The 23rd	Cp182, 4079
3	The 24th	Cp182, 4079
3	The 25th	Cp182, 4079
3	The 26th	Cp182, 4079
2	The 27th	Cp182, 4079
3	The 28th	Cp182, 4079
3	The 29th	Cp182, 4079
2	The 30th	Cp182, 4079

This does not conflict with table 22, and for two watch stations, the twenty-sixth and twenty-eighth, it even confirms the account in the latter. On the basis of this list and table 22, one may suggest that as a rule there were three or four soldiers in the numbered watch stations. The last two watch stations in the list were perhaps exceptions, with each having only two soldiers. Or perhaps it was only at the time of the provisioning that they temporarily had only two soldiers.

Beyond the level of watch stations, a regular *chang* (fortress) is recorded in several wooden documents to have normally had ten soldiers, called *chang-tsu*.[4] In addition, naturally, the commandant, called the *hou-kuan* or *chang-hou*, and the various officers under him, such as the *hou-ch'eng, chang-wei, shih-li, ling-shih, wei ts'ung-shih, wei-shih*, and the like, also resided in the fortress. One document indicates that there were two *ling-shih*, three *wei-shih*, ten *chang-tsu*, and one *ch'ih-hsing* in one *chang*.[5]

Several documents record groups of six to thirty persons working together. Two examples are given here.

> On the *ting-ssu* day of the eleventh month, twenty-four soldiers: one is the supervisor,[6] three are cooks, one is sick, two are storing. These seven persons are not included among the regular hard workers.[7] Seventeen regular hard workers cut 510 bundles of reeds, with each cutting 30 bundles [a day]. As of now, a total of 5,520 bundles of reeds have been accumulated.[8]
>
> 131.21
> pl. 205

On the *chia-ch'en* day of the eighth month, twenty-nine soldiers: one of them is the supervisor, and three are cooks for soldiers. These four persons are not included among the regular hard workers. Twenty-five regular hard workers:

> Two fell trees on the mountain.
> Six store hay.
> Fourteen transport hay totaling 4,020 bundles,
> with each bringing 290 bundles.
> Two weave.[9]
> One . . . (?)[10]

30.19
pl. 241

These documents record the daily work of groups of soldiers stationed in a certain settlement. A detailed analysis of all documents concerning these soldiers shows that most of them were unearthed at the headquarters of the Chia-ch'ü Commandant Area.[11] Therefore, it is evident that groups of soldiers who were working on regular schedules under supervisors were stationed there. As has been discussed, the headquarters of a commandant area such as Chia-ch'ü consisted of two parts: the inner fortress or *chang* and the surrounding *wu-pi*. It is most likely that the ten regular soldiers called *chang-tsu* occupied the inner fortress and were mainly responsible for guarding the headquarters (in addition to miscellaneous assignments), whereas the laboring soldiers were stationed in the *wu-pi* and engaged in manual labor on regular schedules in times of peace.[12] Numbers in the latter group seem to have varied over time.

Many wooden strips also record large numbers of servicemen, including the following.

1. Total 108 officers:
    > Two of them are serving as *hou-kuan* commandant and fort commandant; they receive no regular food rations.
    >> Two committed an infraction and have been imprisoned.
    > [A] total [of] 104 of them are included . . . (?)

    271.22
3436
pl. 271
Cp1434

2. Total seventy *tso-shih* [accessory clerks] are listed on the right:
    > Four of them are ill.
    > Sixty-six are on duty in garrison units . . . (?)

    265.27
2722
pl. 138
Cp1388

3. Total seventy-four officers with salary under 100 *shih* of grain ... (x)

217.76(515)
pl. 356
Cp1193A

4. Total 370 soldiers ... (?)

112.16
3899
pl. 203

5. (x) ... Eighty-five garrison soldiers
    The eleventh month ... (x)

176.41
4302
pl. 240

6. Total eighty-one officers received 170 *shih* of grain.

387.15
Cp1807

7. Total ninety-one officers under the commandant:
    Forty-two of them have already received ... (?)

118.51(250)

8. Total 144 officers: 122,300 [cash?] ...

504.7(267)
Cp1943

9. (x) ... Three hundred 100-*shih* officers.[13]
    200 *tou-shih* officers.[14]
    100 *tso-shih*.[15]

76.29
3549
pl. 180

10. On the first day of the fifth month, 153 soldiers:
    Ten of them ...
    Thirteen are on signal duty.
    Seven are dispatched for special duties.
    Three cook for the officers.[16]

395.9
2126
pl. 104

Most of these documents seem to be the general accounts and reports of soldiers and officers in a certain settlement, not the records of servicemen in one particular garrison center.[17] Numbers 1–5 were discovered at the site of P'o-ch'eng-tzu (Mu-durbeljin), the headquarters of Chia-ch'ü *hou-kuan*; numbers 6–7 were discovered at the site of Ti-wan (Ulan-durbeljin), the headquarters of Chien-shui *hou-kuan*; and number 8 was discovered at the site of Ta-wan (Taralingin-durbeljin), the headquarters of Chien-shui *tu-wei*. It is very likely that these slips were the periodical accounts of duty assignments and food provisions for the total number of servicemen in these *hou-kuan* and *tu-wei* units. The site of discovery of document 9 cannot be positively identified, but judging from the large numbers of 100-*shih* and *tou-shih* and *tso-shih* officers it should be a record of low-ranking officers of a *tu-wei* unit.[18] However, some of these and similar records, particularly numbers 5 and 214.18, are also likely to be the accounts and reports of servicemen in certain large garrison headquarters at a certain time. Both contemporary historical literature and the wooden documents indicate that a considerable number of servicemen indeed resided in the major Chü-yen garrison establishments for various reasons at different times.[19]

In any case, document 10 is definitely an account of the servicemen in one garrison center. Since 153 men were stationed in it, the center must have been at the level of a *chang* or the larger *ch'eng*. Most likely it was a *ch'eng*, the headquarters of a *tu-wei*. The name of this garrison establishment cannot be identified because the site of the discovery of this document is unknown.

Servicemen were not the only residents in the various garrison centers. Families of the military and other civilians also lived there. As is recorded in the following document, the garrison leaders allowed the servicemen from districts outside Chü-yen to have their wives and family with them.

> Officers and soldiers from other districts of the *pu* have their wives and children with them in the headquarters.
>
> 5184

Furthermore, registers and records of provisioning also indicate that servicemen's families lived in the watch stations.[20] But the number of servicemen's families in each of the garrison headquarters is not recorded in the wooden documents.

Regarding the civilians in the garrison headquarters, two documents provide important information.

> Female residents Chou Shu-chün and others of the [*hou-*]*kuan* state that they had borrowed [money?] from the *sui*.
>
> 3851
> pl. 199
> Cp420AB

> ... Female resident Sun Chih of the Li-p'ing *sui* states ...
>
> 4376
> pl. 247

With the original strip broken, only half of the first word on the first document is left. But judging from this half the first word is *hou*. This, together with the fact that it was unearthed at the headquarters of the Chia-ch'ü Commandant Area,[21] indicates that this document is a record of female residents at the said headquarters. The second document is clearly a record of female residents at a watch station.[22] Since these female residents were not referred to as family members of the servicemen or guest residents, they were probably ordinary citizens. In fact, these civilians also had facilities in the garrison settlements. For instance, one document records that five families in the Kuang-ti *hou-kuan* had their own *k'u* (treasury), which was called the Five-Family Treasury (Wu-chia-k'u).[23] According to the two documents, the civilians in the garrison headquarters seem to have been classified or referred to by the places where they resided.

Regarding the civilians in various garrison headquarters, one point of great importance is how they were governed. Several documents record that one of the reasons for a subcommandant, commander, *shih-li*, or other minor officer to receive a "service-time" merit evaluation was his ability to *chih-kuan-min* (administer both officers and civilians). For example:[24]

> Ssu-ma Ch'eng, commander of Ping-shan *sui* of the Chien-shui Commandant Area [with the rank of] *kung-ch'eng*, receives a middle-grade service time (*lao*) of two years, eight months and fourteen days. He is capable of writing and calculating; he administrates both officers and civilians and is quite familiar with the statutes and ordinances. He is classified as a military officer (*wu*). He is thirty-two years of age, seven *ch'ih* and five *ts'un* in height. His home is in Ch'eng-han *li* of Lu-te [District], 600 *li* from the said commandant area.
>
> 13.7(439)

From this document, it is clear that among the various duties of a minor garrison officer was governing the civilian residents in the territory under his control. This seems to be one of the special characteristics of the garrison system.

The previous discussion has shown that the civilian colonists not only settled in the large cities but resided in the garrison settlements of all levels, from the headquarters of a commandant area to that of a commander area. There is even some indication of *li* (ward) organization in the *pu* (or *hou*).[25] This indicates that, although the civilian residents in the garrison units were governed by garrison officers, they seemingly resided mostly in a special quarter of the garrison headquarters. The rooms along the *wu* of the garrison compounds that have been archaeologically explored were probably the residences of these people.

It is difficult to estimate the total population in the various garrison settlements in the Chü-yen region, but some suggestions can be made in light of our preceding discussions. First, we can estimate the number of the servicemen and all other personnel in the garrison unit. If we consider only the period when the development of Chü-yen reached its peak (64 B.C.–A.D. 9), with almost all recorded garrison fortifications and organizations functioning, and assume that each of the 260 *sui* and *t'ing* had on average three soldiers, the total number of soldiers in the garrison stations would be over 790.

As was discussed in the previous section, the *chang* of a *hou-kuan* was regularly stationed with ten soldiers (*chang-tsu*). In addition, the *chang* had a number of laboring soldiers doing various types of work. If we take the number of servicemen of the latter category to be twenty on average, a *chang* would have had thirty soldiers regularly stationed there. In Chü-yen, there were at least seven *chang* (including the one in Chü-yen city) for the seven *hou-kuan* that have been identified with certainty. Therefore, there would have been at least 210 soldiers in the seven *hou-kuan* headquarters.

Thus, the total number of soldiers in the *chang* and *t'ing* and *sui* in Chü-yen would have been one thousand. Interestingly enough, one thousand was precisely the number of soldiers usually under the command of two frontier *tu-wei* (chief commandants) in Han times.[26] Perhaps this is a coincidence, for we have not included the soldiers stationed in the headquarters of Chü-yen and Chien-shui *tu-wei*, and, as was indicated previously, a number of *sui* and *t'ing* often had more than ten soldiers.

If we take document 395.9, cited earlier, as a record of the soldiers in a *tu-wei* headquarters (a fact that is strongly supported by document 26.1, which mentions 182 men under the command of a chief commandant and his marshal (*ssu-ma*) who pursued 90 Hsiung-nu raiders), we may assume that over 150 soldiers were stationed in each of the two *tu-wei* headquarters in the Chü-yen region. Thus, the total number of soldiers in the cities of Chü-yen and Chien-shui would have been 300.

Thus, the total number of soldiers in all the watch stations, *hou-kuan* fortresses, and *tu-wei* cities in the Chü-yen region would have been 1,300. Needless to say, this estimate is a very conservative one. The actual number of servicemen in the garrison units in Chü-yen was, by all indications, larger than this figure.[27] For example, we estimate the total number of servicemen in the watch stations by allowing three men to each. But, as was pointed out previously, the watch stations of cavalrymen actually had from ten to nineteen persons regularly, and some other watch stations had over six soldiers. Furthermore, the watch stations with four servicemen probably outnumbered those with three. So the average of all watch stations that had two, three, or four soldiers was probably around 3.5.

Now we come to estimating the possible number of officers in the Chü-yen garrisons. First, we shall consider those in the seven *hou-kuan*. Document 271.22, cited earlier, seems to indicate that there were 108 officers in the Chia-ch'ü *hou-kuan*, and document 118.51 seems to show 92 officers, including the *hou-kuan* commandant, in the Chien-shui *hou-kuan*. The difference in the totals between the two *hou-kuan* is obviously due to the fact that Chia-ch'ü was the largest of all seven positively identified *hou-kuan* in the Chü-yen region. If we take 108 and 92 as the numbers of officers in Chia-ch'ü and Chien-shui, respectively, and assume that there were 80 officers in each of the other five *hou-kuan*, which were probably smaller than either Chia-ch'ü and Chien-shui, the total number of officers in all seven *hou-kuan* would be 600. This seems to be a reasonable estimate. For if we approach the problem with a different methodology, the result is almost the same. Document 101.26(238) indicates that there were on the average 10 officers in a subcommandant area. Since there were about fifty-two such areas in Chü-yen that have been recorded in the wooden strips, the total number of officers in all the subcommandant areas would have been 520. All the subcommandant areas were under the command of 7 *hou-kuan*. Each *hou-kuan* headquarters had at least 11 officers (1 *hou-kuan*, 1 *hou-ch'eng*, 1 *chang-wei*, 2 *shih-li*, 2 *ling-shih*, 1 *wei t'sung-shih*, and 3 *wei-shih*). Therefore, there were 77 officers in the seven *hou-kuan* headquarters. The total number of officers in the seven *hou-kuan* would then amount to 597 (520 + 77), a number that differs from the above calculation of 600 by only 3.

The seven *hou-kuan* in Chü-yen were under two chief commandants, Chien-shui *tu-wei* and Chü-yen *tu-wei*. The headquarters of a chief commandant, as discussed in an earlier chapter, had an administrative, operations, and clerical staff of five different categories—*yüan, shu, tsu-shih, shu-tso* (or *tso*), and *shih*—and seven subordinate officers—*ch'eng, wei (ch'eng-wei), ssu-ma, ch'i ssu-ma, chia ssu-ma, ch'ien-jen,* and *wu-pai*. Since each of the two *tu-wei* commanded more than three *hou-kuan* and each of the two *tu-wei* headquarters had a physical structure many times larger and more complex than those of the *hou-kuan*, it is quite reasonable to assume that each of the *tu-wei* headquarters had a support staff at least three times larger than the size of the staff at the *hou-kuan* headquarters. Thus, the staff at the *tu-wei* headquarters had at least fifteen members. The total officers of a *tu-wei* headquarters should then number about twenty-three, including the chief commandant himself. If this was the case, the total number of officers in the two *tu-wei* headquarters of the Chü-yen region would have been forty-six.

Adding up the two totals for officers in all the *hou-kuan* and *tu-wei* units in the Chü-yen region, the number would have been 646. If we then add this number to the one for servicemen (1,300), the total number of officers, servicemen, and supporting personnel in the Chü-yen garrison units would have been 1,946.[28]

But, in addition to these regular garrison officers, servicemen, and support personnel, there were, as was discussed earlier, convicts and slaves of varying statuses, private followers, and personal attendants, as well as retired and farming officials and soldiers in the farming establishments, all of whom resided and worked in the Chü-yen garrison settlements but were classified separately. The Chü-yen documents reveal no information about the total number of slaves, private followers, personal attendants, and retired and farming officials in the region. Regarding the convicts, one wooden slip records 370 *fu-tso* convicts and another 50 *ch'ih-hsing*.²⁹ The total is 420, but, as the context of the documents indicates, this comprises only a portion of the convicts working in the Chü-yen garrison settlements.

Since farming was the essential task in the colonization and development of Chü-yen, the farming organization constituted a major establishment in the Chü-yen region.³⁰ One wooden document records that the Hsin-ma Farming Region (*t'ien-kuan*) alone had 1,500 soldiers digging irrigation canals in 85 B.C.³¹ The Hsin-ma Farming Region was located in the Chien-shui Chief Commandant Area. As stated earlier, there were many farming centers in Chü-yen Chief Commandant Area, in the triangle of Chü-yen—Chia-ch'ü—T'ien-pei.³² Information on the number of the farming soldiers in these centers is not available in the wooden documents. However, a wooden document discovered at Mu-durbeljin, the headquarters of the Chia-ch'ü *hou-kuan*, reveals that 140 persons were engaged to dig canals.³³ In addition, the number of such farming experts as cowherds (*mu-shih*) and irrigation soldiers (*ho-ch'ü tsu*) is not indicated in the wooden strips. The officials in the farming organization included the agricultural chief commandant (*nung tu-wei*) or the colonel of military farming (*hu-t'ien chiao-wei*), the farming director (*t'ien-kuan*), the farming commander (*ch'eng, chang-kuan*), the agricultural prefect (*nung-ling*), the foreman clerk of land cultivation (*pieh-t'ien ling-shih*), the accessory clerk of canal supervision (*chien-ch'ü tso-shih*), and so on, but the totals of such officers in the Chü-yen region are unknown. They should have been there in large numbers because one document, 490.10(182), reveals 10 accessory clerks of canal supervision in one farming settlement,³⁴ and there were at least 11 farming directors recorded in the Chü-yen documents,³⁵ each of whom seem to have been assisted by at least 1 clerk of land cultivation.³⁶ Therefore, it seems reasonable to assume that there were over 40 farming officers regularly stationed in the various Chü-yen farming settlements.

Connected to the farming organizations were a series of granaries for storing farm products. These granaries were headed by directors with various official titles, including granary chief (*ts'ang-chang*), granary supervisor (*ts'ang-chien*) or granary head (*chu-ts'ang*), and director (*se-fu*); they were assisted by aides of various classifications, including assistant chief (*tu-ch'eng*), foreman clerks, clerks, clerical assistants, and so forth.³⁷ Once again the total number of such officers in the Chü-yen region is not recorded in the wooden documents, but it seems quite reasonable to assume that there were at least twenty such granary officials in Chü-yen.

The total figures for convicts, servicemen, and support personnel in the farming and granary establishments add up to 2,120. This figure does not include slaves, private followers, personal attendants, and retired officers and skilled workers in the farming settlements. Thus, the actual number of Han who supported or were connected to the garrison organizations must have been considerably higher.

In any event, even with our conservative estimates, the Han forces in the garrison, farming, and granary units in the Chü-yen region must have amounted to at least 4,066.

As was discussed earlier, the Han officers and servicemen from outside Chü-yen were allowed to have their families in their service units. The family members usually included a wife, parents, children, and underage brothers and sisters; they also received food provisions from the garrison administration. Judging from the numbers of registers of their provisions, there seem to have been large numbers of families of servicemen in the various garrison establishments.[38] But specific information about the totals of these servicemen's families in the Chü-yen region is not available. Records of a comparable Han frontier and garrison settlement in the Western Region (Hsi-yü) seem to indicate that the number of officers' and servicemen's family members in the late first century B.C. and early first century A.D. frontier region, which was even more distant and harsher than Chü-yen, was about one-third of the total Han garrison and farming force.[39] But the lack of supporting evidence prevents us from applying this ratio to the Han officers' and servicemen's families in the Chü-yen region.

THE POPULATION OF THE CIVILIAN SETTLEMENTS

The total population of the civilian settlements in Chü-yen is even harder to estimate than that of the garrison establishment. No historical or archaeological sources provide us with any specific information of this sort. We can only work on the problem using such information as the rank of the magistrate of Chü-yen District (*hsien*), the number of *hsiang* (counties), the number of *li* (wards) in Chü-yen, and the population figures generally associated with such units in the established Han institutional framework.

Both the *Table of Officials* (*Pai-kuan kung-ch'ing piao*) in the *Han-shu* and the *Old Han Observances* (*Han chiu-i*) indicate an established Han institutional structure that called the magistrate of a *hsien* (district) with a population of more than 10,000 households *ling* and the magistrate of a *hsien* with a population of less than 10,000 households *chang*.[40] The Chü-yen wooden strips indicate that the district magistrate of Chü-yen was called a *ling* from the earliest date (64 B.C.) of its existence to the last years of the Former Han period.[41] Accordingly, Chü-yen *hsien* should have had a population of more than 10,000 households by the established Han institutional standard. But Ying Shao (fl. A.D. 140–206) maintained that in the border regions acquired and developed during the reign of Emperor Wu sometimes a *hsien* was headed by a *ling* even if it only had a population of "several hundred" (meaning 200 or 300 or more) households. Recently unearthed Han sources in Shantung (Yin-ch'üeh-shan in Lin-i) and Hunan (Ma-wang-tui in Ch'ang-sha) also show large variations in the size of Han *hsien*, ranging from 10,000 to 15,000 and even 20,000 households.[42] As was discussed earlier, Chü-yen was developed as part of the Ho-hsi frontier region in Emperor Wu's time and was established as a *hsien* under the reign of Emperor Hsuan (74–49 B.C.). Naturally, Chü-yen *hsien* was in the category of border *hsien* and was likely to be headed by a *ling* even if its population was not more than 300 households. Thus, we come to see the two possible ranges of the population of Chü-yen *hsien*: either about 300 or more than 10,000 households. But the latter seems unlikely, for the total population of Chang-yeh *chün* in the last years of the Former Han dynasty was only 24,352 households, and it seems very unlikely that half the population resided in Chü-yen. Chü-yen was only one of the ten *hsien* under Chang-yeh *chün*, and was not even its capital district.[43]

If we assume then, that Chü-yen *hsien* had about 300 households, its total population can be estimated in two ways. First, if we use the national average of household size, which was 4.87 persons during the period in question,[44] Chü-yen's total civilian population would have been 1,461 persons. Second, if we use the Chang-yeh average of household size, which was 3.64 persons,[45] Chü-yen's total civilian population would have been 1,092 individuals. Various data regarding family size in the wooden documents lend strong support to the average family size of 3.64 persons in the Chü-yen region, hence the estimate utilizes the lower figure (see table 23). In fact, twenty-eight relevant wooden documents show the following distribution of family sizes. Where the majority of the families in table 23 had 4 persons, the average size of the 28 households is 3.65, a figure that is almost identical to the Chang-yeh average of 3.64.

As was discussed earlier, in the Chü-yen *hsien* there were probably three *hsiang* (counties): Capital County, East County, and West County. If we know the standard population ranges of the county in Han times, we can make estimates of Chü-yen *hsien*'s civilian population accordingly.

However, sections dealing with local government in the *Han-shu* and the *Hou-Han shu* gave no specific figures about the standard population of the county. Other Han and later traditional sources differ on the population of the counties. Their figures range from 500 to 10,000 households, with 647, 1,500, 5,000, and 2,500 as the most common figures within this large range.[46] The views of modern scholars have also been divided on this issue.[47] Ying Shao states that there were 10 *li* (wards) in a county and that each *li* had about 50 families, but other Han sources indicate that a county could have 50 to 100 *li*. In that case, the number of families in a county would have been considerably larger.[48] My view is that in the Former Han period the least number of households required for the establishment of a county was 500, while a larger county would have had a larger population, depending on its location as well as the population size of the district to which it belonged.

As part of a border district, which generally had a smaller population than an interior district,[49] the counties of Chü-yen *hsien* naturally did not have larger populations. The fact that all the county administrators carried the title *se-fu* (county administrator) not *yu-chih* (county administrator with rank) also indicates the small size of the population of Chü-yen *hsien*'s counties because only large counties with a population of more than five thousand households could have a *yu-chih* as administrator in Han times.[50] Thus, we may venture to assume that the population of a county in Chü-yen *hsien* during the period under

TABLE 23. Han Family Size as Recorded in the Chü-yen Documents

Family Identification Number	Number of Persons	Document Numbers
1	2 + 1[a]	Cp202
2	4	Cp203
3	6	Cp218
4	2	Cp392
5	3	Cp395
6	4	Cp766
7	4	Cp955
8	4	Cp1114
9	3	Cp1301
10	4	Cp1273
11	4	Cp2745
12	4	Cp2752
13	3	Cp3281
14	4	Cp3282
15	2	Cp3283
16	3	Cp3287
17	2	Cp3288
18	3 + 1[a]	Cp3289
19	3	Cp3295
20	3 + 1[a]	Cp3298
21	10	Cp4085
22	2	Cp4395
23	2	Cp4789
24	3	Cp4850
25	4	Cp5345
26	3 + 1[a]	Cp9903
27	4	EPT–65: 411
28	4	EPT–65: 478

Note: The average is 103 divided by 28 = 3.68.

Only documents that provide complete and clear information on family size are included. Interpretations of all documents have been checked against their photographs for accuracy.

[a] Implied by the documents.

Pl. 1. Headquarters of the chief commandant of Yü-men Pass (Yü-men *kuan tu-wei*) in western Kansu (Gansu). Han documents were found in its large compound of walls and watch stations in the early part of the twentieth century.

Pl. 2. Remains of a Han oven together with firewood, haystacks, and reeds located in front of the Han headquarters of the chief commandant of the Yü-men Pass, where Han documents were discovered in the 1940s.

Pl. 3. Ruins of the "River Granary City" (Ho-ts'ang ch'eng) about 70 kilometers northwest of Tun-huang in western Kansu. The Great Wall is just behind it to the left, where Han documents were discovered in the early twentieth century.

Pl. 4. Ruins of a Han beacon tower and watch station in the large compound of the "River Granary City," where Han documents were found in the twentieth century. The Han Great Wall can be seen in the background, extending east-west.

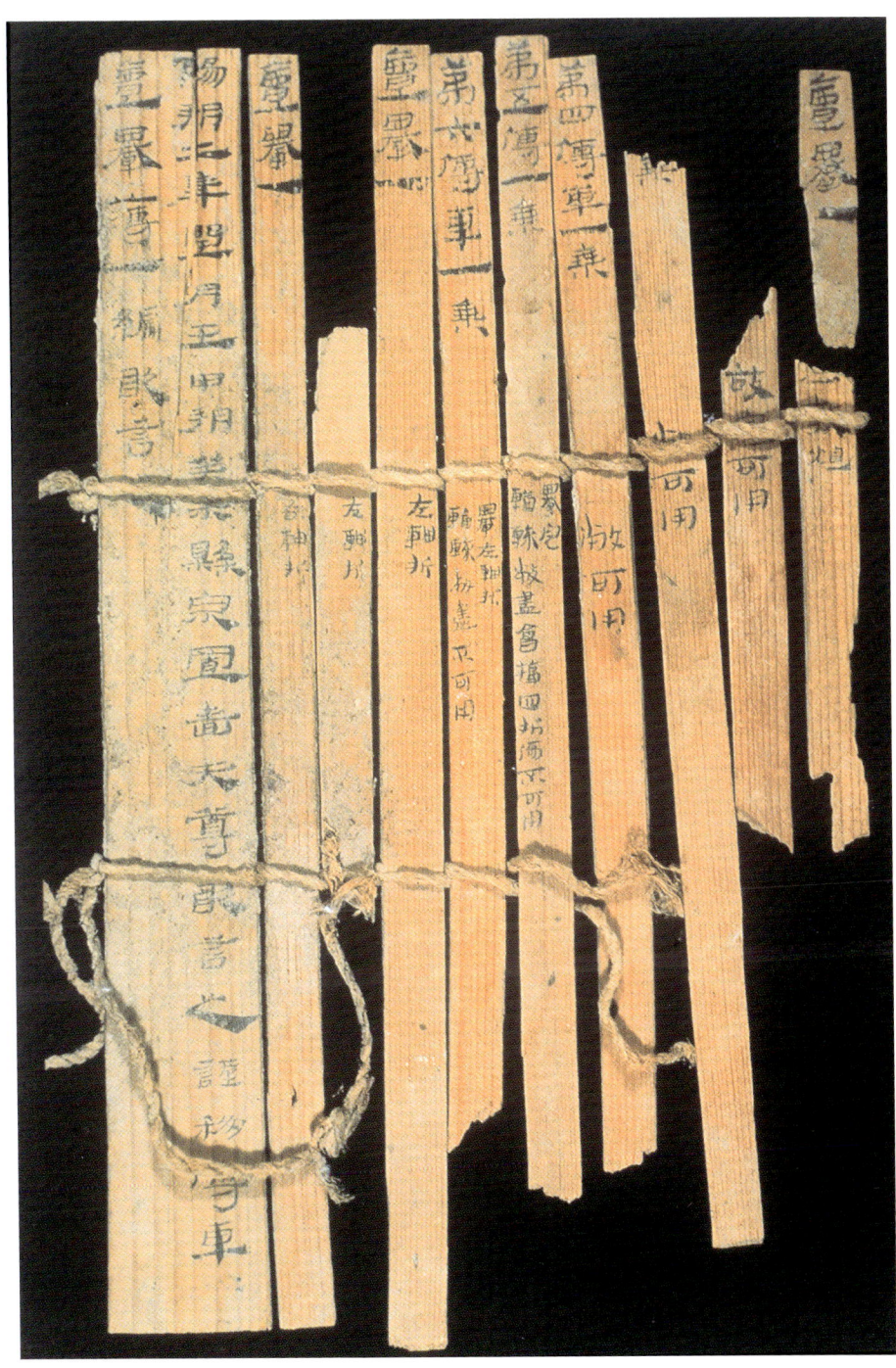

Pl. 5. Register of station carts (*chuan-chü*) dated 23 B.C. in the Han documents discovered in Hsuan-ch'üan Station in Tun-huang, western Kansu.

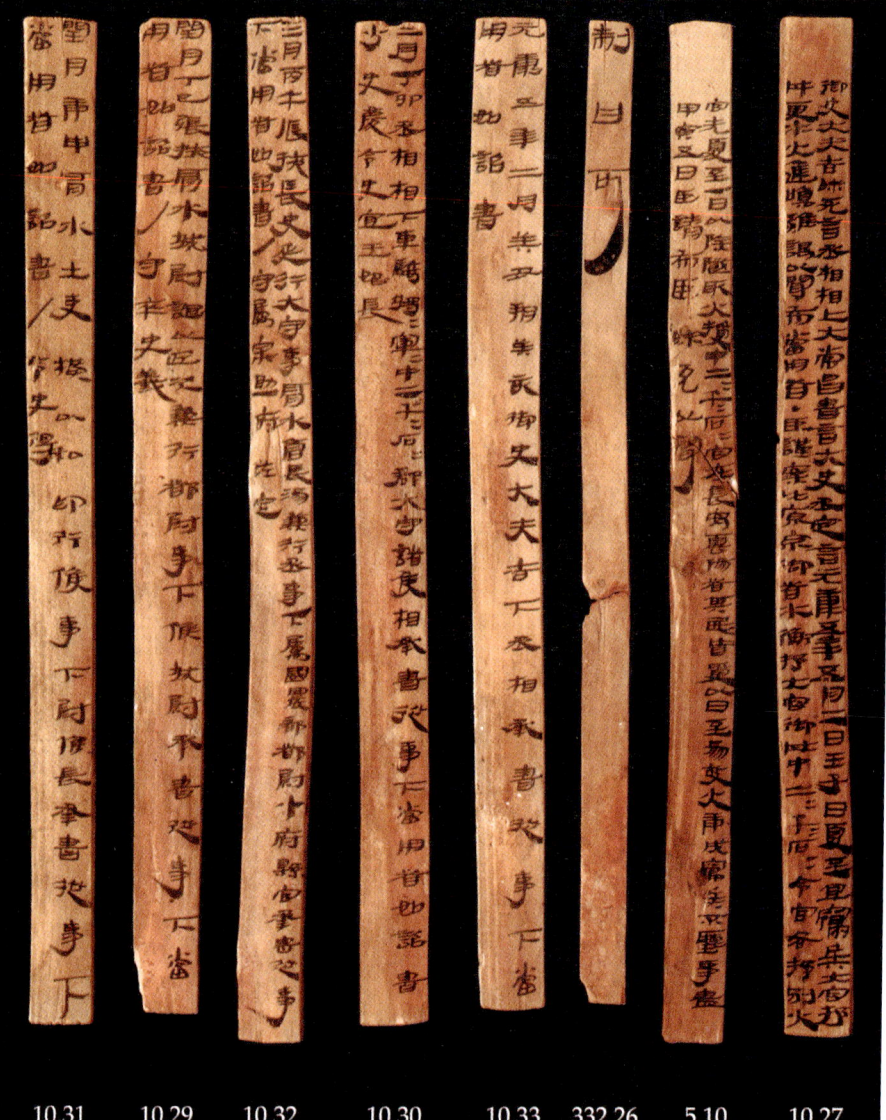

Pl. 6. Imperial decree dated 61 B.C. found in Ti-wan (Ulan-durbeljin) in Chü-yen, the site of the headquarters of the Han Chien-shu commandant (*hou-kuan*, 候官).

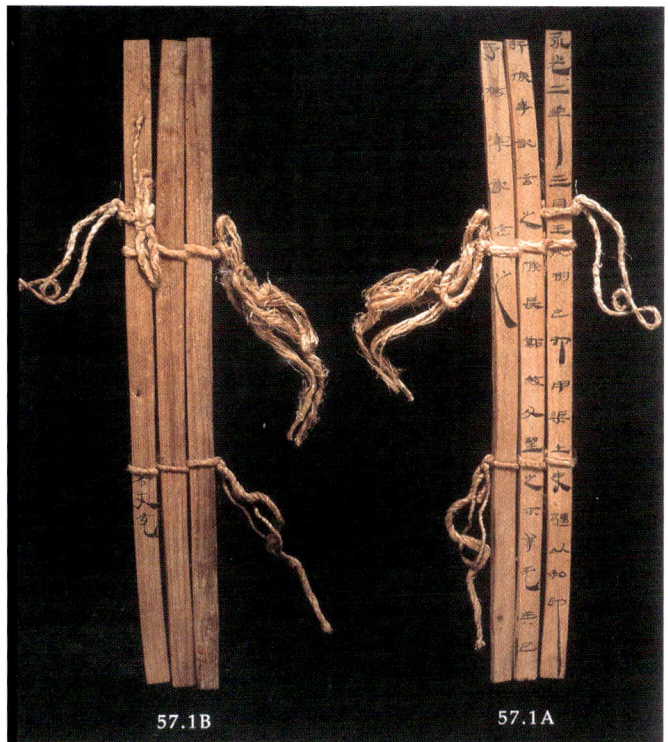

Pl. 7. Docs. 57.1A and doc. 57.1B, dated 42 B.C., are respectively the front and the back of a three-piece staff report on an official's leave on the occasion of his father's death. It was found in P'o-ch'eng tzu (Mu-durbeljin), the site of the Han Chia-ch'ü commandant of the Chü-yen region.

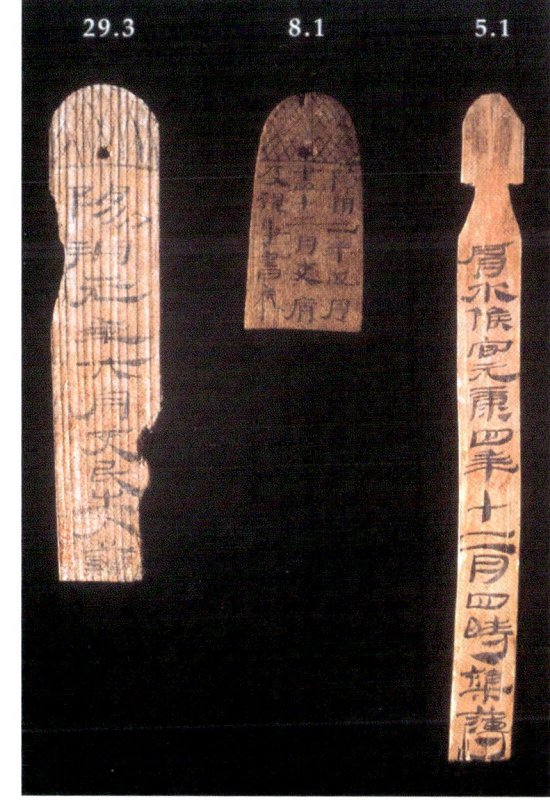

Pl. 8. Three Han documents of different sizes and forms and for various functions found in Chü-yen. Doc. 5.1, dated 62 B.C., is from Chien-shui *hou-kuan* (part of a record book/report). Docs. 8.1 and 29.3 are dated 23 B.C. and 24 B.C., respectively. Doc. 8.1, found at the site of the Han Chia-ch'ü commandant's headquarters, is the cover of an annual report of illnesses and appointments of officials. Doc. 29.3, found at the Chin Pass (Chin-kuan) is a monthly account of officials and civilians crossing the pass.

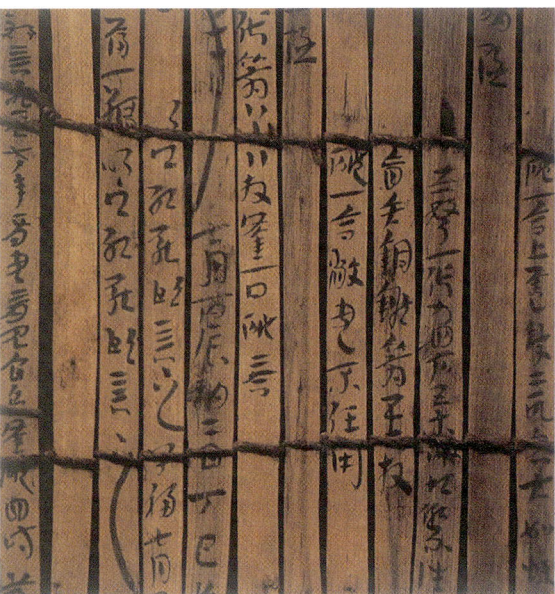

Pl. 9. Register of weapons and related items dated A.D. 93–95, consisting of 77 lines. It was found in Ch'a-k'o erh-t'ieh (Tsakhortei), the site of a commander unit under the jurisdiction of the Han Kuang-ti commandant of Chien-shui in the Chü-yen region.

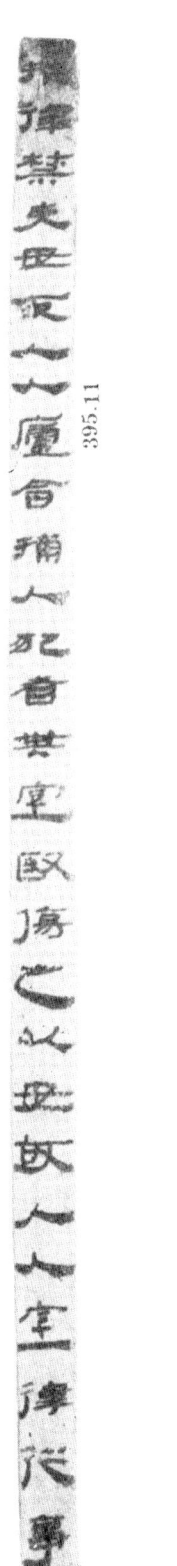

Pl. 10. Two Han documents found in Chü-yen. Doc. 303.18, dated 77 B.C., found in Ta-wan (Taralingin-durbeljin), the site of the headquarters of the Han Chien-shui chief commandant (*tu-wei*) in Chü-yen, concerned the Han conquest of Lou-lan (Lop-nor in eastern Sinkiang) in 77 B.C. in which the Chia-ch'ü commandant Chang was ordered by an imperial decree to send soldiers and female interpreters to Lou-lan and bring the head of the Lou-lan king, assassinated by a Han official, to the imperial capital at Ch'ang-an. The decree also ordered that twenty soldiers and two female interpreters should stay in Lou-lan to help control the area. Doc. 395.11, found in Po-lo Sung-chih (Borotsonch), the site of the headquarters of the Han Sa-ching commandant of Chü-yen, is an article of Han law prohibiting intrusion into private residences by government personnel, that is, the legal idea that "a man's house is his castle."

Pl. 11. Part of the headquarters of the Chia-ch'ü commandant (P'o-ch'eng tzu), where over thirteen thousand documents on wood and bamboo were found from the 1930s to the 1980s. The *chang* (center fortress within) measures 543 square meters. The walls are 4.0 to 4.3 meters thick, and their ruins still stand 4.6 meters high.

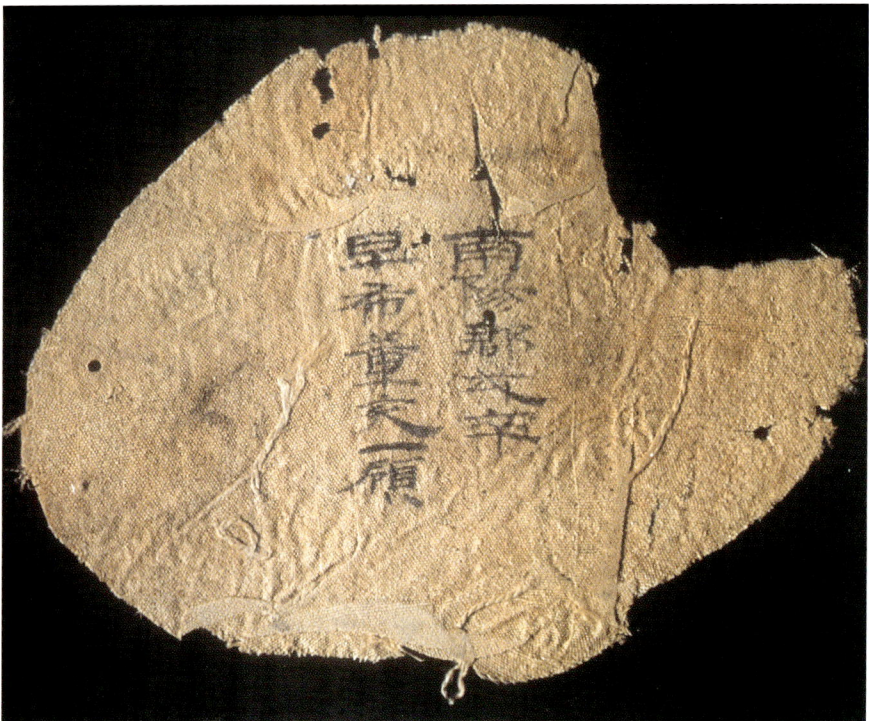

Pl. 12. Han silk document found in P'o-ch'eng tzu, the site of the headquarters of the Han Chia-ch'ü commandant, detailing the clothing of the garrison soldiers from Nan-yang (in modern Honan). A number of Han documents from Chü-yen and Hsuan-ch'üan were written on silk.

consideration was within the range of five hundred to five thousand households. Considering the fact that Chü-yen *hsien* was a frontier region under development and was still protected by large military garrisons, the lower end of this range seems more likely. The higher figures probably referred to the well-developed and densely populated interior districts of the Han empire.

Of the three counties in Chü-yen *hsien*, Capital County was the most important, and it was in existence at the same time as Chü-yen *hsien*.[51] The other two counties, East and West, cannot be accurately dated from the Chü-yen documents, but they were in operation concurrently.[52] It seems that in the process of development of the three Chü-yen counties, Capital County was established first, and only sometime later, when Chü-yen's population and development reached a more advanced stage, were the other two counties gradually instituted.[53] But, judging from the total number of *li* and based on Ying Shao's statement of ten *li* to a *hsiang*, it seems reasonable to assume that all three *hsiang* of Chü-yen *hsien* were active during a certain period of time, particularly during the last decades of the Former Han dynasty. If we assume that each of the *hsiang* had at least 500 households, Chü-yen *hsien* would have had 1,500. Using the Chang-yeh average family size of 3.64 persons, we can place the total population of Chü-yen *hsien* at 5,460 persons. This total is about 6.2 percent of the total population of Chang-yeh (88,731 persons). If we use the 3.68 figure given in table 23, then the total would be 5,520 or 6.22 percent of Chang-yeh's population. The difference is insignificant in this case. This goes nicely with the fact that Chü-yen was only one of the ten districts of Chang-yeh, and also one of the least developed districts.

There were thirty-three *li* in Chü-yen *hsien*. Although these *li* were not established at the same time and some of them even gradually became inactive, they all seem to have been active in the latter part of the period in question. Therefore, if we follow Ying Shao and assume that each *li* had 50 households on average,[54] Chü-yen would have had a total of 1,650 households, and, if we again apply the Chang-yeh average family size of 3.64 persons, Chü-yen would have had a total of 6,006 persons. This total is about 6.8 percent of the total Chang-yeh population (88,731 persons). If the average of 3.68 is used, the numbers would be 6,072 and 6.84 percent, respectively.

We have now made three estimates of the civilian population of Chü-yen *hsien*. It would have had at least 1,092 individuals on the basis of its magistrate's title being *ling*, it would have had 5,460 individuals on the basis of its three counties, and it would have 6,006 individuals on the basis of its thirty-three wards. From the very nature of the basis of our estimate, it seems that the last two figures are the most plausible. Furthermore, the first figure was calculated on the basis of a lower limit, that is, a border district could have had *ling* as the title for its magistrate if it had three hundred households; it does not exclude the possibility of a higher figure. Therefore, we intend to take the last two figures as the most plausible indications of Chü-yen *hsien*'s population. The last two figures are quite close. For reasons that will be explained, we take the higher figure (6,006).[55]

As was discussed earlier, Chang-yeh *chün* had a population of 88,731 individuals in ten districts in the last years of the Former Han dynasty. The average population of a district then was about 8,873 individuals. As a less-developed frontier district, Chü-yen is believed to have had a civilian population less than that of the more developed and older districts of Chang-yeh. This seems to explain the differences between our estimated civilian population of Chü-yen *hsien* and the average district population (8,873) derived from Chang-yeh's total population. But the figure of 6,006 persons is closer to Chang-yeh's average district population of 8,873 individuals than is the figure of 5,460 individuals. For this reason, we take it as the estimated civilian population of Chü-yen *hsien*.

Furthermore, Chü-yen *hsien* became Chü-yen Dependent State (Shu-kuo) of Chang-yeh in the Later Han period. In A.D. 140, it was recorded to have a population of 4,733 individuals (in 1,560 households).[56] The difference between this figure and our estimated population (6,006) of Chü-yen *hsien* in the Former Han times can be explained as the result of a considerable decrease in population in Chang-yeh and throughout the Ho-hsi region in Later Han times.[57] The Later Han figure, however, seems to indicate that our estimated population of Chü-yen *hsien* is not too far from its actual population.

We have no meaningful way to estimate the population of Chien-shui *hsien* in the Chü-yen region. As was discussed earlier, it existed for only a brief period and was not listed in the *Treatise on Geography* in the *Han-shu*; by the last decades of the Former Han dynasty, it had become part of Chü-yen. The only useful population figures recorded in the Chü-yen documents involve the Office of the County Administrator (*se-fu*) of Chien-shui *hsien*, but no information about its counties and wards is given.[58] In consideration of all these factors, we will not venture any estimate of Chien-shui *hsien*'s population. Besides, Chü-yen *hsien*'s population probably already included that of the former Chien-shui *hsien*.

The *hsien* administrative staff also presents a problem in our population estimate. Since most members of this staff were from Chü-yen and hence have already been included in our estimate, and since the *hsien* government in Chü-yen was smaller than those of districts in the interior, there were probably only a handful of officials in the *hsien* government who were not natives of Chü-yen.[59] The total number of such officials can be assumed to have been no more than 10. Thus, the total population in the civilian settlements and under the administration of Chü-yen *hsien* may be estimated at 6,016 individuals.

THE SIZE AND THE DENSITY OF THE CHÜ-YEN POPULATION

In the preceding sections, our investigation of the population size and distribution in the Chü-yen region yields two figures: 4,066 and 6,016 to 6,072. The first figure is the estimate of the number of residents in the garrison and related settlements, and the second is the estimate of the number of civilians under the administration of the *hsien* government in Chü-yen. Based on these figures, we can place the total number of residents in the garrison and civilian establishments in the neighborhood of 10,000. Given the fact that many segments of the Chü-yen population cannot be intelligently estimated, we cannot emphasize enough our understanding that the actual population of Chü-yen in the period of its highest development was higher.[60]

As was noted in an earlier chapter, the Chü-yen region, defined by its Han settlements, covered an area of 9,300 square kilometers. Using this figure to estimate the population density in the region, we reach a figure of about 1.08 inhabitants per square kilometer. This estimate is much higher than the density of 0.70 for the entire Chang-yeh *chün*, as is estimated in modern studies.[61] The difference can be explained by two factors. First, the Chang-yeh population density of 0.70 was calculated from data based on the theoretical territorial boundary, not on the area covered by actual settlements, which was smaller than the area surrounded by the theoretical boundary. Second, Chü-yen had a relatively larger population than some of the regions in Chang-yeh because of its large garrison establishment. Perhaps a combination of both factors is the plausible reason for the larger population density in Chü-yen.

DEMOGRAPHIC CHARACTERISTICS OF THE HAN FRONTIER

Besides size and distribution, the composition of a population—the characteristics and traits that can be observed and measured—provides critical information about the structure and organization of a society. A knowledge of the population composition of Chü-yen can help us understand the Han frontier society in more depth. We turn now to this undertaking.

Demographers generally consider population composition in five major categories: population structure, ethnic characteristics, social and economic characteristics, physiological characteristics, and psychological characteristics.[62] But in practice interest in population composition is generally confined to a relatively few characteristics that are significant from the viewpoint of social problems. The many relevant characteristics can be grouped into two broad classes: demographic characteristics—age, sex, marital status, skin color, and nativity;

and socioeconomic characteristics—education, income, labor force participation, employment status, and occupation. In our discussion of the population composition in Chü-yen, we shall use these two categories as the framework of analysis.

The Chü-yen documents do not provide adequate data for a meaningful analysis of all the individual demographic and socioeconomic characteristics. About some traits there is simply no useful information. Overall, there are more data about the demographic characteristics than the socioeconomic characteristics of the Chü-yen population. For this reason, our analysis will remain sketchy and tentative on some of the issues.

It should be clear from our preceding discussions that the Chü-yen population was composed of two basic groups, the permanent settlers and the short-term or transient settlers. Those who either were born in or had permanently migrated to Chü-yen belonged to the first group; those who went to Chü-yen for garrison service or brief visits belonged to the second group. The transient settlers could become permanent residents of Chü-yen, but, as will be discussed in the next chapter, the Chü-yen residents were forbidden by law to move to the interior. Based on our discussions in chapter 2, we may also assume that almost all of the settlers in both groups were Chinese born because the foreign-born population was under the administration of the Dependent State and its size cannot be intelligently estimated.

In occupation and employment status, the permanent Chü-yen population was predominately agricultural, probably with a very small percentage being merchants, artisans, and other types of tradespeople. But, with the exception of the temporary visitors who went to Chü-yen for nonmilitary reasons, the entire transient population was garrison connected. In a broad sense, this was a military population, even though a large portion of the population in the garrison settlements was engaged in farming and related work. Based on our estimate of the Chü-yen population, we may assume that about 40 percent of the population was military and about 60 percent was agricultural. By the very nature of Chü-yen's economic and military structure as a government-controlled frontier colony, unemployment can be assumed to have been virtually nonexistent.

In education and religion, no specific data are available for a meaningful analysis. But generally some facets of the intellectual and religious dimension of the population composition can be sketched. Education on the Chü-yen frontier was limited to a small segment of the population. Educational materials were limited to those that were basic to daily life, not materials for high intellectual pursuits. These materials included the beginner's lexicons and primers for learning and writing, such as *Ts'ang Hsieh p'ien* and *Chi Chiu p'ien*; calendars; parts of legal codes and ordinances necessary for making administrative decisions; the multiplication tables and related materials for basic arithmetic skills; and some texts necessary for reading and understanding documents. Probably only a handful of people in the civilian and garrison establishments were selected to receive education, but the exact number and its ratio to the entire population are not known, nor is the duration of such an education. Some officials on the frontier evidently had some higher education, for fragments of such classics as the *Book of History* (*Shu-ching*) and the *Book of Changes* (*I-ching*) have been discovered.[63]

Common Chinese folk religion was practiced on the frontier. The worship of the God of the Soil (She) is recorded in the Chü-yen documents. Peachwood charms (*t'ao-fu*) with pictures of the *shen-shu* (*shen-t'u*) and Yü-lü (Yü Lei) gods have been discovered, and fragments of the ancient divination books *Erh-ming shu* and *Mu-yün shu* and commentaries on the *Book of Changes* as well as lines of some unidentifiable ancient fortune-telling works have also been found.[64] Such folk beliefs are assumed to have been universal among the population.

On the most fundamental demographic characteristics—age, sex, marital status, and family size and types—the Chü-yen documents provide either no data or provide too little to warrant a general statement on a specific issue. Take the issue of age as an example. As was discussed in chapter 2, we have information about the age of one hundred people. This sample is too small to be used to estimate the age of the Chü-yen population. Still, on the basis of the established draft age regulations in Former Han times, we know that the age range of the garrison population, slightly less than 40 percent of the Chü-yen population, was 20 to about 56. This is a relatively young population. Interestingly, the median age of servicemen and officers in that limited sample group was 23.5, a figure that is a general indication of a younger population in demographic analysis. Or perhaps this is just a coincidence.

As was noted earlier, the garrison soldiers of a district other than Chü-yen were generally allowed to have their families with them in the garrison settlements. These family members were provided with food by the garrison authorities. Some of the local garrison soldiers were occasionally permitted to have their families with them if their garrison settlements were far from their homes. These families also received food from the garrison administration. The provisions lists of both family groups recorded the recipient's name, age, sex, marital status, and the specific relation to the serviceman or officer with whom the recipient lived in the garrison establishment. These data are invaluable for analyzing demographic characteristics of the population of Chü-yen. Twenty-eight such lists have been found in Chü-yen. They are the source for table 24. Most of the twenty-eight families in the lists came from the districts of Chang-yeh outside Chü-yen, but there is no reason to believe that these families were in any measurable way different from the families in the district of Chü-yen.[65] Furthermore, since these families were of the same period and the lists were discovered in a random way, the family characteristics revealed in these lists are probably representative of the general civilian population of Chü-yen during the period in question, at least from the viewpoint of sampling theory. The various data in the twenty-eight lists are summarized in table 24 by four population variables: age, sex, marital status, and sex ratio (the number of males per hundred females).

We will discuss the age-sex composition first. The table reveals that while the sex ratio among persons under twenty is 52.00, it increases to 150.00 at ages twenty to seventy. This means that women were generally married off or died at an earlier age than men. As can be seen in the overall sex ratio of 88.00 among all age groups, there were more women than men in the population. Interestingly, contrary to the general pattern of sex ratios in modern societies, there were about 20 percent fewer males than females even at ages one to four, an age range that usually carries a sex ratio of 103 to 105 in modern demography.[66] This also indicates that in the Han society of this time baby girls were not discriminated against as they were in later periods of Chinese history by such means as the practice of female infanticide. All of this leads us to think that the sex composition of the population in Han China may have been measurably different from that of the Chinese population in later periods.[67] It is also possible that the sex composition of the Han frontier population was different from that

TABLE 24. Selected Demographic Characteristics of the Population of Chü-yen

Age Group	Males			Females			Sex Ratio
	Number	Married No.	%	Number	Married No.	%	
Ages 1–19							
1–4	4	—	—	5	—	—	80.00
5–10	4	—	—	9	—	—	44.44
11–19	5	3	60	11	7	63.64	45.45
Subtotal	13	3	23.08	25	7	28.00	52.00
Ages 20 and over							
20–30	2	—	—	14	12	92.31	—[a]
31–40	—	—	—	4	4	100.00	—[a]
41–50	3	2	66.67	1	—	100.00	—[a]
51–60	1	1	100.00	—	—	—	—[a]
61–70	—	—	—	1	1	100.00	—[a]
Draft age							
20–57	24	23	95.83	—	—	—	—[a]
Subtotal	30	26	86.67	20	17	85.00	150.00
Unknown	4	—	—	7	3	42.86	57.14
Total	47	29	61.70	52	27	51.92	90.38

[a]Meaningful sex ratios cannot be determined due to uneven data.

of the regular population in the interior, but we have no evidence in any form that this was the case.

The data in table 24 reveal that the percentage of youths under twenty in the sample population is only about 38. Compared to youth ratios in population data of later periods, which usually ranges from 30 to 40 percent, this sample ratio is not unusual.[68] Here the sample data show a Han population not different from later Chinese populations in a critical aspect. We have no reason to believe that this youth ratio was not peculiar to the Chü-yen frontier population.

In marital status, when considering all age groups, the marriage rates for men and women were the same: 56.57 percent. But for persons under twenty the picture is quite different. As table 24 shows, while only three males under twenty were married, seven (28 percent) of the females under twenty were married. The specific age composition of these married women was twelve, fifteen (two persons), seventeen, eighteen (two persons), and nineteen, while the married males (three persons) were nineteen years of age. Thus, women not only married much earlier than men but sometimes at an unusually early age, such as twelve.[69] The marriage rates for adult males and females age twenty and over are about even at 85 to 86.67 percent. It follows from this that men had a higher rate of marriage after age twenty and this rate was high enough to make up the difference between the rates of marriage for men and women under age twenty. The data in table 24 also indicate that 56.57 percent of the entire sample population was married and that teenage marriages only contributed about 10 percent to the total marital status figure. The latter point contrasts sharply with the prevailing understanding that in Han times the age at marriage was usually fourteen or fifteen for women and between fifteen and eighteen for men.[70] Thus, a reexamination of the prevailing conception of the general pattern of age at marriage in the Han period is necessary. A reasonable suggestion seems to be that wealthy people tended to marry earlier than did the common people.

In sum, our data show the marital conditions of the sample population as follows: over half of the people were married; among the married nearly 18 percent had their marriages performed in their youth; men had a higher marriage rate than women; and women had an overwhelmingly higher rate of marriage in youth than men.

The data show no record of concubinage, although the sex ratio of 90.38 is unusually low and a heavy preponderance of females, modern demographers believe, was often accompanied by concubinage (polygyny) in traditional societies.

The data in the twenty-eight lists of provisions supplied to families reveal some significant information about family types on the frontier. Nineteen families are of the nuclear or conjugal type, consisting of the married couple and their unmarried children, and nine are of the extended or joint family type, consisting of two or more nuclear families in various combinations. Thus, about 67.86 percent of the sample population were nuclear families, and only 32.14 percent were extended families.[71] More specifically, five of the nuclear families belong to the primary type, composed of only a husband and wife; the other fourteen belong to the secondary type, composed of the couple and their offspring, which number one to eight (with two being the majority) and whose ages range from one to eighteen. Among the extended families, one was composed of the married couple, their children, and their nineteen-year-old son's wife (age fifteen); one included the married couple, their children, and the husband's parents; one included the married couple and the husband's father; four included the married couple and one or more of the husband's sisters and brothers; and two included the married couple, the husband's parents, and one or more of the husband's sisters and brothers. Thus, among the joint families five were of the lineal type, having two or more generations of married people in one family unit, and four were of the stem type, having the married couple and one or more of the husband's sisters and brothers in one family unit. It is interesting to note that in the last case the age composition of the dependent sisters and brothers is seven, nine, twelve (two persons), thirteen, eighteen, nineteen, and twenty-three. Table 25 provides a summary of the various family types.

As stated earlier, the average size of the twenty-eight families is 3.68 persons. The average family size in Chang-yeh in the last decades of the Former Han dynasty was 3.64 persons. The two figures are almost identical. This reinforces our confidence in the validity of the sample population's being representative of the larger population of Chü-yen as well as of Chang-yeh. At the same time, the national average size of the Han family was 4.87 persons.[72] Thus, on average the families on the frontier were smaller than those in the interior, which generally had about four to five persons.[73]

TABLE 25. Han Family Types as Seen in the Chü-yen Documents

Family Types		Numbers	Percentage of Category	Percentage of Total
Basic	Subtypes			
Nuclear	Primary	5	26.32	19.23
	Secondary	14	73.68	46.15
Subtotal (nuclear)		19	100.00	65.38
Extended	Lineal	5	55.56	19.23
	Stem	4	44.44	15.39
Subtotal (extended)		9	100.00	34.62
Total		28	100.00	100.00

5

THE MAKING OF A HAN FRONTIER REGION

Control and Communication in Chü-yen

THE STABLE DEVELOPMENT and steady growth of a frontier region such as Chü-yen critically depended on the effective operation of the twin institutions of control and communication. Effective organization and control strengthened the stability and security of a frontier region, and efficient and broad systems of internal and external communication kept a frontier region closely connected within and without. Both institutions were keys to the military security, steady economic growth, and continuing development and consolidation of a frontier region. In the Chü-yen region, both systems of control and communication were well organized and developed, and they functioned with great effectiveness. Some of the ideas behind the organization and operation of the two institutions were remarkably modern.

The aims of this chapter are to examine the details of the organization, operation, and effectiveness of the two institutions of control and communication in the Chü-yen region, to explore the development of certain aspects of these institutions into permanent features of Imperial China, and to appraise the historical significance of these institutions in the larger context of Chinese civilization.

CONTROLS ON THE FRONTIER

The Han Pattern of Frontier Control

Early Han troubles with the Hsiung-nu on the northern borders and the Southern Yüeh on the southern borders and their need to deal with these peoples with positive measures caused the Han empire to design systematic frontier policies as a means of reducing border threats.[1] The Han policies were essentially those of border control and development through immigration. The Han policy of border development through immigration followed the plans and tactics instituted in the pre-Ch'in (221 B.C.) and Ch'in (221–207 B.C.) periods, but some of them were modified and expanded by the proposals of Han political thinkers and policymakers in light of the special circumstances and needs of the empire. The Han system of border control, and control of the passage of travelers at key points in general, also made use of the practices of earlier times and included new measures for satisfying special needs.[2] In its complete form and to its full extent, the Han system consisted generally of the following basic components.[3]

1. Control points at key locations on the borders of the empire were established to exercise control over civilian and military traffic and the flow of strategic materials.
2. Passage through the control points was not permitted without a passport.
3. Foreigners, immigrants, and residents of frontier regions were prohibited from entering the border passes without special permission from the central government.
4. Materials of strategic importance—such as weapons of war, young and good horses, metal (especially iron instruments), agricultural implements, special manufactures and precious materials, vehicles, and sometimes even livestock—were not permitted to pass.
5. Markets were held at border passes to allow trade between Chinese and border barbarians, but trade and its frequency were under government control.
6. Certain foreign products were not allowed to be imported from outside the empire.

The Han principles behind these border controls and restrictions seem to have been formulated based on three basic considerations: the control of strategic materials, military and agricultural technology, and manpower. Whereas the first two are easy to comprehend, the third is more complicated. First, the prohibition of Chinese settlers on the frontier from entering the passes was to ensure the stability and hence the continuing development of the Han frontier regions. Second, the fact that civilians, officials, and soldiers were not permitted to use the passes without passports means that the Han government tried to prevent the Chinese from joining its foreign enemies, particularly the Hsiung-nu. Third, the barbarians were not allowed free inward passage because the Han government sometimes questioned the sincerity and allegiance of the foreigners who wished to settle in China and feared that if they were not satisfied with the treatment they received they might abet the Han's enemies (particularly the Hsiung-nu), cause disorder, or even instigate revolts.

This was the general structure of Han border controls. The actual practice varied understandably with time and place. For instance, under Emperor Lü (188–180 B.C.), horses, oxen, and sheep might be allowed, under special circumstances, to go into the kingdom of the Southern Yüeh, but they could only be males for the obvious reason of preventing the propagation of the animals. Under Emperor Wen (180–157 B.C.), in 168 B.C. the passes were actually done away with and passports were no longer used, but in 153 B.C. Emperor Ching (157–141 B.C.) reestablished both the passes and the use of passports and in 146 B.C. a regulation prohibiting young and good horses from going through the border passes was instituted. Under Emperor Wu (141–87 B.C.), in 140–139 B.C. both the passes and the use of passports were done away with again, but in 139 B.C. both institutions were reestablished and, as indicated by events in 121, 108, 103, and 99 B.C., they remained functioning for the rest of Emperor Wu's reign. Under Emperor Chao (87–74 B.C.), in 82 B.C. part of the system of border controls, the prevention of the exportation of horses and crossbows, was relaxed, but the system of passes and passports as a whole continued through Emperor Chao's reign into Emperor Hsuan's reign (74–49 B.C.). In fact, a direct reference to the institution is seen in a decree of 70 B.C. by Emperor Hsuan, when, as a result of a poor harvest, an attempt was made to encourage common people to transport grain to the Ch'ang-an area by allowing those who brought grain by carts or by boats to enter the passes without need of the usual passports. Similar decrees of 23 B.C. and 17 B.C. by Emperor Ch'eng (33–7 B.C.) and an event of A.D. 4 in the reign of Emperor P'ing (1 B.C.–5 A.D.) point to the fact that the system of passes and passports continued through the Former Han period after Emperor Hsuan.[4]

The Han frontier regions, generally territorial acquisitions, were always under strict control for the sake of security and stability. The Chü-yen region was exemplary in this respect. In fact, only through the information on border controls in the wooden documents have modern historians learned the details of border control in Han times.

Measures of Control on the Chü-yen Frontier

For a frontier region, stability is the basis of security. One measure to achieve stability, as was conceived by the Han designers of frontier policy, was strict control of the local population and hence the restriction of mobility.

Registration of Local Population

For the control of the local residents, the garrison organizations and regional governmental authorities required both military personnel and civilians under their jurisdiction to register. The forms of registration varied with the status and position of the registered.

For the regular servicemen—garrison and farming soldiers, hired soldiers, and so on—the general form of registration was as follows.

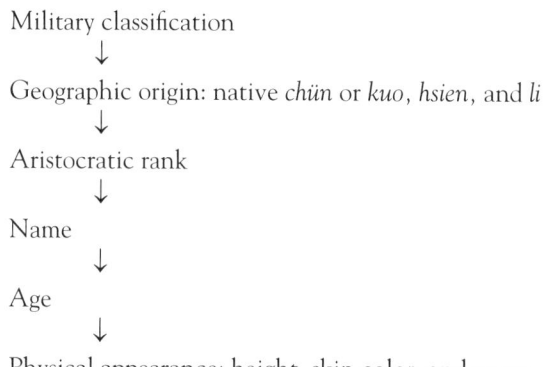

Military classification
↓
Geographic origin: native *chün* or *kuo*, *hsien*, and *li*
↓
Aristocratic rank
↓
Name
↓
Age
↓
Physical appearance: height, skin color, and so on

For the officers, the registers start with their titles and service units, but the rest of the form is the same as those of regular servicemen. The registers of the cavalrymen (*ch'i-shih*) begin with their native *hsien* (district) and give no description of their physical appearance.

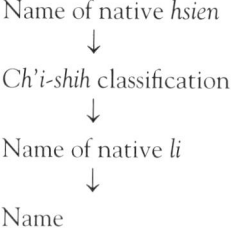

Name of native *hsien*
↓
Ch'i-shih classification
↓
Name of native *li*
↓
Name

Part of the reason for this simplified form is understandable. The name of the *chün* was omitted simply because all the cavalrymen in the Chü-yen garrisons were from Chang-yeh *chün*. But the omission of "physical appearance" from the cavalrymen's registers is not understood, and there are no extant documents to illuminate this point. A few examples of the registers of the three categories are given here to illustrate the actual forms. Documents 1 and 2 are registers of reg-

THE MAKING OF A HAN FRONTIER REGION · 133

ular servicemen; documents 3–5 are those of officers; and document 6 is the register of a cavalryman.

1. Garrison soldier; [from] Ju-nan *chün*, Hsi-p'ing [*hsien*], Chung-hsin *li*; [with the rank of] *kung-ch'eng*; [named] Li Ts'an; age twenty-five [*sui*]; 7 *ch'ih* 1 *ts'un* in height.
   15.22(451)

2. Farming soldier; [from] Tung *chün*, Tung-a [*hsien*], Ch'ang-kuo *li*; [with the rank of] *kuan ta-fu*; [named] Lu Shou; age twenty-eight [*sui*]; 7 *ch'ih* . . . (x)
   43.24(473)

3. Clerical assistant in the office of the Chü-yen chief commandant; [from] Chü-yen [*hsien*], Shih-chih *li*; [named] Wan Shang-shan; age thirty-four [*sui*]; 7 *ch'ih* 5 *ts'un* in height, [of] black [skin color].
   77.81
   2863

4. *Hou* clerk; [from] Han-chung *chün*, Ch'eng-ku [*hsien*], T'i *li*; [named] Li Tung-ch'ang . . . (x)
   43.2(456)

5. Commander of the twenty-eighth *sui*; [from] Chü-yen [*hsien*], Shih-chih *li*; [with the rank of] *ta-fu*; [named] Meng Hsien; age twenty-six [*sui*] . . . (x)
   216.9(434)
   Cp1198

6. [From] Ti-ch'ih [*hsien* of Chang-yeh *chün*]; *ch'i-shih* (cavalryman); [of] Ch'ang-yü *li*; [named] Meng Fu.
   395.1(452)

The complete register of a civilian in Chü-yen takes the following form.

Geographic origin: native *chün*, *hsien*, and *li*
↓
Aristocratic rank
↓
Name
↓
Age
↓
Physical appearance: height, skin color

This form applied only to individuals from a *chün* or *kuo* other than Chang-yeh or Wu-wei, which was a part of Chang-yeh until 72 B.C. For a Chang-yeh (sometimes including the later Wu-wei) resident, the name of the *chün* was deleted. For a Chü-yen resident, both the *chün* and *hsien* entries were also omitted.[5] Three examples are given here to exemplify these forms.

1. [From] Ho-nan *chün*, Ho-nan *hsien*, Pei-chung *li*; [with the rank of] *kung-ch'eng*; [named] Shih Hsiao; age thirty-two [*sui*]; 7 *ch'ih*, 2 *ts'un* in height; [of] black [skin color].
   43.7
   2872
2. [From] Lu-te [*hsien* of Chang-yeh *chün*], Ch'eng-han *li*; [with the rank of] *ta-fu*; [named] Chih Chien-te; aged thirty-two [*sui*]; 7 *ch'ih*, 2 *ts'un* in height; [of] black [skin color].
   37.32
   6826
3. [From] Yang *li*; [named] T'ang Chih; age nineteen [*sui*]; 7 *ch'ih*, 3 *ts'un* in height; [of] tawny [skin color].
   62.34(184)

Document 1 is the register of an individual from outside Chang-yeh *chün*, document 2 is that of a Chang-yeh resident, and document 3 is that of a Chü-yen local.

Followers (*ts'ung-che*), *ch'ih-hsing* (criminals exempted from frontier military and agricultural duties), and regular convicts were also registered. The registers of the followers essentially took the form of the registers of civilians, except for notice of aristocratic rank. The registers of the *ch'ih-hsing* had the same form as those of the followers, though of course with the status *ch'ih-hsing* in place of *follower* at the beginning of the register. The form of the registers of both followers and *ch'ih-hsing* was as follows.

Status
↓
Geographical origin: native *chün*, *hsien*, and *li*
↓
Name
↓
Physical appearance

The register forms of convicts were different because they still had criminal status. The form was also shorter.

Native *hsien*
↓
Convict classification
↓
Age group
↓
Name

The following documents have been translated to show the register forms of followers, *ch'ih-hsing*, and convicts.

1. Follower; [from] Nan-yang [*chün*], Kuan-chün [*hsien*], Hsüan *li*; . . . (x)
   504.10(447)
2. *Ch'ih-hsing*; [from] Tso-p'ing-i [*chün*], Tuo-i [*hsien*], Yeh-lo *li*; [named]
   . . . . (x)[6]
   337.8(442)
   Cp1735
3. [From] Chü-yen [*hsien*]; *fu-tso* convict; *ta-nan*; [named] Wang Chien.
   37.58(455)

It is significant to note that the names of the places on the registers of convicts could be either those of their native places if they were local residents or those of the localities of their current residences if they were not locals. If it was the latter, the places marked on the registers were the ones where the convicts had been assigned for labor. In either case, it was only the current addresses of the convicts that appeared on their registers. This explains the relative briefness of their register forms.

The registers of the local population in the Chü-yen region were detailed and discriminating. And they were reviewed regularly by higher authorities for accuracy. Therefore, they were capable of providing accurate, comprehensive data on the civilian settlers and military personnel in the region, and the garrison and other frontier authorities used such information to better control local population.

Border Control Points and the Use of Passports

In the Chü-yen region, passes and control points were established along the gateways of the region and between large garrison units within it. Among the major passes (*kuan*) frequently seen in the Chü-yen documents were the So Pass (So-kuan) of Chü-yen, the Hsuan-an Pass (sometimes called the Hsuan Pass) of Sa-ching, and the Chin Pass of Chien-shui. The Chin Pass was located at what is now site A32 in Bo Sommarström's report, about half a kilometer north of site A33 (Ti-wan, Ulan-durbeljin), which was the site of Chien-shui *hou-kuan* in Han times. The geographical location of site A32 was situated in such a way that it guarded the northern entrance to the Mao-mu region in ancient times, a fact that accords with the function of the Chin Pass described in the previously translated document 288.7. Figure 6 is a reconstructed plan of the Chin Pass. The exact location of the Hsuan-an Pass is not known, but it was clearly situated in the vicinity of San-ching *hou-kuan* (site P9, Boro Tsonch), and its main function seems to have been to guard the northeastern entrance to the south-

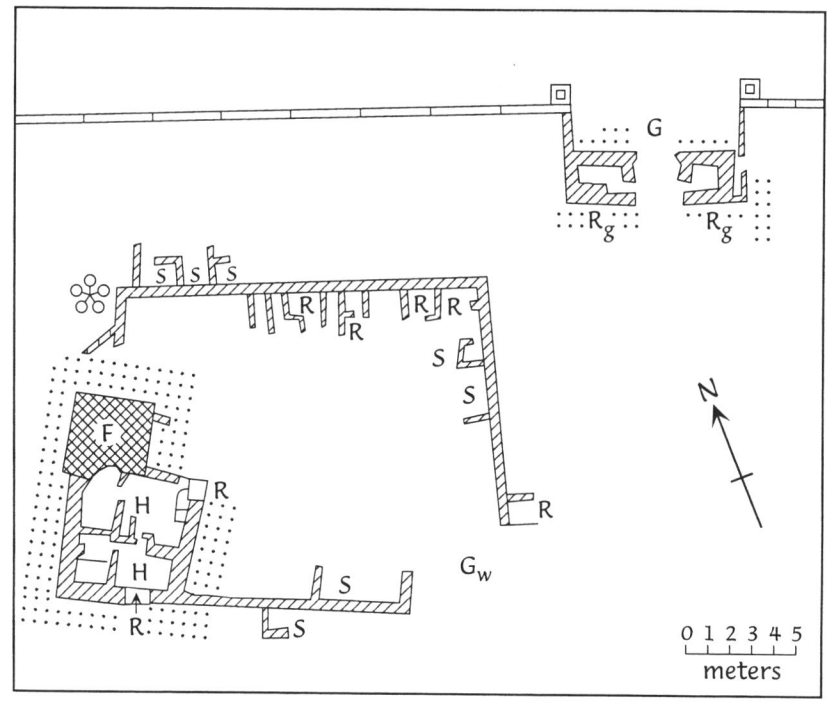

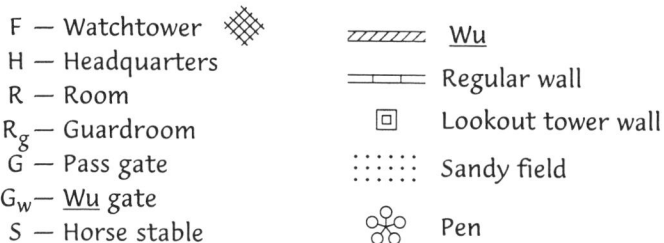

F — Watchtower
H — Headquarters
R — Room
R_g — Guardroom
G — Pass gate
G_w — Wu gate
S — Horse stable

Wu
Regular wall
Lookout tower wall
Sandy field
Pen

Fig. 6. Plan of the Chin Pass establishment

ern region of Chü-yen south of the old Chü-yen Lake. Similarly, the So Pass was probably located somewhere north of the city of Chü-yen (site K799, Khara-Khoto) and guarded the northern entrance to the area that in Han times contained the complex of military and political centers in Chü-yen city (the headquarters of both the Chü-yen *tu-wei* and Chü-yen *hou-kuan*) and the Chia-ch'ü Fortress (the headquarters of the Chia-ch'ü *hou-kuan*).[7]

In the Chü-yen region, the passes were part of the regular garrison establishments. Each of them corresponded to a major watch station and was commanded by a commander or a director of the pass (*kuan se-fu*), who was in turn supported by his pass assistants (*kuan-tso*). The soldiers who guarded and were stationed in the passes were called pass soldiers (*kuan-tsu*).[8]

One of the major assignments of those guarding the passes was the inspection of travelers and their belongings. No one was allowed to go through the passes without a passport or the equivalent travel permit. The passports were issued in three different types, each in the form of a wooden strip: the *kuo-so,* the *chuan,* and the *fu* or *fu-chüan.* The *kuo-so* was a travel notification issued to an individual on government business that entitled him to meals and accommodations at government stations. The *chuan* was a travel permit (passport) issued to civilians for passage through control points. The *fu,* mostly numbered in series, was a pass issued to government personnel and garrison officers and servicemen to allow them, and sometimes their families, to travel within a well-defined frontier or administrative region; *fu* were probably issued to civilians on some occasions.

This classification of travel documents (notifications, passports, and passes) held true in the Chü-yen region (and probably also in the western Ho-hsi region, including part of Chang-yeh, Chiu-ch'üan, and Tun-huang) and only during the period from 43 B.C. to the first years of the Later Han. As will be discussed later in greater detail, the Han system of passes and use of passports generally allowed variations in different regions and times in consideration of special local needs and conditions. The earliest evidence for the use of passports on the western Han frontier dates to about 94 B.C., and after that the clearly dated specimens of travel documents (certificates, passports, etc.) bear the years 78, 64, 50, 43, 28, 12, 11, 5, and 2 B.C. Among these strips, those before 43 B.C. show that the term *kuo-so* was merely part of the text of a *chuan* and always preceded the technical expression *hsien-tao chin-kuan* (passes and fords of the various districts [*hsien* and *tao*]) or similar expressions and therefore really meant "the places [that the traveler] passes." It can reasonably be assumed that by virtue of this special usage in the *chuan,* the term *kuo-so* came to be applied to a specific type of travel document as the system of passports became more complicated and a new type of travel document became necessary. When this transition took place is not revealed anywhere in the Han written and archaeological evidence. But the Chü-yen documents record that the term *kuo-so* had come to mean a specific classification of travel document by 43 B.C. It is historically interesting to note that in Later Han times the *chuan* as a class of travel passport was again combined with the *kuo-so,* only this time *kuo-so* was the appellation and the established procedures for application and use of the *chuan* became the standard practice for the new institution. The *kuo-so* of this new institution was in use as the standard passport from late Later Han times to the tenth century A.D. For this reason, by the end of the Later Han dynasty and the Three Kingdoms period (A.D. 220–65), the origins and the original relationship of *chuan* and *kuo-so* in Former Han times had already become obscure to such learned scholars as Liu Hsi (fl. ca. 200), Li Ch'i (fl. ca. 200), Su Lin (fl. 196–227), Chang Yen (third century), and Ju Shun (fl. 189–265), all of whom disagreed with each other in their interpretations of the two travel documents. The recent discovery of Han wooden documents on the western frontier has provided us with new sources for a better understanding of the extremely difficult and confusing Han institution of travel clearance. However, it should be emphasized that our suggestions about the evolution and practices of the *chuan* and *kuo-so* in Former Han times must remain tentative, and we can only hope that future discoveries of similar documents will shed new light on the problem.[9]

A few examples of *kuo-so*, *chuan*, and *fu* found at Chü-yen are translated here for illustrative purposes. Document 1 is a specimen of *kuo-so*, document 2 is a *chuan* specimen, and documents 3 and 4 are examples of *fu*.

1. Obverse side:

> On the day *i-yu* of the seventh month of the second year of the Yüan-yen period [of Emperor Ch'eng (September 4, 11 B.C.)], Magistrate Shang and Assistant Chung of Chü-yen *hsien* transmit the travel notification (*kuo-so*) [of Wang Feng] to [points of control at] rivers, fords, and passes in the various districts (*hsien* and *tao*) that are en route:
>
>> Commander Wang Feng was appointed with official certificate to purchase riding horses in Chiu-ch'üan, Tun-huang, and Chang-yeh *chün*.[10] He [and his assistants] are entitled to be housed in the government stations,[11] in accordance with statutes and ordinances.
>>
>> [Transcribed and signed by] Acting Foreman Clerk (*ling-shih*) Hsü and Assistant (*ch'eng*) Pao.
>>
>> Forwarded on the day *ting-hai* of the seventh month [September 6, 11 B.C.].

Reverse side:

> The seal of the magistrate of Chü-yen. [Recorded:] Forwarded on the *ting-hai* day of the seventh month [September 6, 11 B.C.].
>
> 170.3A (obverse side) and 170.3B (reverse side)
> 2240 and 2242
> pl. 109, 110

2. On the day *ping-tzu* of the intercalary month beginning on the day *chi-ssu* of the fifth year of the Yung-shih period [the first year of the Yüan-yen period of Emperor Ch'eng; March 4, 12 B.C.], the director (*se-fu*) of North County respectfully submits:

> Ts'u Tzu-tang, of I-ch'eng *li*, states that he needs to do marketing at Chü-yen for his family. According to records, Tzu-tang has not been involved in any criminal cases nor [is he] subject to

THE MAKING OF A HAN FRONTIER REGION • 139

any official summons for judicial investigations. He is qualified to receive a passport (*chuan*), which is to be forwarded to the Chin Pass of Chien-shui and the So Pass of Chü-yen *hsien*. So be it respectfully submitted.

On the day *ping-tzu* of the intercalary month, Assistant P'eng of Lu-te [*hsien*] [approved the request and] forwarded [the passport] to the Chin Pass of Chien-shui and the So Pass of Chü-yen, in accordance with the statutes and ordinances.

[Transcribed and signed by] Head Clerk (*yuan*) Yen, Foreman Clerk Chien.

15.19
pl. 101

3. Issued on the day *chi-yu* of the first month of the fourth year of the Yung-kuang period [of Emperor Yüan; March 4, 40 B.C.]. The travel pass (*fu*) of Chang P'eng-tsu, commander of the Yen-shou Watch Station of the T'o-t'o *hou-kuan*:[12]

Wife, *ta-nü* (adult female), of Wan-sui *li* of Chao-wu [*hsien* of Chang-yeh], named ... (?), age forty-two.

Son, *ta-nan* (adult male), named Fu, age nineteen.

Son, *hsiao-nan* (underage male), named Kuang-tsung, age twelve.

Daughter, *hsiao-nü* (underage female), named Nü-tsu, age nine.

[Daughter-in-law], Fu's wife, named Nan-lai, age fifteen.

They are all black.

29.2
Cp218

4. (x) ... Chia Sheng; of ... *li*; age thirty; 7 *ch'ih*, 3 *ts'un* in height; black [in color]; went out [from the pass], with 2 *shih* of unhusked millet.

Fu Pass no. 681.

11.4
pl. 39

These documents illustrate the forms and procedures of application and issuance of the various passports. In the Chü-yen region, each variety of passport took the form of a wooden strip. The *kuo-so* specimens measure 1.0 to 1.2 Han *ch'ih* in length and 0.6 to 1.8 *ts'un* in width, with the majority being about 1 *ch'ih* by 1 *ts'un*; the *chuan* are generally 0.9 to 1.0 Han *ch'ih* long and 0.5–1.2 *ts'un* wide. The *fu* are of two distinctly different types of sizes: the short ones are 6.1 to 6.2 *ts'un* long and 0.9 to 1.2 *ts'un* wide; the long ones measure 1 *ch'ih* in length by at least half a *ts'un* in width.[13] The actual measurements of the various *kuo-so*, *chuan*, and *fu* specimens show some interesting comparisons with the sizes of such passports and passes mentioned in both the Han literary evidence and the wooden documents. For instance, 6 *ts'un* was prescribed as the length of the *fu*, and this compares with the actual measurements of the short *fu*. But the length of the long *fu* is not mentioned in other written literature. This fact seems to confirm our understanding that the Han institutions allowed a considerable degree of flexibility and variance between theory and practice in their implementation of policy. Similarly, although the prescribed length of the *kuo-so* and *chuan* in the Han code was 1.5 Han *ch'ih*, the actual size of *kuo-so* and *chuan* specimens found in Chü-yen is not longer than 1.2 Han *ch'ih*.[14]

The issuance of the *kuo-so* followed an established procedure. It had to be issued by the office of the bearer. For example, when the traveler was on an assignment for a *hsien* government, the *kuo-so* was issued by the magistrate and his assistant, as was the case in document 1 cited earlier; when the traveler was on an assignment for the *tu-wei* office, the *kuo-so* was issued by the *tu-wei*, as in document 562.3; and when he was on an assignment for a *chün*, it was issued by the governor and his assistant, as in the case of document 303.12AB.

The issuance of the *chuan* followed three steps: (1) the applicant presented his request with a statement of intention and supporting documents to the director (*se-fu* or *yu-chih*) of his county; (2) the county director, and sometimes also his assistant (*tso*), would present, after review and deliberation, the acceptable request to the office of the district magistrate (*hsien-ling*); and (3) the magistrate and/or his assistant, or their temporary substitute or any other appropriate official if both the magistrate and his assistant were not in the district city, would review the application and assume the final responsibility for approving and issuing the *chuan* passport. Whoever approved the *chuan* also put his seal on it.[15]

The procedure for issuing the *fu* passes is not revealed in the Chü-yen documents. But judging from the nature of the *fu* it may be reasonably assumed that they were issued by the office of the bearer in the garrisons. Since the *fu* also served as passes for servicemen and officials for local travel, they were used widely and had to be numbered in an extensive series. The following serves to illustrate the system.[16]

> Six-*ts'un* passes: Dated *chia-ch'en* of the intercalary month of the seventh year of the Shih-yuan period [the first year of the Yuan-feng period of Emperor Chao, 80 B.C.]; from Chü-yen to the Chin Pass [of Chien-shui]; [each] grooved on the side and numbered from 1 to 1,000, with one set having 100; the left-hand part [of each] to be retained at the office, the right-hand part to be forwarded to the Chin Pass, so that only when the two parts match can action be taken.
> [This is] no. 8.
>
> 65.7
> pl. 4

The reference to a numbered series from 1 to 1000 in this piece is seen in similar strips bearing the inscriptions "*Fu* Pass no. 18" (65.9 on pl. 1), "*Fu* Pass no. 23" (11.26 on pl. 39), and "*Fu* Pass no. 117" (Cp1244). The long *fu*—that is, those that measure about 1 *ch'ih* in length by at least half a *ts'un* in width—even carry the inscriptions "*Fu* Pass no. 398" (Cp1505) and "*Fu* Pass no. 681" (11.4 on pl. 39). The two sets of strips clarify our understanding that the series of numbered *fu* indeed reached as high as one thousand.

The *fu* for military officers traveling with their families were not numbered, nor were they grooved on the side.

The practices for the use of the *kuo-so*, *chuan*, and *fu* differed. The *kuo-so* carried the seal of the officer charged with the responsibility of issuance or transmission and was sent directly to the control points (passes and fords) en route prior to the departure of the travelers. Strip 39.2 (pl. 347), measuring 6.3 by 1.5 *ts'un*, and strip 175.20A (pl. 455), measuring 5.5 by 0.95 *ts'un*, are address labels for this type of *kuo-so*. Several fragments seem to be the surviving portions of the dispatches accompanying such transmissions.[17] Upon its arrival at a specific destination, the *kuo-so* was to be opened, and the individual in charge of such duties at a specific pass or ford would also record the fact that the transmission was sealed by a certain authority at the point of origin. On his arrival at the control point, the traveler would be duly identified and checked for the nature and value of his belongings and then be accorded the passage and facilities to which he was entitled. After this, and after the due recording of all necessary information on the obverse side, the *kuo-so* was to be filed as part of the records of the specific point of control.[18]

It may be assumed that on some occasions the *kuo-so* may have been brought directly to the points of control by the travelers, but no strips or fragments from Chü-yen, nor from other frontier regions such as Tun-huang, provide such information.

The *chuan* passports were generally carried by individual travelers, and upon arrival at a point of control, after the checking process had been performed, the travelers were accorded passage, at times with the indication "passage accorded" (*fang-hsing*)—see, for example, strips 505.37A and 505.37B—having been marked on the obverse side of the *chuan*. It seems that some of the *chuan* carried the seals of the authorities who issued them and a label marked *chuan* (see, e.g., strip 257.13, pl. 248). If it was for a long-distance journey, the traveler kept his *chuan* and used it for identification until he reached the main control point guarding the entrance to the locality of his final destination, whereupon he turned it over to the authorities at that control point. In such cases, the authorities at the passes and fords en route copied the text of the specific *chuan* used by each traveler and filed the copy as an official record.

The use of *fu* passes seems to have varied in three ways. For the six-*ts'un fu*, strip 65.7, translated earlier, suggests that a traveler was given the left-hand part of a numbered *fu* by local authorities in Chü-yen and that he would be accorded passage by the authorities of the Chin Pass if his part matched the corresponding right-hand part of the same *fu*. But exactly how the procedure was administered is not clearly recorded. It is assumed that such *fu* did not bear inscriptions. In the Tun-huang region, *fu* were used as passes for military personnel who temporarily left their units on special missions.[19] It seems reasonable to assume that this practice also prevailed in the Chü-yen region and that the *fu* passes also served as identification for military personnel traveling between Chü-yen and the Chin Pass.

The use of the longer *fu* seems to have followed a slightly different procedure. The two surviving specimens, 11.4 and 280.3, show that the position, name, age, and physical characteristics of the users, along with a serial number, were inscribed by one hand on the *fu*. Such *fu* were also split vertically down the center, with the left-hand parts given to the travelers and the right-hand parts presumably forwarded to a major point of control. When a traveler reached the major control point of a frontier region (the Chin Pass in the case of Chü-yen), he would be properly identified, and if the two component parts of his *fu* matched he would be allowed to proceed. His *fu* would be retained at the pass. Before granting outward passage to the traveler, the authorities would check his belongings and record the essential items (such as grain, weapons, animals, and carts) on the *fu*. After passage was allowed, the authorities recorded the traveler's direction by writing *ch'u* (egress) or *ju* (ingress) on the bottom of the *fu*.

How the *fu* for military officers traveling together with their families were used was not recorded on the wooden documents. But it can be inferred from surviving specimens that they were carried by the users, who turned them over to the authorities at the Chin Pass when outward passage was accorded.

It is assumed that at a specified major pass, a pass that controlled the entrance to a region, the travelers were issued appropriate passports or passes if their original ones were retained at the pass. Some of these or similar practices may have been uniform on a nationwide scale, but others may have been just regional. In the Chü-yen region, *fu* and specially issued local *chuan* (see, e.g., CpApp.14) seem to have been used for the latter purpose.

It has been mentioned several times that officials at the control points not only examined and authenticated the passports and passes of travelers but also checked and recorded their belongings. Systematic registers of this were compiled at the passes and fords. These registers included each traveler's name, geographical origin, official position, aristocratic rank, age, physical characteristics, belongings of special importance (grain, weapons, livestock, manufacturers, carts, and so on), and traveling direction. In doing so, the control points also demonstrated their function in preventing the flow of strategic goods to undesirable areas or enemies. Thus, these registers formed the most detailed records of the restrictive controls over the flow of people and strategic materials at the passes and fords, and they were reviewed periodically (generally monthly) and submitted to superior offices.[20] Below is one example of the "tag" (label) of such reports.

> Register of outgoing and incoming officials [and servicemen] and civilians in the sixth month of the first year of the Yang-so period [of Emperor Ch'eng; 24 B.C.].
>
> 29.3A
> 1275
> pl. 60

In an indirect way, these registers also formed a detailed file of the composition and conditions of part of the local population. Together with other means of control, these records provided the local garrison and government authorities with another source of power for ensuring the safety and security of the Chü-yen region.

The passes and the requirement for passports and similar documents in Chü-yen performed a critical role in maintaining order and ensuring security in the region, without which its continuing development would have been seriously jeopardized.

COMMUNICATION ON THE FRONTIER

For the development and garrisoning of a distant frontier region such as Chü-yen, communication is of first importance. While strict control keeps the colony stable and thus provides security, quick and convenient communication binds together the scattered garrison settlements and tightly connects the whole colony to the interior and the central government of the empire. As will be discussed later in detail, archaeological investigation shows that in the Han period a military highway along the Edsen-gol connected the Chü-yen settlements first to central Chang-yeh, the heart of the Ho-hsi region, and then eastward to the interior of the empire and westward to western Ho-hsi and the Western Regions.

Mechanisms and Organization of
Transport and Communication

Carts

In the frontier communications system, a major role was played by carts, which if they were drawn by horses were called *ma-chü* (horse-drawn carts) or if by oxen *niu-chü* (ox-drawn carts).²¹ The shape of a cart was either square or round. The former was called *fang-hsiang-chü* (square cart) and was usually larger; the latter, *yao-chü* (round cart or carriage), was normally smaller.²² The carts were used either for ordinary transportation, in which case they were called *tsai-chü* (transport carts), or in the postal station system, in which case they were called *chuan-chü* (station carts).²³ In general, the *fang-hsiang-chü* were drawn by oxen in the Han period and used as *tsai-chü*, whereas the *yao-chü* were drawn by horses and used as *chuan-chü*. But in the Chü-yen region most of the *fang-hsiang-chü* were actually drawn by horses.²⁴

The majority of carts on the frontier were controlled by the garrisons,²⁵ but some were recorded as having been owned by individuals, including visitors.²⁶ Although most of the government-owned carts were imported from other parts of the empire, the garrison offices sometimes rented carts from local owners known as *tzu-chia* (wealthy people).²⁷

Late in Emperor Wu's reign, carts were brought from the interior prefectures by the government to transport grain and other articles to the frontier regions and were then retained in service on the frontier.²⁸ The Chü-yen documents record a large number of carts from the interior; they were probably brought to Chü-yen during and after this period. The following are two examples.

1. Chang Ch'ang, a garrison soldier from Tung-li *li* of Yeh District [of Wei Prefecture], served in the thirtieth cart.
  28.10
  4087
  pl. 221
2. Wu Yu . . . of the second cart of Kuan-chün District [of Nan-yang Prefecture].
  180.8
  5274
  pl. 318

On the basis of similar documents, the geographical origins of the carts in Chü-yen can be traced. Table 26 is such an attempt. Interestingly enough, this table shows that the carts in Chü-yen were imported from four *chün* and *kuo* located in a region that contains modern southern Hopei, northern Honan, and eastern Shantung, and some areas, such as Pei-ch'iu (in modern Ch'ing-p'ing, Shantung), seem to have supplied more carts than others. This fact leads us to believe that the region at the intersection of the three modern provinces just mentioned was the center of the cart industry in Former Han times. Obviously, there were carts from other *chün* in Chü-yen. Documents 346.36 and 77.7 record cart attendants from Ho-nan *chün* and Lu-te District of Chang-yeh, but reveal no details about the carts.²⁹ Perhaps such documents are yet to be uncovered. It is also of great interest to note that the *chün* and *kuo* that were recorded as having supplied carts were also the areas from which most of the garrison soldiers came. Ch'ing-ho was the only exception. The Chü-yen documents also reveal that the carts on the frontier were numbered and hence were organized into working units. Table 27 shows the numbers of the carts from the first to the thirtieth, though, as indicated, several of the numbers are not recorded in the Chü-yen documents.

The carts were sent from various parts of the Han empire to Chü-yen and were then assigned a number by the garrison offices. For the purpose of identifying its geographical origin, the name of a cart's district was also placed before its number when it was referred to. The general form was as shown on the top of page 146.

TABLE 26. Geographical Origins of Carts in Chü-yen

Chün or *Kuo*	*Hsien*	Document Numbers
Ch'ing-ho[a]	Ts'o	3970
Liang-*kuo*	Tsu-yang	Cp1581
Nan-yang	Kuan-chün	5274
	Hsin-yeh[b]	Cp807
	Yü-yang[c]	7238
Wei	Kuan-t'ao	Cp1662
	Nei-huang	Cp587
	Yüan-ch'eng	7353
	Pei-ch'iu (4 cases)	1173, 3970

[a]The last part of this strip is broken. In the *Treatise on Geography* in the *Han-shu*, both Ts'o District and Pei-ch'iu District are listed under Ch'ing-ho *chün*. But docs. 5835 and 5856 record that Pei-ch'iu District was in Wei *chün*. Also see docs. 311.20, pl. 367; and 311.12, pl. 368. No other Chü-yen documents record any individual from Ch'ing-ho. Moreover, the Chü-yen region was recorded as having had a large number of carts from Wei *chün*. Therefore, it seems certain that the carts mentioned in doc. 3970 were recruited from a district named Pei-ch'iu then located in Wei *chün*. But Pei-ch'iu cannot be found under Wei *chün* in the *Treatise on Geography* in the *Han-shu*. Perhaps the omission was due to the author's oversight. Such oversights were not uncommon in the *Treatise on Geography*. For instance, Ch'ang-p'ing *hsien* is not listed under Huai-yang *chün*, but the Chü-yen wooden documents show that it was a *hsien* in Huai-yang. Furthermore, since Ts'o *hsien* was listed side by side with Pei-ch'iu *hsien* in the Chü-yen documents, it is very likely that the two *hsien* belonged to the same *chün*. It is for this reason that although I have listed Ts'o *hsien* under Ch'ing-ho the possibility of its having been in Wei *chün* must be noted.

[b]One document records the first cart from Hsin-yeh: Yu Hsin-yeh Ti-i chü shih-jen. "Listed on the right are ten persons of the first cart from Hsin-yeh [of Nan-yang *chün*]." 515.16 or 1729, pl. 84. Lao did not decipher the words *yeh-ti* in his transliteration of this document, but the photograph of this slip proves it to be so.

[c]Lao incorrectly reads Yü-yang as Yun-yang in this document.

Name of Original District
↓
Serial Number
↓
Cart

Document 180.8, cited earlier, is an illustration of this form.

Some carts are mentioned in the Chü-yen documents without any indication of their geographical origins.[30] These carts were either of local origin,

TABLE 27. Organization of Carts in Chü-yen

Cart Identification Numbers	Document Numbers	Number of Soldiers Attached
1st	54.24(427)	10
	1277	
	5286	
	5823	
	Cp807	
2d	15.17(423)	
	5274	
3d	74.22(420)	
4th	221.5(427)	
	Cp1581	
	1173	
5th	3970	
6th	6974	20
	6584	
7th	No data	
8th	3123	10[a]
	7353	
9th	3970	
10th	3970	
11th	3970	
12th–14th	No data	
15th	1758	
	Cp987	
16th–18th	No data	
20th	3970	
21st–24th	No data	
25th	1443	
26th–28th	No data	
29th	4032	
30th	9725	
	4087	5

[a]Lao reads this document as follows: Yu Ti-pa chü *shih*. "Listed on the right is the eighth cart, ten . . ." (238.13 or 3123, pl. 150). Its photograph is not clear enough to allow a decipherment of the last word. But from docs. 1277 and 221.52(427) one can infer that this word is *jen* (man).

which made the geographical reference unnecessary,[31] or they were from other parts of the empire but were stationed in a place where the omission of the district name caused no confusion.

The Chü-yen documents also reveal the following information about transportation.

1. ... The fifth elephant. 428.2A
   1173
   pl. 55

2. ... More hired hands in the carts drawn by elephants. 483.13B
   4899
   pl. 287

These two documents seem to indicate that elephants and elephant-drawn carts were in use in the Chü-yen region. But no other details about this interesting issue is found in the wooden strips.[32]

The carts had special registers in the garrisons and hence constituted a special entity in the garrisons' organization.[33]

The carts were manned by *chü-fu* (cart drivers), garrison soldiers, *chü-tsu* (cart soldiers), and *chü-tzu* (cart attendants for officers); they were commanded by *chü-chang* (cart commanders).

Of all the people associated with the carts, the *chü-fu* were the most important in both a functional and an organizational sense. They had the status of garrison soldiers but were recorded on special registers, such as the *chü-fu ming-chi* (registers of *chü-fu*), and received food provisions in a special category. They received weapons and special tools for maintenance and repair of the carts, all of which were duly registered; they drove and took care of the carts; and they were from the localities where the carts had been requisitioned.[34]

Garrison soldiers (*shu-tsu*), often in groups of five or its multiples (ten, twenty, and so on), were assigned to protect each cart and provide the manpower for heavy transport work. The assignment for these soldiers was probably made by local garrison officers when the occasion arose.[35] The *chü-tsu* were also garrison soldiers, but generally they were permanently associated with the carts, as were the *chü-fu*, and there was always one *chü-tsu* for each cart. In this sense, he was an assistant to the *chü-fu* of a cart.[36] The *chü-fu*, *chü-tsu*, and garrison soldiers, along with the cart they served, formed one unit, which we may call the "cart unit"; the commander of the unit was called a *chü-chang*. The units were attached to different garrison posts.[37]

The *chü-tsu* seem to have belonged to a different category. The *chü-tzu* was the attendant who drove and cared for an officer's carriage. Generally they were young, of low status, and seem to have been slaves.[38]

The *ch'ih-hsing* were also assigned to the carts at times, particularly on such long expeditions as taking colonists to the Western Regions from the Ho-hsi area.[39]

Not only were the carts well organized, but they were also well cared for. When not in use, they were parked in garages called *chü-wu* or *chü-k'u*, literally, "storerooms for carts."[40] All the carts were under strict control of the garrison offices. The departure and arrival of a cart were checked and registered at the various checkpoints of the garrison settlements. Permission to leave or enter was required of all the carts. At the checkpoints, a cart's owner and its date of departure or entry were duly recorded. If the cart was leaving the settlements the word *ch'u* (egress) was marked on the register; if it was coming into the settlements, the word *ju* (ingress) was used. Its direction of travel also was recorded at times, so it could be traced if the need arose.[41]

The total number of carts in the Chü-yen region is not known. But one document records that on one occasion 515 carts were assembled in a large lot in the Chia-ch'ü *hou-kuan* for a special mission.[42] The total number of carts in the entire Chü-yen region must understandably have been much larger.

Horses

Horses were another critical means of transportation and communication in the Chü-yen region. As in other parts of the empire, the horses on the frontier were classified according to their specific functions. The horses that drew the *chuan-chü* (station carts) were called *chuan-ma* (station horses), the horses that worked in postal stations were called *i-ma* or *i-ch'i* (postal horses), and those used for security assignments were called *hou-ma* (vigilance horses).[43] In general, horses that drew carts and were not ridden were called *yung-ma* (service horses).[44] There were also special horses reserved for emergencies; these were called *ts'ui-ma* (reserve horses).[45] The horses owned by the government were called *kuan-ma* (government horses), and those owned by private individuals were called *ssu-ma* (private horses).[46] The mounts that belonged to cavalrymen and soldiers in the garrisons were called *tsu-ma* (soldiers' horses).[47]

The Chü-yen documents indicate that a considerable number of minor garrison officers and soldiers had their own horses with them in the garrisons. Table 28 presents a general picture of private ownership among garrison personnel. As is recorded in the wooden documents, garrison officers had their own horses with them.[48] This was naturally due to the shortage of government horses needed to make the garrison system more effective. As these private horses were rendering service to the empire, they were fed at government expense.

For the sake of control, all private and government horses in the garrison settlements were registered according to a special form. The items on the regis-

THE MAKING OF A HAN FRONTIER REGION • 149

ters included the name of the horse's owner, as well as the classification, color, sex, *p'iao* (brand),[49] age, height, grade, and training of the horse. Three examples of such registers are translated here.

1. Yang Pao, the subcommandant of the tenth *hou*: one horse, yellow and white in color, male, five years old . . .[50]

   Cp134
   18.13(428A)

2. One postal horse: red and white in color, male, four years old, 5 *ch'ih* and 8 *ts'un* high, superior grade, well trained.

   142.26(425)

3. One horse: red, male, left *p'iao*, nine years old, 5 *ch'ih* high.

   Cp2069
   510.27(419)

These were the general registers called *ming-chi*.[51] All the garrison offices had to keep these horse registers and submit them regularly to higher offices. The following document is an example of such a report.

On the day *ting-yu* of the tenth month (beginning on the day *keng-ch'en*) of the fourth year of the Ho-p'ing period [of Emperor Ch'eng (25 B.C.)], Commandant Yüeh of the Chien-shui *hou-kuan* respectfully reports:

Register of station and postal horses is respectfully submitted to . . .[52]

Cp1524A

The information on such horse registers provides a sampling of the general characteristics of the horses on the Han frontier. Table 29 presents a summation

TABLE 28. Privately Owned Horses in the Garrisons

Owners (officers and soldiers)	Number of Horses	Document Numbers
Subcommandant (fourth *hou*)	1	122.14(424)
Subcommandant (tenth *hou*)	1	18.13(428A)
Subcommandant	3	46.7(313)
Commander	1	225.4(425)
Officer Sun	1	1166
Hou clerk (*hou-shih*)	3	46.7(313)
Marshal (*ssu-ma*)	2	560.18(420)
Head accounting clerk[a]	1	505.13(421)
Acting *ling-shih*	1	560.11(420)
Cavalryman (*ch'i-shih*)	1	560.8(420)
Hired soldier	1	290.12(272)

[a]See also Ch'en Chih 1960, p. 43.

of these characteristics for horses in the Chü-yen region. The age of the horses ranged from four to sixteen, and the height from 5.7 Han *ch'ih* (1.32 meters) to 7 *ch'ih* (1.62 meters). Judging from the table, it seems that only the postal horses were graded and that they were at times given special training for their assignments.

Because of their special functions, the horses were well taken care of on the frontier. Special stables (*chiu*) were maintained for them in the Chü-yen region. Each large stable was managed by a *se-fu* (director), who was assisted by clerks called *ling-shih*.[53] Under these officials, the *chiu-t'u* (convicts working as stable hands) carried out the chores in the stables.[54] As table 29 shows, individual garrison units had their own horses. Document 3715 further reveals that even a watch station (in this case, the twenty-first *sui*) could have as many as three horses. The horses in the various garrison settlements naturally stayed in the stables of their respective units. But the Chü-yen documents also indicate that there were two major stables in the Chü-yen region. One, called the Chao-wu Stable, was located in the Chien-shui *hou-kuan* in the south; the other, the T'un-yuan Stable, was located in the Chia-ch'ü *hou-kuan* in the north.[55] It seems that these were the two main stables in Chü-yen.

Both government and private horses in garrison service were fed by the government. Feed included barley, millet, *p'ang-huang* (nonglutinous *Panicum mili-*

TABLE 29. Characteristics of Horses on the Chü-yen Frontier

Classification or Owner	Color	Sex	P'iao	Age	Height (ch'ih)	Grade	Training	Document Numbers
Postal horse	Red and white	M	?	4	5.8	Superior	Yes	142.26(425)
Subcommandant	Yellow and white	M	?	5	?	?	?	Cp134
?	?	?	Left	5	5.9	?	?	504.2(422)
Commander	?	M	?	7	5.7	?	?	225.44(245)
Commoner	Variegated	F	?	7–8	?	?	?	62.13(423)
Commoner	Black	F	?	8	?	?	?	62.13(423)
?	White	M	?	7	7.0	?	?	65.12(419)
?	Black	M	?	8	?	?	?	43.9(424)
?	Yellow and white	M	?	9	6.3	?	?	6241
?	Red and black	M	?	9	6.0	?	?	506.3(422)
								Cp1997
?	Red	M	Left	9	5.0	?	?	Cp2069
Commoner (?)	Red	M	?	10	6.0	?	?	53.15(422)
?	?	M	?	11	7.0	?	?	169.10(421)
?	Jet black	F	?	13	?	?	?	154.15(425)
Postal horse (of a *hou-kuan*)	Black and white	M	Left	14	5.8	Middle	?	231.2(425)
Postal horse (of ?)	Red and white (?)	?	Twice	16	?	?	?	Cp878
Postal horse (of a *sui*)	Red	M	?	?	?	?	?	78.36(425)

THE MAKING OF A HAN FRONTIER REGION · 151

aceum), hay, greens, and possibly other unhusked grains. The rates of provision varied with classification and ownership, as well as with the type of feed. Table 30 presents part of this provision system.⁵⁶ The length of the month (twenty-nine or thirty days) seems also to have contributed to this variation. The date of collection was not regular.

In case of a grain shortage, horse owners who were in government service were paid in cash for the equivalent of the normally allotted feed.⁵⁷

Because of their special importance, the horses were under the strict control of the garrison offices. The arrivals and departures of both government and private horses were checked and recorded at the various checkpoints in the Chü-yen region. These records are similar to those of the carts. Two are translated below.

1. Tuan Ch'eng, from Yang-yao *li* of Mao-ling *hsien* [of Yu-fu-feng], age twenty-five, entered from the south with a red female horse on the day *ting-hai* of the twelfth month.
    502.6(422)

2. One small carriage and one red and black, male, nine-year-old, 6-*ch'ih*-high horse entered into . . . at the *pu* time.⁵⁸
    Cp1997
    506.3(422)

As illustrated by these documents, the travel direction, date, and time were all recorded.⁵⁹ The purpose of the checking and recording was to have knowledge of and hence control over the horses entering and leaving the frontier region.

The horses that played a vital role in the frontier region communications system, such as the postal horses, were periodically inspected. Results of the inspections had to be recorded and became part of the governmental documents in the garrison commands. One such record is translated here as an illustration of its form.

TABLE 30. Provisions for Horses in Chü-yen

Classification or Owner	Feed	Monthly Rate	Document Numbers
Postal horse	Barley	3.44 *shih*	302.12(245)
Postal horse	Unhusked grain	3.6 *shih*	192.24(249)
Vigilance horse	Unhusked grain	3.6 *shih*	401.1(248) 63.2(252)
?	Unhusked grain(?)	5.4 *shih*	Cp157
Hou clerk	Unhusked grain	5.8 *shih*	157.2(333)
Officer Sun	Millet	6.0 *shih*	1166
Officer's horse	Greens	30 *shih*	46.7(313)

Book of inspection of the postal horses at the Chiao-nan Station of the T'o-t'o *hou-kuan* in the ninth month of the first year of the Chien-p'ing period [of Emperor Ai; 6 B.C.].

502.7
1767

The postal horses were also graded in the course of inspection.

Oxen

The oxen in the Chü-yen settlements were in two major classifications: *yung-niu* (cart-drawing oxen) and *fu-niu* (land-tilling oxen).[60] A considerable number of the oxen in Chü-yen were under the control of the garrison offices, and they were referred to as *kuan-niu* (government oxen). This was, as was discussed earlier, due to the fact that the central government in Ch'ang-an assigned oxen to the Chü-yen garrison offices for land cultivation.[61]

Private oxen, referred to as *ssu-niu* in the Chü-yen documents, were in the hands of both civilians and garrison personnel. Regarding the latter, one document reveals that a cavalryman owned six strong oxen.[62]

Both government and private oxen in the Chü-yen region were registered on a special form. Among the items recorded were the quantity, grade, color, sex, *chan* (a special identification mark), age, and length of the oxen.[63] Whether any growths or open sores (*chiu*) had developed on an ox's shoulders as a result of drawing the cart was also noted.[64] Three such registers are translated below.

1. One ox: black, male, white head, left *chan*, four years old.[65]

   Cp2118

2. One strong ox: black, male, left *chan*, eight years old, 7 *ch'ih* and 8 *ts'un* long.[66]

   Cp1846

3. ... black, male, left *chan*; no growths.

   Cp2136

The essential features of oxen as seen in the Chü-yen registers are summarized in table 31.

Most of the oxen were black and male. Every one of them seems to have carried the *tso-chan* brand. The known ages range from two to eight. The eight-year-old ox was recorded as having been 7 *ch'ih* and 8 *ts'un* long. That was probably the normal length of an adult ox in Han times. Unlike horses, it was not required to record the height of oxen. This was certainly due to the difference in the functions they performed on the frontier. Evidently, the registration of oxen and horses was undertaken out of functional necessity. As functions varied, so did registration forms.

The ox registers in a garrison settlement were regularly examined and reported to higher or related offices.[67] So the garrisons and their various commanding offices had a fairly accurate account of the oxen in frontier regions.

The oxen were housed in *niu-she* (ox houses or barns).[68] They were cared for by specially assigned personnel.[69] They were fed hay, grain, and other fodder.[70] The basic daily grain ration for an ox was six and two-thirds *sheng* of unhusked grain.[71] But the specifications for the basic daily hay provision were not recorded in the Chü-yen documents.

The comings and goings of oxen were recorded at the frontier checkpoints. The registers were similar to those for carts and horses.[72] The purpose of registration was also the same: control.

Systems of Transportation and Communication

Roadway Transport and Communication

Transportation work played a vital role in keeping the various garrison establishments and other settlements well supplied and supported. Carts, horses, and oxen all shared this work on the frontier, but it was the carts drawn by oxen that, because of their capacity for larger and heavier loads, were given the major responsibility for transporting goods.[73] Horse-drawn carts, and sometimes horses, only occasionally conveyed some commodities of special value such as cash and other valuables. Passenger travel as a rule was by horses and horse-drawn carts, but on occasion ox-drawn carts carried soldiers and the like.

The transportation work in the Chü-yen region comprised both internal (or intraregional) and external (or interregional) lines. Within the region, all the garrison nodes and civilian settlements were connected through various roadways. Essentially, all the cities, fortresses, watch stations, and special settlements discussed in chapter 3 and Bo Sommarström's field report were joined by

TABLE 31. Characteristics of Oxen on the Chü-yen Frontier

Color	Sex	*Chan*	Age	Length (*ch'ih*)	*Chiu*	Document Numbers (in Cp)[a]
?	M	Left	2	?		2196
Black	M	Left	3	7.3		2274
Black	M	Left	3	?	Left/right	2071
Black (white head)	F	Left	4	?		2118
?	?	Left	5	?		2131
Black	M	Left	8	7.8		1846
Black	F	Left	?	?		2218
Black	M	Left	?	?	None	2136
White	M	Left	?	?	None	2280
?	?	?	?	(?).7	Left	2071

[a]For correct interpretations of these documents, see Shen Yuan 1962, p. 426.

multinodal routes.⁷⁴ The main route was the highway running northward along the Edsen-gol from the Mao-mu region to the northernmost major garrison settlement in the Chü-yen region for a total distance of 250 kilometers. Routes of different sizes and varying distances joined the numerous garrison establishments and civilian settlements, and connected them to the main highway—altogether forming a well-connected network of communication routes. Figure 7 illustrates part of this network. Traces of these routes are still visible to modern archaeologists and explorers who do field work in the region.⁷⁵

One of the two main functions of the routes was transportation; the other was communication, which will be discussed later. The main task of regular internal transport included the conveyance of grain (millet, barley, and so on) and other essential commodities for general and military uses. Such transportation assignments were supervised by an officer (such as the *wei-shih* in regular garrison units and the *pieh-t'ien ling-shih* in farming units), and the goods were carried by ox-drawn carts. The general load for grain transport was 25 *ta-shih* in each cart,⁷⁶ and that for hay was 350 bundles. Conveyance was generally from fields to storehouses, between storehouses, from storehouses to garrison offices, and between garrison settlements in the Chü-yen region. For any transportation assignment, the items transported, number of carts used, personnel involved, and so forth were recorded by the concerned offices; any deviation from the established rules would result in the punishment of those officers and soldiers involved.

The following documents have been selected and translated to illustrate the various aspects of the organization and operation of internal transportation systems in the Chü-yen region.

1. The *wei* advises Chien-kuo, subcommandant of the twenty-third *pu*: The number of carts and amount of grain in *shih* and *tou* units should be recorded and reported upon the arrival of "transferred grain" . . .⁷⁷

    145.2
    3681
    Cp809

2. Thirty *shih* of grain were transported to the *hou-kuan* under the supervision of an officer of the tenth *pu*.

    4792

3. Listed on the right are twelve carts that transported grain to the City Granary [of Chü-yen *hou-kuan*]. The total loss due to commutation and waste amounted to 59.5 *shih* of grain.

    Cp1981

4. . . . Thirty-five *hsiao-shih* of barley of the Chien-shui Granary were transported to Chü-yen.

    75.25(276)
    2891

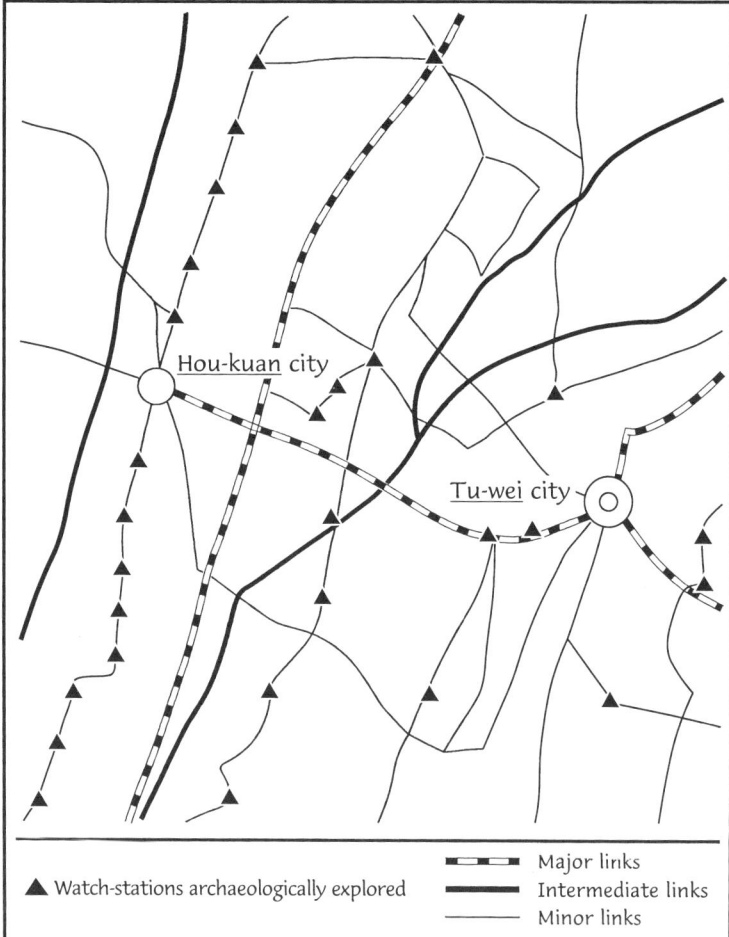

Fig. 7. Communications routes in northern Chü-yen

5. One hundred *ta-shih* of millet were delivered by four carts commanded by *Wei-shih* Li Tsung.
   2785
6. Twenty-five *ta-shih* of millet were delivered by one cart.
   4119
7. One cart made two trips a day; a total of 700 bundles [of hay] was transported, with 350 bundles for each trip.
   261.7
   7248
   pl. 244
8. ... was summoned to the *hou-kuan* office for testimony for failing to transport grain by ox-drawn carts.
   524.10(1)

As carts, immigrants, and garrison and farming personnel in Chü-yen were from different regions of the Han empire and the development of Chü-yen depended on the continuous support (in the form of such items as food, clothing, money, equipment, military supplies, and agricultural tools) of the imperial government and adjacent regions, Chü-yen's lines of external conveyance were vital to its consolidation and growth as a frontier region.[78] They were also a critical component of its communications system. The following documents have been translated to illustrate the various facets of Chü-yen's long-distance transport.

1. Fifty *shih* of barley were delivered by two carts [from Lu-te *hsien* of Chang-yeh], driven by Wang Yü of Ch'ang-lo *li* of Lu-te [and others] under the command of the *wei*[-*shih*].
   253.5
   483
   pl. 25

2. Clothing for garrison soldiers sent from Nan-yang *chün*:
   One long unlined garment of black cloth.[79]
   576.1
   7506
   pl. 472

3. The fifteenth cart from Nei-huang *hsien* [of Wei *chün*] left for Wei *chün*.[80]
   101.29(427)

4. Issued: 7,759 *shih* of "transferred grain" . . .[81]
   99.4
   4540
   pl. 259

5. Ying-chieh belongs [or Ying, all belong] to the *ku-hsia*, preparing the carriages for the retired soldiers . . .[82]
   19.33(82)

As a developing frontier, Chü-yen received support from interior regions of the Han empire, but at the same time it served as an advance station supplying manpower and technological assistance for Han expansion into the Western Regions. Communications lines between Chü-yen and the Han forces and settlements in the Western Regions were maintained. The following documents testify to this fact.

1. Imperial decree to Subcommandant Chang of I-lu *hou* [of Chia-ch'ü *hou-kuan* of Chü-yen *tu-wei*] to dispatch troops:
   Bring the head of the king of Lou-lan to Tun-huang; leave ten soldiers and two female interpreters at Lou-lan.[83]
   303.8
   184
   pl. 10
   Cp1582

2. On the day *i-hai* of the fourth month (beginning on the day *chi-wei*) of the fourth year of the Yüan-k'ang period [of Emperor Hsüan, 62 B.C.], Colonel of Shan-shan and the West [Cheng] Chi, Deputy Marshal Fu-ch'ang, Assistant Ch'ing, [I-hsün] Chief Commandant Ming-chung, Court Gentleman . . . (?)

> It was on the day *kuei-wei* of the fifth month of the second year of the Yuan-k'ang period [64 B.C.], in response to the dispatch from Protector-General [of the Western Regions Cheng Chi], Wei-ch'eng She was sent to command fifty *ch'ih-hsing* with carts managed by them to . . . (?)[84]

118.17
Cp678

These documents concern two critical events in the course of the Han expansion into the Western Regions. The first was about the Han conquest of the Lou-lan state in 77 B.C., during which Fu Chieh-tzu, superintendent of the P'ing-lo Stables, led a small force to the capital of Lou-lan (Lop-nor, Sinkiang); assassinated the king of Lou-lan, An-kuei; and sent his head to the imperial capital at Ch'ang-an. The Han Court then enthroned a new king, Wei-t'u-ch'i; changed the state's name to Shan-shan; and moved its capital to a new site at I-hsun (modern Miran, Sinkiang), where a Han colonial force of forty men was dispatched and shortly afterward a chief commandant was sent to supervise its development.[85] The success of this Han venture placed the control of the eastern gateway to the Western Regions in the hands of the Han and thereby significantly facilitated the Han advance into the interior of the Western Regions.[86] The first document (303.8) indicates that soldiers from the Chü-yen garrisons took part in the Lou-lan expedition and that it was actually the sub-commandant of I-lu *hou* of Chü-yen who brought An-kuei's head to Tun-huang; from there, it was taken to Ch'ang-an through the express system along the imperial highways. Subcommandant Chang returned, with the imperial decree, to his post in the Chü-yen region, where the document was uncovered.[87]

The second document (118.17) indicates that during the critical campaigns of Cheng Chi (fl. 67–49 B.C.) against the Hsiung-nu for control of Chü-shih (modern Yarkhoto, west of Turfan, Sinkiang) from 68 to 64 B.C., which paved the way for eventual Han supremacy in the Western Regions in 60 B.C., the Chü-yen garrisons also sent fifty *ch'ih-hsing* and vehicles to join Cheng Chi's force of fifteen hundred men, which was besieged in Chü-shih by six thousand Hsiung-nu cavalrymen in 64 B.C.[88]

Both documents reveal Chü-yen's communication with the Western Regions and its contribution to the Han expansion in that region. This was still in the early stage of Chü-yen's development.

Documents, in the form of imperial decrees, about the Ch'iang uprising, the

Wu-sun leader Hsiao K'un-mi, and the Hsiung-nu *shan-yü* Hu-han-yeh, all in the period 61–51 B.C., were also uncovered in the Chü-yen region.[89] All of these events directly relate to the emergence of a new Han order in North and Central Asia at that time: the pacification of the Ch'iang (in modern eastern Tsinghai) in 61 B.C., consolidation of Han influence in Wu-sun (the Ili Valley north and northwest of the Tarim Basin) in 53 B.C., and the submission of the Southern Hsiung-nu in 54–51 B.C. The fact that these documents were sent to and kept in Chü-yen indicates that Chü-yen was kept informed of major issues in Han expansion and frontier matters on the one hand and possible Chü-yen involvement in some of these events on the other. In both cases, Chü-yen's distant communications and contacts through its own and the imperial roadways are clearly illustrated by these documents as well as those quoted earlier.

The road from Chü-yen to the imperial capital at Ch'ang-an in the east and the western gate of the Han empire at the Jade Gate Pass (Yü-men *kuan*) is interesting and deserves a closer look. From Chü-yen city to Lu-te (northwest of modern Chang-yeh city, Kansu) of Chang-yeh, the roadway extended for about 1,200 (Han) *li* (roughly 500 kilometers). At Lu-te, the imperial highway ran eastward to Ch'ang-an for 3,250 *li* (1,355 kilometers), and westward to Tun-huang for 800 *li* (336 kilometers) and to the Jade Gate Pass for 918 *li* (or 382 kilometers). The distance from Chü-yen to the Jade Gate Pass was 2,118 *li* (883 kilometers) and to Ch'ang-an, 4,450 *li* (1,885 kilometers). From Ch'ang-an to the Jade Gate Pass, the imperial highway ran for 4,168 *li* (1,738 kilometers) to the Jade Gate, which was 118 *li* (49 kilometers) northwest of Tun-huang.[90] Map 4 shows this connection between the imperial capital at Ch'ang-an and the northwestern frontier.

In the larger context of East-West relations in ancient times, through its attachment to the Ch'ang-an–Tun-Huang route Chü-yen was connected to the Silk Road, which extended from Ch'ang-an through what is now Central Asia and the Near East to Tyre on the eastern shore of the Mediterranean Sea, for a distance of 4,200 miles (roughly 6,757 kilometers) as the crow flies. The road itself ran for something like 6,000 miles (9,654 kilometers), or one-quarter of the length of the equator.[91] In a direct sense, Chü-yen was a part of the Silk Road, for its original development was occasioned by Han China's march into Central Asia, which opened it, and China's consolidation of the frontier regions permanently safeguarded the road in the Ho-hsi Corridor.[92]

The Conveyance of Messages

The fast and convenient conveyance of messages, civilian and military, is of vital importance in placing a frontier region under a system of effective internal and external communication, which is the key to its security and mobility. Chü-yen was a model of success in this respect. Its method of conveying mes-

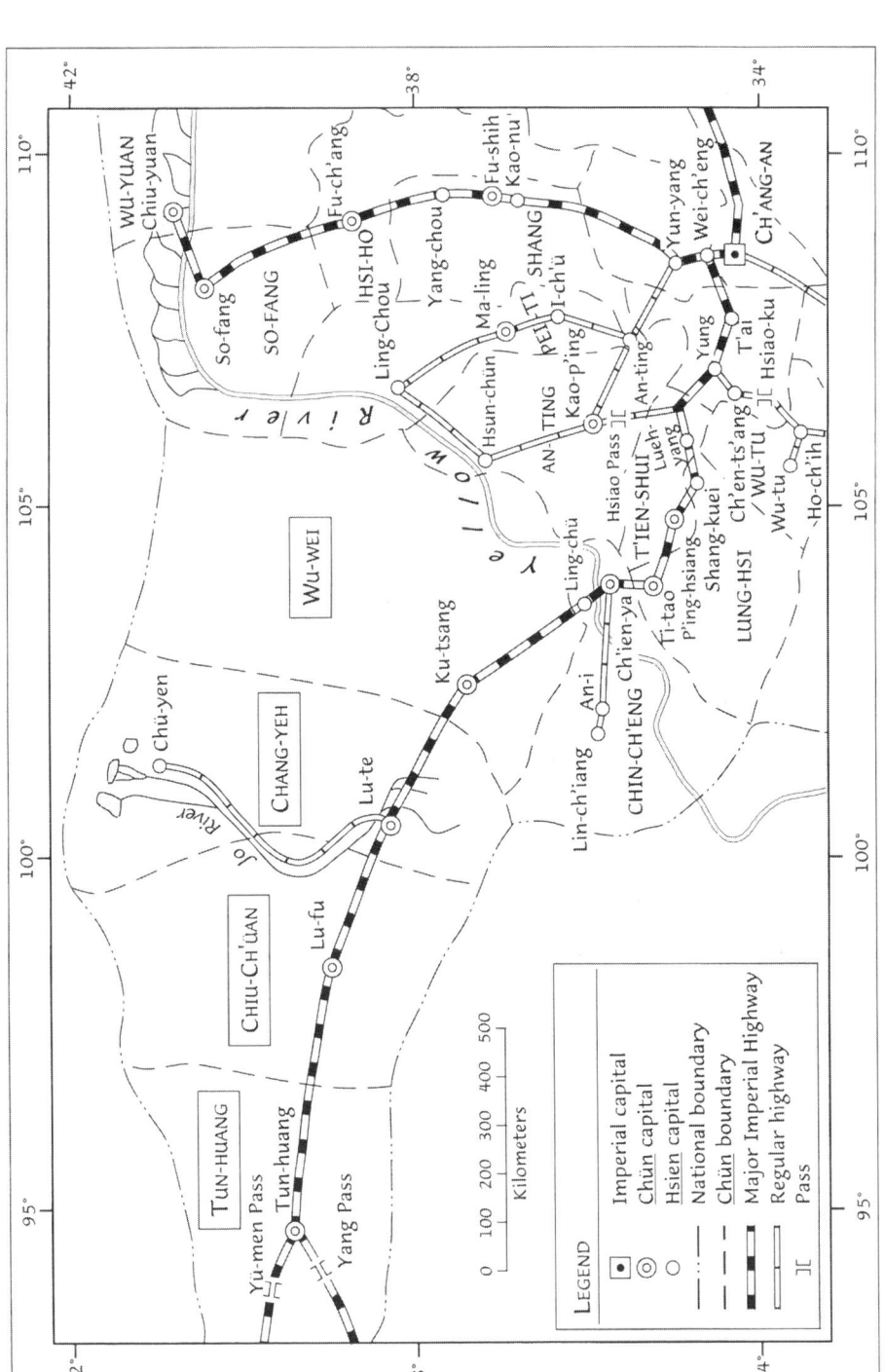

Map 4. The Han Road Network on the Northwestern Frontier

sages had two channels: the regular postal system and the system of defense and war communication.

Postal service in Chü-yen was carried out in two closely connected organizational structures, the regular postal stations (*i* or *so*) and the garrison establishments.[93] The various stations, spaced about thirty *li* (12.5 kilometers) apart, were under the direction of officers called station clerks (*i hsiao-shih*). Under these station clerks were post soldiers (*i-tsu* or *yu-tsu*), who carried out the actual work.[94] Both station clerks and post soldiers were under the command of the Chü-yen garrison authorities and received the same monthly food ration, 3.3 *shih* of millet or 3 *shih* of barley, as did all the other minor officials and soldiers in the garrison establishment.[95] In the post stations, carts (*chuan-chü*) and horses (*i-ch'i*) were kept ready for postal services.

In addition to the postal stations, the various garrison offices also handled messages, and, as was discussed earlier, they even had their own postal horses.

There were four means of transmitting various types of messages in the postal system. The first was termed *i t'ao-tz'u chuan* (transmission of documents through the imperial postal routes). This system transmitted only imperial decrees and orders from the central government to local governments and related offices in the empire. Through it, every part of the Han empire was informed of decisions made at the court and by the central government in Ch'ang-an. The following is an example of such documents uncovered in Chü-yen.

> (?) [Grand Herald Feng] Yeh-wang, Assistant Chung send down [the imperial decree] to the governors of Yu-fu-feng, Han-chung, Nan-yang, and Pei-ti. As soon as you receive this instruction, act accordingly and direct those who should subsequently follow the instruction to do so. The decree is to be transmitted through the imperial postal routes [to the offices named herein], and the said offices should copy it for circulation [among all local units and people]. Those who fail [to do so] (?) [will be punished].
>
> A report on the receipt of the decree is required.[96]
>
> 203.22
3294
pl. 163

This imperial decree was issued between 37 and 34 B.C. when Feng Yeh-wang was the grand herald (*ta hung-lu*).[97] It was next transmitted to the office of the Chang-yeh governor and then to the office of the Chü-yen chief commandant, all through the imperial postal routes.

The second means of conveying messages in Chü-yen was called *i-sui-tz'u hsing* (regional transmission of public notices). This system conveyed only public notices within the Chü-yen region. The notices delivered through this system all were of public interest and had to be made known to the garrison units through which they passed. They were not sealed and were termed *lu-pu* (unsealed public notices). Some of these notices announced military alerts and warnings of possible enemy attack. The following is an example of such documents.[98]

> Dispatch to be transmitted from Kuang-t'ien Watch Station [of Chia-ch'ü *hou-kuan*] to Wang-yuan Watch Station [of T'ien-pei *hou-kuan*], and all the watch stations in between:
>
>> On the *hsin-wei* day of the twelfth month, Subcommandant An of Wu-shang *hou* of Chia-ch'ü [*hou-kuan*] and Scribe Hui-ju respectfully report: At the *tsao-shih* time [roughly 8 to 10 a.m.], soldier (?) of Lin-wu Watch Station [of Chia-ch'ü *hou-kuan*] . . . (x)
>> Each watch station is to copy this dispatch and transmit it to the next watch station. A large group of Hsing-nu have gathered; they might invade the region. Therefore, upon receiving this dispatch [each commanding officer of the region] is to send his men to patrol his territory, instruct the officers and soldiers under his command to signal the alarm, see that the surrounding sandy fields are in good condition, dispatch his men to guard the roads, prohibit [nonmilitary] travel in his territory, make sure the fagots and pennants [for signaling] are ready, and hand out the weapons to be ready for combat. Be completely on the alert and do not let the enemy take any advantage. Each watch station is to be so informed. The loss of life and property is of the gravest concern to all. The above instruction should be complied with as with statutes and ordinances.[99]
>
> 278.7(105–6)
pls. 524–25

The third method of transmitting written communications in the Chü-yen region was termed *i-t'ing-hsing* (regional transmission of general correspondence). It was through this system that routine official and private correspondence was delivered. All the mail thus delivered was sealed and had a mailing label called a *feng-chien* or *chien-shu*.[100] Mail delivery was restricted to local areas, and mail was carried by soldiers of the garrison establishments through a relay system from station to station. It seems certain that this was the most commonly used postal system in Chü-yen. Three examples of the mailing labels, two of which (1 and 2) also include the record of transmission written at the points of destination, are translated here.[101]

1. [Postal Matter]
    To: Sa-ching *hou-kuan*
    To be delivered through the *t'ing*.
        [Mailing recorded:]
        Fu P'u's seal:
            Mail was brought in by soldier Liang on the *i-wei* day of the eighth month.[102]
                                                401.2
                                                2107
                                                pl. 103

2. [Postal Matter]
    To: Chia-ch'ü *hou-kuan*
    To be delivered through the *t'ing*.
        [Mailing recorded:]
        Yang Fang's seal:
            Mail was brought in by soldier T'ung on the *ting-mao* day of the seventh month.
            Two letters [in all].
                                                133.3
                                                4033
                                                pl. 214

3. [Postal Matter]
    To: Petty Officer I in the *hou-kuan* office and Commander Chieh.
    To be delivered by a four-horse post cart through the *t'ing*.[103]
                                                427.1A
                                                7412
                                                pl. 457

The fourth means of delivering correspondence in Chü-yen was termed *i-yu-hsing* (transmission of documents and correspondence through the postal system). The mail in this system was delivered mostly by mounted carriers through the postal stations (*yu*).[104] The Chü-yen documents reveal that the mail sent via the *yu* system was either between two *hou-kuan* of two chief commandant areas (and never of the same chief commandant area) in the Chü-yen region or between Chü-yen and the outside. The following are two examples of the mailing labels and their records of transmission for this category of conveyance.[105]

1. [Postal Matter]
    To: Chien-shui *hou-kuan* [of Chien-shui *tu-wei*]

To be sent through the postal system.
>[Mailing recorded:]
>>Sender: The official seal of the Chang-yeh chief commandant
>>The mail was delivered by soldier Sun Hui [of the Office of the Chief Commandant] on the *keng-wu* day of the ninth month.[106]

74.4(121)
520
pl. 26

2. Horse: One horse, 6 *ch'ih* high.
>[Postal Matter]
>To: Office of the Chü-yen Chief Commandant
>>To be delivered through the postal system.
>>[From: Ch'eng-ao Watch Station of T'o-t'o *hou-kuan* of Chien-shui *tu-wei*][107]

81.8B
7430
pl. 459

As can be seen from these documents, the materials dispatched through the postal system were generally official documents. They were handled by the postal stations in the garrison establishments.

As with the transmission of written communications, the methods of postal delivery also varied on the Chü-yen frontier. In general, local and regular mail was carried by runners and was classified as *tsou-hsing* or *hsing-che tsou* (delivery by couriers).[108] Urgent and distant mail was sent by either mounted carriers or postal carts. Of the four ways of conveying messages just discussed, the first (*i-tao-tz'u chuan*) and the fourth (*i-yu-hsing*) mostly used mounted mail carriers and postal carts, while the other two (*i-sui-tz'u hsing* and *i-t'ing-hsing*) generally employed runners. But there were exceptions to this practice (e.g., document 427.1A cited earlier). Perhaps the basic factor in deciding on the method of postal delivery was the nature, urgency, and weight of the item, as well as the distance to its destination. For instance, heavy items required the use of postal carts, as did distant mail; long-distance mail would have had to be carried by mounted riders, as would urgent messages of war and alarm even over short distances.

The most urgent dispatches were delivered by express post. This type of delivery was termed *li-ma ch'ih-hsing* or *ku-hsing* (express delivery by galloping horses); the official dispatches that required immediate and special delivery by an officer were called *wang-jen ch'ih-piao han* (rush special delivery in a red mailbag).[109] Although the occasion for using such an express delivery was decided by garrison officers in consideration of special circumstances, notice of a military alert and possible enemy invasion can be reasonably assumed to have gone by express delivery.

The procedure for mailing and reception and transmission of the post was systematic and enormously complicated on the Chü-yen frontier. Both private letters and official correspondence and dispatches were first turned over to the *ling-shih* and *wei-shih*, who had charge of postal operations and services in the various garrison offices, or to the clerks at the postal stations in the garrisons.[110] They were then checked, sorted, and collated by the officers and finally sealed in mailing containers termed *feng-han* (dispatch boards) or *shu-nang* (dispatch bags) and sent out to their destinations.[111] After the post had gone, the officers had to write reports on its handling and processing to their superiors.

In most cases, the mail was carried by soldiers or post soldiers. But it was not uncommon to see commanders, subcommandants, *shih-li*, *hou-shih*, or *se-fu* functioning as mail carriers.[112]

The mail was generally marked with its direction—southbound, northbound, eastbound, or westbound mail.[113] In the Chü-yen region, only southbound and northbound mail was involved because of the south-north array of the Han garrison establishments and general settlements in the region.[114]

Once the mail had been sent on its way, officials at all the stops and postal stations through which it passed were required to record the details of its transmission on the mailing label, which served as what was called a "waybill" (*p'ai-tan*) in later periods.[115] The items on the waybill included the exact time of arrival and departure of the mail, the previous stop and the next stop, and the names, organizational affiliations, and identification of the receiver and deliverer of the post. The record was to be examined at the destination of the mail or at any time when a question was raised as to the regularity of the time or stages of its delivery.

Time limits were set for each delivery according to the distance between the locations of origin and destination of the dispatch and the method of its conveyance. When the mail was received at its destination, the time the delivery had taken was compared with the time it should have taken according to the regulations. It would be noted that the delivery was made before, on, or after the allotted time. If the delivery had fallen behind schedule, it was ascertained where the delay had occurred, and the officers at that point were summoned by higher authorities for questioning. If they failed to provide reasonable and acceptable explanations, they would be punished.

When the mail reached its final destination, the officer or soldier handling mail services or postal operations there recorded its arrival and other items related to its delivery on separate wooden strips. He wrote, in small characters, the seal (name) and organizational affiliation and title of the originator, and the condition of his seal if it was broken, on the right-hand side of the original mailing label. He also noted, again in small characters, the date of arrival of the mail and the name, organizational affiliation, and title of the carrier. He then checked all the details of the record of transmission; if no faults were found, he marked the delivery as "satisfactory [according to the established rules]" (*chungch'eng*), but if any aspect of the delivery deviated from the regulations he recorded it as "unsatisfactory [according to the established rules]" (*pu chungch'eng*),[116] and an investigation would then be undertaken. If a return receipt (*chi-ch'ü*) was required, he would take care of it.[117] With this final checking, evaluation, and reply done, the long process of delivering the mail reached its completion.

The following documents have been translated to illustrate the various phases and facets of the procedure of postal delivery.[118]

1. Five letters and three official dispatches:
    Two letters with Wang Hsien's seal.
    One letter with Sun Meng's seal.
    One letter with Ch'eng Hsüan's seal.
    One letter with Wang Ch'ung's seal.
    Two letters with Lü Hsien's seal.
    One letter with Wang Ch'iang's seal.
        On the *kuei-wei* day of the second month, all letters and dispatches have been checked [and recorded] by Ling-shih T'ang Feng.

        214.2
        5745
        pl. 358

2. One northbound, rush and special delivery:[119]
        ... the third year of the Yuan-k'ang period [63 B.C.] ... (x) Commander (?) of Lin-ch'ü Watch Station ... (x)
        At the time of the fourth *fen* of *hun-shih* time [roughly 8 to 10 p.m.],[120] Commander (?) of Ch'eng-hu Watch Station delivered [the mail] to Commander P'u of Ping-shan Watch Station. The delivery has taken 3 *shih* and arrived on schedule. Delivery was satisfactory [according to the established rules].

        502.3
        Cp1912

3. Northbound mail: three letters; one closed dispatch; one open dispatch on board.
        The three letters and the open dispatch on board carry the official seal of the governor of Chang-yeh, to be delivered to the Office [of the Chü-yen Chief Commandant].
        The closed dispatch carries Niu Chün's seal, to be sent to the

clerk of ox affairs of Chang-yeh at the place where he temporarily stays [during his current mission].

At the time of the seventh *fen* of *hsia-pu* time [roughly 4 to 6 p.m.] of the *keng-wu* day of the ninth month, soldier Fu of Lin-mu Watch Station [of Chia-ch'ü *hou-kuan*] received the mail from soldier Hung of Sa-ching Watch Station [of Sa-ching *hou-kuan*]. At the *chi-ming* time [roughly 2 to 4 a.m. of the next day], soldier Ch'ang of Tang-ch'ü Watch Station [of Chia-ch'ü *hou-kuan*] handed the mail to soldier Fu of Shou-hsiang Watch Station [of Chü-yen *hou-kuan*]. The total distance of transmission in the territory of Chü-yen *tu-wei* is 95 *li*; the regulated time limit for delivery is 8 *shih*, 3 *fen*; and the actual time of transmission was 7 *shih*, 2 *fen*.[121]

157.14
Cp916

4. (x) . . . the Office [of the Chief Commandant] is 159 *li* from Hsiang-lu Watch Station [of Sa-ching *hou-kuan*]. The mail was expected to have stayed in the various stations in transit for 1 *shih* and 6 *fen*, and the regulated time limit for transmission is 5 *shih*. Now, it has been delayed for 3 *shih* and 4 *fen*. Explain the reason for this delay.[122]

181.6B
1350
pl. 63

5. The mail was delayed in its delivery. Ch'ang, the subcommandant of the previous stops (watch stations), report to the Office of the Commandant to answer charges.[123]

123.55
3215
pl. 155
Cp687

6. Express delivery to Chien-shui *hou-kuan*.
   [Mailing recorded:]
       The seal was broken.
       The mail was carried in by soldier Wai-jen of . . . (?) on the *ping-yin* day of the twelfth month.[124]

20.1
1496
pl. 73
Cp172

Documents 3 and 4 reveal information about the time limits for transmission of dispatches and correspondence. Document 3 indicates that for a distance of 95 *li* the regulated time of delivery was 8 *shih* and 3 *fen*. One Han *fen* was equivalent to 14 minutes and 24 seconds; 1 *shih* at night was equal to 8 *fen* (or a period of 1 hour, 55 minutes, 12 seconds), and 1 *shih* during daytime equaled 8.5 *fen* (2 hours, 2 minutes, 24 seconds).[125] Therefore, during a 24-hour day, on the average, 1 *shih* corresponded to about 2 hours. Thus, 8 *shih* and 3 *fen* corresponds closely to 16 hours, 43 minutes, 12 seconds, and the mail in this delivery was required to move at the rate of about 5.68 *li* (2.37 kilometers) an hour. In the Han system, this delivery required the post to proceed at the rate of about 11.36 *li* (4.74 kilometers) per Han *shih*. This rate is further confirmed by document 163.19, which reveals a time limit of 11.29 *li* (4.71 kilometers) per Han *shih* for the transmission of a communication from the Chü-yen chief commandant to the office of the Chang-yeh governor.[126] Therefore, we may assume that Han postal carriers on foot were required to move important correspondence at an average rate of a little over 11 *li* (4.59 kilometers) per Han *shih*.

However, two other wooden documents (133.23 and 231.2) indicate different rates of speed for postal delivery. The former document indicates that the time limit for an 80-*li* transmission of a piece of correspondence was set at 9.00 Han *shih*, while the latter document records a time limit of 10.00 Han *shih* for a delivery over the same distance.[127] The respective average rates of distance to be covered per Han *shih*, 8.89 *li* (3.71 kilometers) and 8.00 *li* (3.34 kilometers), are close enough to be considered as slight variants of the same category, which was basically different from that of the 11.36 and 11.29 *li* indicated in documents 157.14 and 163.19.

It is suggested, on the basis of literary evidence, that in Han times the regulated travel distance to be covered while on official business was 60.00 *li* (25.02 kilometers) per day.[128] As an official day generally covered 6 Han *shih*—from

TABLE 32.   Time Divisions in Han Times

Day/Night	Han Times				Modern Times	
	Major Divisions of Night	Twelve Divisions of Day and Night	Variant Names	Number of K'o/Fen	Starting Point of Each Division	
					Exact	Approximate
Night	ping-yeh	(1) yeh-pan	yeh-shih	8.0	Midnight	Midnight
	ting-yeh	(2) chi-ming		8.0	1:55'12" a.m.	2 a.m.
	wu-yeh	(3) p'ing-tan		8.0	3:50'24" a.m.	4 a.m.
Day		(4) jih-ch'u		8.5	5:52'48" a.m.	6 a.m.
		(5) shih-shih	tsao-shih	8.5	7:55'12" a.m.	8 a.m.
		(6) tung-chung	yü-chung	8.5	9:57'35" a.m.	10 a.m.
		(7) jih-chung		8.5	Noon	Noon
		(8) jih-tieh		8.5	2:02'24" p.m.	2 p.m.
		(9) hsia-pu	pu-shih	8.5	4:04'48" p.m.	4 p.m.
		(10) jih-ju		8.5	6:07'12" p.m.	6 p.m.
Night	chia-yeh	(11) huang-hun	hun-shih	8.0	8:09'36" p.m.	8 p.m.
	i-yeh	(12) jen-ting		8.0	9:59'48" p.m.	10 p.m.

jih-ch'u ("sunrise," about 6 a.m.) to *jih-ju* ("sunset," about 6 p.m.)—the regulated rate of distance for official travel, then, was 10.00 *li* (4.17 kilometers) per Han *shih* or 5.00 *li* (roughly 2.09 kilometers) per hour. In comparing this rate with the two previous categories of time limits for transmissions of dispatches and correspondence, we find it to be between the two. That is, the three groups of rates are in the following order in *li* per Han *shih*: (a) 11.36, 11.29; (b) 10.00; and (c) 8.89, 8.00.[129] Since the rate of 10.00 *li* per Han *shih* was for travelers on foot, we may assume that rates (a) and (c) were similarly for couriers on foot. Although the whole range of difference between the four rates in (a) through (c)—from 8.00 to 11.36 *li*—was relatively small, the nature of the correspondence seems to indicate that rate (a) was for dispatches more urgent or important than those conveyed under rate (c). We may point out that the average time limit in rate (a) was about 11.33 *li* (4.72 kilometers) per Han *shih*, while the average time limit in rate (c) was about 8.45 *li* (3.52 kilometers) per Han *shih*. A comparison of the two figures suggests that postal deliveries under rate (a) required the carriers to move faster than did the deliveries under rate (c). It is likely that the best runners were used to carry the more urgent and important communications.

Document 4 (181.6B) indicates that for a distance of 159.00 *li* (66.30 kilometers) the regulated time limit for postal delivery was 5 *shih*. The average rate of travel in this case was 31.80 *li* (13.26 kilometers) per *shih*, or 15.90 *li* (6.63 kilometers) an hour. This rate is about three times any of the rates just discussed. A human runner could not be expected to maintain such a fast pace, hence it must have been the rate for horse post. If this was the case, the horse rate for a 6-*shih* day was 190.20 *li* (79.31 kilometers).[130] It is suggested, on literary evidence, that in Han times for conveyance of most urgent messages a fast-running horse could average 400 to 500 *li* (roughly 167 to 208 kilometers) during a 24-hour day.[131] This rate of horse-post delivery compares with and lends support to our estimated rate based on the Chü-yen documents.

In sum, the Han-regulated distance for transmission of dispatches to be covered by carriers on foot averaged a little over 11 *li* per *shih* and about 66 *li* in a 12-hour day. Mounted carriers averaged 31.80 *li* per *shih*, 190.20 *li* per 12-hour day, and about 400 *li* in a 24-hour day. Although the rate at which dispatches and correspondence was required to move in delivery by postal carts is not recorded in the Chü-yen documents, it should have been very close to that of the horse post.[132] Table 33 summarizes this discussion and gives estimated time limits for conveyance of messages in both a 12-hour and a 24-hour day.

The actual speed of postal transmission varied with individual cases. But the general range of distance covered by carriers can be estimated on the basis of limited information contained in the wooden documents. On foot, the post moved at the speed of from 6.67 to 13.12 *li* per Han *shih*. By horse it traveled at a rate of 18.75 *li* per Han *shih*. Table 34 shows the details of the variations in the actual speed of postal transmission. The table also indicates that, as in the case of the time limits discussed earlier, in practice the more urgent and important posts (documents 157.14 and 317.27) did move faster than the regular post (documents 133.23 and 231.2).

Communication by Signals

The fastest method of communication on the frontier was signaling (*feng-huo*), which was used to send and receive information, mainly of a defense or security nature, to and from neighboring garrison establishments through specially designed signals. In simple terms, the signals included (1) burning, day or night, fagots or firewood piled outside a watch station; (2) sending smoke signals combined with hoisting sails made of silk or other cloth during the day, the former to indicate alarm and the latter to detail the degree of alarm; (3) raising a flaming torch on a pole at night, with one torch used to transmit a simple alarm and additional ones to show the degree of alarm; (4) flashing an "off and on" flame (*li-ho huo*) when besieged at night; (5) beating a drum during the day or at night; and (6) hoisting sails during the day. The last two, and probably also the third, could be used at times as signals of peace.[133] The following documents have been translated to illustrate the operation of the system.

TABLE 33. Time Limits for Transmission of Han Correspondence as Seen in the Chü-yen Documents

	Distance Post Was Carried					
	On Foot			By Horse		
Time	Li	Kilometers	Miles	Li	Kilometers	Miles
Shih	11.36	4.74	2.94	31.80	13.26	8.23
	11.29	4.71	2.92			
	8.89	3.71	2.30			
	8.00	3.34	2.06			
Hour	5.68	2.37	1.47	15.90	6.63	4.12
	5.65	2.36	1.46			
	4.45	1.86	1.16			
	4.00	1.66	1.03			
Twelve-hour day	68.16	28.44	17.66	190.20	79.31	49.41
	67.74	28.32	17.59			
	53.34	22.32	13.86			
	48.00	19.92	12.37			
Twenty-four-hour day	136.32	56.88	35.32	380.40	158.62	98.81
	135.48	56.62	35.18			
	106.68	44.64	27.72			
	96.00	39.84	24.74			

Note: Figures have been rounded to two decimals.

1. Regulations concerning Signaling when Hsiung-nu Enter the Barrier and Penetrate North of the Chin Pass [of Chien-shui *hou-kuan*]:
   When Hsiung-nu are detected, the watch stations outside the barrier should send up smoke signals and raise sail signals: make two smoke signals if [there are] more than five hundred Hsiung-nu.[134]

   288.7
   2390
   pl. 116

2. Commander Liu of Lin-mo Watch Station [of Chia-ch'ü *hou-kuan*] entered [and reported]:
   At the time of *jih-chung* [roughly noon] two sail signals were relayed from the *wu* of Chi-lu Watch Station [of Chia-ch'ü *hou-kuan*]; again, three torch flames were relayed from the *wu* [of the same watch station] at the time of . . . (x)[135]

   126.40(180)
   Cp719

3. On the third day, *ting-wei*, of the eighth month, at the time of *pu-shih* [roughly 4 p.m.] two sail signals were hoisted.

   3.11(214)

4. One torch flame was raised [to signify peace] at the time of *i-yeh* [roughly 10 p.m.], in response to Mu-pi Watch Station, by soldier Kuang.
   One torch flame was raised at the time of *ping-yeh* [roughly midnight], in response to Lin-tao Watch Station, by soldier Chang.

TABLE 34. Speed of Postal Transmission in Chü-yen

Time	Distance Post Was Carried						Document Numbers
	On Foot			By Horse			
	Li	Kilometers	Miles	*Li*	Kilometers	Miles	
Shih				18.75	7.82	4.86	181.6B
	13.12	5.47	3.40				157.14
	12.50	5.21	3.24				317.27
	8.00	3.34	2.07				133.23
	6.67	2.78	1.73				231.2
Hour				9.38	3.91	2.43	181.6B
	6.56	2.74	1.70				157.14
	6.25	2.61	1.62				317.27
	4.00	1.67	1.04				133.23
	3.34	1.39	0.86				231.2

Note: Figures have been rounded to two decimals.

One torch flame was raised at the time of *ting-yeh* [roughly 2
p.m.], in response to Mu-pi Watch Station, by soldier T'ung.

88.19
6212
pl. 392

5. On the *ping-wu* day of the eleventh month of the fourth year ... (x),
[record of] vigilance of the soldiers of the watch station ... (x)

272.32
3155
pl. 152

These documents clarify the routine process of signaling in the garrison establishments. Signaling was one of the regular assignments of soldiers in the garrisons. It was referred to as *chih-hou* (watch and signal duty).[136] The soldiers on such assignments were required to record the details of signaling: (1) the names of the soldiers on duty; (2) the time of signal reception and transmission; (3) the origin and destination of signals received or sent; (4) the types of signals received or transmitted; and (5) the reasons for sending the signals. These records were sent periodically to superior offices for inspection.

Signal communication played a vital role in maintaining the security of the Chü-yen region, which was in need of constant protection from Hsiung-nu raids, and hence every watch station and garrison establishment had at least one watchtower. In fact, with signals traveling at the speed of light (smoke and sail signals) or sound (drum signals), this type of communication was the fastest and most effective means of military defense and operations in early human history.

Upon receiving a warning of possible enemy raids, the garrison officers immediately alerted the people in the region and declared "martial law." This process is detailed in document 278.7, which was translated in the preceding section. In brief, on detecting signals of alarm the soldier on duty reported to the commanding officer of his watch station, who in turn notified the office of the subcommandant. The subcommandant and his head clerk then reported the alarm to the office of the commandant, who issued a notice of alarm to all garrison organizations concerned. "Martial law" was then declared over the area that might be invaded by enemy forces. Such notices were probably copied on a board and posted at places where all residents of the area could read them. These public notices were generally referred to as *pien-shu*.[137] When the local residents had been informed of possible enemy attacks through the *pien-shu*, the process of communication through signaling was complete. The original signals first went through the communications channels of the garrison organizations, which resulted in an alert. Then a general alarm was called by means of written public notices, which informed the inhabitants of the area that there was danger of an invasion.

THE BALANCE BETWEEN CONTROL AND COMMUNICATION

We have examined two vital aspects of the Chü-yen frontier region: the apparatus and practice of rigid control on one hand, and the convenience and rich variety of the communications and transportation systems on the other. Each speaks for a critical aspect of the frontier. The first kept it stable, secure, and well controlled, and the second made it mobile, dynamic, and well connected internally and externally. These two seemingly incompatible aspects actually complemented each other, and the security and development of the Chü-yen region depended on the effective functioning of both. The general principle for the development of a frontier region was strict control, though not at the cost of stagnation, and security, though not at the cost of a loss of mobility and dynamism.

One illustration of this principle at work is a factor that balanced the practice of strict control. Amid the complex regulations that governed the control of people, property, and travel, a statute protecting the rights, privacy, and property of the family is also found in the Chü-yen documents.

Statute on Arresting:

> Officers are forbidden to enter huts or houses to arrest people without an approved reason. People may beat and wound intruders in their houses, and the matter is then dealt with according to the "Statute on Entering People's Houses without an Approved Reason."[138]

395.11
2132
pl. 104

This "Statute on Arresting" (*p'u-lü*) actually warranted the house or its equivalent as the "castle" of the family. The fundamental rights of individuals in the home were secured. In fact, this is probably the world's earliest written legal statute protecting the family and its individual members against unreasonable searches, seizures, and other infringements.[139]

Conclusion

Frontier, Colonization, and Empire

THE LONG PROCESS OF Han western expansion was completed with the full consolidation of the Western Regions in 29 B.C. With it, the larger Han expansion movement that began with Emperor Wu's massive Hsiung-nu campaigns in 129 B.C. came to its full fruition. The Han dynasty had by now acquired over 1.5–1.7 million square miles of new land and reshaped the territorial boundaries of the Chinese empire. It was the largest expansion movement in Chinese history and virtually gave birth to a new China. Since the geographical contour and basic spatial extension of China have since experienced little fundamental change, the Han expansion may be said to have defined the ecology and hence the direction of Chinese society, culture, and history. This is the *longue durée* significance of the Han expansion.

Almost all of the Han expansion was carried out during Wu-ti's reign, mainly from 129 to 90 B.C. Later military expeditions were mostly for the defense and further consolidation of territories acquired in his time. Wu-ti's major campaigns of conquest took place in four regions beyond the Han borders of his day. These were the north and northwest, mainly the land of the Hsiung-nu and Ch'iang and the Western Regions in modern Outer Mongolia, Inner Mongolia, Siberia, Tsinghai, Kansu, Sinkiang, eastern Central Asia, and northern South Asia; the southeast and south, mainly the land of the Yueh in modern southern Chekiang, Fukien, Kwangtung, Hainan Island, Kwangsi, and Vietnam; the southwest, the land of various peoples together called the "Southwest Barbarians" (Hsi-nan i) in Chinese texts, in modern western Szechwan, Kuei-chou, Yunnan, eastern Sikang, and southern Kansu; and the northeast, Ch'ao-hsien (modern Korea). The western expansion—the campaigns and development of the north and northwest regions—has been the central focus of this study. The success of the western expansion was twofold. On the one hand, it was superior military power that led to victory in the military campaigns and hence the acquisition of new land; on the other, it was the Han frontier system—*t'un-t'ien*—that transformed the new land into a permanent part of the empire. Thus, the key structure of Wu-ti's expansion was its special frontier system, and that is the focus of the present study. As already discussed, the Han first put its frontier system into practice in Ho-hsi and gradually refined it into a complex and effective system, as was seen in our examination of the Chü-yen system. This study clearly shows the organizational structure and operational system of the Han frontier at work.

The Ho-hsi campaign was part of a long and expensive Hsiung-nu war during the reign of Wu-ti. But its consequences were far-reaching. First, it acquired a territory of over 265,000 square miles, which proved to be rich in a variety of agricultural and industrial resources, including dairy, lumber, textiles, mining, and agriculture. Second, it extended Han influence far to the west of the Yellow River, and through the thoroughfare of the Ho-hsi Corridor Wu-ti's armies marched to the heart of Central Asia. They conquered, from 108 to 101 B.C., Lou-lan (the Lop-nor region), Lun-t'ou (the Bugur region), and Ta-yuan (Farghana) and finally reached K'ang-chü (Sogdiana). As a result, the nations of the entire Western Regions were shocked and frightened and the kings of most states sent envoys to present tribute to China and had their sons or brothers remain at the Han Court as hostages. China emerged for the first time as an international imperialist power on the Asian continent. Third, after the era of Wu-ti, Ho-hsi, China's gateway to the West, remained a pivot in Chinese–Central Asian and Chinese-Western relations. As such, Ho-hsi played an enormously important role in Chinese political, economic, social, intellectual, religious, and artistic history. To illustrate this point, one needs only to mention, among others, the Silk Road, the role of Ho-hsi in medieval—particularly T'ang (A.D. 618–907)—politics and foreign relations, the introduction of Buddhism via Central Asia, the Ho-hsi learning in the Six Dynasties period (220–589), and the great treasure of art and manuscripts at Tun-huang and Mai-chi-shan. The acquisition of Ho-hsi, then, was indeed the addition of a new frontier to the Han empire that was instrumental in the formation and changes of character and outlook of some areas of Chinese culture and history.

The colonization of Ho-hsi also had a lasting impact. From an economic standpoint, it represented the transformation of an uncultivated land of nomadic pastures into an agricultural domain. Viewed from the perspective of the societal stages of world history, the colonization of Ho-hsi represents the victory of agricultural over nomadic society, a continuing process in North and East Asia, in which the domain of the nomads was gradually shrinking due to the expansion of agricultural civilizations, the result of the clash of civilizations in the *longue durée* world historical perspective. This transformation necessarily produced institutional and other fundamental changes in society.

In the case of Ho-hsi, the transformation was carried out by the Han government through an ingenious design—the *t'un-t'ien* system. The region was populated by emigrants from the "old world" of the Han empire. These colonists, from almost every part of the empire, settled in their new world according to an extremely systematic plan and were rigidly organized in every way. In general, their frontier society was a transplant of the society of the old world. They did not develop a new spirit or a new philosophy of life. In this sense, notwithstanding the far-reaching external impact of the acquisition and development of Ho-hsi, the new world of Ho-hsi was merely an extension of the traditional world of the old east.

The noninnovative nature of the Han frontier society did not make the colonization apparatus less effective. On the contrary, as we have demonstrated, the Han westward expansion proceeded successfully under this system. Not only was Ho-hsi completely colonized in a span of about fifty years, but the frontier was extended far beyond the western boundary of Ho-hsi into a sizable part of Central Asia, including modern Sinkiang and adjacent areas in Central and South Asia. Furthermore, the same system was employed by later dynasties—such as the T'ang, the Yuan (1279–1368), the Ming (1368–1644), and the Ch'ing (1644–1911)—to develop their newly acquired and border regions. The system was even applied in the interior by regional groups or regimes during times of disunion of the Chinese empire. Thus, we may conclude that the Han frontier system is a great heritage in the historical and political context of Imperial China.

Major immediate effects of the western colonization on the Han empire were twofold. The new world absorbed a large segment of the dislocated, economically depressed, and undesirable population of the old east. The emigration thereby reduced the economic burden of the eastern portions of the empire and lessened the potential for unrest and political instability in times of natural disaster and poor harvest. Since the emigration and settling of these colonists were financed by the government, the economic costs were extremely high; to these should be added the expenses of the military expeditions that made the colonization possible. Although exact figures cannot be obtained from the available Han sources, it is reasonable to assume on the basis of various relevant references that at certain times the total annual expenses for the Ho-hsi campaigns and emigrations alone amounted to at least 100 billion in cash. This had tremendous economic and other implications. It was nearly 8.4 times the annual revenue of (about 12 billion) of the Han government prior to Wu-ti's large-scale military campaigns and colonial programs. It is clear that the cost of the acquisition and colonization of Ho-hsi exerted a severe strain on the Han economy.[1] Both Ssu-ma Ch'ien (145–86 B.C.) and Pan Ku (A.D. 32–92) confirmed this point. The two great historians of Han China contended that these skyrocketing expenditures emptied government treasuries and exhausted national economic resources. Together with continued spending on military campaigns and emigration, this financial crisis forced the Han government to institute numerous drastic measures to increase its revenues: additional and new taxes, reform of the currency, reorganization of government monopolies on salt and iron, a new monopoly on liquor, price and market controls (*chün-shu* and *p'ing-chun*), the sale of offices and aristocratic ranks, and forced "voluntary contributions," to mention only a few. New legal measures—often unusually harsh—were also established to enforce these financial schemes. All of these, needless to say, had a lasting impact on the economic conditions and political course of the Former Han empire. As Hsia-hou Sheng (first century B.C.) pointed out in the first year of Hsuan-ti's reign (74–49 B.C.), the Former Han dynasty after Wu-ti was hard put to recover from the economic and political deterioration that resulted from his military campaigns and colonizations. Moreover, almost all of these measures continued through later periods and became permanent features of the economic and governmental institutions of Imperial China.[2]

In a larger historical perspective, the Han frontier system was a long-lasting national and cultural construction that critically affected the development of the Chinese empire. The Han defined their national strength by the boundaries of their frontiers. The success in frontier expansion shaped the geographical boundaries of the Han empire and the cultural boundary between the Han civilization and those that were considered inferior to it. While the outward expansion of the frontier indicated an increase in the influence of the Chinese empire and its culture, the inward retreat implied the opposite. Thus, the frontier often defined the national goals of the Chinese empire, articulated the national imagination of what constituted the Chinese nation and culture, and enunciated its destiny and historical mission as a great empire. As such, the frontier may be seen as one of the most enduring legacies of the Han.

As has been examined in detail, the growth of the Chinese empire was a process of interaction between the center (the empire proper) and the periphery (the frontier regions outside that defined domain) beginning with the early Shang and Chou dynasties. The Shang arose in the frontier region of the Hsia in the seventeenth century B.C. and the Chou in the Shang frontier region in the eleventh century B.C. Later the Ch'in expanded from its original frontier region to unify China and establish its first centralized bureaucratic empire.

During Ch'in and Han times, the pattern of center-periphery interaction was transformed. No longer did the periphery subjugate the center; now the center conquered the periphery and the empire expanded its domain.³ This new pattern of frontier-empire relations began to take shape during the Ch'in dynasty under Shih huang-ti (r. 221–210 B.C.) and completed as a well-defined paradigm under the Han emperor Wu-ti. Thus, with the operation of both patterns—the subjugation of the center by the periphery and the conquest of border regimes (frontier regions) by the center power (the empire)—the Chinese empire strove to maintain its well-conceived territorial configuration, long-established developmental mold, and historical ideal of T'ien-hsia (All under Heaven) during the next two millennia under both Chinese and non-Chinese regimes (e.g., the expansion of the T'ang empire, the conquest of the Sung by the Mongols in 1279, and the rise of the Manchu Ch'ing empire in the seventeenth century).

Major Dynasties and Periods of China

1. THE CLASSICAL AGE (ANCIENT CHINA)

The Hsia (Xia) dynasty	Ca. 2000/1900–1600 B.C. (trad. 2200–1766 B.C.)
The Shang dynasty	Ca. 1600–1100 B.C. (trad. 1766–1122 B.C.)
The Chou (Zhou) dynasty	Ca. 1100–256 B.C. (trad. 1122–256 B.C.)
Western Chou	Ca. 1100–771 B.C.
Eastern Chou	770–256 B.C.
The Spring and Autumn (Ch'un-ch'iu) period	722–468 B.C./770–404 B.C.
The Warring States (Chan-kuo) period	403–221 B.C.

2. THE IMPERIAL PERIOD (IMPERIAL CHINA)

EARLY IMPERIAL

The Ch'in (Qin) dynasty	221–207 B.C.
The Ch'u-Han transition	206–202 B.C.
The Western (Former) Han dynasty	202 B.C.–A.D. 8
The Hsin (Xin) dynasty	A.D. 9–23
The Eastern (Latter) Han dynasty	A.D. 25–220

MIDDLE IMPERIAL

The Three Kingdoms period	
Shu (Shu-Han)	A.D. 221–263
Wei	A.D. 220–265
Wu	A.D. 222–280
The Chin (Jin) dynasty	A.D. 265–280–420

Western Chin	A.D. 265–317
Eastern Chin	A.D. 317–420
The Southern Dynasties period	
The Former (or Liu) Sung (Song) dynasty	A.D. 420–479
The Southern Ch'i (Qi) dynasty	A.D. 479–502
The Southern Liang dynasty	A.D. 502–557
(The Latter Liang dynasty	A.D. 555–587)
The Southern Ch'en dynasty	A.D. 557–589
The Northern Dynasties period	
The Northern Wei dynasty	A.D. 386–534/535
The Eastern Wei	A.D. 534–550
The Western Wei	A.D. 535–557
The Northern Ch'i (Qi) dynasty	A.D. 550–577
The Northern Chou (Zhou) dynasty	A.D. 557–581
The Sui dynasty	A.D. 581–589–618
The T'ang (Tang) dynasty	A.D. 618–907
The Five Dynasties period	
Later Liang	A.D. 907–923
Later T'ang	A.D. 923–936
Later Chin (Jin)	A.D. 936–947
Later Han	A.D. 947–950
Later Chou (Zhou)	A.D. 951–960

LATE IMPERIAL

The Sung (Song) dynasty	A.D. 960–1279
Northern Sung	A.D. 960–1126
Southern Sung	A.D. 1127–1279
The Liao (Khitan) dynasty	A.D. 907–916–1125
The Hsi-Hsia (Xi Xia, Tangut Tibetan) dynasty	A.D. 990–1032–1227
The Chin (Jin, Jurchen) dynasty	A.D. 1115–1234
The Yuan (Mongol) dynasty	A.D. 1279–1368
The Ming dynasty	A.D. 1368–1644
The Southern Ming	A.D. 1645–1662/1683
The Ch'ing (Qing, Manchu) dynasty	A.D. 1644–1911/1912

3. THE REPUBLIC   A.D. 1912–

Notes

PREFACE

1. For detailed studies of these issues, see Chun-shu Chang, *Han-tai pien-chiang shih lun-chi* (Taipei: Shih-hao, 1975), pp. 1–121 (hereafter cited as Chang 1975a); Chun-shu Chang, "Han-tai ssu-ch'ou chih-lu te k'ai-t'o yü fan-chan," *Shih-huo*, new ser., 15, nos. 1–2 (June 1985): 1–14; and Chun-shu Chang, in *Ssu-ch'ou chih-lu wen-hsien shu-lu,* ed. Kansu sheng she-hui k'o-hsueh hsueh-hui lien-ho hui (Lanchou: Lanchou ta-hsueh ch'u-pan she, 1989), pp. 226–27.

2. For a systematic and comprehensive discussion of the discovery and studies of the Han wooden and bamboo documents since 1900, see Chun-shu Chang, "Han-chien te fa-hsien yü cheng-li," *Shih-huo*, new ser., 16, nos. 5–6 (April 25, 1987): 1–19 (hereafter Chun-shu Chang 1987); Chun-shu Chang, "Pa-shih nien lai Han-chien te fa-hsien cheng-li yü yen-chiu," in *Chung-yang yen-chiu yuan ti-erh chieh kuo-chi Han-hsueh hui-i lun-wen chi* (Taipei: Academia Sinica, 1989), pp. 417–40 (hereafter Chun-shu Chang 1989); Chun-shu Chang, "Ch'in-Han shih yü Ch'in-Han chien-tu yen-chiu chung te i-hsieh wen-t'i," in *Min-kuo i-lai kuo-shih yen-chiu te hui-ku yü chan-wang yen-t'ao hui lun-wen chi* (Taipei: National Taiwan University, 1992), pp. 173–77. See also Pien Yü-ch'ien et al., comp., *Pen shih-chi i-lai ch'u-t'u chien-po kai-shu* (Taipei: Wan-chüan lou, 1999), esp. pp. 93–113, which updates my work for the period 1987–93; Ch'en Sung-chang, *Hsiang-kang chung-wen ta-hsueh wen-wu-kuan ts'ang chien-tu* (Hong Kong: Chung-wen ta-hsueh wen-wu kuan, 2001); Ōba Osamu, ed., *Kankan no kenkyū to hatten* (Suita-shi: Kansai University Press, 1993), pp. 12–22 (article by Hsu P'in-fang); and Ōba Osamu, *Mokkan* (Tokyo, 1998).

3. For the discovery, study, and publication of the Chü-yen documents, see Chun-shu Chang 1989, pp. 423–27; and Chun-shu Chang 1987, pp. 5–9. See also *Chü-yen hsin-chien*, introduction; and Hsing I-t'ien, "Fu Ssu-nien, Hu Shih, yü Chü-yen Han-chien te yun-Mei yü fan-T'ai," *Chung-yang yen-chiu yuan li-shih yü-yen yen-chiu so chi-k'an* (*Bulletin of the Institute of History and Philology, Academia Sinica*) (hereafter CYYY) 66, no. 3 (September 1995): 921–52; Hsueh Ying-ch'ün, *Chü-yen Han-chien t'ung-lun* (Lanchow: Kansu chia-yü ch'u-pan she, 1991); and Chien-tu cheng-li hsiao-tsu, *Chü-yen Han-chien pu-pien* (Taipei: Academia Sinica, 1998), pp. 1–5.

4. See Chun-shu Chang 1987, pp. 2–5; and Chun-shu Chang 1989, pp. 419–21, for a

detailed discussion of the history, research, and publication of the Tun-huang documents. See also *Tun-huang Han-chien*, introduction (1: 1–3); *Han-chien yen-chiu wen-chi*, ed. Kansu sheng po-wu kuan (Lanchou, Kansu, 1984), pp. 1–41; and Jao Tsung-i and Li Chün-ming, *Tun-huang Han-chien pien-nien k'ao-cheng* (sometimes titled *Hsin Mang chien chi-cheng*) (Taipei: 1995), pp. 1–10.

5. Chun-shu Chang 1989, p. 423; Chun-shu Chang 1987, p. 5.

6. For the study and publication of the Lop-nor documents, see Chun-shu Chang 1989, pp. 421–22; and Chun-shu Chang 1987, p. 4. See also Hou Ts'an, *Kao-ch'ang Lou-lan yen-chiu lun-chi* (Ürümqi, 1990), esp. pp. 219–333; *Lou-lan Ni-ya*, esp. pp. 1–8; and Meng Fan-jen, *Lou-lan Shan-shan chien-tu nien-tai hsueh yen-chiu* (Ürümqi, 1995), pp. 1–285.

7. For the archaeological work, study, and contents of the Ta-t'ung documents, see Chun-shu Chang 1987, p. 10; and Chun-shu Chang 1989, p. 429.

8. The Hsuan-ch'üan documents have not been published. My use of these documents had constraints under which I agreed to abide. But I have used some of the most important documents for my study and have also quoted some of them. For earlier reports, see *Hsuan-ch'üan Han-chien*. See also Hu P'ing-sheng and Chang Te-fang, *Tun-huang Hsuan-ch'üan Han-chien chien-shih* (Shanghai: Ku-chi, 2001), esp. pp. 200–206.

9. See Chun-shu Chang 1987, pp. 9–19; and Chun-shu Chang 1989, pp. 427–37. In 1983 and 1985, I did archaeological work in the Yung-teng area and found a few wooden documents of the Han period. Another recent discovery is the Yin-wan *Han-chien* (Han era wooden and bamboo documents from Yin-wan), 157 pieces of various sizes uncovered in the spring of 1993 in tombs in Yin-wan Village in the Tung-hai district of Lien-yun-kang in eastern Kiangsu by the sea. These documents, dated from 15 to 10 B.C., provide extremely important materials for the study of the administrative system in the Han local government. See Lien-yun-kang shih po-wu kuan, *Yin-wan Han-mu chien-tu* (Peking: Chung-hua shu-chü, 1996 [1997]), pp. 1–7. All documents discovered in places outside the main areas under study in this book are conveniently collected in *San-chien Han-chien*. See also *Lou-lan Ni-ya*.

10. For a comprehensive discussion of these archaeological finds, see Li Hsueh-ch'in, *Tung-Chou yü Ch'in-tai wen-ming* (Peking: Wen-wu ch'u-pan she, 1981); and Wang Chung-shu, *Han-tai k'ao-ku hsueh kai-shuo* (Peking: Chung-hua shu-chü, 1984). Both Li's and Wang's books are available in English. See Kwang-chih Chang, trans., *Eastern Zhou and Qin Civilizations*, by Li Xueqin (New Haven: Yale University Press, 1985), and *Han Civilization*, by Wang Zhongshu (New Haven: Yale University Press, 1982). See also Chun-shu Chang, "Review of Li Xueqin, *Eastern Zhou and Qin Civilizations*," *American Historical Review* 94, no. 2 (April 1989).

11. For an evaluation of secondary studies on Ch'in-Han China, see Chun-shu Chang, "Ch'in-Han shih yü Ch'in-Han chien-tu yen-chiu chung te i-hsieh wen-t'i," pp. 173–76; and Chun-shu Chang, "Ch'in-Han China in Review," *Studies in Chinese History* 5 (1994): 47–59. At least six hundred monographs and thirteen thousand articles on the Ch'in and Han dynasties have been published in modern times.

CHAPTER I

1. For a systematic discussion of this model, see Chun-shu Chang, "Ku-tai t'un-t'ien chih-tu te yuan-shih yü Hsi-Han Ho-hsi Hsi-yü pien-sai shang t'un-t'ien chih-tu chih fa-chan kuo-ch'eng," in *Ch'ü Wan-li hsien-sheng ch'i-chih jung-ch'ing lun-wen chi* (Taipei, 1978), pp. 563–99 (hereafter Chun-shu Chang 1978). See also chapters 2, 3, and 5 of volume 1 of this book.

2. Chun-shu Chang 1978 has a detailed discussion of this issue (pp. 563–64). See also Yü Hsing-wu, "Ts'ung Chia-ku wen k'an Shang-tai te nung-t'ien k'en-chih," *K'ao-ku* 4 (1972): 40, 41, 45; and Yang K'uan, *Ku-shih hsin-t'an* (Peking, 1965), pp. 160–61.

3. See Chun-shu Chang 1978, p. 565; Fu Ssu-nien, "Chou tung-feng yü Yin i-min," in *Fu Meng-chen hsien-sheng chi*, vol. 4 (Taipei: T'aiwan ta-hsueh, 1952, originally published in 1934), pp. 22–30; the prologue in volume 1 of this book; Chun-shu Chang, "Ch'un-ch'iu Chan-kuo shih-tai chih t'un-t'ien ti-chih yü hsien-chih te ch'u-pu t'an-suo," manuscript; Ch'en P'an, "Ch'un-ch'iu lieh-ch'iang chien-ping k'ao-lueh," *Hsin-ya hsueh-pao* 11, no. 2 (1975): 317–35; Liu Chieh, *Chung-kuo ku-tai tsung-tsu i-chih shih* (reprint; Taipei, 1957), pp. 207–46; and Meng Wen-t'ung, *Chou-ch'in shao-shu min-tsu yen-chiu* (Shanghai, 1958), pp. 8–108.

4. Chun-shu Chang 1978, pp. 565–68; Ch'ü Wan-li, *Shu-yung lun-hsueh chi* (Taipei, 1969), pp. 378–407; Hsu Chung-shu, "Yin-Chou chih-chi shih-chi chih chien-t'ao," CYYY 7, no. 2 (1936): 137–64; Meng Wen-t'ung, "Ku-tai min-tsu hsi-i k'ao," *Yü-kung pan-yueh k'an* 7, nos. 6–7 (June 1937): 13–37; and Chao T'ieh-han, *Ku-shih k'ao-shu* (Taipei, 1956), pp. 141–238, 299–347.

5. *Tso-chuan* (Taipei: Kuang-wen shu-chü, 1963), *chüan* 6, p. 21 (under Hsiang-kung 14), and *chüan* 15, pp. 43–44. For the location of Kua-chou, I have followed Chao T'ieh-han, *Ku-shih k'ao-shu*, pp. 324–26. Old scholarship located Kua-chou in Tun-huang in modern western Kansu Province. Chao's view is more reasonable.

6. For a detailed analysis and documentation of the Ch'in migrations year by year, see Chun-shu Chang 1978, pp. 565–69, 570.

7. See ibid., pp. 569–71, where all Ch'in migrations are listed year by year and analyzed in detail. For a further analysis of the Ch'in patterns and practices of forced population migration, see the prologue in volume 1 of this book.

8. Ssu-ma Ch'ien, *Shih-chi* (1959 ed.; hereafter SC [1959]), pp. 253, 2967; Pan Ku, *Han-shu* (1962 ed.; hereafter HS [1962]), p. 3086; Ssu-ma Kuang, *Tzu-chih t'ung-chien* (1957 ed.), p. 242.

9. SC (1959), pp. 253, 2886; *Shih-chi* (1955 ed.; hereafter SC), p. 462; *Tzu-chih t'ung-chien* (1957 ed.), p. 242.

10. Ch'ang Chü, *Hua-yang kuo-chih* (Shanghai: Shang-wu yin-shu kuan, 1939), p. 35. For the dating of this event, see Chun-shu Chang 1978, p. 570.

11. HS (1962), p. 2286. See also chapter 2.

12. Ibid., p. 2287.

13. Ibid., pp. 2287–89; *Tzu-chih t'ung-chien* (1957), pp. 489–90. The dating of this memorial to 169 B.C. is based on the latter.

14. Chun-shu Chang 1978 (pp. 576–80) has a detailed discussion of the issues discussed here. The organizational structure of the frontier was patterned after the Ch'in and the earlier Ch'i system instituted by Kuan Chung in the seventh century B.C. See the prologue in volume 1 of this book.

15. See Chun-shu Chang 1978, pp. 580–97.

CHAPTER 2

1. The term *Chü-yen region* is used here as it is defined in Bo Sommarström, *Archeological Researches in the Edsen-gol Region, Inner Mongolia*. 2 vols. (Stockholm, 1956–58); and our earlier discussion. After a long process of development, Chü-yen eventually became a *hsien* (district) under the Chang-yeh (Chang-i) *chün*. In consideration of the history of the local administrative system and the evolution of administrative geography

in Former Han China, the term *chün* as a unit of local government is translated as "commandery" if it is dated before 180 B.C., as "province" for 180–90 B.C., and as "prefecture" after 90 B.C. A detailed discussion of this issue and the rationale for this system is given in chapter 4 of volume 1 of this book. Since almost all the *chün* referred to in this study were established after 90 B.C., I have translated it as "prefecture" throughout, with only a few exceptions when this is historically necessary. For a recent examination of the physical geography of the Edsen-gol and the Chü-yen region, also see Ma Hsien-hsing, *Han Chü-yen chih ch'ang-pien* (Taipei, 2001), pp. 27–30; and Erik Norin, comp., *Sven Hedin Central Asia Atlas: Memoir on Maps*, vol. 3: *The Kansu-Hohsi Corridor and the Suloho-Ochinaho Drainage Regions*, by Folke Bergman, with maps and other topographic surveys and images of the Edsen-gol region (Stockholm, 1967).

2. See especially Lao Kan 1960a, pp. 55–56. Other sources on this issue will be cited later.

3. HHS, p. 1337. In Han times, official rank was expressed by the official's salary in terms of so many *shih* of grain, ranging from the 10,000 *shih* to the 100. Actually, the number of *shih* marking the rank of an official did not correspond to his salary. In Former Han times, the officials were generally paid in cash, supplemented at times with a small amount of food, and in the Later Han period they were paid half in cash and half in grain. The recently discovered Yin-wan Han documents throw new light on this issue. See *Yin-wan Han-mu chien-tu*. See also *Wen-wu* 8 (1996): 26–30.

4. Wang Kuo-wei, *Liu-sha chui-chien*, 4 vols. (1914), p. 10 (hereafter cited as Wang Kuo-wei 1914).

5. Lao Kan 1960a, p. 37; L. Carrington Goodrich, trans., "Documents Issuing from the Region of Tun-huang," by Henri Maspero, CYYY 28 (1956): 197–218.

6. See, for example, Michael Loewe, *Records of Han Administration* (Cambridge: Cambridge University Press, 1967), vol. 1, p. 76.

7. For the modern military organization, see Military Service Publishing Co., comp., *The Officer's Guide*, 9th ed. (Harrisburg, PA: Military Service Publishing Co., 1943), p. 33, and *Soldier's Handbook* (Harrisburg, PA: Military Service Publishing Co., 1941), pp. 18–19; National Service Publishing Co., comp., *The R.O.T.C. Manual*, 14th ed. (Washington, DC: National Service Publishing Co., 1931), pp. 16, 45, 70; and U.S. Dept. of the Army, *R.O.T.C. Manual: Operations* (Washington, DC: U.S. Dept. of the Army, 1964), pp. 101–91.

8. It is interesting to note that the organization of the Han garrison system in the Chü-yen region was slightly different from that of the Han garrison in Tun-huang. Some of the official titles found in the Tun-huang documents cannot be found in the Chü-yen documents This again testifies to the understanding that the Han made a special effort to develop specific garrison systems for different frontier regions. In this sense, although the basic structure of the Han garrison systems were the same, each system was unique in its details in order to fit the special local conditions of each frontier region. There were many similar studies after the completion of mine, but all offer different and questionable views. See Wu Ch'ang-lien, *Han-tai pien-chün chang-sui tsu-chih* (Taipei: Wen-hua ta-hsueh, 1983); his review article in *Ming-kuo i-lai kuo-shih yen-chiu yen-chiu te hui-ku yü chan-wang yen-t'ao hui lun-wen chi* (Taipei: Taita, 1992), pp. 179–90; and his article on the numbering of watch stations in *Lao Chen-i hsien-sheng ch'i-shih jung-ch'ing lun-wen chi* (Taipei, 1977). See also Hsing I-t'ien, *Ch'in-Han shih lun-kao* (Taipei: Tung-ta t'u-shu, 1987), the bibliography on *chien-tu* studies, pp. 571–624; Nagata Hedemasa, *Kyoen Kankan kenkyū* (1989); Hsueh Ying-ch'ün, "Han-chien chih-kuan k'ao," in *Ch'in-Han chien-tu lun-wen chi* (Lanchow, 1989), pp. 29–48; and similar articles in the *Chien-tu*

hsueh-pao (Taipei, 1974); *Chien-tu hsueh yen-chiu* (Lanchow, 1996–); and *Chien-tu yen-chiu i-ts'ung* (Peking, 1983–), which present translations of most of Nagata Hedemasa's articles. The articles in the three periodicals generally repeat each other and do not pay attention to each other. For other aspects of the Han system, see Hsu Cho-yun, *Ch'iu-ku lu* (Taipei: Lien-ching, 1982), relevant articles only.

9. It should be pointed out that the various staffs, such as *ling-shih, wei-shih, hou-shih*, and so forth, were composed of military officers rather than civilian officials because they were recorded to have been promoted or transferred to commanding posts. Michael Loewe (1967, vol. 2, p. 387) erred on this point.

10. For a detailed study of these special units, see Chun-shu Chang 1963, pp. 455–66. Other comprehensive studies include Liu Kuang-hua 1988 (*Han-tai Hsi-pei t'un-t'ien yen-chiu*); Ch'en Chih 1986 (*Chü-yen Han-chien yen-chiu*); and Li Ku-yin 1982 (*Han-tai Hsi-pei t'un-t'ien chi-kou ch'u-t'an*). Short articles include Kuan Tung-kuei CYYY 45 (1970); Kuan Tung-kuei CYYY 48 (1977); Chang Jung-fang, "Hsi-Han t'un-t'ien yü si-ch'ou chih lu," in *Chung-kuo shih yen-chiu*, no. 3 (1983); and Chun-shu Chang 1982.

11. A detailed analysis of this is given in Chun-shu Chang 1963, pp. 253–63, 353–82, 402–7; and chapter 4 of this volume.

12. Chun-shu Chang 1963, p. 436.

13. Ibid., pp. 383–86.

14. The final form of table 4 on the whole represents my own interpretation of the rank and pay structure of the Former Han officials in general and the Chü-yen garrison personnel in particular. I have also slightly revised the views I espoused in 1963. The higher rate of cash payment for the same official rank—such as the rate of 1,800 in cash for the *hou-chang*, compared to the rates of 1,600 and 1,200—reflected the salary increases (50 percent) for officials ranked at and below 100 *shih* made in 59 B.C. and for officials ranked at and below 300 *shih* made in 7 B.C. Some of them also seem to reflect the variance of salary rates among the different garrison units. The pay structure in this table represents that of the Former Han period; the officials of the Eastern Han period, as noted in note 3, were paid half in cash and half in grain. In estimating the actual monthly grain payment for garrison officers, I have especially benefited from the discovery of Han wooden documents in Chü-yen in the 1970s and 1980s. These documents include a statement about the official monthly grain pay scale issued in A.D. 27. Since the Eastern Han pay system was adopted after this date, in A.D. 50, this pay scale gives us significant clues about the pay system under the Western Han.

15. My analysis in table 5 represents my interpretation of the administrative structure and possible pay scale of the local governments in Chü-yen based on my research and the works of other scholars. One must bear in mind that the Chü-yen local administrative organizations during the period of our investigation were simpler than those of comparable regions in the interior because Chü-yen was a frontier region protected by extensive garrison forces. My remark on the pay scale issued in A.D. 27 also applies here.

A recent study by Cheng Shih suggests that among county officials the post of *yu-chih* was the creation of a misreading of the Chinese text and did not exist in the Han county administrative structure. This is an incorrect view, as Kao Ming has already pointed out. See Cheng Shih 1978; and Kao Min 1979b. See also Ōba Osamu 1955 (pp. 71–77) for an earlier study of the *se-fu*. Kao Min 1979a is also useful on this issue.

16. This issue is discussed in detail in Chun-shu Chang 1963, pp. 256, 485–86. The title *k'u se-fu* was probably changed to *k'u-tsai* under Wang Mang's Hsin dynasty (A.D. 9–23).

17. For documents concerning the *shang-jen* and *tzu-chia*, see docs. 557.4(169),

267.16(425), 5077, 5732, 4669, Cp1192, and Cp2544. Ch'en Chih (1960, p. 45) maintains that *shang-jen* should read as *p'ang-jen* (*pang-jen*). But the photograph of Cp2544, or 557.4(169), seems to prove the former reading correct. In doc. 214.121, Lao Kan reads the term *tzu-chia* as *tzu-tsu* (214.121[471], 5732). Since its meaning is not understandable, the term *tzu-tsu* has caused speculation among scholars. The editors of the *Chia-pien* read it as *tzu-chia* (Cp1192). A comparison of the photographs of this slip in the *Chia-pien* and Lao Kan 1957 (pl. 356) shows the reading of *tzu-chia* to be correct. For a discussion of *ch'iu-jen* and *yung-jen*, see Lao Kan 1951a, 1960a (pp. 56–57).

18. For the old interpretation of the term *t'ien-tsu* see, for example, Ch'en Chih 1958, p. 5. In the old editions of the *K'ao-shih*, Lao Kan reads *san-chiu jen* (thirty-nine men) in doc. 1746 as *nien-chiu jen* (twenty-nine men) (514.38). The former reading is correct.

19. Doc. Cp1590. See also docs. 510.20(227), 534.6(330), and Cp11.

20. Doc. 140.15(473) or 6605.

21. For the sake of local security and administrative purposes, registration of both military and civil residents was carried out in Chü-yen. The form of the register was varied so as to reflect the status and position of the person being registered. This topic is discussed in detail in Chun-shu Chang 1963, pp. 147–53; and chapter 5 of this volume.

22. Docs. 306.1(256), 194.20(308).

23. Docs. 337.35(255), 229.20(468).

24. Docs. 214.126(399), 214.7(404).

25. HS (1962), p. 221.

26. There are many documents concerning (*ku-li*) Chien in the Chü-yen documents. See, for example, docs. 273.8(331), 308.45(330), and 148.48(321). For the word *shu*, Lao Kan reads *shu* or *yu*; Mori Shikazō reads *yu* (Mori 1959a). This is not correct. The photographs of docs. 295.19 and 148.47 on pp. 394 and 395 in Lao Kan 1957 clearly show that the word is *shu*, which is the ancient form of *shu* according to strips 3851 and 2351.

27. This point is discussed in detail in Chun-shu Chang 1963, pp. 253–60.

28. HS (1962), p. 3244; Lao Kan 1960a, p. 56.

29. Similarly, one wooden document, Cp2042A, reads in part "Tai-pa ju-lü." There was a law governing this procedure. Doc. 505 in Chavannes 1913 indicates that the neglect of this law would result in punishment.

30. Doc. 40.14(466).

31. A *ku-hsia* was a place of execution. See HHS 47, p. 246, including the commentary on this term by Li Hsien (A.D. 651–85). Two other documents also record this term: Cp2179 and 509.16(227). From the content of these documents, a *ku-hsia* seems to have been a garrison office or gathering place. This needs further investigation. See doc. Cp2179 in Ch'en Pang-huai 1961, p. 457. Lao Kan (1949) deciphered this document incorrectly (513.29, p. 504). The photograph of this strip in the *Chia-pien* shows that both the editors of the *Chia-pien* and Ch'en were correct.

32. Lao Kan reads Chü-yen instead of *tsai* (at) in this doc. 285.10(237); *tsai* is the correct reading.

33. Doc. 3498 in Lao Kan 1960a. A similar record is also found in Édouard Chavannes's Tun-huang documents, no. 38 on p. 18 (Chavannes 1913). In this document, Chavannes translated *pa-tsu* as "soldat retraite" and explained it "un soldat qui quitte le service." See also doc. 66 in Chavannes 1913.

34. Docs. 4121–4122(206.24) and 3273. Also compare the phrase "Pa-shih wu-wu" in *Kuan-tzu*, (*Ssu-pu pei-yao* ed.), *chüan*, 8, p. 11. It seems that this regulation is an old military tradition in ancient China.

35. The photograph of this strip is on p. 328 of Lao Kan 1957. *Pan* was incorrectly deciphered as *pien* in Lao Kan 1949, 317.28 (148).

36. This is based on doc. 5355, pl. 325.

37. For another example, see doc. 3273.

38. The full text reads "Tao pa-fu Fu Mu kuo-pi ch'ü" (Going to *pa-fu* Fu Mu's *pi* by the *kuo* [city walls]).

39. For a detailed account of the campaigns, see Chun-shu Chang 1966a, pp. 151–66.

40. HS (1962), p. 2986.

41. The word *ch'ing* in this document is just a polite expression (*mei-ch'eng*). See Ch'en P'an 1947, pp. 323–24. Another possible reading of this document is to consider Wei as a surname ("*Mu-tsu-li* Wei," meaning "Officer Wei who is in charge of hired soldiers"). But the other reading seems to be more plausible according to the context.

42. In Huang Wen-pi's collection of Han wooden documents, one reads "*ying-mu shih* Ch'ang-ling Jen-li *ta-fu* Sun Shang" (Huang Wen-pi 1948, no. 30, p. 201).

> Sun Shang, a hired soldier, from Jen *li* of Ch'ang-ling [District, of Tso P'ing-i] with the rank of *ta-fu*.

The form of this register is the same as those of regular garrison soldiers and farming soldiers in the Chü-yen region. See note 21. Here the *ying-mu-shih* even had the rank of *ta-fu*, the fifth aristocratic rank.

43. Doc. 224.18(49). The decipherment of this document in Lao Kan 1960a is slightly different (no. 3841). I have checked the photograph of this strip on page 198 of Lao Kan 1957 and corrected his mistake.

44. In Chavannes's collection of Tun-huang documents, there are records of *fu-su* (carrying unhusked grains) and *fu-ma* (carrying hemp); see docs. 95 and 96. Chavannes incorrectly deciphered *fu* (to carry) as *mi* (to search for); the photographs of these strips are clear enough to make this correction. However, this error was not corrected in the THHCW. Wang Kuo-wei's reading of the word *fu* is correct (1914, vol. 2, p. 25b).

45. Lao Kan 1960a, no. 5491.

46. Chavannes 1913, nos. 279–81, 282, 283, 286. Wang's study is a detailed one (1914, vol. 2, pp. 25a–b).

47. See Chun-shu Chang 1963, pp. 124–31 (*sheng-tsu*).

48. This study is based solely on the Chü-yen documents and literary evidence. The Tun-huang documents offer no help in our understanding of the term *sheng-tsu*. See ibid.

49. For similar reports, see docs. 536.14(103), 176.18(233), 3126, and 3571. The phrase "kan yen chih" in this document is a customary expression in an official document submitted by a lower office to a higher office. For a detailed discussion of this, see Wang Kuo-wei 1914, vol. 2, p. 5; and Hsia Nai 1948, p. 252.

50. For a similar record, see doc. 4055.

51. Perhaps the word *san* (three) in this document should be *ssu* (four). Lao Kan considers *ti-ko* a single term denoting a granary or treasury (1960a, p. 46). But this slip indicates that there is a distinction between the two; presumably the *ti* is a storeroom for ordinary materials and the *ko* is used for cash and other precious materials.

52. I have revised the interpretation of the original document. The interpretations of this strip in the *Chia-pien* and *Ho-chiao* are partly incorrect. Ch'en Chih's study of this document is also incorrect.

53. For similar records, see docs. Cp8 and 1080.

54. For further examples, see docs. 231.48(223), 203.1(186), Cp1475B, and Cp1307.

55. For an interpretation of the term *fu-chi* in this document, see Yü Hao-liang 1961, p. 455. Yü considers *fu-chi* in this document to be an instruction from the office of the Chang-yeh governor, which is incorrect.

56. Yü Hao-liang 1963a, pp. 44, 46.

57. Ibid., p. 46. References to the *Han-shu* can be found on pp. 272 and 2987 in HS (1962).

58. A *sui* in which a *hou-chang* resided was called a *chu-sui* (head *sui*); see doc. 5463: "ti-shih pu chu-sui chih-so" (The headquarters of the command watch station of the tenth *pu*). See also Lao Kan 1960a, p. 44.

59. *Tang-wang-sheng*, T'o-t'o *sheng*. For another example, see doc. 285.12, pl. 371 (Lao Kan incorrectly read *sheng* as *tang* in doc. 5888).

60. For the form of *sheng* in *tao-sheng* (arrived at the *sheng*), cf. *sheng* in doc. 203.1 on pl. 133 in Lao Kan 1957.

61. Although docs. 2753, 4242, and 9889 record that the *sheng-tsu* were commanded by *sui-chang* (watch station commanders) to go to the *hou-kuan* headquarters, they cannot be interpreted as having belonged to *sui* on this basis. For *sui-chang* are also recorded to have commanded *pu-tsu* (*pu* soldiers) and *chang-tsu* (*chang* soldiers), who definitely did not belong to *sui*. See docs. 4199, Cp508, Cp765, and Cp1291. Perhaps one of the various duties of a *sui-chang* was periodically commanding soldiers of his *hou* or *pu* to go to the *hou-kuan* or any higher office for special service.

62. For the works of *chang-tsu* and *sheng-tsu*, cf. docs. 629, 3955, 4464, 4648, 4670, and 5976.

63. Pl. 317 in Lao Kan 1957. Lao did not use the word *hou* in doc. 5262.

64. Judging from the form, particularly the word *yu* (right), this document is part of an account of soldiers reporting from a lower office to the *hou-kuan*.

65. Yang Lien-sheng 1950, p. 102. Professor Yang's view is a slight revision of his former theory that *sheng* in *sheng-tsu* refers to the *hou-chang* office or the *hou-kuan*.

66. See doc. 78.46 on pl. 213 (*sheng-chiao*), doc. 338.27 on pl. 428 (*sheng-chiao*), doc. 133.11 on pl. 216 (*sheng-fa*), doc. 214.118 on pl. 488 (*sheng-chih*), doc. 254.17 on pl. 229 (*sheng* Tien-pei), doc. 218.11 on pl. 146 (*sheng wei-fu*), doc. 87.8 on pl. 19 (*sheng tsai fu*), doc. 285.1 on pl. 371 (*sheng* Tien-pei), doc. 58.5 on pl. 119 (*sheng chü-tso*), and doc. 551.15 on pl. 121 (*sheng ch'u-tso*). See also Cp431 (*sheng chih*) and Cp1390 (*sheng ch'u*). It should be pointed out that the translation "*hou* headquarters" can also be used to interpret the word *sheng* in these cases.

67. There are still more suggestions. Taking a slightly different view from Yü Hao-liang, Michael Loewe (1967, vol. 1, p. 81; vol. 2, p. 105) holds that *sheng-tsu* "were conscripts detached from their proper units for special duties elsewhere," thus interpreting *sheng* as "to detach [from]." Itō Michiharu (1953, p. 32) suggests the translation "inspection" or "patrol" (*hsun-ch'a*) for *sheng* in doc. 285.1 or Cp1537. These theories either suffer the same criticism as Yü Hao-liang's, such as the translation "detachment," or are too narrow to interpret all the *sheng* documents, as in the case of "inspection."

68. A comprehensive discussion of the *Mu-shih* documents and their interpretation is given in Chun-shu Chang 1965a; and Chun-shu Chang 1977, pp. 171–79. The dating of the *Mu-shih* documents ranges from 88 to 85 B.C.

69. Mori Shikazō 1959a; Chun-shu Chang 1978, p. 588.

70. HS (1962), p. 1139; Nancy Lee Swann, *Food and Money in Ancient China*, trans. and annotated by Nancy Lee Swann (Princeton, 1950), pp. 186–87, 190.

71. HS (1962), p. 229; Dubs, vol. 2, p. 168. English translation is based on Dubs.

72. According to Lao Kan, Minister of Finance Tiao in this document is Fei Tiao, who held this position in the Yung-kuang period of Emperor Yüan (43–39 B.C.). See Lao Kan 1960a, pp. 54, 61.

73. Chun-shu Chang 1965a, p. 3. For the status of the *mu-shih* in the pre-Ch'in era and the Southern and Northern dynasties period, see Chun-shu Chang 1977, pp. 178–79.

74. This term will be discussed later.

75. *Chien* (to see) *hsien* is *hsien* (to be present). See Wang Ch'ung, *Lun-heng chi-chieh*, p. 553. It seems that Alfred Forke missed this point in his translation of the *Lun-heng* (*Lun-heng, Wang Ch'ung's Essays*, vol. 1, 450). See also the *Biography of Wang Mang* in the HS (1962), p. 4158 (Yen Shih-ku's commentary on p. 4159); and HS. In the second wooden document, the use of *chien* (*hsien*) instead of *tsai* (at), as in the first one, seems to be related to the use of *yu* (right). *Chien* was used here to indicate that it was so at the time of the writing of the report.

76. As will be discussed later, doc. 5184 in Lao 1960a indicates "*t'o-hsien min*," meaning that only the family members of people from other districts lived in the *kuan* (the headquarters of a commandant area).

77. Yang Lien-sheng 1950; Yoneda Kenjirō 1954; Mori Shizakō 1960.

78. Yang Lien-sheng 1961, pp. 109–10; 1950, 99–100. Also see the papers of Yoneda Kenjirō, and Mori Shikazō cited in note 77; Fujieda Akira 1955a, p. 327; and Ch'en P'an 1947, pp. 319–21. For the term *ta-nan*, see docs. 1984 and 6797 in Lao Kan 1960a.

79. Docs. 303.9(248), 62.54(452), 123.18(598), 37.58(455), 37.7(626). These terms are also seen in HS (1962), p. 2986; SC (1959), p. 3176; and Huang Wen-pi 1948, p. 204. Doc. 4992 mentions the term *liang-chia-tzu*, but it is a document issued by the central government. Otherwise, *liang-chia-tzu* are not recorded in the Chü-yen documents. In the Tun-huang documents, there are a number of documents with *liang-chia-tzu*. See Édouard Chavannes 1913, nos. 310, 312; and Wang Kuo-wei 1914, vol. 2, p. 22. In *Fu-ping chih-tu k'ao-shih*, Ku Chi-kuang discusses in detail the problem of *liang-chia-tzu* and the private followers in the Han army (1962, pp. 282–90).

80. Doc. 303.9(248); HS (1962), p. 2986.

81. Docs. 123.18(598), 123.34(458).

82. Yü Hao-liang 1961, pp. 451–52.

83. The word *chi* means *chi-nu*, which is another name for the *lien-nu* (crossbow). See Chun-shu Chang 1963, p. 487 (n. 94).

84. Lao Kan 1960a, pp. 56–57.

85. For a discussion of grain provisions for the followers, see Chun-shu Chang 1963, pp. 324–25, 504 (n. 212). For the register form of the followers, see chapter 5 of this volume.

86. Docs. 62.54(452), 504.10(447).

87. Docs. 509.16(227) (recording two *t'u*), 269.7(247), 269.11(254), 3.33(428A) (four *t'u*), 513.29 (ten *t'u*); nos. 259.1, 37.1, 14.26, 34.8, in Lao Kan 1943–44, vol. 1, pp. 73; vol. 2, pp. 18a, 24, 226. A comprehensive discussion of traditional interpretations of the term *t'u* is given in Martin Wilbur, *Slavery in China during the Former Han Dynasty, 206 B.C.–A.D. 25* (Chicago, 1943), pp. 80–81. See also A. F. P. Hulsewé, *Remnants of Han Law*, vol. 1 (Leiden, 1955), p. 130.

88. Doc. 37.1(215) or 6797; pl. 425 in Lao Kan, 1957.

89. Nos. 14.26, 168.19, 40.1 in Lao Kan 1943–44, vol. 2, pp. 26b, 226; vol. 1, p. 84.

For the traditional interpretation of *ch'eng-tan* (building walls or fortifications and standing guard from early dawn) and other technical aspects of this problem, see Chang Cheng-lang 1958, pp. 179–83; Wu Jung-tseng, pp. 193–94; and A. F. P. Hulsewé 1955, pp. 128–30. See also Wei Hung, *Han-chiu-i*, part B, p. 9b.

90. Docs. 14.26(226), 34.8(231), 193.6(392.3), 60.2(449), 37.58(455), 293.9(621).

91. They believed the term *fu-tso* referred to convicts serving three months to one year, especially female convicts. See *Han-chiu-i*, part B, p. 9b; and HS (1962), p. 236 (Li's commentary on the term *fu-tso*).

92. HS (1962), pp. 236, 2286–87, 1135 (*t'u-fu-tso*); Dubs, vol. 2, p. 200, note 14; Édouard Chavannes 1895–1905, vol. 3, p. 180, n. 96, and vol. 3, p. 544, n. 1; Nancy Lee Swann 1950, p. 172; A. F. P. Hulsewé 1955, pp. 240–41; Martin Wilbur 1943, pp. 283–85.

93. A. F. P. Hulsewé 1955, 241.

94. Docs. 188.27(228), 160.10(232), 485.66(234), 227.8(235), 279.21(236), 269.11(254), 237.13(254), 464.3(340), 146.97(342), 71.65(460), 308.19(473), 157.97(515), 268.3(579), 118.17(126), 552.3(128). For the traditional interpretation of *ch'ih-hsing*, see Wu Jung-tseng, "Han hsing-t'u chuan chih tsa-shih," *K'ao-ku* 3 (1977): 193–96, at 194.

95. An example of this is given in doc. 628 in Lao Kan 1960a. It records in part "T'u Hsu Fang, shih-hsing Hu Ch'ang." In his interpretation, Lao Kan reads *ku* rather than *hu*. See the photograph of this strip on p. 31 in Lao Kan 1957. Here the *t'u* and the *ch'ih-hsing* are clearly separate. See also doc. 227.8(235) or 5271.

96. See Chun-shu Chang 1963, pp. 319, 325. The monthly grain provision for the *ch'ih-hsing* was 3 *shih* of *su* (millet). See also docs. 237.13(254), 464.3(340), and 6575.

97. See Chun-shu Chang 1963, p. 152. See also docs. 337.8(142), 71.65(460), 188.27(228), and 552.3(128).

98. In his three decipherments of the original Chinese doc.—118.17(26), 1970, and Lao Kan 1943–44, vol. 1, p. 13b—Lao Kan reads *wu-shih* (fifty) as *wu-ch'ien* (five thousand). This is a mistake. However, when he cited this document in his *K'ao-cheng* Lao gave the correct reading *wu-shih* (1943–44, vol. 1, p. 48; 1960a, p. 23). But most scholars still cite it as *wu-ch'ien*. For *chiang-chü*, the *Chia-pien* reads *chiang-chün* (general), which is a mistake.

99. In A. F. P. Hulsewé's study (1955, p. 242), a list of occasions when the *ch'ih-hsing* were employed is given.

100. HS (1962), pp. 3922–23.

101. See Chun-shu Chang 1963, p. 152. Furthermore, no strips in the Chü-yen documents record that a *fu-tso* received any kind of provisions. Of all the wooden documents, only doc. 487 in Édouard Chavannes 1913 records the *t'u* as receiving grain provisions. Perhaps it only indicates the amount of food the *t'u* should receive. For the convicts in the Tun-huang area, see nos. 536, 92, and 701 in Chavannes 1913.

102. Docs. 337.8(442), 37.58(455), 37.1(215), 227.8(235).

103. Docs. 505.33(371), 5289, 37.35(455).

104. Docs. 37.35(455), 306.16(372), 160.2(558), 8985.

105. Doc. 227.39 or no. 5558 in Lao Kan 1960a, 283.11(474).

106. Doc. 37.35(455). On the same strip, the price of a Han acre is recorded as one hundred in cash; therefore, an adult female slave was equivalent to the price of 200 Han acres of land and an underage male slave 150 acres. For a detailed analysis of this, see Chun-shu Chang 1978, pp. 586–87.

107. See, for example, docs. 15.9(27) and 505.12(421).

108. See, for example, docs. 280.4(419), 62.13(423), and 502.6(422). As doc. 280.4 and other sources indicate, Ching-chao was called Ching-chao-yin in Han times.

109. Docs. 503.17(22), 20.12(20), 148.20(174), 179.9(23), 255.27(173), 183.13(172).

110. Doc. 503.17(22).

111. Doc. 255.27(172).

112. Doc. 40.1(173–74).

113. Lao Kan incorrectly reads *shih* (to loan) as *kuan* (string). The decipherment on which the translation is based is a new one based on a photograph of the original strip. According to the photograph, the first line in the second half of this document was not written at the same time as the rest. The two are probably not related.

114. For a different interpretation of the term *k'o-chü*, see Ch'en P'an 1960, pp. 209–10. Professor Ch'en did not use this document in his study, and he translated *k'o-chü* as "to live at someone's place as an indentured laborer."

115. This translation is based on a new decipherment of the original strip. Neither the editors of the *Chia-pien* (Cp1664) nor Lao Kan (doc. 7110) read this document correctly. For the most recent material on *k'o-min*, see Chü-yen I, p. 31.

116. HHS, p. 312; Chü-yen I, p. 31.

117. According to the *Shih-chi* and the *Han-shu*, after the surrender of the Hsiung-nu in Ho-hsi in 121 B.C. the Han established five Dependent States as habitations for these surrendered people. See HS (1962), p. 176; and SC (1959), p. 2934. Since neither of these histories gives the exact location of the five Dependent States beyond the indication that they were located beyond the old frontier barriers of five northern Han border prefectures, there has long been controversy on this point. See Kamada Shigeo 1949, pp. 287ff; Yen Keng-wang 1961, pp. 157–59; and Lao Kan 1952b, pp. 26–30. Part of this controversy arises from the scholars' failure to understand that some of the five border prefectures in the northwest had their outer boundaries moved several times as a result of the Han military expansion after 120 B.C., that some of the five Dependent States were relocated; and that a few new Dependent States were established after 120 B.C. Lao Kan suggested that the Chang-yeh Dependent State was in Jih-le. This wooden document indicates that the people of a dependent state were already in the area of the second watch station as early as 90 B.C. The colonization of this part of the Chü-yen region did not start until 103 B.C.; consequently, the establishment of a dependent state in this area must have taken place sometime between 103 and 90 B.C. If Lao Kan is right, we may conclude that a new dependent state was established in the Chü-yen region in the earliest stage of its colonization. Like all other Han establishments in the region, it was presumably also under the command of the Chü-yen chief commandant (probably Lu Po-te). But later this Dependent State in Chü-yen probably came under the jurisdiction of the office of the Director of Dependent States (*tien shu-kuo*) in the central government, to which all Dependent States were normally subordinated. In 28 B.C., the Directorate of Dependent States was abolished and incorporated into the Office of the Grand Herald (*Ta hung-lu*), and all the Dependent States came under the jurisdiction of the governments of the various *chün* where they were located. The fact that the Dependent State in Chü-yen had been under the jurisdiction of the Chü-yen chief commandant for only a relatively short period explains the scarcity of wooden documents concerning the affairs of the Dependent State in the Chü-yen region. See HS (1962), p. 735; and Cp34. The other subordinates under the chief commandant of a dependent state included the *ch'eng* (assistant chief commandant) and the *hou* (commandants).

118. Lao Kan 1957, vol. 1, p. 9; Itō Michiharu 1953, p. 49.

119. For a similar example, see HS (1962), p. 3775.

120. A detailed analysis of these documents is given in chapter 5 of this volume.

121. I have arranged the following translations slightly differently than the way they are presented in chapter 5 of this volume.

122. Doc. 1517 in Lao Kan 1960a; pl. 74 in Lao Kan 1957. In the wooden documents of the Chin period found in Niya by Aurel Stein, similar registers of the age and physical characteristics of certain Central Asians (*yueh-chih*) clearly use *hei-se* (black) to describe the skin color, not the hair, of the registrants. These documents are only of the late third century and certainly can be used to affirm our view that *hei-se* in similar Chü-yen registers describes the skin color not the hair color of the registrants. See Aurel Stein 1907, vol. 1, p. 537, docs. N. XV. 53, N. XV. 152. See also Wang Kuo-wei 1914, vol. 3, p. 9 (doc. nos. 29, 31).

123. Chun-shu Chang 1966c; Chun-shu Chang 1977, pp. 180–99.

124. Two persons are recorded to have been above 7 *ch'ih*, but the exact figures are not known because the strips are either broken or damaged. See docs. 6579 and 6574.

125. For studies of the stature of modern Chinese, see Li Chi 1928, pp. 30–33; Alfred Cort Haddon, *The Races of Man and Their Distribution*, rev. ed. (Cambridge, England, 1925), pp. 8, 30; Carlton S. Coon, *The Living Races of Man* (New York, 1965), p. 149; Jui I-fu (Ruey Yifu) 1977, p. 497; and Yang Hsi-mei 1969, pp. 312–13.

126. For an analysis of the doubtful case, see Chun-shu Chang 1966b, pp. 179–80; and Chun-shu Chang 1977, p. 197.

127. Five of the seventeen Ho-hsi natives held orders of rank, with one *shang-tso* from Wu-wei and one *ta-fu* and three *kung-ch'eng* from Chang-yeh. Similarly, five of the interior residents are known to have been rank holders, with two *kung-ch'eng* from Ho-nan and one *ta-fu* each from Ho-nei, Tung, and Wei. The person of tawny color, who was very likely a civilian, cannot be geographically identified.

128. For a detailed discussion of the issue under consideration and the complex racial composition of ancient China, see Chun-shu Chang 1977, pp. 8–14, 199, 200–217 (Yang Hsi-mei).

129. During the period in question, some of the prefectures (*chün*) and kingdoms (*kuo*) functioned for only a limited period and were then given different names and statuses. These changes can be sketched as follows.

> Ch'ang-i *kuo*: Ch'ang-i *kuo* from 97 B.C. to about 73 B.C.; thereafter Shan-yang *chün* until 34 B.C. when the name was changed to Shan-yang *kuo*. It was changed to Shan-yang *chün* again in 27 B.C.
>
> Chi-yin *kuo*: Chi-yin *kuo* from 144 to 52 B.C.; thereafter Ting-t'ao *kuo* until 48 B.C., when it was changed to Chi-yin *chün*. It was Ting-t'ao *kuo* again from 25 to 5 B.C.
>
> Huai-yang *kuo*: Huai-yang *chün* from 169 to 63 B.C.; thereafter Huai-yang *kuo*.
>
> P'ing-kan *kuo*: Established as P'ing-kan *kuo* in 91 B.C. and changed to Kuang-p'ing *kuo* in 56 B.C.
>
> Tung-p'ing *kuo*: Ta-ho *chün* from 116 to 52 B.C.; thereafter Tung-p'ing *kuo*.

The sources for this account are HS 28; Ku Tsu-yü, *Tu-shih fang-yü chi-yao*, *chüan* 2; Hsü T'ien-lin, *Hsi-Han hui-yao*, *chüan* 64; and Hibino Takeo 1953.

130. It is significant to note that while Chang-yeh registers seventeen garrison sol-

diers (see table 9) it records only one farming soldier. This supports the point that some of the farming soldiers were recruited specifically as such. For if they were only garrison soldiers assigned to farming work, more farming soldiers from Chang-yeh would have appeared in this table.

131. This is also true for the Tun-huang garrisons, as is seen in the Tun-huang documents. See THHCW, Henri Maspero 1953; and *Tun-huang Han-chien*. But cf. Wolfram Eberhard's analysis of the Tun-huang data (1955a, pp. 84–86; also 1967, pp. 85–87); Professor Eberhard also lists Ho-nei and Tung-p'ing in modern Hopei, and Chi-yin in modern Honan. He seems to have taken some practice writings and correspondence as the official records of soldiers. In fact, the Tun-huang documents record no Han *soldiers* from the border regions of T'ien-shui, An-ting, Lung-hsi, and Chin-ch'eng.

132. Lao Kan 1960a, p. 56; Ch'en Chih 1958, p. 6.

133. Lao Kan 1960a, p. 56; Yen Keng-Wang 1961, p. 358.

134. The twenty orders of aristocratic rank are as follows.

1. *Kung-shih*
2. *Shang-tsao*
3. *Tsan-niao*
4. *Pu-keng*
5. *Ta-fu*
6. *Kuan ta-fu*
7. *Kung ta-fu* (or *Ch'i ta-fu*)
8. *Kung-ch'eng*
9. *Wu ta-fu*
10. *Tso shu-chang*
11. *Yu shu-chang*
12. *Tso-keng*
13. *Chung-keng*
14. *Yu-keng*
15. *Shao shang-tsao*
16. *Ta shang-tsao*
17. *Ssu-chü shu-chang*
18. *Ta shu-chang*
19. *Kuan-nei hou*
20. *Ch'e-hou* (*t'ung-hou, lieh-hou*)

135. See chapter 1, note 62 of volume 1 of this book.

136. For an examination of some of the issues discussed here, see Sun Yü-t'ang 1937, pp. 46–49; Shimizu Taiji 1930, pp. 4–6; Ōshima Riichi 1955, p. 3; Nishijima Sadao 1961, pp. 141–48; Chun-shu Chang 1978, pp. 573–76; and chapter 1 of volume 1 of this book.

137. See chapter 1 of volume 1 of this book.

138. Chun-shu Chang 1963, pp. 295–97; Ch'en P'an 1951b; Ch'en Chih 1958, pp. 24–25; Chun-shu Chang 1978, p. 586.

139. For examples of bestowals of aristocratic rank, see Nishijima Sadao 1961, pp. 206–7.

140. For a similar record, see doc. 162.6(513). For the record of this particular bestowal of rank by Emperor Yuan in the *Han-shu*, see HS (1962), p. 288.

141. Several additional remarks can be made about the translation of this document.

1. Michael Loewe reads *she-ling* in this document as a single term (1960, p. 119). Obviously, this is questionable. It should read "*she, ling-ssu*" (see the text in the *Yuan-ti-chi* in the *Han-shu* cited later in this note). There are several other examples in the *Hou-Han shu* that can serve to validate this reading. They are cited in Nishijima Sadao 1961, pp. 90–92. Doc. 162.14(478) also provides evidence for this point.
2. According to the *Han-chiu-i*, "*Ssu (min) chueh i-chi*" should be "to bestow *kung-shih* on the commoners"; "*Ssu (min) chueh erh-chi*," *shang-tsao*; "*Ssu (min) chueh san-chi*," *tsan-niao*; and so forth. See *Han-chiu-i*, B, p. 6a; and Nishijima Sadao 1961, pp. 220–21. Lao Kan's decipherment of this slip was incomplete. Loewe says: "The significance of the words *san-chi* is not understood" (p. 120). But, according to the photograph of this slip and the method of bestowing ranks, Nishijima Sadao (1961, p. 223) reconstructs this part as: "*i-ch'ou chao ssu-chueh san-chi*." This is correct.
3. This event is also recorded in the *Yuan-ti-chi* in the *Han-shu*: "*Ta-she T'ien-hsia, ssu-min-chueh i-chi*" (HS, 1962, p. 288).

Dubs's translation reads as follows (Dubs, vol. 2, p. 321).

Let a general amnesty [be granted] to the Empire, and [let there be] granted to the common people, one step in noble rank.

142. For the record of these particular bestowals of aristocratic rank in the *Han-shu*, see HS (1962), pp. 223, 229, 242, 243, 254, 255, 257, 259. See also Nishijima Sadao 1961, pp. 206, 233, 275.

143. The *niao* (bird) in *Luan-niao* in the document under consideration was traditionally considered to be a *wu* (crow); the photograph of this strip proves that *niao* is the correct reading.

144. HS (1962), p. 2652.

145. Kamada Shigeo 1949, pp. 33–63; Michael Loewe 1960, p. 105.

146. SC (1959), p. 2794.

147. For the technical details of this point, see Chun-shu Chang 1966b, pp. 190–92.

148. Of the twenty orders of aristocratic rank, only the highest, *lieh-hou*, was recorded to have been hereditary, though generally with a reduced fief, in Han written literature. There is no evidence that the other orders were also hereditary. The same was true of the Ch'in system. See Liao Pai-yüan 1973, pp. 102, 163–70.

149. For the Chü-yen documents, see, for example, docs. 501.1(447), 50.15(453), 157.9(498), 509.18(428B), 62.1(452), 211.17(168), and 517.1(445). For sources in the *Shih-chi* and *Han-shu*, see SC (1959), pp. 214, 2337, 3094; and HS (1962), pp. 141, 549.

150. For contemporary views, see HS (1962), pp. 141 (156 B.C.), 2152 (122 B.C.); and SC (1959), p. 3094 (122 B.C.).

151. *Han chiu-i*, B, p. 9b. For a detailed discussion of the reading of the text in the *Han chiu-i*, see Chun-shu Chang 1966b, pp. 190–92.

152. Ju Shun's and Yen Shih-ku's views can be found in the commentaries on the *Shih-chi* and *Han-shu*. See SC (1959), pp. 217, 3078; and HS (1962), pp. 141, 550, 2142.

153. Li Ch'i's commentary on the *Han-shu*. See HS (1962), p. 141. Wang Ming-sheng's view is found in his *Shih-ch'i shih shang-chueh*, vol. 1, p. 10. Wang made a clear distinction between *tuo-chüeh* (to be deprived of noble rank) and *mien-kuan* (to be dismissed from office) and believed that a person whose noble rank was taken away could

still keep his official post. See Chun-shu Chang 1966b, p. 235, for a detailed discussion of this point.

154. HS, p. 80; Dubs, vol. 1, p. 312.

155. Tung Yüeh, Ch'i-kuo k'ao, p. 349; Shen Chia-pen, Han-lü che-i, in Shen Chi-i hsien-sheng i-shu, sec. 10, pp. 14b–15a. The views of modern scholars have generally followed one of these sources and hence are omitted here.

156. Lao Kan incorrectly reads shih-wu as wu-shih (fifty); the photograph in the Chia-pien clearly indicates that shih-wu is correct.

157. In the last edition of the Shih-wen, Lao Kan deciphers Chao An-ta in this document instead of Chao An-shih.

158. Under the Huai-yang kuo in Han-shu 28B, there are districts called Ning-p'ing and Hsin-p'ing but not Ch'ang-p'ing. According to the wooden documents, there was certainly a Ch'ang-p'ing District in Huai-yang (docs. 1474, 1477, 1481, 1479; pl. 71). There are two possible explanations for this: (1) Ch'ang-p'ing in the wooden documents is incorrect or either Ning-p'ing or Hsin-p'ing in the Han-shu is incorrect; and (2) Huai-yang Prefecture has a territory that is different, either partly or wholly, from that of Huai-yang kuo. I prefer the first explanation.

159. Lao Kan did not interpret this as Huang.

160. For more examples of similar registers of shih-wu, see docs. 211.17(168) and 62.1(452). For further study of this issue, see Chun-shu Chang 1963, pp. 147–51.

161. Compare the interpretation of shih-wu given by Liu Hai-nien in 1978. Without reference to recent studies of the term, Liu reaches the conclusion that shih-wu simply referred to adult males (age twenty to sixty) *without* or *deprived of* aristocratic rank. This partly contradicts our conclusion. Liu did not consult the Chü-yen documents for his study. See Liu Hai-nien 1978, pp. 58–62, esp. p. 61. One Tun-huang document also records an officer who was a shih-wu. A clear discussion of this case is given in Wang Kuo-wei 1914, vol. 2, pp. 10a–10b. For other brief discussions of the term shih-wu, see Moriya Mitsuo 1957, pp. 94–96; and Nishijima Sadao 1961, pp. 217–18.

162. See also SC (1959), p. 232; HS, p. 80; Dubs, vol. 1, p. 312; and Nishijima Sadao 1961, pp. 247–63. A wooden document discovered in 1974 at P'o-ch'eng-tzu gives further credence to my interpretation of nan-tzu. See Chü-yen I, p. 31.

163. It must be noted at this point that some scholars hold that there was a distinction between shih-wu and nan-tzu; others reject such a view. For instance, Hulsewé indicates that he has been unable to discover whether there was a distinction between the two. See A. F. P. Hulsewé 1955, pp. 217–18.

164. This translation is based on my new reading of the original controversial text, which differs from readings suggested by other scholars on Han institutions. For my detailed discussions of other possible readings and the bases for my own reading, see Chun-shu Chang 1966b, pp. 190–92. For the Chinese text, see Han chiu-i, B, p. 9b.

165. Hsün Yüeh (A.D. 148–209), Ch'ien-Han chi, p. 39. In the Han-shu version of this passage, the word mien is read as wan (to complete). On the basis of the reading in the Ch'ien-Han chi, Wang Hsien-ch'ien (1842–1918) suggests that wan in the Han-shu should be changed to mien (HS, p. 61). Shen Chia-pen also makes this point. Perhaps such a change is unnecessary. The word mien in the Ch'ien-Han chi really meant mien-lao (exemption from mutilating punishment for the elderly), and hence wan and lao all meant the same thing in this case. For a discussion of the Han institution of mien-lao, see Chun-shu Chang 1966b, p. 192; for Shen Chia-pen's view, see his Han-lü che-i, pp. 14b–15a.

166. See, for example, Hsün Yüeh, *Ch'ien-Han chi*, p. 93 (141 B.C., Emperor Ching); HS (1962), pp. 258 (62 B.C., Emperor Hsuan); and 356 (A.D. 4, Emperor P'ing). See also HS (1962), p. 1106.

167. Evidently, seventy was the standard determination for old age (*lao*) in ancient China. This was clearly defined in the classic *Li-chi* (Book of Rites) and the dictionary *Shuo-wen chieh-tzu* (Script Explained and Characters Elucidated) by Hsü Shen (fl. A.D. 100–121). See *Li-chi*, pp. 6–7; and *Shuo-wen chieh-tzu*, p. 422. The *Chou-li* (Institutes of the Chou) also mentions that the *lao* people were exempt from punishment. See *Chou-li* (Taipei, 1956), p. 216.

168. For details of the controversy over the Former Han draft age, see Hamaguchi Shigekuni 1931, 1933, 1935a; Lao Kan 1942a; Yang Lien-sheng 1961, pp. 85–118 (originally published in 1950 in HJAS); Nishida Taichirō 1950; Ōba Osamu 1952; Nishimura Genyu 1953; and Yoneda Kenjirō 1957. Also see Li Yüan-ch'eng, "Han-tai fu-i k'ao," pp. 25a–36b; Ho Ch'ang-ch'ün 1937, 1962; and Sun Yü-t'ang 1937. In the introduction to his work of 1953, Henri Maspero also gives a brief account of the Han military system (L. Carrington Goodrich 1956, pp. 199–200), but it is merely a translation of Ju Shun's theory recorded in his commentary on the *Han-shu* 7. Obviously, Maspero did not consult the studies of Hamaguchi and the new materials in the wooden documents. See also Chun-shu Chang 1963, pp. 184–95.

169. The two officers were Fan Hung and Feng K'uang. Fan was appointed *wei-shih* of the Chia-sh'ü *hou-kuan* at the age of twenty-one during the Kan-li period (53–50 B.C.) of Emperor Hsuan's reign. At the age of twenty-one, Feng was already commander of the third *sui* of the Chia-ch'ü *hou-kuan* in the third year (A.D. 16) of Wang Mang's T'ien-feng period (A.D. 14–19) when he was transferred to the post of commander of Hsun-pei *sui* of the Chia-ch'ü *hou-kuan*. See doc. 285.3(486) or 5879, pl. 370; and doc. 225.11(468) or 5125, pl. 308 (T'ien-feng *yuan-nien* in Lao Kan's transliteration should be corrected to read T'ien-feng *yuan-nien* and *hsun-pei* to *chih-pei*). For the dating of Fan Hung, see Mori Shikazō 1955, which is a study of Fan Hung. See also Yang Lien-sheng 1961, p. 112; and Chun-shu Chang 1963, pp. 187–90.

170. For a detailed analysis of the Han system of conscription, see Chun-shu Chang 1963, pp. 184–95.

171. See docs. 148.43(320) or Cp868, 275.20(325) or Cp2545, and 362.32(470). The *ti-ch'i ting chang* (commander of the seventh watch station) in the first document was deciphered as *ti-shih t'ing chang* (commander of the tenth watch station) in the 1949 edition of the *Shih-wen*, and it still was not corrected in the 1960 edition (doc. no. 6219). The plate of this strip on p. 393 of Lao Kan 1957 shows that *ch'i* (seven) is the correct reading.

172. See docs. 506.13(435), 5355, and 317.21(148).

173. See docs. 285.3(486), 136.43(158), 185.16(465), 127.35(34), and 206.7(306); and Mori Shikazō 1955. The latter is a lengthy study of Fan Hung, but my interpretation differs from Mori's. See also note 169 in this chapter. For another record of the title *chu-kuan ling-shih* (chief clerk), see doc. 71.43 or 3373, in which Lao incorrectly reads *chu* (chief) as *wang* (king) and leaves the words *ling-shih* (clerk) undeciphered. Ho-chiao's reading is correct.

174. See docs. 34.21(199) and 128.2(286).

175. See docs. 275.21(355), 278.9(338), 273.24(319), 273.8(331), and 275.23(336). The word *yen* in doc. 275.23 was variously deciphered as *chien* and *chih* by Lao Kan. The photograph of the original strip on p. 490 in Lao 1957 shows the word to be *yen*. By com-

paring this with the photographs of the word *yen* in other strips (273.8 on p. 440 in Lao 1957, 273.24 on p. 389), I have deciphered this word as *yen*.

176. See docs. 557.8(334), 148.1(332), and 275.23(336); and Mori Shikazō 1959a, pp. 141–48. As was pointed out earlier, Mori incorrectly deciphers *shu* as *yu*. In fact, the word *yu* is clearly different from the word *shu*, as in doc. 3271, pl. 160.

177. Ho Ch'ang-chün (1962) has given us a detailed treatment of the abolition of the system of conscription and the rise of professional army in the early Later Han. See also Ch'ien Wen-tzu (fl. A.D. 1192–1215), *Pu Han ping-chih*, p. 418.

178. See chapters 3 and 4 of this volume.

179. For an examination of one doubtful case indicating that a *ch'i-shih* may have been from the prefecture of An-ting and the reason for its exclusion from our analysis, see Chun-shu Chang 1966b, pp. 195–96.

180. For the approximate location of the districts of Chang-yeh, see Yang Shou-ching, *tse* 2; and map 1 this volume.

181. This has been analyzed in detail in Chun-shu Chang 1966b, pp. 194–95.

182. See Lao Kan 1960a, p. 56.

183. For the technical details of this point, see Chun-shu Chang 1966b, pp. 196–97.

184. The original document should read "*Chin ch'u-wei Lu-te ch'i-shih*."

185. In reference to officials, the word *ch'u* means "to leave an old post to take a new post or office"; see Ju Shun's commentary on the *Han-shu* in HS (1962), p. 145.

186. Ibid., p. 2877.

187. Ibid., p. 2971.

188. HS, p. 528; SC (1959), p. 1430.

189. SC (1959), p. 1431.

190. For references to *ch'i* and *ch'i-ping* (horsemen), often over tens of thousands in a single campaign, in the accounts of these expeditions, see HS, pp. 1153–62; and Chun-shu Chang 1966a, pp. 151–66. Through careful examination of these accounts, the difference between the usage of *ch'i-shih* and *ch'i* can be clearly discerned.

191. This issue was discussed in detail in chapter 2 of volume 1 of this book.

192. HS, p. 1413.

193. Chun-shu Chang 1966a, pp. 167–72.

194. The basic sources for this statement are HS, pp. 853–62, 1339–40, 1344; Ch'ien Wen-tzu, *Pu Han ping-chi*, pp. 411–12; and *Han chiu-i*, B, p. 5b. I have reorganized the picture presented in these sources on the basis of modern geographic scholarship and my own study of the Han military and economic structure.

CHAPTER 3

1. Lao Kan 1957, vol. 1, p. 9; Lao Kan 1960a, 38; Itō Michiharu 1953, pp. 48–49; Fujieda Akira 1954, p. 637. Hibino Takeo (1953, p. 62) suggests that the *hou* and *sui* are in a parallel position, but both the Tun-huang and the Chü-yen documents indicate that the *hou* is superior to the *sui*, and several strips record *sui* under *hou*. See L. Carrington Goodrich 1956, pp. 209–12; and docs. 133.23(289), 40.20(299), and 6.7(197).

2. Ch'en Meng-chia's picture of the Chü-yen garrison settlements differs from this somewhat. He suggests different modern locations for the Han settlements, for example, site A8 for both the headquarters of the Chü-yen chief commandant and the Chia-ch'ü *hou-kuan*, A1 for the T'ien-pei *hou-kuan*, K710 for the Chü-yen *hou-kuan*, P9 for the Sa-ching *hou-kuan*, A24 for the Kuang-ti *hou-kuan*, and A33 for the Chien-shui *hou-kuan*.

In addition, he proposes adding three more *hou-kuan* to the system: adding Che-lu to the Chü-yen *tu-wei* and Ts'ang-shih and Yü to the Chien-shui *tu-wei*. Ch'en's system was strongly challenged by Nagata Hidemasa. I am not convinced by Ch'en's reasoning either. See Ch'en Meng-chia 1963b, esp. pp. 106–7; Ch'en Meng-chia 1964, esp. pp. 86–94; and Nagata Hidemasa 1974a, esp. pp. 164–75. I have assigned site A38 (Man-Han *ch'eng* of the "Two-Town" area called Shuang-ch'eng-tzu) for the Kuang-ti *hou-kuan*. See Sommarström, *Archeological Researches*, vol. 2, pp. 361–63. For other extensive studies of this topic, see my discussions in chap. 4 of this volume, especially concerning the works of Wu Ch'ang-lien, Nagata Hedemasa, Hsueh Ying-ch'ün, and others.

I still maintain that the city of Chü-yen was in what was later Khara-Khoto (i.e., site K799). Evidently it was called Chü-yen Lake city (Chü-yen tse ch'eng) at one time during its development. The *Chü-yen hsin-chien* has several documents that indicate this. Thus, the city must have been close to Chü-yen Lake.

3. Lao Kan has not touched upon this question. Itō Michiharu (1953, pp. 42–43) and Yoneda Kenjirō (1953a, pp. 50–60) mentioned it but failed to point out the main questions involved: whether a numbered *hou* is just another name for a word *hou* or indicates a separate *hou* and whether *pu* is just another name for a *hou*. It should again be pointed out that the term *pu* here obviously does not mean the same thing as its definition in the *Pai-kuan-chih* in the *Hou-Han-shu*.

4. See also doc. 24.2(291).

5. Docs. 198.19(494), 210.2(496), 2711.

6. There are also the eighteenth *hou*, the sixth *hou*, and the second *hou* (docs. 4956, 3263, 5357), but they are seen only once, and the photographs of these strips (on pp. 159 and 325 in Lao Kan 1957) are not clear enough to make new interpretations. The eleventh *hou* is seen twice, but its interpretation is questionable and the photographs (docs. 3260 and 3632, pls. 159 and 184) are not clear enough for examination. Lao Kan also mistransliterated the twenty-third *hou-chang* as the fifteenth *hou-chang* in doc. 4569, pl. 325. Ch'en Meng-chia (1964, p. 92) suggests one more numbered *pu*: the thirty-seventh. But its existence is highly doubtful, for no wooden strip directly refers to it. For the fourth *pu*, see also Chü-yen I, pp. 3–4.

7. For examples of Ping-t'ing *pu* and Ping-t'ing *hou-chang*, see docs. 2716, 4091, and Cp1562.

8. This key document was previously incorrectly deciphered as Ping-t'ing *ti shih-san* pu (Ping-t'ing, thirteenth *pu*); see doc. 45.15(490).

9. Lao Kan 1957, vol. 1, pp. 9–11; Itō Michiharu 1953, pp. 48–49. With reference to table 17, the subcommandant areas Tung-kuo, Hsin-ma, and Chien-shui are not listed in Lao 1957 and Itō Michiharu 1953. Lao also lists the Chung subcommandant area as unknown. Ch'en Meng-chia suggests fifty-three *hou* (see Ch'en Meng-chia 1964, esp. pp. 79 and 108), but the identification of some of them is questionable.

10. For a discussion of the *t'ing* or *sui*, see Lao Kan 1948c; and Ho Ch'ang-ch'ün 1940.

11. See Ch'en Meng-chia 1963b, pp. 80–81, 83; and Ch'en Meng-chia 1964, pp. 79, 108. Ch'en believes that there were originally over three hundred *sui* in the Chü-yen region (1963b, p. 83). See also Sommarström, *Archeological Researches*, p. 28. See docs. 40.20(299) (six *sui*); 133.23(289), T'un-yüan *hou* (five *sui*); 288.6(452) (six *sui*); 6.7(197) (six *sui*); 40.20(299); and 4079 or Cp182, twenty-third *pu* (eight *sui*).

12. Docs. 75.30(475), 557.8(334–335).

13. Doc. 557.5(334).

14. See Chun-shu Chang 1963, pp. 337–45.

15. In the 1960 edition of the *Shih-wen* (5160), Lao reads the original Chinese document as "Erh-shih i sui (twenty-first *sui*)." The photograph of this strip on p. 310 in Lao Kan 1957 indicates that "Erh-shih erh sui (twenty-second *sui*)" is the correct reading. See also doc. 65 in Henri Maspero 1953, which indicates a distance of about 4.6 Han *li* (1.9 kilometers) between the *sui*.

16. One Han *li* is equal to 417 meters.

17. Doc. 24.15(199). The Ping-t'ing *sui* was probably on the border between the Chia-ch'ü and T'ien-pei commandant areas (see doc. 4952 in Lao Kan 1960a). From docs. 4185 and 3593, it is clear that from the sixth *sui* up to the thirty-seventh all lie in the territory of the Chia-ch'ü Commandant Area. Probably, the thirty-eighth *sui* also belonged to Chia-ch'ü. One document (5125 in Lao Kan 1960a) also records that the third *sui* was in Chia-ch'ü.

18. Mori Shihazō 1955, 140. See also the later elaboration on the theory by Nagata Hidemasa (1964, esp. pp. 146–55 and attached chart); and Yoneda Kenjirō 1953, pp. 59ff. Yoneda maintains that the numbered *hou* headquarters occupied the same barrack as the southernmost *sui* under them. For example, the headquarters of the fourth *hou* was in the fourth *sui*. Ch'en Meng-chia suggests that the fourth *pu* had the first, second, third, and fourth *sui*; the seventh *pu* had the fifth to the seventh *sui*; the tenth *pu* had the eighth to the tenth *sui*; the eleventh *pu* had the eleventh to the thirteenth *sui*; the seventeenth *pu* had the fourteenth to the seventeenth *sui*; the eighteenth *pu* had the twenty-third to thirtieth *sui*; and the thirty-seventh *pu* had the thirty-first to thirty-eighth *sui*. Since the existence of some of the *pu* in this system is questionable, the validity of the theory is also doubtful. See Ch'en Meng-chia 1964, p. 76.

19. See, for example, docs. 34.21(199) and 24.15(199).

20. Besides the three, the counties of Kuang-ming, T'ao, and Pei are also referred to in the Chü-yen documents. But the documents indicate that they either belonged to other districts or were not known for certain to have been under Chü-yen District. For a more detailed account of the *hsiang-li* organization in the Chü-yen region, see Chun-shu Chang 1977, pp. 131–42.

21. Ying Shao, *Feng-su t'ung i-wen*, in Lu Wen-shao, p. 645. For a detailed discussion of this point, see Chun-shu Chang 1977, pp. 132–36; and the discussion of population in Chü-yen in chapter 4.

22. See docs. 140.5(87), 37.51(37), 77.42(450), and 759.

23. Bo Sommarström 1956–58 (Khara-Khoto and site A35), pp. 190–93, 343.

24. Lao Kan 1939, pp. 164–65; 1948, 518.

25. Bo Sommarström 1956–58, pp. 315, 45; Chü-yen I, p. 2 (for Chia-chü *hou-kuan*). See also the new measurement made by Kansu sheng wen-wu kung-tso tui in the 1970s (*Chü-yen hsin-chien*, p. 1 and map).

26. See Chü-yen I, pp. 3, 4, 5.

27. Some watchtowers were even smaller. Professor Lao Kan observed one tower that measured only 3.33 meters wide. See Lao Kan 1960a, p. 42. It could be that the tower in question was already ruined.

28. Compare the archaeological reports of Tun-huang and the Lop-nor area in Aurel Stein 1933, pp. 163–92, Aurel Stein 1921, vol. 2, p. 654, vol. 3, pp. 34–41; Huang Wen-pi 1948, pp. 105–12; and Folke Bergman 1945, pp. 135–51. For different sizes and other measurements of the various Chü-yen fortifications, see Ch'en Meng-chia 1963, pp. 81–82.

29. Lao Kan 1960a, p. 38; doc. 99.1(204). Chü-yen I, p. 4 (the fourth *sui* was also the headquarters of the fourth *hou*).

30. Docs. 238.3(594), 46.12(498), 126.40(180).

31. Calculated from data in doc. 175.9(190) or 3472, pl. 173; and Chü-yen I, pp. 3–5.

32. Lao Kan 1960a, p. 43. For a discussion of the *wu* or *pi*, see pages 44–45.

33. Doc. 68.63(195). The two terms could be interpreted as the gates of the inner and outer *wu*, but this is probably better.

34. Modern scholarship on the *li* system in Han times is extensive. See, for example, Ōbata Tatsuo 1942; Sogabe Shizuo 1949; Lao Kan 1950a, 1954; Wang Yü-ch'üan 1954; Wang Chia-wu 1954, pp. 135–64; Yang Shu-fan 1955; Miyazaki Ichisada 1960, 1962; Koga Noburu 1972, pp. 51–55; and Matsuimoto Yoshimi 1977, pp. 199–214. However, all except two of these scholars (Wang Chia-wu and Miyazaki) have focused their attention on the administrative aspects of the *li* and make no attempt to study its physical form. Wang Chiao-wu and Miyazaki Ichisada have analyzed the physical form of the *li* in their respective works, but neither used the Han wooden documents as sources. For this reason, they have been limited in their understanding of the *li* in Han times. A detailed account of the *li* as both an administrative unit and a residential division based on the Han era wooden documents is given in Chun-shu Chang 1965b. See also the discussion of *li* in chapter 5 of this volume.

35. The translation follows a new interpretation based on a photograph of the original strip in Lao Kan 1957. Lao's interpretation(doc. 3007) is slightly different.

36. Folke Bergman 1945, pl. 22b (between pp. 144 and 145). Aurel Stein and Folke Bergman considered this a remnant of a ruined fortress. In a study of the names of *hsiang* and *li* as recorded in all Han era documents, Ho Shuai-ch'üan composed a list of all the *hsiang* and *li* in the various *chün* and *kuo* and also proposed a plan of a Han *li*. His *li* diagram is the shape of a square in a city. See Ho Shuai-ch'üan, "Han-chien Hsiang-li Chih chi-ch'i yen-chiu," *Ch'in-Han chien-tu lun-wen chi* (Lanchou, 1989), pp. 183–86. It is possible that some interior cities may have had uniformly square *li* in Han times, and they definitely did in later times (such as the city of Ch'ang-an in T'ang times), but this would have been geographically and economically impossible for the *li* in Chü-yen city and its environs. I think the *li* in the Chü-yen region must have had varied shapes and that the one proposed here was one of them.

37. HS, p. 980; see also Wang Hsien-ch'ien's commentary in HS.

38. The word *ssu* in the original document was interpreted as *ho* in the *Chia-pien*. The photograph shows that *ssu* is the correct reading. Lao Kan read it as *ssu* but mistook *che* as *chi*; see doc. 127.7(228).

39. The editors of the *Chia-pien* incorrectly read *ssu* as *li* in the original document.

40. Ch'en Chih 1958, p. 60.

41. Docs. 2116, 160.11(464), 4218.

42. Sommarström, *Archeological Researches*, pp. 346, 347–49, 355.

43. Lao Kan 1960a, p. 46.

44. Docs. 4062, 5432, 5492, Cp1135, Cp1701.

45. Professor Chou Fa-Kao has a section on the *t'ing-pu* in his *Chin-wen ling-shih* (pp. 153–57). Since he used only one wooden document in his study, his interpretation of the term does not seem to fit the cases given here.

46. The term *chü-tso* means "to settle in some place," which differs from the term *k'o-tso*, which means "to reside temporarily in some place." See my discussion of the term *k'o-tzu* in chapter 2 of this volume. (This strip was broken, and only half of the word *tso*

is left. There is a possibility that the word is *yen*, but this change does not affect our interpretations here.)

47. In both Lao Kan 1949 and Lao Kan 1960a, this document (no. 5514) was deciphered incorrectly. This new decipherment was made according to the photograph of the original strip in Lao Kan 1957.

48. From the literary evidence of the Han period, the Tu-t'ing was located outside the capital of either a prefecture or a district. It was quite common in the interior of the empire. See Lao Kan 1950a, p. 130; and 1960a, p. 18.

49. For examples, see documents in Lao Kan 1949, pp. 119–67; Chü-yen *tu-wei fu* (The Headquarters of the Chü-yen Chief Commandant); and Chien-shui *tu-wei fu* (The Headquarters of the Chien-shui Chief Commandant).

50. Docs. 254.18(234), 3868, 5184, 287.22(467), 40.21(154).

51. See above, note 49.

52. Doc. 14.26A(226) or Cp2333A. For the term *ssu-she*, see HHS 54, 312, and the commentary by Li Hsien.

53. Docs. 816(195), 106.27(200), 206.26(200), 194.17(209), 82.1(211), 214.108(219), 8260, 4650 (compare this one with 4655), Cp1377. For a recent interpretation of the term *t'ing-pu*, see Fang Shih-ming 1973, p. 53.

54. Docs. 194.17(209), 214.108(219), 82.1(211), 106.27(200), 206.26(200).

55. See Bo Sommarström 1956–58, maps 2 and 3; Folke Bergman 1945, pp. 136ff.; and map 2 in this volume.

56. Chü-yen I, pp. 5, 10; Chun-shu Chang 1978, pp. 583–84.

57. It is interesting to note that the Mongolian name for Ta-wan (site A35), where Chien-shui city, the headquarters of the Chien-shui chief commandant, was located, is Taralingin-durbeljin, meaning "Walled Enclosure near the Agriculture Settlement." Archaeological fieldwork has uncovered abundant traces of an ancient cultivation, such as fields and canals, in the neighborhood of the site. See Bo Sommarström 1956–58, pp. 343–57; Aurel Stein 1928, pp. 412–13; and Folke Bergman 1945, pp. 136–37. See also Chun-shu Chang 1978, pp. 586–88; and Ch'en Kung-jo and Hsü P'ing-fang 1963.

58. In addition to earlier discussions, see also Chun-shu Chang 1977, pp. 176–77; 1978, p. 587–88.

59. For a detailed analysis of this point, see chapter 5 in this volume.

60. This was calculated from data in the Han-shu and Lao Kan's estimate of the total area of Chang-yeh. See HS (1962), p. 1613; and Lao Kan 1935c, p. 218.

61. In formulating the conceptual framework used in my analysis in this section, particularly the concepts of node, a nodal dominance relationship, and the central-place system, I have greatly benefited from modern studies in economic geography and settlement analysis. A few of these are listed here to register my scholarly indebtedness: John C. Lowe and S. Moryadas, *The Geography of Movement* (Boston, 1975); Brian J. L. Berry and Frank E. Horton, *Geographic Perspectives on Urban Systems* (Englewood Cliffs, NJ, 1970); Gerald Kraft, John R. Meyer, and Jean-Paul Valette, *The Role of Transportation in Regional Economic Development* (Lexington, MA, 1971); and Roger Minshull, *Regional Geography: Theory and Practice* (London, 1971).

62. Here it must be clarified again that although I have used the term *planned migration* in this study, I have not used it with the same meaning as conventional definitions in modern migration studies (e.g., William Petersen 1955, 1958). As I pointed out in chapter 1, traditional Chinese frontier migrations, such as the one under consideration

in this study, represented a unique type. They are not covered by the modern typology of migration, which has generally classified migration as "primitive," "forced," "impelled," "free," or "mass" on the basis of the variables involved. As our analysis has clearly demonstrated, none of these classifications can adequately describe the pattern of Chinese frontier migration because the Chinese system was a combination of three basic features: forced and/or free migration, government-controlled and supported transfer and settlement, and government awards and protection.

CHAPTER 4

1. Docs. 303.23(248), 303.31(253). The watch station was called Kan-hou, which was likely one of the centers for cavalrymen. The *Chia-pien* editors read doc. 276.3 (Cp1488) as *yu ti san sui shih-jen,* which means "ten soldiers in the third *sui.*" This is a mistake. It should be *yu ti-san chü shih-jen,* meaning "ten men with the third cart." Lao Kan reads them as *yu ti san pai ch'i-shih jen* and *yu ti san-pai shih jen* in Lao Kan 1949 and 1960a, 276.13(517) and 8280, respectively. Cf. similar information in the Tun-huang documents (nos. 279–283, 286, and 288 in THHCW).

2. See docs. 99.1(204), 214.37(317), 157.2(333), and 55.3(128). See also the discussions in chapter 2 in this volume.

3. The editors of *Chia-pien* read *nien-ch'i* (twenty-seven) as *nien-liu* (twenty-six) in the original Chinese document, which is a mistake. The photograph of this strip is clear enough for this correction.

4. Docs. 267.22(233), 267.17(233), 26.21(325), 3706, 5976. Lao Kan reads the last document differently. I have checked the photograph of this slip in Lao Kan 1957 (p. 377).

5. Doc. 26.21(325), pl. 414. See also doc. 139.36(50) or Cp947; note 4; and the discussions in chapter 2.

6. *Tso-chang* in the original Chinese document means "to be a supervisor over a group of soldiers working on a fixed schedule." See doc. 3085, pl. 148.

7. According to Yen Shih-ku's commentary in the *Biography of K'ung Kuang* in the *Han-shu,* the word *chieh* means *mien* (HS [1962], 3355–56). Thus *chieh-ch'u* in the original Chinese document is *mien-ch'u,* meaning "to be released or excluded from." This is in accord with the context of the document.

8. This translation follows a new decipherment based on the photograph of the original document in Lao Kan 1957. Neither of Lao's two decipherments of this document, 133.21(230) and 3933, is correct.

9. Based on Lao's 1949 version of this document, Ch'en Chih (1958, p. 19) interprets this in the original Chinese document as "being in charge of the ornamental articles of horses," which is a mistake.

10. This translation follows a new decipherment based on the photograph of the original slip. In his two decipherments of this document, in the 1949 edition of the *Shih-wen* (doc. 30.19 on p. 232) and the 1960 edition of the *Shih-wen* (doc. 4322), Lao failed to make the correct interpretation.

11. Chun-shu Chang 1963, pp. 248–52, 482–85, nn. 54–63. These documents provide detailed information on the daily lives of the laboring soldiers in Chü-yen. For a detailed study of this, see Chun-shu Chang 1977, pp. 143–70.

12. According to the wooden documents, besides garrisoning, the military colonists performed types of work classified as *sheng-tso* and *ting-tso* (scheduled hard work), and

hai-tso (inspection). The first two were discussed earlier. For the last, see doc. 286.2 on p. 300 of Lao Kan 1957; and Chun-shu Chang 1963, 484, n. 60.

13. These were officials with an annual salary of 100 *shih* of grain. For a detailed analysis of the rank order and salary scale of officers in the garrisons, see Chun-shu Chang 1963, chap. 5, sec. 2A, esp. tables a and b; and chapter 2 of this volume.

14. In the Later Han period, the *tou-shih* officials received a salary of 1.2 *tou* of grain per day (or a monthly salary of eleven *shih* of grain according to a different source). But the issue is unclear for the Former Han period. See HS (1962), p. 743 (Yen Shih-ku's commentary); and Ying Shao, *Han kuan-i*, pt. A, p. 35a.

15. The upper part of this wooden strip is missing. A *tso-shi* received a monthly salary of 8 *shih* of grain in Eastern Han times. See Ying Shao, *Han kuan-i*, pt. A, p. 35a. Information about the salary scale of the *tso-shih* in Western Han times is not available. See also chapter 2 of this volume.

16. This translation follows a new decipherment based on the photograph of the original strip in Lao Kan 1957. Neither of Lao's two decipherments of this document, 395.9(228) and 2126, is correct.

17. See also docs. 3904, Cp1193B, Cp1314, 7352, 161.5(305), and 214.18(239) or 7352 and 3960.

18. Judging from its number, 71.29, it is probably a record of the Chü-yen *tu-wei*.

19. HS (1962), pp. 2451, 2455; doc. 3307 (Cp 410).

20. For records of this, see the previous discussions of servicemen's families in the garrison settlements; and Chun-shu Chang 1963, 337–42 (on grain provisions for family members).

21. *Chia-pien* (p. 115) lists this document as being discovered at P'o-ch'eng-tzu.

22. Since the first two words of the original Chinese document are not legible, the superior offices of the Li-p'ing watch station are unknown, nor has such information been found in other documents.

23. Doc. 1282 or 29.10, pl. 60. For a detailed discussion of this issue, see Chang Chung-shu 1963, chap. 5, sec. 1A. The wooden slip is dated 24 B.C.

24. For the term *chih-kuan-min*, see Shih-chi 121 (SC [1959], p. 3122). For further examples, see docs. 179.4(446), 49.9(481), 37.57(455), and 3239. This register form is not seen in the cases of high-ranking officials, being unique to minor garrison officers. See also Chang Shun-shu 1977, pp. 165–67. According to Lao Kan, the word *wu* in the original Chinese document is meant to indicate that the subject is a military officer, a *wu-li*. See Lao Kan 1960a, 17–18.

25. Doc. 89.42(478). This document indicates that Chung-kuan *li* was in the Chü-yen *pu*.

26. A *tu-wei* on the frontier in the Western Regions was said to have commanded 500 soldiers. See Hsu Sung, p. 3569. The total of 500 men is 200 less than the regular troops under the command of a *chiao-wei* of foot soldiers in the imperial capital. See *Han-kuan*, p. 8. It is also interesting to note that under a *chiao-wei* of foot soldiers there were 73 officers, in addition to the 700 soldiers. The ratio between soldiers and officers was 9.59 to 1. But evidently such was not the case on the frontier and in frontier campaigns. For instance, in General Chao Ch'ung-kuo's (137–52 B.C.) campaign against the Ch'iang in 61 B.C., in a memorial to Emperor Hsuan (74–49 B.C.), the general mentioned 10,000 soldiers and officers under 9 *chiao-wei* of foot soldiers. If a *chiao-wei* of foot soldiers commanded 700 soldiers, there were 6,300 soldiers under the 9 *chiao-wei* and the rest of the force—3,700 men—should be officers. Therefore, there were about 411 officers under

the command of a *chiao-wei*, and the ratio between officers and soldiers was 1.71 to 1. See HS (1962), p. 2987.

27. For instance, see Chü-yen I, p. 10 (EJT 28:63). But this document may be a general account, not a reference to a specific time period.

28. Of the total of 1,946 military personnel, the ratio between soldiers and officers is 1,300 to 646 (or about 2 to 1). Compared to the ratio between officers and soldiers in Chao Ch'ung-kuo's forces mentioned in note 26, this ratio is understandable and reasonable. If we do not consider the soldiers in the headquarters of Chü-yen and Chien-shui *tu-wei*, the ratio between soldiers (1,000) and officers is 1.55 to 1, which is even closer to the previously mentioned ratio of 1.71 to 1 in Chao Ch'ung-kuo's forces. Therefore, on the Han frontier the number of officers generally amounted to about 50 percent of the number of soldiers. Perhaps this was due to the fact that the troops on the frontier, which were generally divided into smaller working units to cover a large area, needed more direction and guidance from officers in their garrison and noncombat assignments. For example, in the Chü-yen frontier system, a watch station with no more than four soldiers could have 4 officers (1 commander and 3 *ling-shih*).

29. See chapter 2 of this volume for a discussion of convicts and slaves.

30. For a detailed discussion of the organization and work of farming activities in Chü-yen, see Chun-shu Chang 1963, chap. 5, sec. 5 ("Land Cultivation"); and 1978, pp. 585–88.

31. See chapter 2 of this volume for a discussion of farming soldiers. There is good reason to believe that all fifteen hundred soldiers belonged to the Hsin-ma Farming Region because one of its many subordinate units is recorded to have commanded seventy soldiers. See doc. 513.25 or 1468, pl. 70. Furthermore, as was discussed earlier, the massive use of farming officials and soldiers for the development of new and border territories was the long-established Han policy. For instance, in 119 B.C. sixty thousand farming officials and soldiers were sent to develop the area west of the Yellow River from So-fang to Ling-chü.

32. See also Ch'en Kung-jou 1963; Ch'en Meng-chia 1963b, pp. 101–2; and Chun-shu Chang 1963, chap. 5, sec. 5 ("Land Cultivation").

33. See doc. Cp1501; and Chun-shu Chang 1977, p. 161.

34. Doc. 490.10(182). See also Chun-shu Chang 1977, p. 161.

35. A list and discussion of these farming units can be found in Chun-shu Chang 1963, chap. 5, sec. 2.1, docs. a–n.

36. This is based on information in docs. 47.5 or 173 (pl. 9) and 310.19 or 211 (pl. 12).

37. A detailed account of the organization and operation of the granary system in Chü-yen is given in Chun-shu Chang 1963, chap. 5, sec. 2.1.

38. For a detailed study of food provisions for servicemen's families in the various Chü-yen garrison units, see ibid., sec. 2.2B.

39. HS (1962), p. 3926. The calculation is based on the fact that the total Han garrison and farming force under the *Wu-chi chiao-wei* was said to have numbered fifteen hundred men.

40. See HS (1962), p. 742; and *Han chiu-i,* pt. A, p. 6b. For secondary studies of the problem, see T'ao Hsi-sheng and Shen Chü-ch'en, pp. 187–88; Tseng Tzu-sheng, pp. 240–42; Yen Keng-wang 1961, p. 217; Lao Kan 1954; Ts'ai Hsing-an, p. 32; and Ch'ü Chao-ch'i, pp. 1–2. See also Rafe de Crespigny 1967, p. 63. The *Han-shu* indicates that the monthly salary of the *ling* ranged from 600 to 1,000 *shih* of grain and that of the *chang*

from 300 to 500 *shih;* but the *Han chiu-i* records that while the monthly salary of the *ling* was 600 to 1,000 *shih* of grain, that of the *chang* was 300 to 400 *shih.* The slight difference between the two versions was the result of the elimination of the 500-*shih* salary from the Han salary scale in 23 B.C. See also Ying Shao, *Han kuan-i,* pt. A, p. 32b.; and HHS (1963), p. 3623.

41. See docs. 313.44(10), dated 64 B.C.; 190.1(74), dated 31 B.C.; 140.9(38), dated 26 B.C.; 32.6 (25), dated 16 B.C.; and 170.3 (168–169), dated 11 B.C. The dating of these documents indicates that Chü-yen was probably headed by a *ling* from the beginning of its *hsien* status. See also Chun-shu Chang 1977, pp. 89–91.

42. Ying Shao, *Han kuan-i,* pt. A, p. 32b; *Yin-ch'ueh shan Han-chien,* pp. 7–8, 89ff. (documents of pre-Ch'in times); *Chung-kuo ku-tai ti-t'u chi,* vol. 1 ("Ti-hsing t'u" and "Chu-chün t'u"); Hunan po-wu kuan, *Ch'ang-sha Ma-wang-tui Han-mu* (Ch'angsha: Hunan jen-min, 1979), maps in question; *Wen-wu* 4 (1984): 27–36. The Yin-ch'ueh-shan documents were discovered in 1972 and the Ma-wang-tui maps, in 1973. See also Li Hsueh-ch'in, *Chien-po i-chi yü hsueh-shu shih* (Taipei, 1994), pp. 372–73.

43. HS (1962), p. 1613; Chun-shu Chang 1977, pp. 92–93.

44. This is based on the population figures for households and persons in A.D. 2. See Chun-shu Chang 1975a, pp. 66–67.

45. HS (1962), p. 1613; Chun-shu Chang 1977, p. 92. The total number of households and persons in Chang-yeh was, respectively, 24,352 and 88,731 according to the A.D. 2 census.

46. See HS (1962), pp. 3341 and 3346 (which indicate 600 households for Lo-an County) and 706 (which indicates 647 households for Lo-an County); HHS (1965), p. 3624; Hao Ching, *Hsü hou-Han shu,* pp. 1485–86; *Han-kuan,* p. 7a; and Ch'ien Ta-hsin, p. 182. See also HS (1962), p. 1121 ("In ancient times a *hsiang* consisted of 12,500 households"); Nancy Lee Swann 1950, p. 125; and Liu Hsing-t'an, p. 12.

47. See, for example, Lao Kan 1950a, p. 134; Yang Shu-fan 1955, esp. p. 50; Wang Chia-wu, pp. 21–22; Hibino Takeo 1955, esp. pp. 23–25, 35–38; Koga Noburo, pp. 51–53; and T'ao Hsi-sheng and Shen Chü-ch'en, pp. 189–90.

48. See Ying Shao, *Feng-su t'ung i-wen* (Lu Wen-ch'ao ed.), p. 645; and the sources cited in n. 42. The Yin-ch'ueh-shan documents indicate that there were 50 households in a *li.* The Ma-wang-tui maps indicate that there were 108 in a large *li*, 35 to 50 in middle ones, and only 12 in a small one.

49. Wu Chia-wu, p. 81, indicates that the large *hsien* in the interior had a population ranging from 30,000 to 80,800 households. Ying Shao, *Han kuan-i,* pt. A, p. 32b. The Yin-ch'ueh-shan documents indicate that the large *hsien* had 20,000 households, the middle one 15,000, and the small one 10,000.

50. According to the *Han-kuan* (p. 7a), only the administrators of large counties with populations of more than 5,000 households were called *yu-chih.* The title *yu-chih* appears in the Chü-yen wooden documents but is not associated with any of the three Chü-yen counties. See docs. 313.44(10), 181.2(19), 181.10(19), 81.10(83), 495.18(6).

51. Docs. 313.44(10), 181.21(19), 495.12(6).

52. Doc. 4977.

53. It was not uncommon in early Han times for a district to have just one county. See Wang Chia-wu, pp. 68–82.

54. It is generally agreed among scholars that Ying Shao's statement reflected the institution of the Former Han period. During the Later Han period, the number of households in a *li* was increased to 100. Accompanying this change was a general reduc-

tion in the total number of *hsiang* and *li* to half that of the Former Han period. For instance, in A.D. 2 there were 6,622 *hsiang* for a national population of 59,594,978 persons, but in 157 A.D. there were only 3,681 *hsiang* for a national population of 56,486,856 persons. However, the Yin-ch'ueh-shan documents (from tombs of Wu-ti's time) show 100 *li* in a county. Since these documents are of the fourth century B.C., the 100-*li* county was clearly an old ideal. Other suggestions about the number of households in a *li* from ancient times to the Han dynasty included 25, 72, and 80. For traditional sources on the problems discussed here and modern studies, see Ying Shao, *Feng-su t'ung i-wen* (Lu Wen-ch'ao ed.), p. 645; HHS (1965), pp. 3533–34, 3625; HS (1962), pp. 742–43, 1640; Fu Wu-chi, p. 12; Chun-shu Chang 1975a, pp. 66, 68; Tseng Tzu-sheng, p. 244; Huang-fu Mi, pp. 120–21; *Chin-shu,* p. 275; Tu Yu, p. 39; Ku Yen-wu, *Jih-chih lu,* vol. 4, pp. 102–3; Liu Hsing-t'ang, esp. pp. 8–11; Lao Kan 1950a, esp. pp. 133–34; Wang Chia-wu, pp. 79–80, 143–44; Yang Shu-fan 1955, pp. 49–50; Lan Kan 1960a, pp. 41–42; Lao Kan 1935b, esp. pp. 180–81; Wan Kuo-ting, pp. 124–25; Makino Tatsumi, pp. 197–98; Hans Bielenstein 1947, esp. pp. 126–27, 135; and John D. Durand, esp. pp. 216–19.

55. Needless to say, this figure does not include visitors and temporary residents of Chü-yen, who were usually not counted in the Han population registers.

56. HHS (1965), p. 3521. The average household size was 3.034.

57. In A.D. 140, the total population of the Ho-hsi region was only about 53.77 percent of the population in A.D. 2. In the Chang-yeh area, the Later Han population was only about 36.68 percent of the Former Han population. But population changes in different districts must have varied with location, economic conditions, and the effects of administrative reorganization. See Lao Kan 1935c, p. 236, for an analysis of the Later Han data. I have recalculated the population data collected by Professor Lao Kan and have come up, after all necessary adjustments, with the following data for the ratio between the Later Han (A.D. 140) and the Former Han (A.D. 2) population figures for the four *chün* of Ho-hsi: Tun-huang had about 76 percent of its Former Han population, Chang-yeh had 36.68 percent, Chiu-ch'üan had 70 percent, Wu-wei had 32.3 percent.

58. Cf. docs. 37.51(37), dated 52 B.C.; 140.5(87); 77.42(450); and 759.

59. For a detailed account of the *hsien* administrative staff in interior districts, see Yen Keng-wang 1961, vol. 1, pp. 216–23.

60. Needless to say, the size of the non-Chinese population in the Chü-yen region cannot be meaningfully estimated either.

61. Lao Kan 1935c, p. 218.

62. Theoretical treatment and comparative applications of the various demographic concepts and terms used here and in the section that follows can be found in T. Lynn Smith and Paul E. Zopf Jr., 1970, chap. 3; Charles B. Nam and Susan O. Gustavus 1976, chap. 6; Edward G. Stockwell 1970, chap. 6; and Louis Henry 1976, chap. 2.

63. A detailed analysis of these aspects is given in Chun-shu Chang 1963, pp. 475–76, 532.

64. See ibid., pp. 473–75, 531–32.

65. Another such list was discovered in P'o-ch'eng-tzu in 1974, but it was not published. See Chü-yen I, p. 27.

66. See, for example, Louis Henry 1976, pp. 10–11; T. Lynn Smith and Paul E. Zopf Jr., 1970, pp. 196–202; and Charles B. Nam and Susan O. Gustavus 1976, pp. 195–97.

67. The low sex ratios among both adults and youth in our sample present a sharp contrast with similar data on sex ratios in early modern and modern China. For instance,

Professor Ho Ping-ti's study of the Chinese population in these periods reveals that the sex ratios among children under sixteen were not only always over 110 but mostly over 120 and the sex ratios among people of all ages were larger than 105, ranging from 107 to 156. According to the most comprehensive 1953 census data, males constituted 51.82 percent and females 48.18 percent of the total population, for a sex ratio of 107.5. See Ho Ping-ti 1959, pp. 41–46, 57–64, 95–97.

68. For youth ratios in the Chinese populations of later periods, see Ho Ping-ti 1959, pp. 41–46, 57–64, 95–97.

69. Modern scholars generally believe that, except for cases of child marriage, in Han times a woman was usually married at the age of fourteen or fifteen. Mentions of women being married at the ages of thirteen, fourteen, fifteen, and sixteen can be found in the Han written literature. But marriage of a woman at twelve is not mentioned in any written Han documents. Men were married at a relatively older age than women, usually between fifteen and eighteen. For a detailed analysis of the issue of age at marriage in ancient China and in Han times, see Ch'en Ku-yüan 1936, pp. 125–27; and Yang Shu-ta 1933, pp. 24–31. According to records in the Han literature, child marriage occurred only in the palace. In one case, the ages were eight for an emperor (Chao, 95–74 B.C., r. 87–74 B.C.) and six for an empress (née Shang-kuan). It is interesting to note here that Emperor Hui (211–188 B.C., r. 195–188 B.C.) issued an edict in 189 B.C. decreeing that any unmarried woman between fifteen and thirty was to be taxed at five times the normal rate. See also HS (1962), p. 91.

70. See note 68 for the prevailing view.

71. For the theoretical treatment of the various terms and concepts in the sociological analysis of family types that I have employed in my analysis, see Norman W. Bell and Ezra V. Vogel 1960, pp. 1–33; William J. Goode 1964, chaps. 5–7; George P. Murdock 1949, chaps. 1–2; and Clifford Kirkpatrick 1955, chap. 4.

72. For a detailed discussion of this and related issues, see Chun-shu Chang 1975a.

73. The average Han family size of four to five persons is smaller than what has been traditionally assumed by scholars. See Chun-shu Chang 1975a; and Ch'ü-yen T'ung-shu 1972, pp. 3–9. The Chü-yen data on family size serve to correct the long-held misunderstanding that children under two years of age were normally omitted by the Chinese census takers, which would amount to 6 to 8 percent of the total population. For an example of this misunderstanding, see T. H. Hollingsworth 1969, p. 66. On this issue, the Yin-wan Han documents shed no light either. While they provide good information on the number of officials in Tung-hai *chün* (in modern eastern Kiangsu), they do not give local population figures. See *Yin-wan Han-mu chien-tu*.

CHAPTER 5

1. For details of the Hsiung-nu and Southern Yüeh challenges to the Han in the earlier reigns of the dynasty, see the earlier chapters of this volume; and Ch'ü Tui-chih 1944, pp. 134–37.

2. For studies of the establishment and functions of the passes in pre-Ch'in times, see Ch'ü Shou-yüeh 1958, pp. 161–65; Ch'en P'an 1975, pp. 132b–133a; *Meng-tzu*, p. 403; *Sun-tzu*, p. 211; and *Ch'in hui-yao*, pp. 408–9.

3. HS (1962), pp. 123–24 (including the commentaries by Chang Yen, Ju Shun, Li Ch'i, and Yen Shih-ku), 2320–21 (including Ying Shao's commentary), 588, 2905, 3848, 3851, 3925; HHS (1965), pp. 293, 2140; *Lieh-nü chuan*, *chüan* 5, p. 9b; *Hsi-Han*,

p. 671; Ch'ü Hsüan-ying 1928, pp. 80–83; Ch'ü Hsüan-ying 1938, pp. 751–53. See also the information provided by Han wooden documents found in Tun-huang and Chü-yen to be discussed in the next section.

4. HS (1962), pp. 123–24, 143, 204, 222, 245, 313, 318, 601, 2320–21, 2379, 2699, 2819, 3650, 3851, 3925. See also the various commentaries on the issues mentioned in these pages. I have calculated the dating of some of the events by consulting other relevant sources.

5. This general rule was not always observed, however. Sometimes both the *chün* and *hsien* were given in a register of a local resident, and only the name of the *hsien* was written on the register of an individual from an interior *chün* of the empire. See docs. 5188, 4457, and 311.28(477).

6. Lao Kan read Tuo-i as Tai-yü, and the editors of *Chia-pien* followed him. Tai-yü *hsien* is not found in the current text of the *Treatise on Geography* in the *Han-shu*. Ch'en Chih (1959, p. 121) suggests that Tai-yü was the colloquial form of Tuo-i. For the register form of hired soldiers, see Huang Wen-pi 1948, p. 201.

7. For wooden documents concerning the various passes, see, for example, docs. 15.19(27), Cp110, CpApp14A, Cp2434 (or 4144 or 206.2 on pl. 225), and 140.5(87). For a different interpretation of the three passes in Chü-yen, see Ch'en Meng-chia 1963b, pp. 103–5. Basically, Ch'en holds that the Hsuan-an Pass in doc. 206.2 is a mistranscription for the So Pass of Chü-yen *hsien* made by Lao Kan and the editors of the *Chia-pien* and that the So Pass was the major pass of the Chü-yen *tu-wei*. On the first point, the pictures of doc. 206.2 in Lao Kan 1957 and the *Chia-pien* fail to support his view. On the second point, Ch'en has based his theory on doc. 218.32, which reads in Lao Kan 1949 "Chü-yen-hsien chieh i-shu" (p. 624). The picture of this slip in pl. 418 in Lao Kan 1957 seems to show that Ch'en was probably correct, although it is not clear enough to take *kuan*, instead of *hsien* as the definitive reading. If *kuan* is indeed the correct reading in this document, and it is very likely so since the context would seem to indicate that it refers to the So Pass in Chü-yen. For the geographical location and current condition of site A32, see Bo Sommarström, 1956–58, vol. 2, pp. 305–8, pl. XXd; and Chü-yen I, pp. 4–5.

8. See, for example, docs. 191.1(10), 223.10(4), 276.8(479–480), 562.3(15), and 2573. See also Fujieda Akira 1954, p. 652. For passes that were of major importance to a large territory or the whole empire, such as the Jade Gate and Yang Passes, the organization was more complex than for those in Chü-yen and they were directed by a chief commandant of a pass (*kuan tu-wei*) or a lesser prefect of a pass (*kuan-ling*). See docs. 8872 (585.1 in pl. 552) and 5850 or 56.7(81); Fujieda Akira 1954, p. 652; and Ch'en Meng-chia 1964, pp. 58–59. For the most important passes in Former Han times, see *Hsi-Han*, pp. 670–72. See also *Ta-T'ang liu-tien*, *chüan* 30, pp. 41–42.

9. The problem of the types, uses, and procedures for issuance of the various travel documents (passes, passports, permits, certificates, and so on) in the Former Han period has been one of the most difficult, confusing, and controversial subjects in the study of Han institutions. Since the Later Han, numerous commentaries and works have been written on it, but they often disagree and raise more questions than they answer. My tentative suggestions here are based on my reading of the wooden documents found in the Chü-yen and Tun-huang regions and extensive reading of primary and secondary sources on this problem. But the emphasis is on the former because they are the original Han travel documents and later studies tend to offer differing and sometimes confusing interpretations. Among the most useful modern studies are Ch'en Chih 1959, pp. 9–10, 165–66; Ch'en Chih 1962c; Wang Chung-ying 1975; Wan Ssu-nien, pp. 51–69 (article

by Naitō Tōrajirō); Wang Kuo-wei 1914, supplement, pp. 5a–6a; Lou Tsou-i 1939, pp. 100–103; Yanai Wataru, pp. 137–40; Ōba Osamu 1954b; and Lao Kan 1960a, pp. 3–5. Among other important written primary sources and secondary studies are HS (1962), pp. 123–24 (including commentaries by Chang Yen, Ju Shun, Li Ch'i, and Yen Shih-ku), 359–60 (including commentaries by Li Ch'i and Yen Shih-ku), 2819 (including commentaries by Su Lin and Chang Yen), 3560 (including Yen Shih-ku's commentary); HS (1955), p. 145 (including various commentaries); *Tung-Han*, pp. 95–96; *Chou-li cheng-i*, vol. 8, pp. 12–13 (including commentaries by Cheng Hsüan, Chia Kung-yen, and Sun I-jang); Liu Hsi, pp. 90, 91 (see Nicholas C. Bodman 1954, pp. 3–5, for the dating of the book); *Ta-T'ang liu-tien*, p. 150; Hung Mai, vol. 4, p. 91; *Shuo-wen chieh-tzu* (1963 ed.), p. 96; Ch'ü Hsuan-ying 1928, pp. 80–82; Yang K'an, p. 33; Yang Shen, p. 82; Hsia Nai 1948, pp. 245–46; Ch'en P'an 1947, pp. 327–28; Ch'en P'an 1952, p. 352; Ch'en Chih 1958, pp. 20–21; Dubs, vol. 1, pp. 252–53; and Dubs, vol. 3, p. 84. A few other relevant sources on specific aspects of the large problem of Former Han travel clearances, which have already been cited or will be, are omitted here. The wooden documents from Chü-yen carefully examined in this study include 562.3A (pl. 47), Cp1584AB, 140.1AB (pl. 412, pl. 413); Cp1167AB, 170.3AB (pl. 109, pl. 110), 39.2 (pl. 347), 80.10 (pl. 376), 506.20AB (pl. 23, pl. 24), 218.34 (pl. 146), 218.1 (pl. 418), 37.21 (pl. 425), 175.20A (pl. 455), 516.29 (pl. 376), 257.13 (pl. 248), 15.19 (pl. 101), 334.20AB (pl. 58, pl. 59), Cp1892AB, CpApp14, 65.10 (pl. 1), 65.9 (pl. 1), 65.7 (pl. 4), 11.4 (pl. 39), 11.26 (pl. 39), Cp103, 29.1 (pl. 60), Cp218, Cp1244, Cp1505, Cp1716, 15.8 (pl. 100), 218.34 (pl. 146), 516.29 (pl. 376), 81.10 (pl. 376), 37.21 (pl. 425), 218.1 (pl. 418), and 45.28 (pl. 131), Cp589. The documents from Tun-huang examined include nos. 80, 81, 82, 83, and 315 in Chavannes 1913; and no. 3 in Hsia Nai 1948.

In the *Biography of Chung Chün* (fl. ca. 122–111 B.C.), the *Han-shu* mentions the *hsu* passport. The commentaries of Chang Yen and Su Lin say that it was written on silk and divided. The *hsu* passport then functioned as follows. The traveler was issued half of the passport at the pass of a region to continue his journey into that region; on his return journey, he would duly turn this part of the passport over to the authorities of the pass, and if it matched the other half he was permitted to pass. See HS (1962), p. 2819. However, the use of the *hsu* passport is not mentioned anywhere in either the Chü-yen or Tun-huang documents. It seems that in these frontier regions the wooden *fu* and *chuan* were used in place of the silk *hsu*, and the main reason for this seems to have been that silk was too precious on the frontier to use for passports.

Needless to say, the *chuan* and *fu* used as travel papers discussed in this section were different from the *chuan* and *fu* used as official and military credentials in Han times.

10. The Chinese text reads "i *chao-shu mai ch'i ma* Chiu-ch'üan Tun-huang Chang-i chün." The term *chao-shu* in this context was a technical usage in Han public documents, and it did not necessarily mean "imperial decree." Lao Kan transcribed *ch'i-yüeh* (seventh month) in this document as *shih-yüeh* (tenth month). *Ch'i-yüeh* is the correct reading.

11. The Chinese text reads *tang-she chuan-she*. This was a technical term in Han passports. The travelers named in them were entitled to lodging and sometimes transportation at the government stations (*chuan-she*). For detailed discussions of this, see Lao Kan 1960a, pp. 18–19; Ch'en P'an 1952, pp. 354–55; Ch'en Chih 1962c, p. 146; Ōba Osamu 1954b, pp. 22–23; Hamaguchi Shigekuni 1935b; and Hsia Nai 1948, p. 245. For the use of the *chuan-she*, see Lao Kan 1947, p. 91 (commentary by Wang Yü-ch'üan); and Pai Shou-i, pp. 98–99.

12. Lao Kan incorrectly deciphered Chang P'eng-tsu as Sun Shih in doc. 1274.

Doc. 1273 (29.1 in pl. 60) is Sun Shih's *fu* (and included his wife, daughter, and sister).

13. For the *kuo-so*, see docs. Cp1584AB (303.12), 140.1AB (pls. 412, 413), Cp1167AB (213.28), 170.3AB (pls. 109, 110), 80.10 (pl. 376), and Cp 1873(506.20AB); for the *chuan*, see 516.29 (pl. 376), 15.19 (pl. 101), 334.20AB (pls. 58, 59), and Cp1892AB (505.27AB); for the *fu*, see 29.1 (pl. 60), 29.2 (pl. 60), 65.7 (pl. 1), 65.9 (pl. 1), 65.10 (pl. 1), 11.26 (pl. 39), 11.4 (pl. 39), and Cp1505 (280.3). Examples of actual measurements of a few complete specimens, unbroken on either end, include: (1) *kuo-so*: 1 *ch'ih* by 1.8 *ts'un*, 1 *ch'ih* by 1 *ts'un*, 1.2 *ch'ih* by 0.6 *ts'un*, 1 *ch'ih* by 0.85 *ts'un*; (2) *chuan*: 9.4 by 1.2 *ts'un*, 1.05 *ch'ih* by 0.5 *ts'un*; and (3) *fu*: 6.1 by 1.1 *ts'un*, 6.1 by 1.2 *ts'un*, 6.2 by 0.9 *ts'un*, 6.2 by 1 *ts'un*, 7.8 by at least 0.5 *ts'un*, 1 *ch'ih* by at least 0.5 *ts'un*. For the broken ones, a few examples show that the width of the *kuo-so* ranges from 0.95 to 1.1 *ts'un* and the width of the *chuan*, from 0.5 to 0.9 *ts'un*. The length of the *fu* is 6.2 *ts'un*. The various *kuo-so* and *chuan* were originally issued from different parts of the Han empire (such as Chü-yen and Lu-te of Chang-yeh, Lu-fu of Chiu-ch'üan, Ch'ang-an, Lo-yang of Ho-nan, and Yang-chai of Ying-ch'uan) and at different times from 78 to 2 B.C., but there is no evidence that the time or place of issuance followed a particular convention for the size of these passports.

14. For the prescribed length of the *fu*, see docs. 7, 9, 782, 1441; SC (1959), p. 237; Ch'en P'an 1975, p. 42; and *Shuo-wen chieh-tzu* (1963 ed.), p. 96. For the standard size of the *kuo-so* and *chuan* prescribed in the Han Code, see Ju Shun's (fl. A.D. 189–265) commentary on *Han-shu* 12 in HS (1962), pp. 359–60 (Dubs, vol. 3, p. 84) and Ch'eng Shu-te, p. 75. For the different interpretations of the use of *chuan*, see HS (1955), p. 145; Pai Shou-i, p. 99; Wan Ssu-nien, p. 53 (article originally written in Japanese by Naitō Torajirō); and Yanai Wataru, p. 137. For the benefit of comparison, these are the sizes of three complete *fu* found at Tun-huang: 1 *ch'ih* by 0.39 *ts'un*, 1 *ch'ih* by 0.43 *ts'un*, and 1 *ch'ih* by 0.43 *ts'un*. They are comparable to their counterparts found at Chü-yen. See docs. 81, 82, 83 in Chavannes 1913.

15. See, for example, docs. 15.9, Cp1167AB, 140.1AB (pls. 412, 413), and Cp1982AB (in this document, *chien* should be corrected to read *chuan*.); and 334.20AB (pls. 58, 59).

16. The original Chinese text of the following document has the date *chia-ch'en*, but the intercalary month of the first year of Yuan-feng, beginning on the day *jen-shen* (April 26), does not contain the day *chia-ch'en*, which can be found in the next month and should be May 28. The intercalary month of this year contains three days beginning with the "heavenly stem" *chia*, namely, *chia-hsu* (April 28, 80 B.C.), *chia-shen* (May 8), and *chia-wu* (May 18). So it seems that the scribe erred in using *chia-ch'en* for one of these three dates. Unfortunately, the key words in two similar pieces in this series—65.10 (pl. 1) and 65.9 (pl. 1)—are not clear enough to allow a correction. For the meaning of the term *ts'ung-shih*, see *Shih-ching* (b), p. 1072; Bernard Karlgren, *The Book of Odes*, p. 157.

17. See, for example, docs. 562.3(15), 45.28(36).

18. Because these passports were kept at the passes and fords through which the travelers passed, they and their fragments were uncovered, often in groups, in the places that were the sites of ancient points of control for the Han frontier regions in Ho-hsi, of which both Tun-huang and Chü-yen, the two regions where the largest quantities of wooden documents have been uncovered, were parts. The practice of using the *kuo-so* just discussed is best illustrated by strips 140.1A and 140.1B on pls. 412 and 413.

19. Docs. 80, 81, 82, 83 in Chavannes 1913; see also THHCW (1949), p. 15.

20. For examples of such registers, see Chun-shu Chang 1977, pp. 182–85; and docs.

5962, 50.20(185) and CpApp14. For clarification of the procedure for reporting to superior offices, see docs. 148–49 and 150 in Chavannes 1913 (also in THHCW [1949], p. 24). See also Wang Kuo-wei 1914, supplement, pp. 5a–6a. For reports of the *fu* in regular accounts of the garrisons, see 394.2 (490) and 210.28 (496). For the routine inventory and inspection of the *chuan* in the garrison units, see docs. 1635 and 3028.

21. See docs. 1258 and 340.24(426). The horse-drawn carts were mostly counted in *sheng* units and the ox-drawn carts in *liang* units. See the documents cited earlier and 340.27(426), 335.15(420), 53.15(422), 54.11(421), 280.4(419), 280.3(419), 62.32(423), 62.13(423), 1258, 505.9(422), 340.24(426), 212.69(428A), and Cp966. The driving of an ox cart was called *ch'ih*. See docs. 403.12(421), 218.45(426), 67.3(603), 418.1(32), and 1258. To attend or manage a cart was called *chiang-chü*. See docs. Cp678, 1782, 1840.

22. See, for example, docs. Cp1708, 53.15(422), and 505.9(422). For a detailed discussion of this problem, see Lao Kan 1960a, p. 20; Ch'en P'an 1952, p. 368; HS 12 (1962), pp. 359–60 (including Yen Shih-ku's commentary on p. 360); and SC (1955), pp. 3729–30 (including the various commentaries).

23. See, for example, docs. 212.69(428A) and 174.29(382). For a detailed study of the *chuan-chü*, see Hamaguchi Shigekuni 1960; and Mori Shikazō 1957.

24. See, for example, docs. 53.15(422), 62.13(423), and 62.43(423).

25. The government-controlled carts were probably called *kuan-chü*. See doc. 167 in Maspero 1953.

26. See, for example, docs. 62.13(423), 67.3(603), 280.4(419), 280.3(419), 62.32(423), 25.2(424), and 42.13(426).

27. See, for example, docs. 4469, 5077. In these documents, Lao incorrectly deciphers *chia* as *tsu*. Docs. 1561, 1770, 1776, and 1540 also seem to have been records of hired carts; see Chun-shu Chang 1963, pp. 508–9, n. 251.

28. *The Biography of Liu Ch'ü-li*, in HS (1962), pp. 2879–80.

29. See docs. 346.36 (or 1782), pl. 88; and 77.7 (or 1840), pl. 89. Lao and the editors of *Chia-pien* incorrectly deciphered the word *chü* (cart) in doc. 346.36 as *chün* (army) (Cp1766). See also Ch'en Chih 1960, p. 44.

30. See docs. 54.24(427), 1277, 5286, 15.17(423), 74.22(420), 221.5(427), 6974, 6584, 3123, 1758, 1443, 4032, 9725, and 4087.

31. See doc. 54.24(427). Such cases are similar to those personnel registers that omitted the names of *chün* and *hsien* for local natives.

32. On the basis of the photographs of the two strips, I have reconstructed documents 428.2A and 483.13B as records of *hsiang-chü* (elephant-drawn carts). Recent archaeological reports and scholarly studies show that elephants were native to North China until early Chou times in about the eleventh century B.C. They were captured and trained to draw carts, assist with farm work, and fight in battle. They became extinct in North China as the forest cover was reduced and the human population increased. They continued to exist in South China, though after the third century B.C. they were generally to be found only in pockets in the remoter parts of the Yangtze watershed and southern frontier regions, particularly in mountainous areas such as southern Hupeh, Kwangtung, and Fukien. Elephants still were found occasionally in the middle Yangtze and Huai River regions, but in North China they were traditionally believed to have become extinct in the third century B.C. Now the Chü-yen documents indicate the possibility that in late Former Han and early Later Han times elephants were still used to draw carts, and possibly for other useful purposes, even on the northwestern frontiers of the Han

empire. This is one of the most surprising and significant discoveries in the study of the Chü-yen slips. For early mentions of and stories about elephants in ancient China, see Hsü Shen (b), p. 198; Ou-yang Hsün, pp. 1643–44; and Hsü Chien, pp. 698–99. For important recent studies of elephants in China, see Hsü Chung-shu 1935; Tu Hsü eh-chih; Lo Chen-yü 1927, p. 30b; Kuo Mo-jo 1965, pp. 512–13; Ch'en Meng-chia 1956, pp. 555–57; Yang Chung-chien and Liu Tung-sheng, p. 147; Edward H. Schafer 1957; Schafer 1963, pp. 79–83; Schafer 1967, pp. 224–26; H. G. Creel, pp. 74–76; Carl W. Bishop 1921; Li Chi, pp. 22, 37, 38; and Chang Kwang-chih 1977, p. 252.

33. See, for example, doc. 43.25B (or 6691), pl. 420.

34. See docs. 10075, 7468 (Lao incorrectly reads *chü-fu* as *chü-yu* in this document), 1443, 5778, 3368, 7328, 10111, 5286, 5329, Cp708, Cp1581, and 4032. See also Ch'en P'an 1961, p. 63. Among the weapons and tools the *chü-fu* received were metal arrowheads, saws, cauldrons, *kung* (a particular part of the hub of a wheel), *fu*-style axes (axes whose edge and handle are parallel), *chin*-style axes (axes whose edge is at ninety degrees to the handle), and large and small pincers.

35. For the *shu-tsu* attached to carts, see docs. 1277, 6974, 4087, 6584, and 9725.

36. Ch'en P'an (1974, p. 74) holds that *chü-tsu* was another name for *chü-fu*. But documents 10075 and 7468 clearly show that they were different. Both documents list *chü-fu* and *chü-tsu* side by side. If the two terms were synonymous, they would not be listed separately in such a manner in these documents:

1 . . . commanding *chü-fu* and *chü-tsu* . . .	484.67
	10075
	pl. 601
2. The Huan-hsi *sui*: *chü-fu* and *chü-tsu* . . .	83.5A
	7468
	pl. 465

37. See docs. Cp1662 and 7468.

38. Ch'en P'an (1961, pp. 60–63) holds that a *chü-tzu* was a young cart attendant. This view is only partly correct. As stated earlier, the *chü-tzu* was a cart attendant, but he was specifically an attendant on an officer's carriage (doc. 206.27). Doc. 14.12(476) shows that a man named Shih Ssu, age twenty-five, attended the carriage of an officer named Lan. Shih Ssu was probably a *chü-tzu*. If such was the case, the *chü-tzu* were not necessarily very young. In 1969, a tomb at Lei-t'ai in Wu-wei of Kansu was opened. Dated to the period A.D. 168–210, the tomb yielded, among numerous valuable items, ninety-eight bronze figures of horses and chariot and carriage models. Eight of the horses and figures of male and female slaves were inscribed. These inscriptions indicate that the carriages were attended by *chiang-chü nu* (slave carriage attendants). It seems that the *chiang-chü nu* were of the same class as the *chü-tzu*. See Kan Po-wen, p. 17; and Kansu sheng po-wu-kuan, p. 105.

39. See, for example, doc. Cp678 quoted and translated in chapter 3 of volume 1 of this book. For a discussion of this, see Lao Kan 1960a, p. 23.

40. For *chü-wu*, see Cp345; for *chü-k'u*, see doc. 280.4(419). See Li Shan's (d. A.D. 689) commentary on the usage of the word *k'u* in the *Wen-hsüan* (vol. 1, p. 48) and docs. 1234 and 1258.

41. See docs. 25.2(242), 41.28(420), 505.13(421), 62.13(423), 505.9(423), 53.15(422), 502.6(422), 505.12(421), and 506.3(422).

42. See Chun-shu Chang 1963, chap. 5, sec. 3.1.D (p. 370); and doc. 9637.

43. For *chuan-ma*, see docs. 212.69(428A), 303.22(253), and 503.19(265). For *i-ma* or *i-ch'i*, see docs. 78.36(425), 231.2(245), 192.24(249), and 521.28(216). For *hou-ma*, see docs. 90.30(427), 515.45(422), and 401.1(248).

44. See docs. 53.15(422), 505.9(423), and 25.2(424).

45. See doc. 497.2(265). For a discussion of the term *ts'ui-ma*, see Yü Hao-liang 1961, p. 452. Yü holds that *ts'ui-ma* were *fu-ma* (secondary horses). Needless to say, the word *ts'ui* in this context meant "secondary," "reserve," "contingent," "deputy," and so on.

46. Docs. 19.1(421), 46.7(313). Doc. 44.15(424) records the term *nan-ma* (southern horse). Perhaps the horses were also referred to by their geographical origins. This nomenclature was definitely related to the grading of horses in Han times. For such grading, see Tsou Chieh-cheng, pp. 41–42. According to the Chü-yen documents, the price of a regular horse was around five thousand in cash, but the price of a *yung-ma* was about four thousand. See docs. 554.2(548), 229.1(174), 5871, 4128, 3338, and 37.35(455); see also Mori Shikazō 1957, pp. 252–53.

47. See, for example, doc. 560.8(420).

48. See, for example, doc. Cp1191.

49. Such words as *p'iao*, *chan*, and *ch'ieh*, which all mean "to cut," are often associated with the registers or records of horses, oxen, and donkeys in the Chü-yen and Tun-huang documents. For registers of oxen, see my later discussion; for the use of the word *ch'ieh*, see THHCW, no. 341 (Chavannes incorrectly deciphered *hsin* [horse in purple] as *p'ien* [parallel] in this document). When these words were used, they were often preceded by directional words (such as *tso*, "left") and numbers (such as *liang*, "two"), which indicated the side of the animal that received such actions and their number. Shen Yüan (1962, p. 427) maintains that the words *p'iao* and *chan* were synonymous with the word *hsiao* (to cut) but offers no interpretation of the meaning of *p'iao* and *chan* in the context of the horse and ox registers and records in the Chü-yen documents. It seems to me that the use of the word *ch'ieh* in the Tun-huang documents throws light on our understanding of the problem. Doc. 341 in THHCW mentions a certain male animal marked by *liang ch'ieh*. The function of the word *ch'ieh* in this document is the same as that of the words *p'iao* and *chan* in the horse and ox registers. *Ch'ieh* means "to take something away." The words *p'iao* and *chan* generally mean "to stab, cut, or puncture." Putting together the meanings of the three words, the whole process can be understood as one of operating on the animals and leaving certain permanent marks on them. But the shape and function of the marks remain unknown, as does the exact nature of the operation. And the two aspects seem to be related. If the purpose of the operation was for identification, a simple process of branding by cauterization would have been enough. If the purpose was removal of the reproductive organs, the more complicated operation of castration or spaying would have been required. The latter case seems less likely, for according to the *Shuo-wen chieh-tzu*, which was completed ca. A.D. 100 by Hsu Shen, in Han times the castration of horses and oxen was called *sheng* and *chien* (or *kai*), respectively. (On this, see Hsu Shen [b], pp. 29, 30, 201. See also Chia Ssu-hsieh, p. 92; Shih Sheng-han 1957, p. 61; and Shih Sheng-han 1962, pp. 68–69.) Therefore, it seems very likely that the words *p'iao*, *chan*, and *ch'ieh* signified the operation of branding. The three words were apparently peculiar to three different categories of animal: *p'iao* to horses, *chan* to oxen, and *ch'ieh* to donkeys. However, the three processes of branding seem to have differed. For horses and donkeys, the process of branding, as the words *p'iao* and *ch'ieh* suggest, may have been simply one of shaving the hair then cauterizing the skin with special markings, but for oxen the process, as the word *chan* suggests, may have been

one of notching the left—always the left—horn in different ways. The Ch'in statutes on bamboo slips discovered in 1975 at Shui-hu-ti of Yun-meng hsien in Hupeh lend strong support to both interpretations. One legal document concerned with horse thievery mentions a case in which the expression yu-p'iao (right p'iao) was taken as a critical mark of identification, and another document concerned with litigation over the ownership of oxen uses the expression yu-chüeh (having horns) as a critical mark of identification. The context of both expressions corresponds to that of the words p'iao and chan in the registers and records on Chü-yen wooden slips. Cf. especially doc. 512.25, (pl. 66) or Cp2131. See Chun-shu Chang 1963, pp. 513–14; and Yun-meng Ch'in-chien, pt. 3, pp. 34–35. See also Wang Meng-ou 1966 (pp. 10–13), which suggests that chan was a physiognomic remark; and Michael Loewe 1967 (vol. 2, p. 302), which suggests that chan and p'iao referred to the cutting of the horns of the animals. Loewe's suggestion raises no questions with oxen, but it would hardly apply to horses. Wang's suggestion is also questionable. No surviving ancient texts or remarks on the physiognomy of horses, including the Hsiang-ma ching (Physiognomy of Horses), discovered at Ma-wang-tui of Ch'ang-sha in Hunan in 1973, contain the word p'iao. See Hsiang-ma ching, pp. 17–22; Chuang-tzu, pp. 186–87; Lü-shih ch'un-ch'iu, pp. 225–26; Chia Ssu-hsieh, pp. 75–87; Ou-yang Hsün, pp. 1611–20, 1625–28; and Hsü Chien, pp. 701–6.

50. The word huang in the original Chinese document was incorrectly deciphered in the Chien-pien and by Lao Kan.

51. Mori Shikazō (1957) also discussed the horse registers of the Chü-yen region, but his analysis was limited without the benefit of Lao Kan 1957 and the Chien-pien, which had not been published at that time.

52. The word yueh (month) in the original Chinese document was incorrectly deciphered as kuan (official, office) in the Chien-pien.

53. See docs. 51.23(475), 174.17(290), 212.65(481), 9018, 20.11(9), and 174.17(290). Both Ōba Osamu (1955, p. 64) and Mori Shikazō (1957, p. 239) mistook the se-fu of a stable for a district official. Docs. 20.11 and 174.17 clearly indicate that he was not the latter.

54. See doc. 198.13(428C).

55. See Chun-shu Chang 1963, pp. 377–78. It is interesting to note that T'un-yuan was also the place where the T'un-yuan Granary was located. The T'un-yuan Stable was seemingly closely connected with the granary. Perhaps T'un-yuan was a center of both food supplies and horses for the northern Chü-yen region. Officer Sun, mentioned in doc. 1166, was the chief clerk of the T'un-yuan Granary (doc. 297.17, pl. 325). Some scholars also mistakenly identified Chao-wu Stable as part of the administration of Chao-wu hsien. See Fujieda Akira 1954, p. 654.

56. See also docs. 192.24(249), Cp1593, Cp1921, 32.15(267), 303.23(248), 2378, and 3976. Detailed discussions of this can be found in Chun-shu Chang 1963, pp. 378–82, 514. The monthly rates for p'ang-huang and hay cannot be calculated with certainty. But it seems that the rate for p'ang-huang should have been very close to that for unhusked grain (see doc. 507.3A, pl. 116) and the rate for hay should have been about five to nine bales a day (see doc. 3976). For special methods of horse feeding, see Chia Ssu-hsieh, p. 82.

57. See, for example, doc. 269.6(247).

58. Part of the document was broken and lost. Lao Kan and the editors of Chien-pien incorrectly read ch'ih as chang in the Chinese original. The pu time corresponded roughly to 4 to 6 p.m. A detailed description of time divisions in the Han period will be given later.

59. See also docs. 25.2(242) and 505.13(421).

60. See, for example, docs. 509.20(264), 2210, 2820, and Cp181B.

61. Detailed discussions of the organization and work of land cultivation in the Chü-yen region can be found in Chun-shu Chang 1963, pp. 455–72.

62. Doc. 517.7(426) or 5922. Local oxen were also for sale. Doc. 2820 records that the price of a *fu-niu* was three thousand in cash, and Cp181B indicates that the price of a *yung-niu* was the same. See also 116.1(429).

63. For a discussion of the meaning of the word *chan*, see n. 49.

64. The original Chinese expressions are *chiu tso-yu* or "growths on both shoulders" (510.28, pl. 71, Cp2071), *chiu tso-chien* or "growths on the left shoulder" (517.16, pl. 84; Cp2264), and *wu-chiu* or "no growths on either shoulder" (515.24, pl. 120; Cp2136; 520.2, Cp2280). The interpretation presented here is based on my understanding of the words *chiu* and *nao* or *chiao* in the *Shuo-wen chieh-tzu* ([b], pp. 114, 119), *Chou-li* ([a], pp. 259–60), and *I-li* (chap. 38, pp. 6b, 4a). My early experiences with farming in a traditional Chinese village in North China is also helpful in my understanding of these difficult expressions. Recent discoveries of various models of ox-drawn carts have also greatly enhanced our understanding of the problem. See *Hsin Chung-kuo ch'u-t'u wen-wu*, pl. 84; *Kan Po Wen*, pl. 6; and *Kansu sheng po-wu kuan* 1974, pl. 7. Michael Loewe (1967, vol. 2, pp. 302, 305, 307) suggests that *chiu* means "to cauterize." This seems to be another possible interpretation. But if the cauterization was for branding the theory encounters difficulties. For in some of the ox registers (e.g., docs. 510.28, 520.2, and 512.34) both *tso-chan* and *chiu* or *wu-chiu* occurred and if *tso-chan*, as discussed earlier, signified a branding mark there was no need for a cauterization mark as a sign of branding. The indication of *wu-chiu* is even more inexplicable. Therefore, the expression *chiu* in these registers clearly had a different purpose. Since growths affected the condition, and hence the grading, of the oxen, it seems reasonable to assume that the various remarks on the direction and existence of *chiu* in ox registers or records were for grading purposes. For the deciphering of the ox registers, see also Shen Yuan 1962, p. 62.

65. *Chia-pien* incorrectly reads *ch'ih* (age) as *shou* (head) in the original Chinese document. Lao Kan incorrectly reads *t'ou* as *p'in* and *ch'ih* as *shou* in the 1960 version of his transliteration (doc. 1467), and he also reads *ch'ih* as *shou* in the 1949 version (doc. 512.6 on p. 428B).

66. In this document, Lao Kan incorrectly read *t'e* (male) as *shun* (yellow ox), *ch'ih* (age) as *shou*, and *hsieh* (length) as *ch'ih*; he also left *li* and *tso* undeciphered. See doc. 491.8(429). The editors of *Chia-pien* followed Lao's version but changed the blank for *tso* to *hsien*.

67. See, for example, doc. Cp255.

68. See doc. Cp8444.

69. Doc. 512.1 or 1449.

70. Docs. 6989, 217.13(328), 509.20(264) or Cp2037. For doc. 509.20, Lao mistook *tang* for *shang* (reward) and *sheng-ta* for *tou-chiao*.

71. See doc. Cp2037.

72. See, for example, docs. 41.28(420) and 280.3(419).

73. Lao Kan 1960a, p. 20.

74. See particularly map 2 ("The Edsen-gol Region") and map 3 ("The Archaeological Remains of the Etsina Oasis") in Bo Sommarström 1956–58, vol. 1; and map 3 in this volume.

75. See particularly Huang Wen-pi 1948, pp. 59–60; and Bo Sommarström 1956–58.

76. The *Chiu-chang suan-shu*, vol. 2, pp. 23, 24. For a detailed discussion of the dat-

ing and related problems of the *Chiu-chang suan-shu,* see Joseph Needham et al. 1954–, vol. 3, pp. 24–27; Li Yen, *Chung-kuo suan-hsueh shih* (Reprint; Taipei: Shangwu, 1955), pp. 13–18; and Ch'ien Pao-tsung, *Chung-kuo shu-hsueh shih* (Peking: K'o-hsueh, 1964), pp. 32–33.

77. "Transferred grain" is a translation of the technical term *chuan-ku.* The word *chuan* was incorrectly deciphered as *fu* in Lao Kan 1960a and *Chia-pien.*

78. For a detailed analysis of the financial and economic conditions and their relationship with the central government, see Chun-shu Chang 1963, chap. 5, sec. 2, especially pp. 287–90.

79. This document was discovered at the site of P'o-ch'eng-tzu, the headquarters of the Chia-ch'ü *hou-kuan.* The editors of *Chia-pien* incorrectly read Wei *chün* as Wei *tu* in the original Chinese document (Cp587).

80. For a detailed study of the servicemen's clothing system and the supply of clothes and clothing materials by different regions of the empire, see Chun-shu Chang 1963, pp. 300–312. The regions that supplied clothing materials to Chü-yen were centers of Han China's textile industries, including Kuang-han, Ho-nei, Tu-nei, and Wei.

81. This translation follows a new decipherment of the document based on photographs of the slip: "Ch'u *chuan-ku* ch'i-ch'ien ch'i-pai wu-shih chiu shih." Both Lao Kan 1949 (99.4 on p. 298) and Lao Kan 1960a mistranscribed this document by leaving *ch'i* (seven) and *shih* (bushel) undeciphered.

82. This document was discussed in chapter 2.

83. I-lu *hou* belonged to Chia-ch'ü *hou-kuan*; its headquarters was located at I-lu *sui.* Lao Kan deciphered *shih-jen* (ten soldiers) in the original document as *nien-jen* (twenty soldiers). Lao Kan considers the female interpreters mentioned in this document to be non-Chinese (1960a, p. 23).

84. This translation is based on a decipherment of this long wooden document; both Lao Kan and the editors of *Chia-pien* transcribed a slightly different version. *Chi* in the original document refers to Cheng Chi (fl. 67–49 B.C.); *chief commandant* refers to the chief commandant of I-hsun of Shan-shan.

85. HS (1962), pp. 230, 3002, 3877–78. The name of the king of Lou-lan is given as An-kuei in *Han-shu* 7 (*Chao-ti chi*) and as Ch'ang-kuei in *Han-shu* 96A (*Hsi-yü chuan*). The discrepancy is likely the result of a copyist's error. See also Yen Shih-ku's commentary on this issue in HS (1962), p. 3879.

86. Chun-shu Chang 1978, sec. 5, presents a systematic examination of the Han expansion in the Western Regions.

87. The document was discovered at Ta-wan. Presumably, the decree was handed to the Chien-shui *tu-wei* by Subcommandant Chang when he entered the Chü-yen region from the south.

88. A detailed discussion of this development is given in Chun-shu Chang 1978, sec. 5 (on stages of Han expansion in the Western Regions). See also HS (1962), pp. 3005, 3922–24; *T'ung-chien,* pp. 827–29; and Shen Wei-hsien, p. 15. My interpretation of the wooden document is different from the one in Lao Kan 1960a, p. 23.

89. Docs. 267.19(59), Cp1803, Cp2361. I tentatively date these documents to 60 B.C., 53 B.C., and 51 B.C., respectively, on the basis of their contents and the history of the events surrounding the persons mentioned in them.

90. The distances between the key points in Ho-hsi and from Ch'ang-an to these points in Han times are calculated from information in HS (1962), p. 3875; HHS (1962), pp. 3403, 3520–21; *Kua-ti chih,* p. 262; Ku Tsu-yü, *ts'e* 20, p. 31a; Hsü Sung, p.

3467; and Lao Kan 1960a, pp. 32–33. As was discussed earlier, the Jade Gate Pass, the western gate of the Han empire, was located in what is now called Hsiao-fang-p'an or TXIV in Aurel Stein's report. The distance between Chü-yen and Lu-te was variously suggested as 1,200 and 1,530 li. The estimate of 1,530 li (roughly 638 kilometers) was suggested in the *Kua-ti chih*, compiled under the auspices of Li T'ai in A.D. 642, and that of 1,200 li was suggested in the *Tu-shih fang-yü chi-yao* by Ku Tsu-yü (1631–92). The difference between the two suggestions is due to the different ways of figuring the distance. The T'ang estimate evidently reflected the distance of actual travel from Chü-yen to Chang-yeh (the T'ang name for the Han Lu-te) in the seventh century, and Ku Tsu-yü's estimate reflected seventeenth-century conditions. Both estimates do not in any way reflect the distance as the crow flies. The modern distance by road between the two points is actually less than 1,000 li. For this reason, I have used Ku Tsu-yü's estimate in my study. The *Kua-ti chih* (p. 227) also suggested that the distance from the Han Lu-te to Chü-yen Lake (Chü-yen *tse*) was 1,064 li (roughly 443 kilometers). One Chü-yen document discovered in P'o-ch'eng-tzu indicates that the distance from a certain *hou-kuan* to a certain other place was 1,063 li, or roughly 443 kilometers (doc. 49.9[481]). One wonders whether the reference to Chü-yen Lake in the *Kua-ti chih* might really refer to some other place in the Chü-yen region such as Chia-ch'ü *hou-kuan*. The other possibility is that doc. 49.9 was transferred to P'o-ch'eng-tzu from a location on the shore of Chü-yen Lake. Neither suggestion is supported by other wooden documents. The Chü-yen documents also suggest that the distance from the Chien-shui *hou-kuan* to Lu-te was 600 li (roughly 250 kilometers). See docs. 13.7(439) and 37.57(455). Chü-yen hsin-chien EPT–59: 582 is a waybill posting the distance between stations (*shih*) from Ch'ang-an to Chü-yen in Ho-hsi. It lists nineteen stations but not in the right order. Some parts are certainly missing. It refers only to stations, not cities or large garrison settlements. For example, it says there are only 90 Han li between Chü-yen and Lu-te. Unless the missing parts are found, this document is useless for our research. Doc. EPT–50: 10 indicates that the distance between Ming-sha Ward and Lu-te was 1,060 Han li, further confirming our view. However, the recently unearthed (1990–93) Han documents (dated 111 B.C.–A.D. 107) in the Han Hsuan-ch'üan Station (*chih*) 64 kilometers east of Tunhuang in Hsiao-ku *hsien* show the distance from there to several stations and places and the distance between eleven stations in Chiu-ch'üan (694 Han li or roughly 286 kilometers). Unfortunately, many critical parts and some key information are also missing. As the documents stand now, the most useful for my study is the distance from Hsuanch'üan to Chang-yeh Station (not Lu-te of Chang-yeh *chün*), 1,275 li (Han), or roughly 526 kilometers, and to Ch'ang-an, 4,080 li or roughly 1,685 kilometers. Doc. V 92 DXT 161: 39 AB contains the word *Chang-yeh*, which must refer to the station in Chang-yeh *hsien* of Wu-wei *chün* since Lu-te, the capital of Chang-yeh *chün*, which was sometimes referred to as Chang-yeh in Han documents, a common convention in early times, was only 800 li (Han) from Tun-huang. All these figures generally confirm my own calculations. The minor differences are due to the fact that the figures in the Hsuan-ch'üan document were the distances between stations (*chih*) and not the distance via the imperial highway. Stations were often located some distance off the highway, and some of them were far from any regular transportation route. T'ang Tsung-i published a solid study of the roads and communication routes in Han times, but it, too, is useless for our research, although it is very good for other parts of the Han empire. See T'an, *Han-tai kuo-nei lulu chiao-t'ung k'ao* (Hong Kong: Hsin-ya yen-chiu so, 1967).

91. Sven Hedin 1938, p. 228.

92. In researching and writing this section, I consulted the following works for comparative purposes: John C. Lowe and S. Moryadas, *The Geography of Movement* (Boston, 1975); Jean Labatut and Wheaton Jane Lane, eds., *Highways in Our National Life* (Princeton, 1950); Gerald Kraft, *The Role of Transportation in Regional Economic Development* (Lexington, MA, 1971); Norman E. Lee, *Travel and Transport through the Ages* (Victoria, Australia, 1951); Albert C. Leighton, *Transport and Communication in Early Medieval Europe, A.D. 500–1100* (Newton Abbot, Devon, England, 1972).

93. See doc. 18.18(108) and 6241.

94. See docs. 413.3(271), 562.1A(263), and 3271. See also Lao Kan 1948a, p. 75; Lao Kan 1960a, pp. 2–3, 20; Lou Tsou-i 1963, p. 124; and Mori Shikazō 1957, pp. 238–42.

95. Docs. Cp185, 6241, 413.3(271), Cp2358B, 1767, and 64; Chun-shu Chang 1963, pp. 318–20. See also Lao Kan 1948, p. 91 (Wang Yü-ch'üan's comments); Pai Shou-i, pp. 89–99; Lou Tsu-i 1939, pp. 98–99; and Ch'en Meng-chia 1963b, p. 105. However, it must be pointed out that the postal system on the frontier had been, as already noted, simplified to fit local conditions. The classification of *t'ing* (lodge), *yu* (post house), *i* (post station), and *chuan* (government station) used in the interior of the Han empire was too unpractical to be followed in a frontier region such as Chü-yen.

96. Several points in the original document need clarification. Yeh-wang, at the beginning of the document, refers to Feng Yeh-wang, who was the grand herald (*ta hung-lu*) from 37 to 34 B.C. (HS [1962], pp. 820, 3302). Therefore, this document must have been issued and transmitted to the frontier in that period. The phrase *ch'eng-shu ts'ung-shih hsia tang-yung-che* was a technical term in Han official documentary writings; it indicated that the document in question was an imperial decree or government order issued by the court or the central government to lower offices in the empire. (This phrase was changed to *chu-che hsing-shih* in later periods.) For detailed discussions of the Han documentary style in this respect, see Wang Kuo-wei 1914, vol. 2, p. 2b; Lao Kan 1960a, p. 7; and Chavannes 1913, pp. 41–43 (Chavannes, however, mistakes *ch'eng* for *feng* in his documents nos. 136, 138, 143, 291, 450). The phrase *pieh-shu hsiang-pao* (sometimes just *pieh-shu*) corresponds to *shu-tao ming-pai pu* (sometimes just *ming-pai pu*) in similar documents. It indicates that the decree or order had to be copied for circulation among concerned units or people or both. The phrase *shu-tao-yen* was also a common technical term in Han official documents. It appeared at the end of a document to indicate the requirement for a return receipt (cf. docs. 513 and 8297). A general procedure for transmitting imperial decrees in Han times was as follows: they went first from the imperial secretary to the chancellor, then from the chancellor to officials of the full 2,000-*shih* rank, officials of the 2,000-*shih* rank, governors, and chancellors of the feudal kingdoms. These officials would then direct their offices to copy the imperial decrees and send them to their subordinate officials, whose offices in turn would do the same, sending the decrees farther down in the official hierarchy, with the process continuing until they reached the lowest levels. With respect to the Chü-yen region, the imperial decrees could either be sent first to the office of the Chang-yeh governor and then to the office of the Chü-yen magistrate or the office of the Chü-yen chief commandant or both or they could be sent directly from the central government to the office of the Chü-yen chief commandant, all depending on the nature of the decrees and their timing. In any case, when the Chü-yen chief commandant received the imperial decrees he would direct his office to copy them and would see to it that they were transmitted down the ladder of the garrison hierarchy from commandants to subcommandants to commanders.

For a discussion of the procedures for transmitting imperial decrees and government orders, see Lao Kan 1960a, pp. 7–8, 33; and Ōba Osamu 1961, pp. 11–12. Ōba's study is particularly useful because he reconstructed the procedure for the transmission of an imperial decree in a sequence of wooden documents dated 61 B.C.: docs. 590(10.27), 401(5.10), 872(332.26), 1445(10.33), 588(10.30), 556(10.32), 557(10.29), and 559(10.31), which are arranged in order of their sequence of transmission.

97. See note 96. For more examples of this, see docs. 3250, 3135, and 3294. It seems that this type of transmission went through both the *t'ing* and the *i* in Chü-yen. See doc. 419.

98. For other examples, see docs. 1846, 2322, 5074, 7150, 7475, 7628, 7632, 7599, 7669, 7610, Cp1626, Cp852, 41.25(155), and 308.25(157). For a detailed discussion of this subject, see Chun-shu Chang 1963, pp. 387–89.

99. This translation basically follows the decipherment in Lao Kan 1949. The original document was written on a *ku* (goblet), and its photographs are on pp. 524–25 in Lao Kan 1957. In Lao Kan 1960a, the decipherment of this document is divided into eight separate fragments, docs. 8219, 8220, 8227, 8232, 8238, 8239, 8241, and 8247. A complete and revised version of this document can be found in Chun-shu Chang 1977, p. 153. For the interpretation of *ching feng-huo* in this document, see Ch'en P'an 1960, p. 209. My translation here is tentative, of course, for this is probably the most difficult piece in the Chü-yen documents.

100. For a detailed examination of this, see Lao Kan 1960a, p. 3.

101. See also docs. 1322, 2125, 3634, 3856, 3877, 5352, 5433, 5717, 145.13(147), and Cp1431.

102. The term *i-lai* in the original Chinese text was a technical term used in the system of postal delivery. It means "[the said soldier] came with [the mail]."

103. For the meaning of *sheng* in the original document, see Ju Shun's commentary in *Han-shu* 13 (1962, pp. 57–58).

104. For studies of the *yu* system in Han times, see Hamaguchi Shigekuni 1935b; Sogabe Shizuo 1956; Ho Ch'ang-ch'ün 1940; Lou Tsu-i 1963, pp. 123–25; Pai Shou-i, pp. 94–96; Lao Kan 1948a; Lan Kan 1950a, and Yen Keng-wang 1961, pp. 60–61. Needless to say, as in many other respects, the frontier postal system and other organizations of conveyance did not follow the system used in the interior. For instance, the distance between two postal stations was generally fixed in the interior, but the wooden documents do not show that such was the case in Chü-yen. This is quite understandable, for, as the Han frontier system was designed to be functional and the general needs and geographical conditions of the frontier regions (whether Chü-yen or the Western Regions) and the interior were generally different, a fixed and indiscriminate application of the same system under differing local conditions would have destroyed the original purpose of the system.

105. See also docs. 5495, 7397, 7400, 7589, 21.3(159), 363.1(160), 4590, and 3838.

106. The word *fu* in the original Chinese document is incorrectly deciphered as *su* by Lao Kan and as *ping* by the editors of *Chien-pien* (Cp456). Both Lao Kan and the editors of *Chia-pien* also read *chang* as *keng*.

107. Document 81.8A (or 7420) shows that this correspondence was sent from Ch'eng-ao Watch Station of T'o-t'o *hou-kuan*.

108. See, for example, docs. 5628, 5528, and 4498.

109. See, for example, docs. 1496, 7634, and 5752; and Chun-shu Chang 1963, pp. 394–95. *Li-ma ch'ih-hsing* was a technical term in the Han postal system indicating

"urgent delivery." It does not mean that the mail was delivered by an officer riding a speedy horse. Mori Shikazō misunderstood this point in his article of 1957 and identified the *ch'i-li* in doc. 15.24(451) as the *li* in *li-ma ch'ih-hsing* (Mori Shikazō 1957, pp. 240–41). Actually the *ch'i-li* in Han times was a guard not a postal officer. See *Han-shu* 76 (1962, p. 3212). A speedy horse could run 400 to 500 (Han) *li* (roughly 166 to 208 kilometers) a day. See Lao Kan 1948a, p. 75. For the *wang-jen ch'ih-piao han*, see doc. Cp1912. The term literally means "dispatches to be sent in a red mailbag as fast as one would run for one's life." The most urgent mail was always delivered in red or red and white mailbags. It was also called *pen-ming-shu*, literally "mail to be transmitted as fast as possible without taking a rest." See HS (1962), p. 3416.

110. See docs. 311.6(153), 136.44(158), 136.39(158), 136.43(158), 259.1(151), 214.34(152), Cp914, Cp925, Cp932, and Cp1023.

111. For the collation of official documents and dispatches, see Ch'en P'an 1952, pp. 368–69; 1947, pp. 328–30.

112. See, for example, docs. 393, 5707, 4497, 109.9(122), 284.4(121), and 5496, where *wei-shih* should read *hou-shih*.

113. Lou Tsu-i 1963, pp. 126–30; Lao Kan 1960a, pp. 31–33. Detailed discussions of this and the preceding aspects may be found in Chun-shu Chang 1963, pp. 365–68.

114. Lao Kan 1960a, pp. 31–33.

115. For the *p'ai-tan* of later periods, see John K. Fairbank and Ssu-yü Teng 1961, p. 9. See also Lou Tsu-i 1963, pp. 134–35, 137.

116. For a detailed explanation of the usage of *chung-ch'eng* and *pu chung-ch'eng* in Ch'in and Han times, see Ch'en P'an 1977, pp. 104b–105a. For examples in wooden documents, see docs. Cp994, Cp1912, 137.1 (143–44), 55.11(56), 229.24 on pl. 291, 2702 on pl. 339, and 56.37 on pl. 368.

117. See, for example, doc. Cp1914.

118. See also docs. 1535, 2746, 2920, 5339, Cp1910AB, Cp767, Cp1912, 188.21(146), 231.2(148), 505.39(124), 506.1(124), and 506.16(124).

119. For the meaning of *wang-jen ch'ih-piao han*, see note 109.

120. The time divisions of a day in Han times is a complex subject. Lao Kan (1960a, pp. 67–73; 1969, esp. pp. 356–67), Ch'en P'an (1947, pp. 335–38), Ch'en Meng-chia (1965b, esp. pp. 113–32), and others have made significant contributions to our understanding of this issue. On the basis of these studies (which often disagree with each other) and my own research, a general picture can be drawn as follows. The whole day, divided into twenty-four "hours" in modern times, was in Han times divided into twelve major periods called *shih*, each equaling roughly two present-day hours: *yeh-pan* (or *yeh-shih*), *chi-ming*, *p'ing-tan*, *jih-ch'u*, *shih-shih* (or *tsao-shih*), *tung-chung* (or *yü-chung*), *jih-chung*, *jih-tieh*, *hsia-pu* (or *pu-shih*), *jih-ju*, *huang-hun* (or *hun-shih*), and *jen-ting*. The whole 24-hour day was also divided into 100 smaller units called *k'o* or *fen*, each corresponding to 14 minutes and 24 seconds in our modern system. In the Han system, the daytime consisted of the seven periods from *p'ing-tan* through *huang-hun* and the nighttime was composed of the other five periods. Each period in the daytime had almost exactly 8.5 *k'o* (or *fen*), whereas each period in the nighttime had only 8 *k'o*. There were a total of just under 60 *k'o* in the daytime and exactly 40 *k'o* in the nighttime. The 40-*k'o* nighttime was also divided into five parts, namely, *chia-yeh*, *i-yeh*, *ping-yeh*, *ting-yeh*, and *wu-yeh*, each having 8 *k'o*. The details of the Han system of time division is summarized in table 32.

121. The word *ch'ü* in *tang-ch'ü* (watch station) in the original Chinese document

was left undeciphered in *Chia-pien*, and the word *ch'i* (seven) in *ch'i-fen* was misread as *shih* (ten).

122. Lao Kan read *chiang* as *ch'u*, *ch'ih* as *chin*, *ssu* (four) as *jih* (day), and *wu-shih* (fifty) as *nien* (twenty) in the original Chinese document. The term *chieh-ho* appears in many wooden documents (e.g., Cp390, 716, 1015, and 1757). Yü Hao-liang (1961, p. 454) holds that *ho* was used for *ho* (duty) and the term *chieh-ho* means "to be released from one's post or duty." But Yen Shih-ku suggested in his commentary on *Han-shu* 81 that *chieh-ho* meant *fen-shu* (to explain a mistake or argue a point). Yen Shih-ku was correct. See HS (1962), p. 3346.

123. Lao Kan read *shu-ming* (several) as *she-ming* (names of people who received amnesty) in the original Chinese document.

124. Lao Kan and the editors of *Chia-pien* deciphered the words *yin-p'o* (seal broken) as *chia-ch'en* in the original document. The photograph of the two words is not very clear, but it still shows more of the form of *yin-p'o* than of *chia-ch'en*. Furthermore, similar documents, some of which were cited earlier, show that the writing in this line always consists of the seal (name), organizational affiliation, and title of the originator (or sender) of the mail. In the event that the seal was broken, two words—*yin-p'o*—were written in its place. See docs. 4876 and 4901. Therefore, *yin-p'o* is taken as the correct interpretation.

125. See note 120.

126. Doc. 1962 in Lao Kan 1960a, photograph on pl. 95, also on p. 127 in Lao Kan 1949.

127. See Cp767 for doc. 133.23(199); and doc. 5381 and pl. 327 for doc. 231.2, which is also on p. 148 of Lao Kan 1949.

128. Lao Kan 1960a, pp. 20, 33.

129. Doc. 317.27(148), or 5390, may also be a key document for studies of the time limits for the transmission of correspondence, but its key words are undecipherable and hence it does not provide any information of critical importance. It does, however, indicate that the time limit for the postal delivery in question was not over 12.5 *li* (5.21 kilometers) per Han *shih*.

130. Compare the distance to be covered at the ordinary rate for horse post in Ch'ing times (A.D. 1644–1911) examined in John K. Fairbank and Ssu-yü Teng 1961, esp. pp. 17–18. However, the Ch'ing *li*, equivalent to 576 meters, was larger than the Han *li*. See Ch'en Meng-chia 1966, p. 42; and Tseng Wu-hsiu 1964, p. 177. It is interesting to note here that the Han rate for horse post was almost identical to the T'ang (A.D. 618–907) rate. This is one of the institutional continuities from the Han to the T'ang. For the T'ang rate, see Li Shu-t'ung 1977, p. 223.

131. Lao Kan 1948, pp. 74–75.

132. HS (1962), pp. 57–58 (including Ju Shun's commentary).

133. Lien-sheng Yang 1961, pp. 147–48; Lao Kan 1960a, pp. 34–37; Chun-shu Chang 1977, pp. 144–48.

134. Lao Kan left *so* undeciphered.

135. Lao Kan and the editors of *Chia-pien* read the second *jih* (day) in the phrase *jih jih-chung shih* as *hsi* (west), that is, "*jih hsi-chung shih*," in this document. *Jih* seems to be the correct reading.

136. See doc. 183.7(180).

137. For a detailed discussion of the *pien-shu*, see Ch'en P'an 1960, pp. 212–14. See also Lao Kan 1960a, p. 3.

138. Lao Kan read *ku* (former) as *hui* (or) in the original Chinese document. For a new interpretation of this document, which the present translation follows, see Chun-shu Chang 1977, p. 155.

139. A detailed discussion of this statute and related problems is given in Chun-shu Chang 1971, pp. 6, 12; and 1975a, pp. 67–68, 70, n. 7. A similar text is quoted in Cheng Hsüan's (A.D. 127–200) commentary on the *Chou-li*, which reads:

> Those who, without an approved reason, enter into people's houses or huts, or board their carriages or boats, or drag other people to commit legal offenses, can be resisted and killed, without liability.

For a discussion of this text and its translation, see Chun-shu Chang 1975a, pp. 68, 70, n. 7. See also Ch'eng Shu-te, p. 62; and *Chou-li cheng-i*, pp. 83–84. The basic ideas contained in this passage and the Han statute had their origins in pre-Ch'in times. The *Mo-tzu* mentions some ordinances that prohibited the *san-lao* and other officials and people from entering into residences without credentials (vol. 3, pp. 369–70).

CONCLUSION

1. For detailed discussions of these issues, see chapters 1, 2, and 5 and the conclusion to volume 1 of this book.

2. See the conclusion to volume 1 of this book.

3. The large issue of center versus periphery in early China, particularly in Shang and Chou times, was explored in the prologue to volume 1 of this book.

Glossary

THE FOLLOWING GLOSSARY is a highly selective one. It includes a small number of key terms, phrases, names, and titles in the text and notes but omits the names of persons and titles of books that appear in the bibliography and that are generally familiar to the specialists or raise no controversy among the experts in the various fields.

An-hsi 安息
An-i 安邑
An-ting 安定
An-yang 安陽

ch'an (shan) 禪
chan-pu 占卜
chang 長
chang 丈
chang 障
Ch'ang 昌
Chang Ch'ien 張騫
Ch'ang Hui 常惠
Chang T'ang 張湯
Chang Tz'u-kung 張次公
Ch'ang-an 長安
Ch'ang-shui 長水
Ch'ang-shui chiao-wei 長水校尉
Ch'ang-wu hou 昌武侯
Chang-yeh (Chang-i) 張掖
Chao 趙

Chao An Chi 趙安稽
Chao Ch'ung-kuo 趙充國
Chao Hsin 趙信
Chao I-chi 趙食其
Chao Kuo 趙過
Chao P'o-nu 趙破奴
Chao Pu-yü 趙不虞
Chao Shih-ch'eng 趙始成
Chao T'o 趙陀
Ch'ao Ts'o 鼂錯
Ch'ao-hsien 朝鮮
ch'ao-hui 朝會
Ch'e-shih (also Chü-shih) 車師
Ch'en T'ang 陳湯
Chen-p'an 真番
Cheng 鄭
Cheng 政（正）
cheng 正
Ch'eng 丞
ch'eng 城
Ch'eng 程

Cheng Chi 鄭吉
Cheng Hsuan 鄭玄
Ch'eng Wan 成娩
Ch'eng-chi 成紀
Ch'eng-Chou 成周
ch'eng-kuo 城郭
Cheng-so 正朔
Ch'eng-wang 成王
Ch'i 弃
Ch'i 契 (Hsieh, name)
ch'i (chi) 騎
Chi chiao-wei 己校尉
Chi-li 季歷
Ch'i-lien *shan* 祁連山
Chi-pin 罽賓
Ch'i-shan 岐山
ch'i shih 騎士
chi-ssu 祭祀
Chia I 賈誼
Chia-ch'ü 甲渠
Chia-ku wen 甲骨文
Ch'iang 羌
Chiang Shang 姜尚
Chiang Yuan 姜嫄
chiang-chün 將軍
Ch'iang-Han 強漢
Ch'iang-jen 羌人
Chiao-chih 交趾
Chiao-ho *ch'eng* 交河城
chiao-wei 校尉
Chieh 桀
chieh 節
Chieh-chih 捷枝
chieh-ho 解何
Chieh-ho 介和
chien 監
ch'ien 錢
ch'ien-jen 千人
chien-keng 踐更
Chien-shui 肩水
chien-tu 簡牘
Chien-wei 犍為
chih 置
chih kuan-min 治官民
chih lü-ling 知律令
Chih-chih *ch'eng* 郅支城
Ch'ih-ku *ch'eng* 赤谷城
Chin 金
chin 錦
chin 津
Ch'in 秦
Ch'in Hu 秦胡
Ch'in-jen 秦人
Ching-chao 京兆
Ching-chao-yin 京兆尹
Chiu-chen 九真
Chiu-ch'üan 酒泉
Ch'iu-tzu 龜茲
Chiu-yuan 九原
ch'iung-lu 穹廬
Chou 周
Chou 紂
Chou Kung 周公
Chou-jen 周人
Chou-yuan 周原
Ch'u 楚
ch'ü 曲
ch'u-chün 初郡
Chü-fu 車父
chü-kuo 居國
Ch'ü-lei 渠勒
Ch'ü-li 渠犁
chü-tso 居作
Chü-yen 居延
chuan 傳
Chuan-Hsu 顓頊
chuan-she 傳舍
chueh 爵
chün 郡
Chün-ch'en *shan-yü* 軍臣單于
Chün-chi *chiang-chün* 浚稽將軍
chün-hsien 郡縣

chün-shih 軍市
chün-shih ling 軍市令
chün-shu 均輸
Ch'ung 崇
chung-ch'eng 中程
Chung Chün 終軍
Chung-hang Yueh 中行說
Ch'ung-ho *hou* 重合侯
Chung-hua 中華
Chung-kuo 中國
Chung-kuo jen 中國人
Chung-shan 中山
chung-ti 中的
Chung-yuan 中原

Erh-shih ch'eng 貳師城
Erh-shih *chiang-chün* 貳師將軍
erh-yeh 二業

Fan Tai 范代
fang (*pang*) 方
fang-shih 方士
feng 烽, 燧, 㷭
feng 封
Feng 豐, 鄷
Feng Feng-shih 馮奉世
feng-chien 封建
Feng-ch'iu 封丘
feng-huo 烽火
feng-kuo 封國
fu 傅
fu 符
fu 賦
Fu Lu Chih 復陸支
fu-ch'ien 賦錢
Fu-chü *chiang-chün* 浮沮將軍
fu-lao 父老
fu-ma ssu-ts'ung 負馬私從
fu-se 服色

Hai 亥

Han 漢
Han 韓
Han Kuei-tang 韓隤當
Han T'ui-tang 韓頹當
Han Yen-nien 韓延年
Han Yueh 韓說
Han-chia 漢家
Han-chien 漢簡
Han-chung 漢中
Han-hai 翰海
Han-jen 漢人
Han-min-tsu 漢民族
Han-ti 漢帝
Han-t'ing 漢廷
Han-tsu 漢族
Hao 鎬
Hao Hsien 郝賢
Ho Po 河伯
ho-ch'in 和親
Ho-hsi 河西
Ho-nan 河南
Ho-nei 河內
Ho-t'ien 和田, 和闐
Ho-tung 河東
hou 侯, 候
Hou-Chi 后稷
hou-kuan 候官
Hou-t'u 后土
Hsi Po 西伯
Hsi-ho 西河
Hsi-shui 漆水
Hsi-yü 西域
Hsi-yü Tu-hu 西域都護
hsia tang-yung che 下當用者
hsiang 鄉
hsiang-chü 象車
Hsiao-ku 效穀
hsiao-shih 小石
hsien 縣
hsien-kuan 縣官
Hsien-pi 鮮卑 (also Hsien-pei)

Hsien-yang 咸陽
Hsin 新
Hsin-Ch'in-chung 新秦中
Hsin Ch'ing-chi 辛慶忌
hsing 姓
hsing-kuo 行國
hsing-shih 姓氏
hsing-tsu 姓族
Hsiu-Ch'u 休屠
Hsiung-nu 匈奴
Hsu Lu 徐盧
Hsu Tzu-wei 徐自為
Hsuan-ch'üan 懸泉
Hsuan-t'u 玄菟
Hsun Chih 荀彘
hsun-li 循吏
Hu 胡
hu 斛
Hu Ch'iang Chiao-wei 護羌校尉
Hu Ch'ung-kuo 壺充國
Hu Wu-huan Chiao-wei 護烏桓校尉
Hu-ch'i 胡騎
Hu-Han-yeh 呼韓邪
Hu-shih 胡市
hu-tiao 戶調
Hua 華
Hua-Hsia 華夏
Hua-jen 華人
Huai-nan 淮南
Huang 皇
Huang 湟
huang 黃
Huang-Lao 黃老
Huang-men 黃門
huang-ti 皇帝
Huang-ti 黃帝
Huang-T'ien 皇天
Hun-yeh *wang* 昆邪王，渾邪王
Huo Ch'ü-ping 霍去病

i 夷

I (yi) 邑
I Chi Hsien 伊即軒
I-chih 驛置
I-ch'ü 義渠
I-hsun 伊循
i-i-chih-i 以夷制夷
i-i-fa-i 以夷伐夷
i-ma 驛馬
i-tsu 驛卒
I-ts'ung Hu 義從胡
i-wan 億萬
I-wu ssu-ma 伊吾司馬

jen 人
Jen Li-cheng 任立政
Jen-ch'eng 任城
jih-chi pu 日記簿
Jih-nan 日南
ju chao-shu 如詔書
ju lü-ling 如律令
ju-ku-shih 如故事
Jung 戎
jung 戎

K'ai-ling *hou* 開陵侯
Kan Yen-shou 甘延壽
kan yen-chih 敢言之
kan-lan 問闌
kan-lan 干蘭（杆蘭）
K'ang-chü 康居
Kao Pu Shih 高不識
Kao Yü 高圉
Kao-ch'ang pi 高昌壁
keng-fu 更賦
keng-tsu 更卒
ko 戈
k'o 客
k'o-min 客民
k'o-she 客舍
k'o-tzu 客子
K'u 嚳

Ku Kung T'an Fu 古公亶父
K'u-ch'e (Kucha) 庫車
ku-li 故吏
k'u-li 酷吏
Ku-mo 姑墨
Ku-shih 姑師
ku-shih 故事
K'uai-chi 會稽
kuan 關
kuan 官
Kuan Chung 管仲
kuan-sai 關塞
kuan-she 館舍
kuan-shih 官市
kuei 鬼
kuei 軌
Kuei Jung 鬼戎
Kuei-shan 貴山
K'un-mi 昆靡(彌)
K'un-mo 昆莫
K'un-wu 昆吾
kung 功
Kung Fei 公非
Kung Liu 公劉
Kung Tsu 公祖
kung-lao 功勞
Kung-sun Ao 公孫敖
Kung-sun Ho 公孫賀
Kung-sun Jung-nu 公孫戎奴
kuo 國
Kuo Ch'ang 郭昌
kuo-chia 國家
kuo-jen 國人
kuo-so 過所

lan-ch'u 蘭出
lan-ju 蘭入
lao 勞
Lao-shang *shan-yü* 老上單于
li 禮
li 里

li 吏
Li Ch'e 李哆
Li Chü 李沮
Li Hsi 李息
Li Kan 李敢
Li K'o 李克
Li Kuang 李廣
Li Kuang-li 李廣利
Li K'ui (also Li K'uei) 李悝
Li Ling 李陵
Li So 李朔
Li Ssu 李斯
Li Ts'ai 李蔡
li-cheng 里正
li-jen 里人
li-yueh 禮樂
Liang-shan 梁山
lien 連
ling 令
Ling-chü 令居
ling-shih 令史
Liu Ch'e 劉徹
Liu Pang 劉邦
Lo-i 洛邑 (雒邑)
Lo-lang 樂浪
Lou-chuan 樓專
lou-ch'uan 樓船
Lou-lan 樓蘭
Lu 魯
Lu Chia 陸賈
Lu Chiang 陸疆
Lu Po-te 陸博德
Lu T'o-chih 陸它之
Lu T'o-fu 陸它父
Lu-te 虅得
Lun-t'ai 輪台
Lun-t'ou 侖頭
Lung Chiang 隆疆
Lung-hsi 隴西

Ma T'ung 馬通

mai-ti-ch'üan 買地券
Man-i ti 蠻夷邸
Mao-tun (Modun) 冒頓 (Modu 墨毒)
Mien Ch'en 綿臣
min 民
Ming-t'iao 鳴條
mu-chu 木主
mu-mien 木棉
mu-shih 牧士
mu-shih 募士

Nan-tou-mi 難兜靡
Nan-yueh 南粵 (南越)
nei 內
nei-chün 內郡
nei-shih 內史
nei-shu 內屬
neng-shu k'uai chi 能書會計
ni-lü 逆旅
Nuo-ch'iang 婼羌 (also Juo-ch'iang)

pa 霸
Pa 巴
pa-tsu 罷卒
Pai I 伯夷
pai-hsing 百姓
pan-liang 半兩
P'an-yü 番禺
pang 邦
pao-sai 保塞, 葆塞
Pao-sai man-i 葆塞蠻夷
Pao-sai wai-man-i 葆塞外蠻夷
P'ei 沛
Pei-chün 北軍
Pei-ti 北地
pi 壁
pi 鄙
p'i 匹
pi-hsia 陛下
Pi-lu 卑陸

pien-hu 編戶
pien-hu ch'i-min 編戶齊民
Pin 邠
P'ing-ch'eng 平城
p'ing-chun 平準
ping-fa 變法
P'ing-yang 平陽
Po 亳
P'o 僰
po-shih 博士
Po-teng (Pai-teng) 白登
pu 布
pu 部
P'u Ching 僕黥
Pu K'u 不窋
P'u P'eng 僕朋
P'u Ta 僕黕
P'u-ch'ang hai 蒲昌海 (Yen-tse)
pu-ch'ü 部曲
P'u-lei 蒲類
pu-luo 部落
P'u Tuo 僕多

sai-wei 塞尉
San-fu 三輔
san-lao 三老
San-tsung 三嵏
Sang Hung-yang 桑弘羊 (also Sang Hung-hsiang)
se-fu 嗇夫
Sha-ch'a (Sha-ch'e) 沙車
Sha-chü 沙車 (also Sha-ch'e, Sha-ch'a, So-chü)
Shan (Tan) 撣
Shan Kuo 山國
Shan-shan 鄯善
shan-yü 單于
Shang 商
Shang Chia Wei 上甲微
Shang Ch'iu-ch'eng 商丘成
Shang chün 上郡

GLOSSARY • 229

Shang Yang 商鞅
Shang-fang 尚方
Shang-jen 商人
Shang-ku 上谷
Shang-kuan Chieh 上官桀
Shang-kuei 上邽
Shang-ti 上帝
Shao-fu 少府
she 社
she-chu 社主
shen 神
Shen Pu-hai 申不害
Shen-tu 身毒
sheng 聖
sheng 升
sheng 省
sheng t'ien-tzu 聖天子
sheng-tsu 省卒
shih 氏
Shih 史
shih 石
Shih huang-ti 始皇帝
shih-che 使者
Shih-che chiao-wei 使者校尉
shih-jen 市人
shih-li 士吏
shih-tsu 氏族
shih-tsu 士卒
shih-wu 什伍, 仕伍, 士伍
Shu 蜀
shu-chia tsu 戍甲卒
shu-kuo 屬國
Shu-kuo tu-wei 屬國都尉
Shu-lei 疏勒 (So-lo)
shu-min 庶民
Shu-pu 蜀布
Shu-sun T'ung 叔孫通
shu-tao yen 書到言
shu-t'ien tsu 戍田卒
shu-tsu 戍卒
Shun 舜

So-chü (Sha-ch'a, Sha-ch'e) 莎車
So-fang 朔方
Sou-su tu-wei 搜粟都尉
Ssu 姒
Ssu-fu ts'ung-ma 私負從馬
ssu-huo 祀火
ssu-kuan 私館
Ssu-ma 司馬
Ssu-nung 司農
ssu-shih 私市
ssu-ts'ung 私從
Su Chien 蘇堅
Su Wu 蘇武
suan 算
suan-fu 算賦
sui 隧（燧）, 隊
Sui Ch'eng 遂成
sui ch'u mu chu shui ts'ao pu shih t'ien-tso 隨畜牧逐水草不事田作
sui-chang 隧長
sui-chang 隧障
Sun Wu 孫武
Sung 宋

ta chiang-chün 大將軍
Ta Ch'in 大秦
Ta Yüeh-chih 大月氏
Ta-Chien 大前（煎）
Ta-Han 大漢
Ta-Hsia 大夏
Ta-i 大乙
ta-p'i 大辟
ta-shih 大石
ta-shih chi 大事記
Ta-sou 大搜
ta-tsung 大宗
Ta-yuan 大宛
Tai 代
Tai 邰
T'ai Wang 太王
t'ai-hsueh 太學

tai-mao 玳瑁 (*tai-mei*)
T'ai-p'u 太僕
T'ai-shan 泰山
t'ai-shih 太史
tai-t'ien 代田
T'ai-yuan 太原
Tan 僤
Tan-yang 丹陽
tao 道
Ti 氏
Ti 帝
Ti 狄
Ti 邸
Ti 第
Ti-Hsin 帝辛
ti-kuo 帝國
Ti-tao 狄道
t'ieh-kuan 鐵官
Tien 滇
T'ien 天
T'ien Ch'ien-ch'iu 田千秋
T'ien Fen 田蚡
T'ien-ming 天命
T'ien-shui 天水
T'ien-ti 天帝
t'ien-t'ien 天田
t'ien-tsu 田卒
T'ien-tzu 天子
T'ien-wang 天王
Tien-yen *shan* 填顏山
t'ing 亭
t'ing-chang 亭長
t'ing-chuan 亭傳
Ting-hsiang 定襄
t'ing-shih 亭市
tou 斗
Tou I-ju 豆意如
Tou Ying 竇嬰
ts'ai-kuan 材官
tsan 贊
Tsang 牂

Ts'ang-hai 蒼海
Tsang-k'o 牂柯
Ts'ang-wu 蒼梧
Ts'ao Hsiang 曹襄
Tso P'ing-i 左馮翊
tsu 族
tsu 卒
Tsu-mo 且末 (also Chü-mo)
Tsung-Chou 宗周
tsung-fa 宗法
Tsung-pu 賨布
ts'ung-shih 從事
tsung-tsu 宗族
t'u 徒
t'u-chu 土著
T'u-fan 吐蕃 (often misread as T'u-po)
Tu-hu 都護
Tu-ling 杜陵
t'u-t'eng 圖騰
Tu-wei 都尉
Tuan Hui-tsung 段惠宗
tui 隊
t'un-chang 屯長
t'un-ch'i 屯騎
Tun-huang 敦煌
t'un-t'ien 屯田
Tung Chung-shu 董仲舒
Tung Yueh 東越 (東粵)
Tung-Hu 東胡
Tung-ou 東甌
T'ung-p'u 僮僕
T'ung-p'u tu-wei 僮僕都尉
tzu 子
Tzu-ch'an 子產
tzu-chia 訾家

wai 外
wai-ch'en 外臣
wai-chün 外郡
wai-kuo 外國

wang 王
Wang Hai 王亥
Wang Hsien 王險
Wang Hui 王炈
Wang Shen-sheng 王申生
wei 尉
Wei 魏
Wei 渭
Wei 衛
Wei Ch'ing 衛青
Wei Man 衛滿
Wei Shan 衛山
Wei-li 尉犁（尉黎）
Wei-li chih-tao 爲吏之道
Wei-su 尉須
Wei-t'ou 尉頭
wen 文
Wen Ting 文丁
wen-li 文吏
Wen-su 溫宿
Wen-*wang* 文王
Wen-wu Ting 文武丁
wu 武
wu 塢
Wu Ch'i 吳起
Wu chiao-wei 戊校尉
Wu Hsu-lu 唯徐虛
Wu-chi chiao-wei 戊己校尉
wu-chün 五鈞
wu-hsing 五行 (*wu-heng*)
Wu-huan 烏桓
Wu-lei 烏壘
wu-li 武吏
wu-shu 五銖
Wu-sun 烏孫
Wu-t'an tzu(chü)-li 烏貪訾距離
Wu-ti 武帝
Wu-wang 武王
Wu-wei 武威
Wu-yuan 五原

Yang-kuan 陽關
yang-tsu 養卒
Yao 堯
yeh 野
Yeh-che 謁者
Yeh-lang 夜郎
Yen 燕
Yen-ch'i 焉耆
yen-chih 閼氏
Yen-chih *shan* 焉支山
Yen-jan 燕然
yen-kuan 鹽官
Yen-men 雁門
Yen-tse 鹽澤
yi 邑 (also I)
Yin-jen 殷人
Yin-tun 因敦
Yin-yü *chiang-chün* 因杅將軍
Ying Cheng 嬴政（正）
Ying-ch'uan 潁川
ying-mu shih 應募士
yu 郵
Yu Fu-feng 右扶風
Yu Hsien-wang 右賢王
Yu I 有易
Yü-ch'eng 郁城
yu-chiao 游徼
yu-chih 有秩
Yu-t'ing 郵亭
Yü-men 玉門
Yü-men *kuan* 玉門關
Yu-pei-p'ing 右北平
Yü-t'ien 于闐
Yü-tse 魚澤
Yü-wu 余吾
yuan-shu 爰書
Yueh-ch'i *chiao-wei* 越騎校尉
Yueh-chih (often misread as Jou-chih) 月支（月氏）
Yun-chung 雲中
Yun Tu 雲都

Han-chien *Terms*

THIS SHORT LIST includes only special terms and characters in the wooden and bamboo documents that have been discussed in the notes and the text. Other terms, names, and special expressions may be found in the glossary.

An Kuei 安歸

Ch'a-k'o erh t'ieh 查柯爾帖
chan 斬
chang 長
chang 章
chang 障, 鄣
Ch'ang Kuei 嘗歸
Chang P'eng-tsu 張彭祖
chang-li 長吏
Ch'ang-ling 長陵
Ch'ang-p'ing 長平
chang-sai 障塞
chang-tsu 障卒
chao 詔
Chao An-shih 趙安世
Chao An-ta 趙安達
chao-shu 詔書
Che-lu 遮虜
ch'eng 稱
ch'eng 城
ch'eng 丞

ch'eng-shu ts'ung-shih hsia tang-yung che 承書從事下當用者
ch'eng-tan 城旦
cheng-tsu 正卒
chi 迹, 跡
chi 積
ch'i 黍
Chi 吉 (Cheng Chi) 鄭吉
ch'i-li (chi-li) 騎吏
chi-ming 雞鳴
chi-nu 積弩
ch'i-shih 騎士
ch'i-yueh 七月
chia 家
chia 假
chia-ch'en 甲辰
chia-hsu 甲戌
chia-shen 甲申
chia-tsu 甲卒
chia-wu 甲午
chia-yeh 甲夜
chiang 降

233

234 • HAN-CHIEN TERMS

chiang-chü 將車
chiang-chü-nu 將車奴
ch'iang-nu 強弩
chiao 茭
chiao (nao) 橈
chiao-lo-chü 繳絡具
ch'ieh 拣
chieh i shu 謁移書
chieh-ch'u 解除
chieh-ch'u 界出
chieh-ho 解何
chien 檢
chien 犍
chien 見 (as *hsien* 現)
Chien (name) 建
ch'ien-chang 千長
chien-keng 踐更
Chien-shui 肩水
chien-tsai 見在 (*hsien-tsai* 現在)
chih 隻
chih 制
ch'ih 齒
ch'ih 遲
ch'ih 持
chih kuan min 治官民
chih lü-ling 知律令
chih-chi 治擊
Chih-pei 止北
ch'ih-piao 赤表
chih-so 治所
chin 進
chin 今
chin (ax) 斤
ch'ing 卿
ching feng-huo 驚烽火
ch'ing-hei 青黑
Ch'ing-ho *chün* 清河郡
chiu 久
chiu tso-chien 久左肩
chiu tso-yu 久左右
ch'iu-jen 就人 (僦人)

chu 主
chü (also *lü*) 間
chü 居
ch'u 出
ch'u 除 (*ch'u-wei* 除為)
ch'ü 曲
chu-che hsing-shih 主者行施
ch'ü-ching 渠井
chü-fu 車父
chü-k'u 車庫
chu-kuan ling-shih 主官令史
chu-sui 主隧
chü-tso 居作
ch'u-tso 出作
chü-tsu 車卒
chü-wu 車屋
Chü-yen *kuan* 居延關
Chü-yen *tse* 居延澤
chü-yu 車又
chuan 傳
chuan-chü 傳車
chuan-ku 傳穀
chuan-ma 傳馬
Ch'ueh-Hu 卻胡
chui lo-chü 綴絡具
chün 軍
Chung-kuan li 中官里

fa-chiao 伐茭
Fan Hung 范弘
fei ta-t'ou 肥大頭
Fei Tiao 非調
fen 分
fen-shu 分疏
feng 奉
Feng 馮
Feng K'uang 馮匡
Feng Yeh-wang 馮野王
fu 府
fu (to assist) 輔
fu (ax) 斧

HAN-CHIEN TERMS • 235

fu 冘 (another form of 負)
fu-chi 府記
fu-ma 負麻
fu-ma 副馬
fu-su 負粟
fu-tso 復作

hei 黑
Hei-ch'eng 黑城
hei-se 黑色
ho 荷
ho 何
ho 和
hou-ma 候馬
hou-shih 候史
hsi 西
Hsi-min 徙民
hsia-pu 下舖
hsiang 象
hsiang-chü 象車
Hsiang-ma ching 相馬經
hsiao 削
Hsiao-fang-ch'eng 小方城
hsiao-nan 小男
hsiao-nu 小奴
hsieh 絜
hsien 現
hsien 閑
Hsin-p'ing 新平
Hsin-yeh 新野
hsu 繻
Hsu Fang 許放
Hsuan-ch'üan *chih* 縣(懸)泉置
hsun-ch'a 巡察
hsun-pei 巡北
Hu Ch'ang 胡敞
Huan-i sui 驩喜隧 (Huan-hsi *sui*)
huang 騜
huang-hei 黃黑
huang-hun 黃昏
hui 或

hui-yueh 會月
hun-shih 昏時

i-ch'i 驛騎
i-lai 以來
i-ma 驛馬
i-ts'ung 義從
i-yeh 乙夜

Jen-li 仁里
jen-shen 壬申
jen-ting 人定
jih-chi 日迹, 日跡
jih-chi 日積
jih-ch'u 日出
jih-chung 日中
jih-chung-shih 日中時
jih-hsi 日西
jih-jih chung-shih 日日中時
jih-ju 日入
Jih-lei 日勒
jih-tieh 日昳

kai 犗
kan yen chih 敢言之
kao 誥
keng 更 (also *ching*)
keng-tsu 更卒
k'o 刻
k'o-tzu 客子
ku 故
ku 觚
k'u 庫
Ku-hsia 鼓下
ku-li 故吏
kuan 貫
kuan (head office) 官
kuan nu-p'ei 官奴婢
kuan tu-wei 關都尉
kuan-chü 官車
kuan-ling 關令

k'un-ch'ien 髡鉗
kung 釭
kung-ch'eng 公乘 (*kung-sheng*)
kung-shih 公士
kuo 郭
kuo-pi 郭辟
kuo-so 過所

lao 老
Lei-t'ai 雷台
li 力
li-men 里門
lien-nu 連弩
liang 兩（輛）
liang chia tzu 良家子
liang ch'ieh 兩拑
ling 令
ling-shih 令史
lu 廬
lü 律
lü (also *chü*) 閭
Luan-niao 鸞鳥

Ma-wang-tui 馬王堆
Mao-mu 毛目
mei-ch'eng 美稱
mi 覓
mien 免
mien 面
mien-ch'u 免除
mien-lao 免老
ming-chi 名籍
mu-shih 牧士
mu-tsu li 募卒吏

nan-ma 南馬
nao 橈
niao 鳥
Ning-p'ing 寧平
nu 奴
nu 弩

nü 女

pa 罷
pa-fu 罷復
pan 辦
P'an-ho 番和
p'ang-jen (*pang-jen*) 旁人
pei-chang 百長
Pei-ch'eng 北城
Pei-ch'iu 貝丘
pei-ju 北入
pen-ming shu 奔命書
pi 辟
p'iao 剽
pieh-shu hsiang-pao 別書相報
pien 辨
p'in 牝
ping 病
p'ing-tan 平旦
Ping-t'ing 鉼庭
ping-yeh 丙夜
P'o-ch'eng-tzu 破城子
Po-lo-sung-chih 博羅松治
pu 簿
pu (*hou* 候) 部
pu sheng-jen 不勝任
pu-ch'ü 部曲
pu-keng 不更
pu-shih 餔食
pu-tsu 部卒

Sa-ching 卅井
san-chi 三級
san-lao 三老
sha-t'ien (*t'ien-t'ien* 天田) 沙田
shang 賞
shang-tso 上造
shao-li 少吏
she, ling-ssu 赦, 令賜
she-ling 赦令
she-ming 赦名

HAN-CHIEN TERMS • 237

sheng 省
sheng 乘, 騬
sheng chih 省治
sheng ch'u 省出
sheng Tien-pei 省殄北
sheng tsai Fu 省在府
sheng Wei-fu 省尉府
sheng-chiao 省茭
sheng-fa 省伐
sheng-kuan 省官
sheng-ta 升大
sheng-tso 省作 (sheng as office)
sheng-tso 省作
sheng-tsu 省卒
shih 貰
shih 石
shih (two hours) 時
shih-hsing (ch'ih-hsing) 施刑, 弛刑
shih-li 士吏
shih-nan 使男
shih-nü 使奴
shih-pu 食簿
shih-shih 食時
shih-yueh 十月
shou 首
shu 屬
Shu 舎 (ancient form of 舒)
shu-ming 數名
shu-tao ming-pai pu 書到明白布
shu-tao-yen 書到言
shu-tso 書佐
Shuang-ch'eng-tzu 雙城子
Shui-hu ti 睡虎地
shun 犉
so 索
ssu 私
ssu (min) chueh i-chi 賜民爵一級
ssu nu-p'ei 私奴婢
ssu-ts'ung 私從
su 粟
su 宿

Sun Shang 孫尚
Sun Shih 孫時

ta-nan 大男
ta-nu 大奴
ta-she T'ien-hsia 大赦天下
Ta-wan 大灣
tai-fu (ta-fu) 大夫
tai-t'ien 代田
Tai-yü 帶羽
tang 當
Tang-ch'ü 當曲
tang-she chuan-she 當舍傳舍
Tang-wang sheng 當往省
tao-pi 刀筆
tao-sheng 到省
ti-ko 邸閣
ti-mu 地畝
Ti-wan 地灣
T'ien-feng yuan-nien 天鳳元年
t'ien-kuan 田官
T'ien-pei 殄北
t'ien-sai 田塞
t'ien-she 田舍
ting 亭
ting pu 亭部
ting-tso 定作
ting-yeh 丁夜
t'o-hsien min 他縣民
T'o-t'o sheng 橐佗省
t'ou 頭
tou-chiao 斗茭
tsai 在
ts'ai-kuan 材官
ts'ang 倉
ts'ang 藏
Ts'ang-shih 倉石
tsao-shih 早食
tsao-t'ou 槖頭
Ts'o 厝
tso 左

tso (tsuo) 作
tso 坐
tso-chan 左斬
tso-chang 作長
tso-shih 佐史
tsu 卒
tsu-shih 卒史
ts'ui 萃
ts'ung-shih 從事
t'u 徒
t'u-fu-tso 徒復作
tu-t'ing 都亭
t'un-t'ien 屯田
T'un-yuan 吞遠
tung-chung 東中
tung-ju 東入
Tuo-i 袂衶
tzu-chia 訾家
tzu-tsu 資卒

Wa-yin-t'o-ni 瓦因托尼
wan 完
Wan-sui li 萬歲里
wang-jen 亡人
wang-jen ch'ih-piao han 亡人赤表函
wei 未
Wei (name) 尉
Wei chün 魏郡
Wei tu 魏都
wei-shih 尉史
wei-shih 未使
wei-tsu 衛卒

wu 塢
wu 毋, 勿, 無
wu-chiu 毋久
wu-hai 無害
wu-pi 塢辟
wu-se 物色
wu-yeh 戊夜

Ya-Hu 厭(壓)胡
yao-chü 軺車
yeh-pan 夜半
yeh-shih 夜時
yeh-ti 野第
Yeh-wang 野王
yen 延
yen 夒
Yen-nien 延年
yih-min 移民
yin-p'o 印破
ying-mu shih 應募士
yu 郵
Yü 庾
yu tsu i-jen sheng-kuan 右卒一人省官
yu-chueh 有角
yü-chung 隅中
yu-p'iao 右剽
Yü-yang 育陽
yuan 援
Yun-meng hsien 雲夢縣
Yun-yang 賣陽
yung-jen 傭人

Selected Bibliography

TITLES LISTED IN the sections "Abbreviations" and "Basic Sources, Conventions, and Style of Citing Han Wooden and Bamboo Documents" are excluded from the Western-, Japanese-, and Chinese-language sections. While the "Basic Sources" section is included in the "Sources" at the end of Volume 1, it is in the front matter in this volume.

For a book of such magnitude, it is impossible to include an exhaustive bibliography. Thus, here I have listed only about one-third of the works cited in the book. They are the most important primary and secondary sources, the ones that deal directly with the Han wooden and bamboo documents and issues in Ch'in and Han society, institutions, and empire building. Some standard reference works and materials cited merely to substantiate minor points have been excluded. Articles in collections generally are not listed separately under individual authors. Theoretical works, cited mostly in the appendixes, have generally been excluded as well. The same is true of all but a few of the standard reference works cited in the prologue and appendixes 2 and 3 in volume 1. All the Chinese and Japanese items cited in the prologue in the text and in the notes include English translations. This is also the case with "Abbreviations" and "Basic Sources" entries.

This bibliography is divided into three categories of languages: "Works in Western Languages," "Works in Japanese," and "Works in Chinese." With few exceptions, translated works are listed under the translators' names, not those of the original authors.

ABBREVIATIONS

Chun-shu Chang 1963   "The Colonization of the Ho-hsi Region: A Study of the Han Frontier System." Ph.D. diss., Harvard University, 1963.

Chun-shu Chang 1966a   "Military Aspects of Han Wu-ti's Northern and Northwestern Campaigns," HJAS 26 (1966): 148–73.

Chun-shu Chang 1966b   "The Han Colonists and Their Settlements on the Chü-yen Frontier," TH 5, no. 2 (December 1966): 154–269. Reprinted as Michigan Papers in Chinese Studies, no. 25. Ann Arbor: Center for Chinese Studies, University of Michigan, 1967.

Chun-shu Chang 1967a   "Han-tai Ho-hsi Ssu-chün te Chien-chih nien-tai yü k'ai-t'uo kuo-ch'eng te t'ui-ts'e" (On the Dating and Developmental Stages of the Four Prefectures of Ho-hsi), CYYY 37, no. 2 (1967): 681–749.

Chun-shu Chang 1975a   *Han-tai pien-chiang shih lun-chi* (Studies in Han Frontier History). Taipei: Shih-huo, 1975.

Chun-shu Chang 1978   "Ku-tai t'un-t'ien chih-tu te yuan-shih yü Hsi-Han Ho-hsi Hsi-yü pien-sai shang t'un-t'ien chih-tu chih fa-chan kuo-ch'eng" (The Origins of the Agricultural Colony System and China's Establishment of It in the Frontier Regions of Ho-hsi and Hsi-yü [the Western Regions]), in *Ch'ü Wan-li hsien-sheng ch'i-chih jung-ch'ing lun-wei chi* (Taipei: Lien-ching, 1978), pp. 563–99.

Chun-shu Chang 1989   "Pa-shih-nien lai Han-chien te fa-hsien cheng-li yü yen-chiu" (The Discovery and Studies of Han Wooden and Bamboo Documents in the Last Eighty Years [1900–1989]), in *Chung-yang yen-chiu-yuan ti-erh chieh kuo-chi Han-hsueh hui-i lun-wen chi* (Taipei: Academia Sinica, 1989), pp. 417–40.

Ch'ien Wen-tzu   *Pu Han ping-chih* (A Treatise on the Han Military System). In *Pu-pien*, pp. 407–23.

Ch'in-mu chu-chien   *Shui-hu-ti Ch'in-mu chu-chien* (The Ch'in Bamboo Documents from Shui-hu-ti [of Yun-meng, Hupeh]), comp. Shui-hu-ti Ch'in-mu chu-chien cheng-li hsiao-tsu. Peking: Wen-wu, 1978.

CHS   *Ch'in Han shih chi chung-ku shih ch'ien-ch'i yen-chiu lun-wen-chi* (Essays on the History of China from 221 B.C. to A.D. 907), ed. Ta-lu tsa-chih she. Taipei: Ta-lu tsa-chih she, 1960.

Cp   *Chü-yen Han-chien chia-pien* (The Han Wooden and Bamboo Documents from Chü-yen, Pt. 1), ed. Institute of Archaeology, Chinese Academy of Sciences. Peking: K'o-hsueh ch'u-pan she, 1959.

CSK   *Ch'üan Shang-ku San-tai Ch'in-Han San-kuo Liu-*

	ch'ao wen (Complete Writings from High Antiquity to the Six Dynasties), ed. Yen K'o-chün. 9 vols. Taipei: Shih-chieh shu-chü, 1963.
CYC	*Chü-yen Han-chien Shih-wen ho-chiao* (Collected Collations of Old Deciphered Texts of the Han Wooden and Bamboo Documents from Chü-yen), ed. Li Chün-ming et al. 2 vols. Peking: Wen-wu ch'u-pan she, 1987.
CYYY	*Chung-yang yen-chiu yuan li-shih yü-yen yen-chiu so chi-k'an* (Bulletin of the Institute of History and Philology, Academia Sinica).
Dubs	*The History of the Former Han Dynasty*, by Pan Ku. Translated by Homer H. Dubs. 3 vols. Baltimore: Waverly Press, vol. 1, 1938; vol. 2, 1944; vol. 3, 1955.
HHS	*Hou-Han-shu* (History of the Later Han Dynasty), by Fan Yeh. *Po-na* ed., Wang Hsien-ch'ien ed., *Hou-Han-shu chi-chieh* ed. 2 vols. Taipei: I-wen yin-shu kuan, 1955.
HHS (1965)	*Hou-Han-shu* (History of the Later Han Dynasty), punctuated and ed. Sung Yun-pin et al. 12 vols. Peking: Chung-hua shu-chü, 1965.
HJAS	*Harvard Journal of Asiatic Studies*.
HK	*Han-kuan ch'i-chung* (Seven Treatises on Han Institutions), ed. Sun Hsing-yen. 1884 ed.
HP	*Han-pei chi-shih* (Comprehensive Annotations on Han Era Tomb and Stone Inscriptions), by Kao Wen. Kaifeng: Honan Ta-hsueh, 1985.
HS	*Han-shu* (History of the [Former] Dynasty), by Pan Ku. *Po-na* ed., Wang Hsien-ch'ien ed., *Han-shu pu-chu* ed. 2 vols. (Taipei: I-wen yin-shu kuan, 1955).
HS (1962)	*Han-shu* (History of the [Former] Han Dynasty), punctuated and ed. Hsi-pei ta-hsueh li-shih hsi. 12 vols. Peking: Chung-hua, 1962.
Hui-pien	*Li-tai ko-tsu chuan-chi hui-pien* (A Collection of Monographs on the Minority Nationalities and Border Peoples in the Dynastic Histories), ed. Chien Po-tsan et al. Peking: Chung-hua, 1958.
MH	*Les memoires historiques de Se-ma Ts'ien*, trans. and annotated by Édouard Chavannes. 5 vols. Paris: Leroux, 1895–1905. 6 vols. Paris: Maisonneuve, 1967–69.
Pu-pien	*Erh-shih-wu shih pu-pien* (Supplements to the Twenty-five Dynastic Histories). Vols. 1–2. Shanghai: K'ai-ming Shu-tien, 1935.

RR	*Ritsumeikan Literature Review*.
SC	*Shih-chi* (Historical Records). *Po-na* ed. Ed. Takigawa Kametarō. *Shiki kaichu kōshō* (Historical Records Annotated and Collated), 10 vols. Peking: Wen-hsueh ku-chi k'an-hsing she, 1955.
SC (1959)	*Shih-chi* (Historical Records), punctuated and ed. Ku Chieh-kang et al. 10 vols. Peking: Chung-hua shu-chü, 1959.
Shen Wei-hsien	*Ch'ien-Han Hsiung-nu piao* (A Chronological Table of the Hsiung-nu in the Former Han Period). In *Pu-pien*, pp. 1753–74.
SPPY	*Ssu-pu pei-yao* (Collectanea of the Classics and Most Essential Works in Four Classifications).
SPTK	*Ssu-pu ts'ung-k'an* (Collectanea of the Classics and Most Essential Works in Four Classifications).
ST	*San-tai Ch'in-Han Wei-Chin shih yen-chiu lun-chi* (A Collection of Essays on the History of the Hsia, Shang, Chou, Ch'in, Han, Wei, and Chin Dynasties), ed. Ta-lu tsa-chih she. Taipei: Ta-lu tsa-chih she, 1966.
SZ	*Shigaku zasshi* (Journal of Historical Science).
TG	*Tōyō gakuhō* (Reports of the Oriental Society).
TH	*Tsing Hua Journal of Chinese Studies*, new series.
THG	*Tōhō gakuhō* (Journal of Oriental Studies).
TK	*Tōyōshi kenkyū* (Journal of Oriental Studies).
TLT	*Ta-lu tsa-chih* (Continent Magazine).
Watson	*Records of the Grand Historian of China*, trans. Burton Watson. 2 vols. New York: Columbia University Press, 1961. New ed. 3 vols. Hong Kong: Chinese University Press, and New York: Columbia University Press, 1993. Volumes 1 and 2 of new edition are reprints of 1961 edition. Volume 3 is new. Translations from the *Shih-chi*.
YTL	*Yen-t'ieh lun* (Discourses on Salt and Iron), by Huan K'uan. Ed. Wang Li-ch'i. *Yen-t'ieh lun chiao-chu* (YTL Annotated and Collated). Shanghai: Ku-tien wen-hsueh ch'u-pan she, 1958.

WORKS IN WESTERN LANGUAGES

Allan, Sarah. *The Heir and the Sage: Dynastic Legend in Early China*. San Francisco, 1981.

Ames, Roger T. *The Art of Rulership: A Study in Ancient Chinese Political Thought.* Honolulu, 1983.
Bailey, H. W. "Ttangara." *Bulletin of the School of Oriental and African Studies* 8, vol. 4 (1937): 883–921.
———. "Recent Work in 'Tokharian.'" *Transactions of the Philological Society* 1947: 126–53.
Barfield, Thomas J. *The Perilous Frontier: Nomadic Empires and China.* Cambridge, MA, 1989.
———. *The Nomadic Alternative.* Englewood, NJ, 1993.
Barnard, Noel. *Bronze Castings and Bronze Alloys in Ancient China.* Canberra: Australian National University, 1961.
Barnett, Michael Keith. "The Han Philosopher Yang Xiong: An Appeal for Unity in an Age of Discord." Ph.D. diss., Georgetown University, 1983.
Bell, Norman W., and Ezra V. Vogel, eds. *The Family.* Glencoe, IL, 1960.
Bergman, Folke. *Archaeological Researches in Sinkiang.* Stockholm, 1939.
———. *Travels and Archaeological Field-Work in Mongolia and Sinkiang.* Stockholm, 1945.
Berry, Brian J. L., and Frank E. Horton. *Geographic Perspectives on Urban Systems.* Englewood Cliffs, NJ, 1970.
Bielenstein, Hans. "The Census of China during the Period 2–742 A.D." *Bulletin of the Museum of Far Eastern Antiquities* 19 (1947): 125–63.
———. *Emperor Kuang-wu and the Northern Barbarians.* Canberra, 1956.
———. "The Chinese Colonization of Fukien until the End of T'ang." In *Studia Serica Bernhard Karlgren Dedicata*, ed. Soren Egerod and Else Glahn, 98–122 (Copenhagen, 1959).
———. *The Bureaucracy of Han Times.* Cambridge: Cambridge University Press, 1980 [1981].
Bishop, Carl W. "The Elephant and Its Ivory in Ancient China." *Journal of the American Oriental Society* 41 (1921): 290–306.
Blakeley, Barry B. "Regional Aspects of the Socio-political Development in the Spring and Autumn Period: Clan Power in a Segmentary State." Ph.D. diss., University of Michigan, 1970.
———. *Functional Disparity in the Socio-political Traditions of Spring and Autumn China.* Leiden, 1980. Reprinted from the *Journal of Economic and Social History of the Orient*, nos. 20, 22.
———. "Recent Developments in Chu Studies." *Early China* 11-12 (1985–87): 371–79.
Bodde, Derk. *Festivals in Classical China.* Princeton, 1977.
———. *China's First Unifier: A Study of the Ch'in Dynasty as Seen in the Life of Li Ssu.* Leiden: Brill, 1938. Reprinted in 1967.
Bodman, Nicholas C. *A Linguistic Study of the Shih-ming.* Cambridge, MA, 1954.

Boulnois, Luce. *The Silk Road*. Trans. Dennis Chamberlain. New York, 1966.
Cantor, Norman C. *Inventing the Middle Ages*. New York, 1991.
Chang, Chi-yun. "Weapons and War Materials in Chinese History." *Chinese Culture* 6, no. 1 (October 1964): 1–23.
Chang, Chun-shu. "The Rediscovery of the Shang and the Origins of the Shang Civilization: An Historian's Review of Outstanding Issues and Literature." *Thought and Word* 10, no. 4 (November 1972): 93–102.
———. "Emperorship in Eighteenth-Century China." *Journal of the Institute of Chinese Studies* (Chinese University of Hong Kong) 7, no. 2 (1974a): 551–72.
———. "The Chinese Family in Han Times." *Early China* 1 (1975b): 65–70.
———. *The Making of China: Main Themes in Premodern Chinese History*. Englewood Cliffs, NJ: Prentice-Hall, 1975c.
———. "War and Peace with the Hsiungnu in Early Han China: The Hsiungnu Challenge (200–133 B.C.) and the Origins of Han Wu-ti's Military Expansion." In *Essays in Commemoration of the Eightieth Birthday of Professor T'ao Hsi-sheng*, 611–98. Taipei: Shih-huo ch'u-pan she, 1979.
———. "Qin-Han China in Review: The Field, New Frontiers, and Next Assignment." *Studies in Chinese History* 4 (1994): 47–59.
Chang, Chun-shu, and Shelley Hsueh-lun Chang. *Crisis and Transformation in Seventeenth-Century China*. Ann Arbor, 1992.
Chang, Kwang-chih. *The Archaeology of Ancient China*. Rev. eds. New Haven, 1968, 1977, 1986.
———. *Early Chinese Civilization: Anthropological Perspectives*. Cambridge, MA, 1976.
———. *Shang Civilization*. New Haven, 1980.
———. *Art, Myth, and Ritual: The Path to Political Authority in Ancient China*. Cambridge, MA, 1983.
Chang, Kwang-chih, ed. *Studies of Shang Archaeology: Selected Papers from the International Conference on Shang Civilization*. New Haven, CT, 1982a.
Chang, Kwang-chih, trans. *Eastern Zhou and Qin Civilizations*, by Li Xueqin. New Haven, 1985a.
Chang, Kwang-chih et al., trans. *Han Civilization*, by Wang Zhongshu. New Haven, 1985b.
Chatterjee, Partha. *The Nation and Its Fragments: Colonial and Postcolonial Histories*. Princeton, 1993.
Chavannes, Édouard. "Les pays d'Occident d'après le *Heou Han chou*." *T'oung Pao*, 2d ser., 8 (1907): 149–234.
———. *Notes on Ancient Chinese Documents*, by É. Chavannes, A. Stein, and others. 1940. Reprinted from *New China Review* 4 (1922).
Ch'en, Kenneth. *Buddhism in China: A Historical Introduction*. Princeton, 1964.
Cheng, Te-k'un. *Archaeology in China*. Vol. 3: *Chou China*. Cambridge, England, 1963.

Cheng, Tsai-fa, William H. Nienhauser Jr., and Robert Reynolds, trans. *The Grand Scribe's Records (Shih-chi by Ssu-ma Ch'ien)*. Vol. 1: *Basic Annals of Pre-Han China*; Vol. 7: *The Memoirs of Pre-Han China*. Bloomington, IN, 1994.

Chi, Ch'ao-ting. *Key Economic Areas in Chinese History*. Reprint. New York, 1963.

The Chinese Classics. Ed. and trans. James Legge. 5 vols. Reprint. Hong Kong: Hong Kong University Press, 1961.

Ch'ü, T'ung-tsu. *Laws and Society in Traditional China*. Paris and the Hague, 1961.

———. *Han Social Structure*. Ed. Jack L. Dull. Seattle, 1972.

Conrady, August. *Die chinesischen Handschriften-und sonstigen Kleinfunde Sven Hedins in Lou-lan*. Stockholm, 1920.

Coon, Carlton S. *The Living Races of Man*. New York, 1965.

Creel, Herrlee Glessner. *The Birth of China: A Study of the Formative Period of Chinese Civilization*. London, 1936.

———. *The Origins of Statecraft in China*. Vol. 1: *The Western Chou Empire*. Chicago, 1970.

De Crespigny, Rafe. *Official Titles of the Former Han Dynasty*. Canberra, 1967.

———. *Northern Frontier: The Policies and Strategy of the Later Han Empire*. Canberra, 1984.

De Groot, J. J. M. *Die Hunnen der vorchristlichen Zeit*. Berlin, 1921.

———. *Die Westlande Chinas in der vorchristlichen Zeit*. Ed. O. Franke. Berlin, 1926.

DeWoskin, Kenneth J., trans. *Doctors, Diviners, and Magicians of Ancient China: Biographies of Fang-shih*. New York, 1983.

Di Cosmo, Nicola. "Ancient Inner Asia Nomads: Their Economic Basis and Its Significance in Chinese History." *Journal of Asian Studies* 53, no. 4 (1994): 1092–1126.

Dobson, W. A. C. H. "Some Legal Instruments of Ancient China: The Ming and the Meng." In *Wen-lin*, ed. Chow Tse-tsung, 269–82. Madison, 1968.

Dubs, Homer H. *A Roman City in Ancient China*. London, 1957.

Durand, John D. "The Population Statistics of China, A.D. 2–1953." *Population Studies* 12 (March 1960): 209–56.

Duyvendak, J. J. L. "An Illustrated Battle-Account in the History of the Former Han Dynasty." *T'oung Pao* 34, no. 4 (1939): 249–64.

Eberhard, Wolfram. "Bermerkungen zu statistischen Augnaben der Han Zeit." *T'oung Pao* 36, no. 1 (1936): 1–24.

———. *Kultur und Siedlung der Randvölker Chinas* (*T'oung Pao* Supplément 36). Leiden: Brill, 1942a.

———. *Lokalkulturen im alten China*. Vol. I: *Die Lokalkulturen des Nordens und Westens* (*T'oung Pao* Supplément 37). Leiden, 1942b.

———. "Notes on the Population of the Tun-huang Area." *Sinologica* 4, no. 2 (1955a): 69–90.

———. "The Origin of the Commoners in Ancient Tun-huang." *Sinologica* 4, no. 3 (1955b): 141–51.

———. *Conquerors and Rulers: Social Forces in Medieval China*. Leiden, 1965.

———. *Settlements and Social Change in Asia*. Hong Kong: Hong Kong University Press, 1967.

———. *A History of China*. Rev. ed. Berkeley, 1969.

———. *China und seine Westlichen Nachbarn*. Darmstadt, Germany, 1978.

Eikemeier, Dieter, and Herbert Franke, eds. *State and Law in East Asia*. Wiesbaden: Otto Harrassowitz, 1981.

Eisenstadt, S. N. *The Political Systems of Empires: The Rise and Fall of Historical Bureaucratic Societies*. New York, 1963.

Eley, Geoffrey, and Ronald G. Suny, eds. *Becoming National: A Reader*. New York, 1996.

Eno, Robert. *The Confucian Creation of Heaven: Philosophy and the Defense of Ritual Mastery*. Albany, 1990.

Fairbank, John K. *China, A New History*. Cambridge, MA, 1992.

Fairbank, John K., ed. *The Chinese World Order: Traditional China's Foreign Relations*. Cambridge, MA, 1968.

Fairbank, John K., and Ssü-yu Teng. *Ch'ing Administration: Three Studies*. Cambridge, MA, 1961.

Fitzgerald, Charles P. *The Southern Expansion of the Chinese People*. New York, 1972.

Forke, Alfred, trans. *Lun-heng: Wang Ch'ung's Essays*. 2 vols. Reprint. New York: Praeger, 1962.

Franke, Otto. *Beiträge aus chinesischen Quellen zur Kenntniss der Türkudker und Skythen Zentralasiens (Abhandlungen der Königlich Preussischen Akademie der Wissenschaften zu Berlin)*. Berlin, 1904.

Frye, Richard N. *Heritage of Central Asia: From Antiquity to the Turkish Expansion*. Princeton, 1996.

Fung, Yu-lan. *A History of Chinese Philosophy*. Trans. Derek Bodde. Vol. 2. Princeton, 1975.

Gale, Essen M., trans. *Discourses on Salt and Iron*, by Huan K'uan. Taipei: Ch'eng-wen Ch'u-pan she, 1967.

Gellner, Ernest. *Nation and Nationalism*. Oxford, 1983.

Giles, Lionel, trans. *Sun Tzu on the Art of War*. London, 1910.

Goode, William J. *The Family*. Englewood Cliffs, NJ, 1964.

Goodrich, L. Carrington, trans. "Documents Issuing from the Region of Tun-huang," by Henri Maspero. *Bulletin of the Institute of History and Philology, Academia Sinica* 28 (1956): 197–218.

Gottschang, Karen Turner. "Chinese Despotism Reconsidered: Monarchy and

Its Critics in the Ch'in and Early Han Empires." Ph.D. diss., University of Michigan, 1983.
Graff, David A. "Early T'ang Generalship and the Textual Tradition." Ph.D. diss., Princeton University, 1995.
Haddon, Alfred Cort. *The Races of Man and Their Distribution.* Rev. ed. Cambridge, England, 1925.
Haloun, Gustav. "Zur Ue-tsi Frage." *Zeitschrift der Deutschen Morgenländischen Gesellschaft* 91 (1937): 247–318.
Hedin, Sven. *Across the Gobi Desert.* Trans. H. J. Cant. New York: Dutton, 1932.
———. *The Silk Road.* Trans. F. H. Lyon. New York: Dutton, 1938.
———. *The Wandering Lake.* Trans. F. H. Lyon. London: Routledge, 1940.
Henning, W. B. "Argi and the 'Tokharians.'" *Bulletin of the School of Oriental and African Studies* 9, no. 3 (1938): 545–71.
Henry, Louis. *Population: Analysis and Models.* Trans. Etienne van de Walle and Ellis F. Jones. New York, 1976.
Hermann, Albert. *Die alten Seidenstrassen zwischen China und Syrien.* Göttingen, 1910.
———. *Das Land der Seide und Tibet im Lichte der Antike.* Leipzig, 1938.
Hervouet, Yves. *Un poète cour sous les Han: Sseu-ma Siang-jou.* Paris, 1967.
Hirth, Friedrich. "The Story of Chang K'ien, China's Pioneer in Western Asia." *Journal of the American Oriental Society* 37, no. 1 (May 1917): 89–116, 117–32 (Chinese text), 133–36 (Chronology), 137–52 (Index).
Ho, Ping-ti. *Studies on the Population of China, 1368–1953.* Cambridge, MA, 1959.
———. *The Cradle of the East: An Inquiry into the Indigenous Origins of Techniques and Ideas of Neolithic and Early Historic China, 5000–1000 B.C.* Hong Kong: Chinese University Press; Chicago: University of Chicago Press, 1975.
———. "The Chinese State: A Search for the Roots of Its Authoritarianism." Paper presented at the Irvine Seminar on Social History and Theory, Irvine, CA, April 1988.
Hobsbawm, Eric J. *Nation and Nationalism since 1870: Programme, Myth, and Reality.* New York, 1990.
Hollingsworth, T. H. *Historical Demography.* New York, 1969.
Houn, Franklin W. "The Civil Service Recruitment System of the Han Dynasty." *Tsing-hua Hsüeh-pao,* new ser., 1 (1956): 138–64.
Howorth, Henry H. "The Westerly Drifting of Nomads, from the Fifth to the Nineteenth Century: Part XII, The Huns." *Journal of the Anthropological Institute of Great Britain and Ireland* 3 (1874): 453–75.
Hsiao, Kung-ch'üan. *A History of Chinese Political Thought.* Trans. F. Mote. Princeton, 1978.

Hsu, Cho-yun. *Ancient China in Transition: An Analysis of Social Mobility, 722–222 B.C.* Stanford, 1965a.

———. "The Changing Relationship between Local Society and the Central Political Power in Former Han, 206 B.C.–8 A.D." *Comparative Studies in Society and History* 7, no. 4 (July 1965b): 358–70.

———. *Han Agriculture: The Formation of Early Chinese Agrarian Economy (206 B.C.–A.D. 220)*. Seattle: University of Washington Press, 1980.

Hsu, Cho-yun, and Katheryn M. Linduff. *Western Chou Civilization*. New Haven, 1988.

Hudson, Geoffrey Francis. *Europe and China: A Survey of Their Relations from the Earliest Time to 1800*. Boston, 1961.

Hulsewé, A. F. P. *Remnants of Han Law*. Vol. 1. Leiden, 1955.

———. "Han Times Documents: a Survey of Recent Studies Occasioned by the Finding of Han Times Documents in Central Asia." *T'oung Pao* 45, nos. 1–2 (1957).

———. "Quelques considérations sur le commerce de la soie au temps de la dynastie des Han." In *Mélanges de sinologie offerts a Monsieur P. Demiéville*, vol. 2, 117–36. Paris, 1974.

———. "The Problem of the Authenticity of *Shih-chi*, Chap. 123: The Memoir on Ta Yuan." *T'oung Pao* 61 (1975): 83–147.

Hulsewé, A. F. P., trans. *China in Central Asia: The Early Stage, 125 B.C.–A.D. 23*, by Pan Ku. Leiden: Brill, 1979.

———. *Remnants of Ch'in Law: An Annotated Translation of the Ch'in Legal and Administrative Rules of the 3rd Century B.C. Discovered in Yun-meng Prefecture, Hu-pei Province, in 1975*. Leiden: Brill, 1985.

Idema, W. L., and E. Zürcher, eds. *Thought and Law of Qin and Han China: Studies Dedicated to Anthony Hulsewé on the Occasion of His Eightieth Birthday*. Leiden: Brill, 1990.

I-li (*Book of Etiquette and Ceremonial*). Trans. John Steele. Reprint. Taipei: Ch'eng-wen, 1966. Originally published in 1917.

Jachid Sechin and Van Jay Seymons. *Peace, War, and Trade along the Great Wall*. Bloomington, IN, 1989.

Jansen, Clifford J. *Readings in the Sociology of Migration*. London, 1970.

Kamada, Shigeo. "The Han Emperor's Policy of Oppressing Kingdoms." *Memoirs of the Research Department of the Toyo Bunko* 21 (1962): 77–95.

Karlgren, Bernhard. *Some Fecundity Symbols in Ancient China*. Stockholm, 1930.

———. *Legends and Cults in Ancient China*. Stockholm, 1946.

Karlgren, Bernhard, trans. *The Book of Odes*. Stockholm, 1950a.

Karlgren, Bernhard. *Glosses on the Book of Odes*. Stockholm, 1964.

Karlgren, Bernhard, trans. *The Book of Documents*. Stockholm, 1950b.

Karlgren, Bernhard. *Glosses on the Book of Documents*. Stockholm, 1948–49.

Keightley, David N. *Sources of Shang History: The Oracle Bone Inscriptions of Bronze Age China.* Berkeley, CA, 1978a.

———. "The *Bamboo Annals* and Shang-Chou Chronology." *Harvard Journal of Asiatic Studies* 38, no. 2 (December 1978b): 423–38.

———. *The Ancestral Landscape: Time, Space, and Community in Late Shang China, ca. 1200–1045 B.C.* Berkeley, 2001.

Keightley, David N., ed. *The Origins of Chinese Civilization.* Berkeley, 1983.

Kierman, Frank A., and John K. Fairbank, eds. *Chinese Ways in Warfare.* Cambridge, MA, 1974.

Kirkpatrick, Clifford. *The Family as Process and Institution.* New York, 1955.

Knechtges, David, trans. *Wen Xuan; or, Selection of Refined Literature.* 2 vols. Princeton, 1982. Reprinted in 1996.

Kohn, Hans. *Nationalism: Its Meaning and History.* New York, 1955.

Konow, Sten. *Kharoshthi Inscriptions with the Exception of Those of Asoka. Corpus Inscriptionum Indicarum,* vol. 2, pt. 1. Calcutta, 1929.

———. "Notes on Indo-Scythian Chronology." *Journal of Indian History* 12, no. 1 (April 1933): 1–46.

Koslov, P. K. *Die Mongolei, Amdo und die tote Stadt Charachoto.* Berlin, 1925.

———. *Comptes rendus des expéditions pour l'exploration du Nord de la Mongolie.* Leningrad, 1927.

Krader, Lawrence. *Peoples of Central Asia.* 3d ed. Bloomington, IN, 1971.

Kraft, Gerald. *The Role of Transportation in Regional Economic Development.* Lexington, MA, 1971.

Labatut, Jean. *Highways in Our National Life.* Ed. Jean Labatut and Wheaton J. Lane. Princeton, 1950.

Lamar, Howard, and Leonard Thompson, eds. *The Frontier in History: North America and Southern Africa Compared.* New Haven, 1981.

Lao, Kan. "The Division of Time in the Han Dynasty as Seen in the Wooden Slips." *Bulletin of the Institute of History and Philology, Academia Sinica* 39 (1969): 351–68.

Lattimore, Owen. *Inner Asian Frontiers of China.* Boston, 1951.

———. *Studies in Frontier History: Collected Essays, 1928–1958.* London, 1962.

Lau, D. C., trans. *Confucius: The Analects.* New York: Penguin, 1979.

———. *Mencius.* New York: Penguin, 1970.

———. *Lao Tzu: Tao Te Ching.* New York: Penguin, 1963.

Laufer, Berthold. *Sino-Iranica: Chinese Contributions to the History of Civilization in Ancient Iran, with Special Reference to the History of Cultivated Plants and Products.* Reprint. Taipei: Ch'eng-wen, 1967. Originally published in 1919.

Lee, Norman E. *Travels and Transport through the Ages.* Victoria, Australia, 1951.

Legge, James, trans. *The Chinese Classics.* 5 vols. Reprint. Hong Kong: University of Hong Kong Press, 1960.

———. *The Four Books.* Reprint. New York: Paragon, 1966.
Leighton, Albert C. *Transport and Communication in Early Medieval Europe, A.D. 500–1100.* Newton Abbot, Devon: David and Charles, 1972.
Lewis, Mark Edward. *Sanctioned Violence in Early China.* Albany, 1990.
———. *Writing and Authority in Early China.* Albany, 1999.
Li, Chi. *The Formation of the Chinese People.* Cambridge, MA, 1928.
———. *The Beginnings of Chinese Civilization.* Seattle, 1957.
———. *Anyang.* Seattle, 1977.
Lindner, Rudi Paul. *Explorations in Ottoman Prehistory.* Ann Arbor, 2007.
Liu, Pak-yuen. *Les institutions politiques et la lutte pour le pouvoir au milieu de la dynasties des Han antérieurs.* Paris: Collège de France, 1983.
Loewe, Michael. "Some Notes on Han-Time Documents from Chü-yen." *T'oung Pao* 47, nos. 3–5 (1959): 294–322.
———. "The Orders of Aristocratic Rank of Han China." *T'oung Pao* 48, nos. 1–3 (1960): 97–174.
———. "The Measurement of Grain during the Han Period." *T'oung Pao* 49, nos. 1–2 (1961a): 64–95.
———. *Military Operations in the Han Period.* London, 1961b.
———. "Some Notes on Han-Time Documents from Tun-huang." *T'oung Pao* 50 (1963): 150–89.
———. "Some Military Despatches of the Han Period." *T'oung Pao* 51, nos. 4–5 (1964): 335–54.
———. "The Wooden and Bamboo Strips Found at Mo-chü-tzu (Kansu)." *Journal of the Royal Asiatic Society* 1–2 (1965): 13–26.
———. *Records of Han Administration.* 2 vols. Cambridge, England, 1967.
———. *Everyday Life in Early Imperial China during the Han Period, 202 B.C.–A.D. 220.* New York, 1970.
———. *Crisis and Conflict in Han China, 104 B.C. to A.D. 9.* London: Allen and Unwin, 1974.
———. *Ways to Paradise: The Chinese Quest for Immortality.* London: Allen and Unwin, 1979.
———. *Chinese Ideas of Life and Death: Faith, Myth, and Reason in the Han Period (202 B.C.–A.D. 220).* London: Allen and Unwin, 1982.
———. *Divination, Mythology, and Monarchy.* Cambridge: Cambridge University Press, 1994.
Loewe, Michael, and Edward L. Shaughnessy, eds. *The Cambridge History of Ancient China: From the Origins of Civilization to 221 B.C.* Cambridge, England, 1999 [2000].
Lowe, John C., and S. Moryadas. *The Geography of Movement.* Boston, 1975.
Mabbett, Ian, ed. *Patterns of Kingship and Authority in Traditional Asia.* London: Croom Helm, 1985.

Maenchen-Helfen, Otto. "The Yueh-chih Problem Re-Examined." *Journal of the American Oriental Society* 65, no. 2 (April–June 1945): 71–81.

Mair, Victor H. *The Bronze Age and Early Iron Age Peoples of Eastern Central Asia.* 2 vols. Washington, D.C., 1998 [1999].

———. *The Tarim Mummies: Ancient China and the Mystery of the Earliest People from the West.* London and New York, 2000.

Major, John S., trans. *Heaven and Earth in Early Han Thought: Chapters Three, Four, and Five of the Huainanzi.* Albany, 1993.

Mauss, Marcel. *The Gift: Forms and Functions of Exchange in Archaic Societies.* Trans. Ian Cunnison. London: Cohen and West, 1966.

McGovern, William Montgomery. *The Early Empires of Central Asia.* Chapel Hill, North Carolina, 1939.

McLeod, Katrina C. D., and Robin D. S. Yates. "Forms of Ch'in Law: An Annotated Translation of the *Feng-chen shih*." *Harvard Journal of Asiatic Studies* 41, no. 1 (June 1981): 111–68.

Minshull, Roger. *Regional Geography: Theory and Practice.* London, 1971.

Miyazaki, Ichisada. "Les Villes en Chine a l'époque des Han." *T'oung Pao* 48, no. 4.5 (1960): 376–92.

Mori, Shikazō. "Han-Time Documents from Chü-yen with Particular Reference to Those Discovered by Ulan-durbeljin." Trans. Michael Loewe. *Acta Asiatica* 3 (1962a): 1–15.

Mote, F. W. "The Growth of Chinese Despotism, A Critique of Wittfogel's Theory of Oriental Despotism as Applied to China." *Oriens Extremus* 8 (1961): 1–41.

Murdock, George P. *Social Structure.* New York, 1949.

Nam, Charles B., and Susan O. Gustavus. *Population: The Dynamics of Demographic Change.* Boston, 1976.

Needham, Joseph. *The Development of Iron and Steel Technology in China.* London, 1964.

Needham, Joseph, et al. *Science and Civilization in China.* 7 vols. Cambridge, England, 1954–.

Nicolson, Harold. *Diplomacy.* New York, 1964.

Parker, Edward Harper. *A Thousand Years of the Tartars.* London, 1895. 2d ed., New York, 1924.

Petersen, William. *Planned Migration: The Social Determinants of the Dutch-Canadian Movement.* Berkeley and Los Angeles, 1955.

———. "A General Topology of Migration." *American Sociological Review* 23 (June 1958). Reprinted in Clifford J. Jansen, ed., *Readings in the Sociology of Migration*, 49–68. London, 1970.

Pirazzdi-t'Serstevens, Michèle. *La Chine des Han.* Bern, Switzerland, 1982. English translation by Janet Seligman, *The Han Dynasty.* New York, 1992.

Pokora, Timotheus, trans. *Hsin-lun (New Treatises) and Other Writings by Huan T'an (43 B.C.–28 A.D.)*. Ann Arbor, 1975.
Poo, Mu-chou (P'u Mou-chou). *In Search of Personal Welfare: A View of Ancient Chinese Religion*. Albany, 1998.
Průšek, Jaroslav. *Chinese Statelets and the Northern Barbarians, 1400–300 B.C.* Prague: Academia, 1971.
Puett, Michael. *The Ambivalence of Creation: Debates concerning Innovation and Artifice in Ancient China*. Stanford, 2001.
Pulleyblank, E. G. "The Consonantal System of Old Chinese." *Asia Major*, new ser., 60, pt. 1 (April 1962): 58–144; pt. 2 (December 1962): 206–65 (appendix, "The Hsiung-nu Language," pp. 239–65).
———. "The Wu-sun and Sakas and the Yüeh-chih Migration." *Bulletin of the School of Oriental and African Studies* 33, no. 1 (1970): 154–60.
Queen, Sarah A. *From Chronicle to Canon: The Hermeneutics of the Spring and Autumn according to Tung Chung-shu*. Cambridge: Cambridge University Press, 1997.
Rickett, W. Allyn, trans. *Guanzi: Political, Economic, and Philosophical Essays from Early China—A Study and Translation*. 2 vols. Princeton, 1985; reprint, 1998.
———. *Kuan-tzu: A Repository of Early Chinese Thought—A Translation and Study of Twelve Chapters*. Hong Kong: Hong Kong University Press, 1965.
Sage, Steven F. *Ancient Sichuan and the Unification of China*. Albany, 1992.
Said, Edward W. *Orientalism*. New York, 1978.
———. *Culture and Imperialism*. New York, 1993.
Schafer, Edward H. "War Elephants in Ancient and Medieval China." *Oriens* 10 (1957): 289–91.
———. *The Golden Peaches of Samarkand: A Study of T'ang Exotics*. Berkeley and Los Angeles, 1963.
———. *The Vermilion Bird: T'ang Images of the South*. Berkeley and Los Angeles, 1967.
———. *Shore of Pearls*. Berkeley and Los Angeles, 1970.
Schindler, B. "Preliminary Account of the Work of Henri Maspero concerning Chinese Documents on Wood and on Paper Discovered by Sir Aurel Stein on His Third Expedition to Central Asia." *Asia Major* 1, no. 2 (1950): 216–72.
Schram, S. R., ed. *The Scope of State Power in China*. Hong Kong: Chinese University Press, 1985.
Schwartz, Benjamin I. *The World of Thought in Ancient China*. Cambridge, MA, 1985.
Seaman, Gary, and Daniel Marks, eds. *Rulers from the Steppe: State Formation on the Eurasian Periphery*. Los Angeles, 1991.
Seligman, C. G. "The Roman Orient and the Far East." In *Annual Report of the Smithsonian Institution*, 96–98. Washington, D.C., 1938.

Shafer, Boyd C. *Nationalism: Myth and Reality*. New York, 1955.
Shaughnessy, Edward L. *Sources of Western Zhou History: Inscribed Bronze Vessels*. Berkeley, 1991.
———. *Before Confucius: Studies in the Creation of the Chinese Classics*. Albany, 1997.
Shih, Sheng-han. *A Preliminary Survey of the Book Ch'i-min yao-shu*. Peking, 1962.
Shulze, Hagen. *States, Nations, and Nationalism: From the Middle Ages to the Present*. Trans. William E. Yuill. Cambridge, MA, 1994.
Sinor, Dennis. *Introduction à l'étude de l'Eurasie Centrale*. Wiesbaden: Otto Harrassowitz, 1963.
———. *Inner Asia: History, Civilization, and Languages*. Bloomington: Indiana University Press, 1969.
Sinor, Dennis, ed. *The Cambridge History of Early Inner Asia*. Cambridge: Cambridge University Press, 1990.
Smith, Anthony D. *Theories of Nationalism*. New York, 1971.
Smith, T. Lynn, and Paul E. Zopf Jr. *Demography: Principles and Methods*. Philadelphia, 1970.
Snyder, Louis, ed. *The Dynamics of Nationalism: Readings in Its Meaning and Development*. New York, 1964.
Sommarström, Bo. *Archeological Researches in the Edsen-gol Region, Inner Mongolia*. 2 vols. Stockholm, 1956–58.
Stein, Aurel. *Ancient Khotan*. 2 vols. Oxford, 1907.
———. *Ruins of Desert Cathay*. 2 vols. London, 1912.
———. *Serindia*. 5 vols. Oxford, 1921.
———. *Innermost Asia*. 4 vols. Oxford, 1928.
———. *On Ancient Central-Asian Tracks*. London, 1932.
Stockwell, Edward G. *Population and People*. Chicago, 1970.
Sun, I-tu Zen, and John de Francis, eds. *Chinese Social History*. Reprint. New York, 1966.
Swann, Nancy Lee. *Food and Money in Ancient China*. Trans. and annotated by Nancy Lee Swann. Princeton, 1950. (*Han-shu, chüan* 24) (With related texts *Han-shu, chüan* 91 and *Shih-chi, chüan* 129).
Sylwan, Vivi. *Investigation of Silk from Edsen-gol and Lopnor*. Stockholm, 1949.
Tarn, W. W. *The Greeks in Bactria and India*. Cambridge, England, 1938.
Tinios, Pantelis Ellis. "Sure Guidance for One's Own Time: Pan Ku and the Tsan to *Han-shu* 94." *Early China* 9–10 (1983–85): 184–203.
———. "Pan Ku, the Hsiung-nu, and *Han-shu* 94." Ph.D. diss., University of Michigan, 1988.
Tsien, Tsuen-hsuin. *Written on Bamboo and Silk*. Chicago, 1962.
Twitchett, Denis C., and Michael Loewe, eds. *The Ch'in and Han Empires, 221 B.C.–A.D. 220.* (*The Cambridge History of China*, vol. 1). Cambridge, England, 1986.

Van Zoeren, Steven. *Poetry and Personality: Reading Exegesis and Hermeneutics in Traditional China.* California: Stanford University Press, 1991.

Waldron, Arthur. *The Great Wall of China: From History to Myth.* Cambridge, England, 1990.

Walker, Richard L. *The Multi-state System of Ancient China.* Hamden, CT, 1953.

Wallacker, Benjamin E. "Dethronement and Due Process in Early Imperial China." *Journal of Asian History* 21, no. 1 (1987): 48–67.

Wang, Ching-ju. "Arsi and Yen-ch'i, Tokhri and Yüeh-chih." Trans. Achilles Fang. *Monumenta Serica* 9 (1944): 81–91.

Wang, Yü-ch'üan. "An Outline of the Central Government of the Former Han Dynasty." *Harvard Journal of Asiatic Studies* 12, nos. 1–2 (June 1949): 134–87.

Watson, Burton. *Ssu-ma Ch'ien: Grand Historian of China.* New York, 1958.

Watson, Burton, trans. *Courtier and Commoner in Ancient China.* New York, 1974. Selections from the *History of the Former Han* by Pan Ku.

Weber, Max. *From Max Weber: Essays in Sociology.* Ed. H. H. Gerth and C. Wright Mills. New York, 1958.

———. *On Charisma and Institution Building: Selected Papers.* Ed. and introduced by S. N. Eisenstadt. Chicago and London: University of Chicago Press, 1968.

Whittaker, C. R. *Frontiers of the Roman Empire: A Social and Economic Study.* Baltimore, 1994.

Wiens, Herold J. "Cultivation Development and Expansion in China's Colonial Realm in Central Asia." *Journal of Asian Studies* 26, no. 1 (November 1966): 67–88.

———. *Han Chinese Expansion in South China.* Hamden, CT, 1967. Originally published in 1954.

Wilbur, Martin. *Slavery in China during the Former Han Dynasty, 206 B.C.–A.D. 25.* Chicago, 1943.

Wittfogel, Karl A. *Oriental Despotism: A Comparative Study of Total Power.* New Haven, 1957.

Wu, Hung. *The Wu Liang Shrine: The Ideology of Early Chinese Pictorial Art.* Stanford, 1989.

Wylie, Alexander. "History of the Heung-no in their Relations with China." *Journal of the Anthropological Institute of Great Britain and Ireland* 3 (1874): 401–52; 5 (1876): 41–80. Translation from the *Han-shu.*

———. "History of the South-Western Barbarians and Chaou-S'en." *Journal of the Anthropological Institute of Great Britain and Ireland* 9 (1880): 53–87, 87–96. Translation of "Memoir of Yen Ts'ou," *Han-shu* 64, with an introduction by Henry H. Howorth.

———. "Notes on the Western Regions." *Journal of the Anthropological Institute of Great Britain and Ireland* 10 (1881): 20–73; 11 (1882): 83–115. Translation from the *Han-shu.*

Yang, Lien-sheng. *Money and Credit in China: A Short History.* Cambridge, MA, 1952.

———. "An Inscribed Han Mirror Discovered in Siberia." *T'oung Pao* 42, nos. 3-4 (1953): 330-40.

———. "Notes on Maspero's *Les documents Chinois de la Troisième Expédition de Sir Aurel Stein en Asie Centrale.*" *Harvard Journal of Asiatic Studies* 18, 1-2 (June 1955): 142-58.

———. *Studies in Chinese Institutional History.* Cambridge: Harvard University Press, 1961.

———. *Les aspects économiques des travaux publics dans la Chine impériale.* Paris: College de France, 1964.

———. *Excursions in Sinology.* Cambridge: Harvard University Press, 1969.

Yates, Robin D. S. "Some Notes on Ch'in Law." *Early China* 11-12 (1985-87): 243-75.

Yü, Ying-shih. "Life and Immortality in the Mind of Han China." *Harvard Journal of Asiatic Studies* 25 (1964-65): 80-122.

———. *Trade and Expansion in Han China: A Study in the Structure of Sino-Barbarian Economic Relations.* Berkeley, 1967.

———. "Han Foreign Relations." In *The Cambridge History of Ancient China: From the Origins of Civilization to 221 B.C.,* ed. Michael Loewe and Edward L. Shaughnessy. New York: Cambridge University Press, 1999.

———. "The Hsiung-nu." In *The Cambridge History of Early Inner Asia,* ed. Denis Sinor. New York: Cambridge University Press, 1990.

Zürcher, Erik. *The Buddhist Conquest of China: The Spread and Adaption of Buddhism in Medieval China.* 2 vols. Leiden: Brill, 1959.

WORKS IN JAPANESE

Abe Takeo 安部健夫. *Chūgokujin no tenka kannen* 中國人の天下觀念. Kyoto, 1956.

Amano Motonosuke 天野元之助. "Chūgoku bosei ko" 中國畝制考. *Tōa keizai kenkyū* 3 (1958): 1-36.

———. *Chūgoku nōgyō shi kenkyū* 中國農業史研究. Tokyo, 1962. Rev. ed. 1979.

Chūgoku kōdaishi kenkyū kai, ed. 中國古代史研究会. *Chūgoku kōdaishi kenkyū* 中國古代史研究. 3 vols. Kyoto, 1960-69.

Ebata Shinichirō 江幡真一郎. "Seikan no kanryō kaikyū" 西漢の官僚階級. *Tōyōshi kenkyū* 9, nos. 5-6 (1952): 401-22.

Egami Namio 江上波夫. *Yūrashia kodai hoppō bunka kyōdō bunka ronkō* ユーラシア古代北方文化：匈奴文化論考. Kyoto, 1948.

Fujieda Akira 藤枝晃. "Kankan shokkan hyō" 漢簡職官表. *Tōhō gakuhō* 25 (October 1954): 630-57.

———. "Chōjō no mamori" 長城のまもり. *Natura et Cultura* 自然と文化 2 (May 1955a): 239–344.

———. "Shaku 'ken sho yō hoku' hoka" 釋"見署用穀"ほか. *Tōyōshi kenkyū* 14, nos. 1–2 (July 1955b): 151–56.

Fujita Takao 藤田高夫. "Kandai no gunkō to shasetsu" 漢代の軍功と爵制. *Tōyōshi kenkyū* 53, no. 2 (September 1994): 33–54.

Fujita Tōyōhachi 藤田豐八. *Tōzai kōshō-shi no kenkyū* 東西交渉史の研究. Vol. 2. *Seiiki hen* 西域篇. Tokyo, 1933.

Fukui Shigemasa 福井重雄. *Kandai kanri tōyō seido no kenkyū* 漢代官吏登用制度の研究. Tokyo, 1988.

Hamaguchi Shigekuni 濱口重國. "Senkō to kakō" 踐更と過更. *Tōyō gakuhō* 19, no. 3 (December 1931): 84–107. Supplement, *Tōyō gakuhō* 20, no. 2 (December 1932): 140–46.

———. "Shin-kan jidai no yōeki rōdō ni kansuru mondai" 秦漢時代の徭役労働に關する問題. In *Ichimura Hakushi koki kinen Tōyōshi ronsō*, 1025–45. Tokyo, 1933.

———. "Kan no chōhei-tekiri ni tsuite" 漢の徵兵適齢に就いて. *Shigaku zasshi* 46, no. 7 (July 1935a): 43–63.

———. "Kandai no densha" 漢代の傳舍. *Tōyō gakuhō* 22, no. 4 (August 1935b): 45–68.

———. "Kandai ni okeru kyōsei rōdō kei sono ta" 漢代に於ける強制労働刑その他. *Tōyō gakuhō* 23 (February 1936): 53–105.

———. "Kandai no den 漢代の傳. In *Wada Hakushi koki kinen Tōyōshi ronsō*, 741–51. Tokyo, 1961.

———. *Tō ōchō no senjin seido* 唐王朝の賤人制度. Kyoto, 1966.

Haneda Akira 羽田明. "Tenden bengi" 天田辨疑. *Tōyōshi kenkyū* 1, no. 6 (August 1936): 35–38.

———. "Shin-shin-chū to yu-chū 新秦中と楡中. *Tōyōshi kenkyū* 4, nos. 4–5 (June 1939): 67–69.

Harada Yoshito 原田淑人. "Shina kodai kansatsu no hentetsu hō" 支那古代簡札編綴法. *Tōhō gakuhō* 6 (February 1936): 61–72.

———. *Kan Rikuchō no fukushoku* 漢六朝の服飾. Tokyo, 1937.

Harada Yoshito, and Komai Kazuchika 駒井和愛. *Shina koki zukō* 支那古圖器考. 2 vols. Tokyo, 1932, 1937.

Harada Yoshito 原田淑人 et al. *Rakurō* 樂浪. Tokyo, 1930.

Hayashi Minao 林巳奈夫. *Kandai no bunbutsu* 漢代の文物. Kyoto, 1976.

Hibino Takeo 日比野丈夫. "Kankan shoken chimei kō" 漢簡所見地名考. *Tōyōshi kenkyū* 12, no. 3 (March 1953): 93–103.

———. "Kasei shigun no seiritsu ni tsuite" 河西四郡の成立について. In *Silver Jubilee Volume of the Zinbun kagaku kenkyūsyo, Kyoto University* (Kyoto, 1954): 120–40.

———. "Gō-tei-ri ni tsuite no kenkyū" 郷亭里についての研究. *Tōyōshi kenkyū* 14, nos. 1–2 (July 1955): 23–42.

———. "Kandai no seihō hatten to ryōkan kaisetsu no jiki ni tsuite" 漢代の西方発展と兩關開設の時期について. *Tōyōshi kenkyū* 27 (March 1957): 31–58.

———. *Shinkan teikoku* 秦漢帝國. Tokyo, 1966.

Hiranaka Reiji 平中苓次. *Kyoen Kankan kōshō saimoku* 居延漢簡考證細目. Vol. 1. Kyoto, 1955.

———. *Chūgoku kodai no densei to zeisei* 中國古代の田制と税制. Kyoto, 1967.

Iriye Keishirō 入江啓四郎. *Chūgoku koten to kokusaikō* 中國古典と國際法. Tokyo, 1966.

Ise Sentarō 伊瀬仙太郎. *Chūgoku Seiiki keieishi kenkyū* 中國西域經營史研究. 2d ed. Tokyo, 1968.

Ishida Mikinosuke 石田幹之助. "Shia seisui hakken no mokkan ni tsuite" 支那西陲發現の木簡について. *Shoen* 1 (1937).

Itō Michiharu 伊藤道治. "Kandai Kyoen sensen no tenkai" 漢代居延戰線の展開. *Tōyōshi kenkyū* 12, no. 3 (March 1953): 29–49.

Itō Tokuo 伊藤得男. "Kandai no yū ni tsuite" 漢代の郵について. *Tōyō gakuhō* 28, no. 3 (August 1941): 124–37.

———. "Kandai no yōeki seido ni tsuite" 漢代の徭役制度について. *Palaeologica* 3, no. 2 (1959a): 144–60.

———. "Nihyaku shijū ho ichi-bo sei shikō no igi" 二四〇歩一畝制施行の意義. *Bunka kiyō* 4 (October 1959b): 113–25.

———. "Nihyaku shijū ho ichi-bo sei no kigen" 二四〇歩一畝制の起原. *Shūkan Tōyōgaku* 2 (1959c): 24–40.

Iwai Hirosato 岩井大慧. "Oreru-Sutain Kyō daisanji Chua tanken shōrai bunsho no *kōshaku*" オーレルスタイン卿第三次中亜探險将来文書の考釋. *Gakutō* 51, no. 10 (October 1954).

Kamada Shigeo 鎌田重雄. *Kandai shi kenkyū* 漢代史研究. Rev. ed. under the title *Shin-Kan seiji seido no kenkyū* 秦漢政治制度の研究. Tokyo, 1962.

———. "Kandai no shōsho kan" 漢代の尚書官. *Tōyōshi kenkyū* 26, no. 4 (March 1968): 113–37.

Katō Shigeshi 加藤繁. *Shina keizai-shi kōshō* 支那經濟史考證. 2 vols. Tokyo, 1952. Chinese translation: *Chung-kuo ching-chi shih k'ao-cheng* 中國經濟史考證, by Wu Chieh 吳杰. Peking, 1959.

Katō Shigeshi, trans. *Shiki Heijunsho, Kanjo Shokkashi yakuchū* 史記平準書、漢書食貨志譯注. Tokyo, 1942.

Kawakatsu Yoshi 川勝義雄. "Kyoen Kankan nenpyō" 居延漢簡年表. *Tōyōshi kenkyū* 12, no. 3 (1953): 1–8.

Kimura Masao 木村正雄. *Chūgoku kodai teikoku no keisei* 中國古代帝國の形成. Tokyo, 1965.

Koga Noburu 古賀登. "Kan Choanjō no kensetsu puran" 漢長安城の建設プラン. *Tōyōshi kenkyū* 31, no. 2 (September 1972): 28–60.

Kojima Sukema 小島祐馬. "Kan no Butei to Shina rekidai zaiseisaku" 漢の武帝と支那歴代財政策. *Tōa keizai kenkyū* 4, no. 1 (January 1920): 1–15; no. 2 (February 1920): 143–60.

Kurihara Tomonobu 栗原朋信. "Ryo-Kan jidai no kanmin-shaku ni tsuite" 両漢時代の官民爵について. *Shikan* 22–23 (1940): 27–59; 26–27 (1941): 109–46.

———. *Shin-Kan shi no kenkyū* 秦漢史の研究. Tokyo, 1960.

Kuwabara Jitsuzō 桑原隲藏. *Tōzai kōtsūshi ronsō* 東西交通史論叢. Tokyo, 1933.

Maeda Masana 前田正名. *Kasai no rekishi Chirigakuteki kenkyū* 河西の歴史地學的研究. Tokyo, 1964.

Makino Tatsumi 牧野巽. *Shina kazoku kenkyū* 支那家族研究. Tokyo, 1944.

Masubuchi Tatsuo 増淵龍夫. "Kandai ni okeru minkan hitsujo no kōzō to ninkyō no shūzoku" 漢代における民間牧序の構造と任侠の習俗. *Hitotsubashi Review* 25, no. 5 (November 1951): 97–139.

———. *Chūgoku kodai no shakai to kokka* 中國古代の社會開と國家. Tokyo, 1959.

Matsuda Hisao 松田壽男. "Kyoen no Hakutei" 居延の白亭. In *Wada Hakushi kanreki kinen Tōyōshi ronsō*, 641–52. Tokyo, 1950.

———. "Tōzai kōtsūshi ni okeru Kyoen ni tsuite no kō" 東西交通史における居延についての考. *Tōhōgaku ronshū* 1 (February 1954): 1–25.

———. *Kodai Tenzan no rekishi chirigaku teki kenkyū* 古代天山の歴史地理學的研究. Tokyo, 1956.

Matsuda Kazusei 松田一政. "Saika no shito Kara-hoto no chōsa no gaiyō ni tsuite" 西夏の死都カラホトの調査の概要について. *Tōhō gakuhō* 19 (November 1950): 136–56.

Matsumoto Yoshimi 松本善海. "Shin-Kan jidai ni okeru tei no hensen" 秦漢時代における亭の変遷. *Tōyō bunka kenkyūjo kiyō* 3 (1952): 157–99.

———. *Chūgoku sonraku seido no shiteki kenkyū* 中國村落制度の史的研究. Tokyo, 1977.

Mikami, Tsugio 三上次男 and others ed. *Chūgoku Kodaishi no sho mondai* 中國古代史の諸問題. Tokyo, 1954.

Miyazaki Ichisada 宮崎市定. *Tōyō ni okeru soboku shugi no minzoku to bummei shugi no shakai* 東洋に於けるる素朴主義の民族と文明主義の社會. Tokyo, 1940.

———. "Kandai no risei to Tōdai no bōsei" 漢代の里制と唐代の坊制. *Tōyōshi kenkyū* 21, no. 3 (1962): 27–50.

Mizuno Seiichi 水野清一 and Egami Namio. *Nai-Mōko Chōjō chitai* 内蒙古長城地帯. Tokyo, 1935.

Mori Shikazō 森鹿三. "Kyoen Kankan kenkyū josetsu" 居延漢簡研究序説. *Tōyōshi kenkyū* 14, no. 3 (March 1953): 1–11.

———. "Reishi Kō ni kansuru bunsho" 令史弘に関する文書. *Tōyōshi kenkyū* 14, nos. 1–2 (1955): 137–50.

———. "Kyoen-kan ni mieru uma ni tsuite" 居延簡に見える馬について. *Tōhō gakuhō* 27 (1957): 233-54.

———. "Kyoen shutsudo no issatsu sho ni tsuite" 居延出土の一冊文書について. In *Ishishima Sensei koki kinen Tōyōgaku ronsō*, 551-64. Osaka, 1958.

———. "Kyoen Kankan no shūsei" 居延漢簡の集成. *Tōhō gakuhō* 29 (1959a): 139-54.

———. "Kyoen no sōki-kan" 居延の早期簡. *Bokubi* 92 (1959b).

———. "Kyoen shutsudo no sotu kazoku rinmeiseki ni tsuite" 居延出土の卒家屬廩名籍について. In *Hashimoto Hakushi koki kinen Tōyōgaku ronsō*, 342-53. Kyoto, 1960.

———. "Shinkan Kyoen Kankan kōhen ni yosete" 新刊居延漢簡甲編によせて. *Kyokutō shoten shohō* 1-2 (1962b).

———. *Tōyōgaku kenkyū* 東洋學研究. Kyoto, 1970.

———. *Tōyōgaku kenkyū Kyoen Kankan hen* 東洋學研究：居延漢簡篇. Kyoto, 1975.

Moriya Mitsuo 守屋美都雄. *Chūgoku kodai no kazoku to kokka* 中國古代の家族と社會. Kyoto, 1968.

Nagata Hidemasa 永田英正. "Kyoen Kankan hōsui kō" 居延漢簡燧隧考. *Tōhō gakuhō* 36 (October 1964): 143-66.

———. "Kandai no shugi" 漢代の集議. *Tōhō gakuhō* 43 (March 1972): 97-136.

———. "Kyoen Kankan no shūsei" 居延漢簡の集成. *Tōhō gakuhō* 46 (1974a): 161-88; 47 (1974b): 243-300.

———. *Kyoen Kankan no kenkyū* 居延漢簡の研究. Kyoto, 1989.

Nakada Koru 中田薫. "Ritsurei hō teikei no hattatsu ni tsuite hokō" 律令法體系の發達について補考. *Hōseishi kenkyū* 3 (1952).

Niida Noboru 仁井田陞. "Chūgoku baibaihō no enkaku" 中國買賣法の沿革. *Hōseishi kenkyū* 1 (1951).

———. "Sutain daisanji Chūa tankan shōrain no Chūgoku bunsho Masupero no kenkyū" スタイン第三次中亜探險将来の中國文書マスペろの研究. *Shigaku zasshi* 64, no. 6 (June 1955): 592-603.

———. *Chūgoku hōseishi kenkyū* 中國法制史研究. 4 vols., 1959-64.

Nishida Taichirō 西田太一郎. "Kan no seisotsu ni tsuite" 漢の正卒について. *Tōyō no shakai to bunka* 1 (1950): 185-203.

———. "Kan no seisotsu ni kansuru sho mondai" 漢の正卒に関する諸問題. *Tōhō gakuhō* 10 (April 1955): 37-47.

Nishijima Sadao 西嶋定生. *Chūgoku kodai teikoku no keisei to kōzō* 中國古代帝國の形成と構造. Tokyo, 1960.

———. *Shin-Kan teikoku* 秦漢帝國. Tokyo, 1974.

———. *Chūgoku keizai shi kenkyū* 中國經濟史研究. Rev. ed. Tokyo, 1975. Originally published in 1966.

———. *Chūgoku kodai no shakai to keizai* 中國古代の社會と經濟. Tokyo, 1981.

Nishimura Genyū 西村元祐. "Kandai no yōeki seido" 漢代の徭役制度. *Tōyōshi kenkyū* 12, no. 5 (September 1953): 47–68.

———. "Kandai no kishi—shi, sotsu no mondai ni kanren shite" 漢代の騎士—士、卒の問題に關連して. *Ryūkoku shidan* 44 (1958).

Nunome Chōfū 布目潮渢. "Hansen hankoku ron" 半錢半穀論. *Ritsumeikan Literature Review* 148 (September 1957): 1–21.

Ōba Osamu 大庭脩. "Zaikan kō" 材官考. *Ryukoku shidan* 36 (1952): 76–87.

———. "Kandai ni okeru kōji ni yoru shōshin ni tsuite" 漢代における弘次による昇進について. *Tōyōshi kenkyū* 12, no. 3 (March 1953): 14–28.

———. "Kandai kanri no kinmu kitei" 漢代官吏の勤務規定. *Seishin joshi daigaku ronsō* 4 (March 1954a): 50–75.

———. "Kandai no kansho to pasupōto" 漢代の關所とパスポート. *Tōzai gakutsu kenkyūsyo ronsō* 16 (October 1954b).

———. "Kan no shokufu" 漢の嗇夫. *Tōyōshi kenkyū* 14, nos 1–2 (July 1955): 61–80.

———. "Kyoen shutsudo no shosho satsu to shosho dankan ni tsuite" 居延出土の詔書斷簡について. *Tōzai gakushu kenkyūjo ronsō* 52 (1961): 1–36.

———. *Mokkan* 木簡. Kyoto, 1979.

———. *Shin Kan hōseishi no kenkyū* 秦漢法制史の研究. Tokyo, 1982.

———. *Kankan kenkyū* 漢簡研究. Kyoto, 1992.

———. *Mokkan* 木簡. Tokyo, 1998.

Ōba Osamu, ed. *Kankan kenkyū no genjō to tenbō* 漢簡研究の現状と展望. Suita-shi, 1993.

———. *Kyoen Kankan sakuin* 居延漢簡索引. Suita-shi, 1995.

Obata Tatsuo 小畑達雄. "Kandai no sonraku sonshiki ni tsuite" 漢代の村落組織について. *Tōa jimbun gakuhō* 1, no. 4 (1942): 370–91.

Ogata Isamu 尾形勇. "Kandai tondensei no ichi kōsatsu" 漢代屯田制之一考察. *Shigaku zasshi* 72, no. 4 (April 1963): 1–30.

Okazaki Takashi 岡崎敬. "Kandai henkyō heishi no hifuku ni tsuite" 漢代邊境兵士の被服について. *Tōyōshi kenkyū* 12, no. 3 (March 1953): 64–81.

———. "Chūgoku kodai no kamado ni tsuite" 中國古代のかまどについて. *Tōyōshi kenkyū* 14, nos. 1–2 (July 1955): 103–22.

Ōshima Riichi 大島利一. "Tonden to daiden" 屯田と代田. *Tōyōshi kenkyū* 14, nos. 1–2 (July 1955): 1–22.

———. *Shiba Sen* 司馬遷. Tokyo, 1972.

Satō Taketoshi 佐藤武敏. "Shunjū Sengoku jidai no seitetsugyō" 春秋戰國時代の製鉄業. In *Chūgoku kodaishi kenkyū*, ed. Chūgoku kodaishi kenkyūkai, 103–25. Tokyo, 1960.

———. *Chūgoku kodai kōgyōshi no kenkyū* 中國古代工業史の研究. Tokyo, 1962.

———. "Zenkan no kokuda" 前漢の穀價. *Jimbun kenkyū* 18, no. 3 (1968): 22–38.

———. *Chōan* 長安. Tokyo, 1971.

Sekino Takashi 關野雄. *Chūgoku kōkogaku kenkyū* 中國考古學研究. 2d ed. Tokyo, 1963.

Shimizu Tajii 清水泰次. "Kandai no tonden" 漢代の屯田. *Tōa keizai kenkyū* 14, no. 3 (July 1930): 10–14; 4 (May 1933): 1–4.

Shiratori Kiyoshi 白鳥清. "Dokuro inki shiyō no fūzoku to sono dempa" 髑髏飲器使用の風俗と其の傳播. *Tōyō gakuhō* 20, no. 3 (March 1933): 121–44; 4 (May 1933): 139–55.

Shiratori Kurakichi 白鳥庫吉. *Seiikishi kenkyū* 西域史研究. Vol. 1. Tokyo, 1941.

Shodō Zenshū 書道全集. 3 (Tokyo: Heibonsha, 1931), pp. 2–3. New ed. in 1958, vol. 2, pp. 22–31.

Sogabe Shizuo 曾我部靜雄. "Toshi ribō sei no seiritsu katei ni tsuite" 都市里坊制の成立過程について. *Shigaku zasshi* 58, no. 6 (1949).

———. "Kandai ni okeru yūtei haichi no kankaku ni tsuite" 漢代に於ける郵亭配置の間隔について. *Bunka* 20, no. 6 (November 1956): 20–26.

Takatori Yūji 鷹取祐司. "Kandai sanrō no henka to kyōka" 漢代三老の變化と教化. *Tōyōshi kenkyū* 53, no. 2 (September 1994): 1–32.

Takikawa Seijirō 瀧川正次郎. "Jōdai hōsui kō" 上代燧燈考. *Shigaku zasshi* 61, no. 10 (October 1952): 934–49.

Tamura Jitsuō 田村實造. *Hoku Ajia ni okeru rekishi sekai no keisei* 北アジアにおける歴史世界の形成. Kyoto, 1956.

Tōyōshi kenkyū kai 東洋史研究會. "Kan-doku kenkyū bunken mokuroku" 簡牘研究文献目錄. *Tōyōshi kenkyū* 12, no. 3 (March 1953): 9–10; 14, nos. 1–2 (July 1955): 157.

Tsukamoto Zenryū 塚本善隆. *Chūgoku Bukkyō tsūshi* 中國佛教通史. Vol. 1. Tokyo, 1968.

Tsuruma Kazuyuki 鶴間和幸. "Shin Shikōtei Ryō kensetsu no jidai" 秦始皇帝陵建設の時代. *Tōyōshi kenkyū* 53, no. 4 (March 1995): 30–54.

Uchida Gimpu 内田吟風. "Gesshi (Getsushi) no Bakutoria (Bactria) seni ni kansuru chiriteki nendai teki kōshō" 月氏のバクトリア遷移に關する地理的年代的考證. *Tōyōshi kenkyū* 3, no. 4 (April 1938a): 29–56; 5 (June 1938b): 29–51; 6 (September 1938c): 59–63.

———. *Kodai no Mōko* 古代蒙古. Tokyo, 1950.

———. *Hoku Ajia shi kenkyū* 北アジア史研究. Kyoto, 1975.

Uchida Ginzō 内田銀蔵. *Nihon keizai shi no kenkyū* 日本經濟史の研究. Tokyo, 1924.

Umehara Sueji 梅原末治. *Kodai hoppōkei bumbutsu no kenkyū* 古代北方系文物の研究. Kyoto, 1938.

———. *Mōko Noin-Ura hakken no ibutsu* 蒙古ノインウラ發現の遺物. Tokyo, 1960.

Utsunomiya Kiyōyoshi 宇都宮清吉. *Kandai shakai keizai shi kenkyū* 漢代社會經濟史研究. Tokyo, 1955. Rev. ed. 1967.

———. *Chūgoku kodai chūseishi kenkyū* 中國古代中世史研究. Tokyo, 1970.
Yamada Shōhō 山田勝芳. *Shin Kan zaisei shunyū no kenkyū* 秦漢財政收入の研究. Tokyo, 1993.
Yoneda Kenjirō 米田賢次郎. "Kandai henkyō no soshiki" 漢代邊境の組織. *Tōyōshi kenkyū* 12, no. 3 (March 1953a): 50–63.
———. "Kyoen Kankan to sono kenkyū seika" 居延漢簡とその研究成果. *Palaeologia* 2, no. 3 (August 1953b): 252–60; 3, no. 2 (June 1954): 174–83.
———. "Kandai henkyō heishi no kyūyo ni tsuite" 漢代邊境兵士の給與について. *Tōhō gakuhō* 25 (October 1954): 141–60.
———. Chōbo yori mitaru Kandai no kanryō soshiki ni tsuite" 帳簿より身たる漢代の官僚組織について. *Tōyōshi kenkyū* 14, nos. 1–2 (July 1955): 81–102.
———. "Kandai yōeki nissū ni kansuru ichi shiron" 漢代徭役日數に關する一試論. *Tōhō gakuhō* 27 (March 1957): 189–212.
———. "Nihyaku shijū ho ichi-bo sei no seiritsu ni tsuite" 二四〇步一畝制の成立について. *Tōyōshi kenkyū* 26, no. 4 (March 1967): 33–66.
Yoshida Mitsukuni 吉田光邦. "Kyū to do" 弓と弩. *Tōyōshi kenkyū* 12, no. 3 (March 1953): 82–92.
———. "Kankan ni dai" 漢簡二題. *Tōyōshi kenkyū* 14, nos. 1–2 (July 1955): 123–36.
Yoshida Torao 吉田虎雄. *Ryō-kan sozei no kenkyū* 兩漢租稅の研究. Osaka, 1932.
Yoshinami Takashi 好並隆司. "Kan-Kan kōhanki ni okeru kōtei shihai to kanryōsō no dōkō" 前漢後半期における皇帝支配と官僚層の動向. *Tōyōshi kenkyū* 26, no. 4 (March 1968): 138–59.
———. *Shin-Kan teikokushi kenkyū* 秦漢帝國史研究. Tokyo, 1978.

WORKS IN CHINESE

An Tso-chang 安作璋. *Han-shih ch'u-t'an* 漢史初探. Shanghai, 1955.
An Tso-chang and Hsiung T'ieh-chi 熊鉄基. *Ch'in-Han kuan-chih shih-kao* 秦漢官制史稿. 2 vols. Chinan: Ch'i-lu shu-she, 1985.
Chai Yun-sheng 翟云升. *Chiao-cheng ku-chin jen-piao* 校正古今人表. In *Pu-pien* 1, pp. 369–83.
Chan-kuo ts'e 戰國策. 1st ed., *Kuo-hsueh chi-pen ts'ung-shu*. 2d ed., Shangai: Ku-chi, 1978. 3d ed., *Chi-chu hui-k'ao*. 3 vols. Nanking, 1985.
Chan Li 展力 et al. "Shih-t'an Yang-chia wan Han-mu ch'i-ping yung" 試探楊家灣漢墓騎兵俑. *Wen-wu* 10 (1977): 22–26.
Chan Li-po 詹立波. "Sun Pin ping-fa ts'an-chien chieh-shao" 孫臏兵法殘簡介紹. *Wen-wu* 3 (1974a): 40–46.
———. "Lueh-t'an Lin-i Han-mu chu-chien *Sun Tzu ping-fa*" 略談臨沂漢墓竹簡孫子兵法. *Wen-wu* 12 (1974b): 13–19.
Chang Cheng-lang 張政烺. "Han-tai te t'ieh-kuan t'u" 漢代的鉄官徒. *Li-shih chiao-hsueh* 1 (1951): 17–22.

———. "Ch'in-Han hsing-t'u te k'ao-ku tzu-liao" 秦漢刑徒的考古資料. *Pei-ching ta hsueh hsueh-pao, Jen-wen k'o hsueh* 4 (1958): 179–83.

Chang Ch'i-yun et al. 張其昀. *Chung-hua Min-kuo ti-t'u chi* 中華民國地圖集. Taipei: Kuo-fang yen-chiu yuan, 1959–62.

Chang Ch'un-shu 張春樹. *Chung-kuo ku-tai te she-shen* 中國古代的社神. Taipei: Taita, 1956.

———. "Chü-yen Han-chien chung so-chien te mu-shih" 居延漢簡中所見的牧士. *Ta-lu tsa-chih* 30, no. 9 (May 1965): 1–3.

———. "Han-tai pien-ti shang hsiang ho li te chieh-kou" 漢代邊地上鄉和里的結構. *Ta-lu tsa-chih* 32, no 3 (February 1966c): 1–5.

———. "Chü-yen Han-chien chung so-chien te Han-tai jen te sheng-hsing yü fu-se" 居延漢簡中所見的漢代人的身型與膚色. In *Ch'ing-chu Li Chi hsien-sheng ch'i-shih lun-wen chi*, vol. 2, 1033–45. Taipei, 1967.

———. "Han-tai pien-sai shang li-tsu te jih-ch'ang kung-tso" 漢代邊塞上吏卒的日常工作. *Shih-huo*, new ser. 1, no. 2 (May 1971): 1–12.

———. "Shih-lun Han Wu-ti shih t'un-t'ien Hsi-yü Lun-t'ou te wen-t'i" 試論漢武帝時屯田西域侖頭的問題. *Ta-lu tsa-chih* 48, no 4 (April 1974b): 1–4.

———. *Ch'in-Han shih-ch'i Ssu-lu k'ao-ch'a tzu-liao* 秦漢時期絲路考查資料. 2 vols. Lanchow, 1982.

———. "Han-tai ssu-ch'ou chih-lu te k'ai-t'uo yü fa-chan" 漢代絲綢之路的開頭與發展. *Shih-huo*, new ser. 15, nos. 1–2 (June 1985): 1–14.

———. "Han-chien te fa-hsien yü cheng-li" 漢簡的發現與整理. *Shih-huo*, new ser. 16, nos. 5–6 (April 1987): 1–19.

———. "Ch'in-Han shih yü Ch'in-Han chien-tu yen-chiu chung te i-hsieh wen-t'i" 秦漢史與秦漢簡牘研究中的一些問題. In *Min-kuo i-lai kuo-shih yen-chiu te hui-ku yü chan-wan yen-t'ou hui lun-wen chi*, 173–77. Taipei: National Taiwan University, 1992.

———. "Hsi-yü ku-ti chin-shih" 西域古地今釋. Manuscript.

———. "Ch'in Shih-huang hsin-chuan" 秦始皇帝新傳. Rev. ed. of 1985 Lanchow ed. Manuscript.

Chang Chün-yueh 張君約. *Li-tai t'un-t'ien k'ao* 歷代屯田考. Shanghai, 1939.

Chang Hsin-ch'eng 張心澂. *Ch'un-ch'iu kuo-chi kung-fa* 春秋國際公法. Peking, 1924.

———. *Wei-shu t'ung-k'ao* 偽書通考. 2 vols. Shanghai: Shang-wu yin-shu kuan, 1954.

Chang Hsing-lang 張星烺. *Chung-hsi chiao-t'ung shih-liao hui-pien* 中西交通史料彙編. Reprint. Taipei: Shih-chieh shu-chü, 1962.

Chang Kwang-chih 張光直. *Shang-Chou ch'ing-t'ung ch'i yü ming-wen te tsung-ho yen-chiu* 商周青銅器與銘文的綜合研究. Taipei: Chung-yang yen-chiu yuan, 1973a.

———. *Mei-shu shen-hua yü chi-ssu* 美術神話與祭祀. Taipei: Tao-hsiang ch'u-pan she, 1973b.

———. *Chung-kuo ch'ing-t'ung shih-tai* 中國青銅時代. Hong Kong: Chung-wen ta-hsueh, 1982b; Taipei: Lien-ching, 1983; *erh-chi*, Peking: San-lien, 1990.

———. *Chung-kuo k'ao-ku hsueh lun-wen chi* 中國考古學論文集. Taipei: Lien-ching, 1995.

Chang Mu 張穆. *Meng-ku yu-mu chi* 蒙古游牧記, with additional notes by Ho Ch'iu-t'ao. Taipei, 1959.

Chang Wei-hua 張維華. "Han Chang-yeh chün Li-chien hsien te-ming chih lai-yuan" 漢張掖郡驪靬縣得名之來源. *Ch'i-ta kuo-hsueh chi-k'an* new ser. 1, no. 1 (November 1930): 1–18.

———. "Han chih pien-sai k'ao-lueh" 漢置邊塞考略. *Ch'i-lu hsueh pao* 1 (1941).

———. "Han Ho-hsi Ssu-chün chien-chih nien-tai k'ao-i" 漢河西四郡建置年代考疑. *Chung-kuo wen-hua yen-chiu hui-k'an* 中國文化研究彙刊 2 (September 1942): 31–42.

———. *Lun Han Wu-ti* 論漢武帝. Shanghai, 1957.

———. *Han-shih lun-chi* 漢史論集. Chinan: Ch'i-Lu shu-she, 1980.

Chang, Wen-hu 張文虎. *Chiao-k'an shih-chi chi-chieh so-yin cheng-i cha-chi* 校勘史記集解索隱正義札記. 3 vols. Peking: Chung-hua, 1977.

Ch'ang Chü 常璩. *Hua-yang kuo-chih* 華陽國志. *Ts'ung-shu chi-ch'eng ch'u-pien* ed.

Ch'ang Jen-hsia 常任俠. *Ssu-ch'ou chih-lu yü Hsi-yü wen-hua i-shu* 絲綢之路與西域文化藝術. Shanghai: Wen-i ch'u-pan she, 1981.

Ch'ang Pi-te 昌彼得. "Hsi-Han te ma-cheng" 西漢的馬政. *Ta-lu tsa-chih* 5, no. 3 (August 1952): 11–15.

Chao Ch'ao 趙超. *Han Wei Nan-pei ch'ao Mu-chih hui-pien* 漢魏南北朝墓誌彙編. Tientsin: Ku-chi, 1992.

Chao I 趙翼. (a) *Kai-yü ts'ung-k'ao* 陔餘叢考. Reprint. Taipei: Shih-chieh shu-chü, 1960.

———. (b) *Nien-erh shih cha-chi* 廿二史劄記. 2 vols. Peking: Chung-hua shu-chü, 1963.

Chao Jung-lang 趙榮烺. "Han-chien li-p'u" 漢簡曆譜. *Ta-lu tsa-chih* 2, no. 10 (May 1959): 26, 40.

Chao Shih-ch'ao 趙世超. *Chou-tai kuo-yeh kuan-hsi yen-chiu* 周代國野關係研究. Taipei: Wen-chin, 1993.

Chao T'ieh-han 趙鐵寒. *Ku-shih k'ao-shu* 古史考述. Taipei: Cheng-chung shu-chü, 1965.

Ch'en Chih 陳直. *Liang-Han ching-chi shih-liao lun-ts'ung* 兩漢經濟史料論叢. Shensi, 1958.

———. *Shih-chi hsin-cheng* 史記新証. Tientsin: Jen-min ch'u-pan she, 1959.

———. "Chü-yen Han-chien chia-pien shih-wen chiao-cheng" 居延漢簡甲編釋文校正. *K'ao-ku*, no. 4 (1960): 43–45.

———. "Kan-su Wu-wei Mo-tsui-tzu Han-mu ch'u-t'u yü-chang shih-chien t'ung-k'ao" 甘肅武威磨咀子漢墓出土玉杖十簡通考. *K'ao-ku*, no. 3 (1961): 160–62, 165.

———. "Chü-yen Han-chien kai-shu" 居延漢簡概述. *Li-shih chiao-hsueh*, no. 4 (1962a): 2–4.

———. "Liu-shih-nien-lai wo-kuo fa-hsien chu-mu-chien kai-shu" 六十年來我國發現竹木簡概述. *Li-shih chiao-hsueh*, no. 9 (1962b): 2–5.

———. "Han-Chin kuo-so t'ung-k'ao" 漢晉過所通考. *Li-shih yen-chiu*, no. 6 (1962c): 145–48.

———. "Ch'u-t'u wen-wu ts'ung-k'ao" 出土文物叢考. *Wen-wu* 6 (1972): 38–39.

———. *Han-shu hsin-cheng* 漢書新証. Reprint. Tientsin: Jen-min ch'u-pan she, 1979. Originally published in 1959.

———. *Mu-lu ts'un-chu* 摹廬(盧)存著. Chinan, Shantung: Ch'i-Lu shu-she, 1981.

———. *Chü-yen Han-chien yen-chiu* 居延漢簡研究. Tientsin: Ku-chi ch'u-pan she, 1986.

Ch'en Chu-t'ung 陳竺同. *Liang-Han ho Hsi-yü teng-ti te ching-chi wen-hua chiao-liu* 兩漢和西域等地的經濟文化交流. Shanghai: Jen-min ch'u-pan she, 1957.

Ch'en Hsiao-chiang 陳嘯江. *Hsi-Han she-hui ching-chi yen-chiu* 西漢社會經濟研究. Shanghai, 1936.

Ch'en Kao-yung 陳高傭. *Chung-kuo li-tai t'ien-tsai jen-huo piao* 中國歷代天災人禍表. 2 vols. Shanghai: Chi-nan ta-hsüeh, 1939.

Ch'en Ku-yuan 陳顧遠. *Chung-kuo hun-yin shih* 中國婚姻史. Reprint. Taipei, 1966.

Ch'en Kung-jou 陳公柔 and Hsu P'in-fang 徐蘋芳. "Kuan-yü Chü-yen Han-chien te fa-hsien ho yen-chiu" 關於居延漢簡的發現和研究. *K'ao-ku*, no. 1 (1960): 45–53.

———. "Ta-wan ch'u-t'u te Hsi-Han t'ien-tsu pu-chi" 大灣出土的西漢田卒補記. *K'ao-ku*, no. 3 (1963): 156–61.

———. "Wa-yin t'o-ni ch'u-t'u lin-shih chien te cheng-li yü yen-chiu" 瓦因托尼出土廩食簡的整理與研究. *Wen-shih* 13 (1981).

Ch'en Meng-chia 陳夢家. *Yin-hsu Pu-tz'u tsung-shu* 殷墟卜辭綜述. Peking, 1956.

———. "Han-chien so-chien feng-li" 漢簡所見俸例. *Wen-wu* 5 (1963a): 32–41.

———. "Han-chien k'ao-shu" 漢簡考述. *K'ao-ku hsueh-pao* 1 (1963b): 77–110.

———. "Han-chien so-chien Chü-yen pien-sai yü fang-yü tsu-chih" 漢簡所見居延邊塞與防禦組織. *K'ao-ku hsueh-pao* 2 (1964): 55–109.

———. "Yü-men kuan yü Yü-men hsien" 玉門關與玉門縣. *K'ao-ku*, no. 9 (1965a): 469–77.

———. "Han-chien nien-li piao hsu" 漢簡年曆表續. *K'ao-ku hsueh-pao* 2 (1965b): 103–49.

———. "Mu-chih yü li-chih" 畝制與里制. *K'ao-ku*, no. 1 (1966): 36–45.

———. *Han-chien chui-shu* 漢簡綴述. Peking: Chung-hua shu-chü, 1980.

Ch'en Nai-hua 陳乃華. "Lun Ch'i-kuo fa-chih tui Han-chih te ying-hsiang" 論齊國法制對漢制的影響. *Chung-kuo shih yen-chiu* 2 (1977): 38–44.

Ch'en P'an 陳槃. "Han-Chin I-chien ou-shu" 漢晉遺簡偶述. *Bulletin of the Institute of History and Philology, Academia Sinica* 16 (1947): 309–41; 23 (1952): 349–83.

———. "Han-chin I-chien ou-shu hsu-k'ao" 漢晉遺簡偶述續考. *Ling-nan hsueh-pao* 10, no. 1 (December 1949): 53–82.

———. "Man-t'an ti-ch'üan" 漫譚地券. *Ta-lu tsa-chih* 2, no. 6 (March 1951a): 3.

———. "Yu Han-chien chung chih chün-li ming-chi shuo-ch'i" 由漢簡中之軍吏名籍說起. *Ta-lu tsa-chih* 2, no. 8 (April 1951b): 15, 19, 32.

———. "Ku-chu-chien tsai wen-shu fang-mien chih ying-yung" 古竹簡在文書方面之應用. *Ta-lu tsa-chih* 4 (February 1953a): 5–8.

———. "Hsien-Ch'in Liang-Han chien-tu k'ao" 先秦兩漢簡牘考. *Academic Review* 學術季刊 1, no. 4 (June 1953b): 60–72.

———. "Hsien-Ch'in Liang-Han po-shu k'ao" 先秦兩漢帛書考. *Bulletin of the Institute of History and Philology, Academia Sinica* 24 (1953c): 185–93.

———. "Han-chien sui-i" 漢簡碎義. *Ta-lu tsa-chi* 15, no. 4 (August 1957): 1–6.

———. "Han-chien sheng-i chih hsü" 漢簡勝義之續. *Bulletin of the Institute of History and Philology, Academia Sinica* 4 (1960): 205–18.

———. "Han-chien sheng-i" 漢簡勝義. *Tsing Hua Journal of Chinese Studies* new ser. 2, no. 2 (June 1961): 60–67.

———. *Ch'un-ch'iu ta-shih piao lieh-kuo chueh-hsing chi ts'un-mieh piao tsuan-i* 春秋大事表列國爵姓及存滅表譔異. 7 vols. Taipei: Academia Sinica, 1966.

———. *Pu-chien yü Ch'un-ch'iu ta-shih piao chih ch'un-ch'iu fang-kuo kao* 不見於春秋大事表之春秋方國稿. 2 vols. Taipei: Academia Sinica, 1970.

———. "Han-chien sheng-i tsai-hsü" 漢簡勝義再續. *Bulletin of the Institute of History and Philology, Academia Sinica* 43 (1971): 773–803.

———. *Han-Chin i-chien shih-hsiao ch'i-chung* 漢晉遺簡識小七種. 2 vols. Taipei, 1975.

———. *Lieh-kuo chien-ping k'ao* 列國兼併考. In *Chung-kuo shang-ku shih tai-ting kao*, 207–79. Taipei: Academia Sinica, 1985.

Ch'en Pang-huai 陳邦懷. "Chü-yen Han-chien chia-pien chiao-yü" 居延漢簡甲編校語. *K'ao-ku*, no. 10 (1960).

———. "Chü-yen Han-chien chia-pien chiao-yü tseng-pu" 居延漢簡甲編校語增補. *K'ao-ku*, no. 8 (1961): 456–57.

———. "Chü-yen Han-chien ou-t'an" 居延漢簡偶談. *K'ao-ku*, no. 10 (1963): 565–66.

———. "Chü-yen Han-chien k'ao-lüeh" 居延漢簡考略. *Chung-hua wen-shih lun-ts'ung* 2 (1980): 83–94.

Ch'en Shu-kuo 陳戍國. *Ch'in-Han li-chih yen-chiu* 秦漢禮制研究. Changsha: Hunan chiao-yü, 1993.

Ch'en Wei-liang 陳煒良 et al. *Chia I yen-chiu* 賈誼研究. Hong Kong: 1958.

Ch'en Yin-k'o 陳寅恪. *Sui-T'ang chih-tu yuan-yuan lueh lun kao* 隋唐制度淵源略論稿. Shanghai: Ku-chi, 1980a.
———. *T'ang-tai cheng-chih shih shu lun kao* 唐代政治史述論稿. Shanghai: Ku-chi, 1980b.
———. *Chin-ming kuan ts'ung-kao* 金明館叢稿. 2 vols. Shanghai: Ku-chi, 1980c.
———. *Han-liu t'ang chi* 寒柳堂集. Shanghai: Ku-chi, 1980d.
Cheng Chao-ching 鄭肇經. *Chung-kuo shui-li shih* 中國水利史. Reprint. Taipei: Shang-wu yin-shu kuan, 1966.
Cheng Liang-shu 鄭良樹. *Chu-chien po-shu lun-wen chi* 竹簡帛書論文集. Peking: Hung-hua shu-chü, 1982.
Cheng Shih 鄭實. "Se-fu k'ao" 嗇夫考. *Wen-wu* 2 (1978): 55–57.
Ch'eng I 成一 et al. *Ssu-ch'ou chih-lu man-chi* 絲綢之路漫記. Peking: Hsin-hua shu-tien, 1981.
Ch'eng Shu-te 程樹德. *Chiu-ch'ao lü k'ao* 九朝律考. Shanghai: Chung-hua shu-chü, 1955.
Ch'i Hsia 漆俠. *Ch'in-Han nung-min chan-cheng shih* 秦漢農民戰爭史. Peking: San-lieu, 1979.
Ch'i Yü-chang 祁玉章. *Chia Tzu t'an-wei* 賈子探微. Taipei: San-min shu-chü, 1969.
Chia I 賈誼. *Hsin-shu* 新書. SPPY edition.
Chia-ku wen-pien 甲骨文編. Comp. Sun Hai-po 孫海波 et al. Peking: Chung-hua, 1965.
Chia Ssu-hsieh 賈思勰. *Ch'i-min yao-shu* 齊民要術. Wan-yu wen-k'u ed. 2 vols.
Chien-tu hsueh-hui pien-chi pu 簡牘學會編輯部. *Chü-yen Han-chien hsin-pien* 居延漢簡新編. Taipei: Chien-tu hsueh-hui, 1981.
Ch'ien Chien-fu 錢劍夫. *Ch'in-Han huo-pi shih kao* 秦漢貨幣史稿. Wuhan: Hupei jen-min, 1986.
Ch'ien Mu 錢穆. "Chou-ch'u ti-li k'ao" 周初地理考. *Yenching Journal* 10 (December 1931): 1958–85.
———. *Hsien-Ch'in Chu-tzu hsi-nien k'ao-pien* 先秦諸子繫年考辨. Rev. ed. 2 vols. Hong Kong: Hsiang-kang ta-hsueh ch'u-pan she, 1956.
———. *Ch'in-Han shih* 秦漢史. Hong Kong, 1957.
———. *Liang-Han ching-hsueh chin-ku wen p'ing-i* 兩漢經學今古文評議. Hong Kong: Hsin-ya, 1958.
———. *Shih-chi ti-ming k'ao* 史記地名考. Reprint. Hong Kong: T'ai-p'ing, 1962. New ed. Taipei: San-min, 1984.
———. *Chuang-Lao t'ung-pien* 莊老通辨. Reprint. Taipei: San-min, 1973. Originally published in 1971.
Ch'ien Pao-tsung 錢寶琮. *Chung-kuo shu-hsueh shih* 中國數學史. Peking, 1964.
Ch'ien Ta-hsin 錢大昕. *Nien-erh shih k'ao-i* 廿二史考異. 2 vols. Shanghai: Shang-wu yin-shu kuan, 1975.

Chin Shao-ying 金少英. *Han-chien i-t'an chi ch'i-t'a* 漢簡臆談及其他. Lanchou, Kansu, 1978.

Chin-shu 晉書. Comp. Fang Hsuan-ling 房玄齡 et al. Taipei: I-wen yin-shu kuan, 1955.

Ch'in Shih-huang ling ping-ma yung 秦始皇陵兵馬俑. Comp. Ch'in Shih-huang ling ping-ma yung po-wu kuan. Peking: Wen-wu, 1983.

Ch'in Shih-huang ling ping-ma yung k'eng 秦始皇陵兵馬俑坑. Comp. Shensi k'ao-ku yen-chiu so. 2 vols. Peking: Wen-wu, 1988.

Ch'in yung hsueh yen-chiu 秦俑學研究. Comp. Ch'in Shih-huang ping-ma yung po-wu kuan. Sian: Shensi jen-min chia-yü ch'u-pan she, 1996.

Ch'in-hui-yao 秦會要. *Ch'in-hui-yao ting-pu* 秦會要訂補. By Sun K'ai 孫楷, rev. with additions by Hsu Fu 徐復. Chung-hua shu-chü ed. Peking, 1959.

Ch'ing-shih kao 清史稿. *Ch'ing-shih kao chiao-chu* ed. 15 vols. Taipei: Kuo-shih kuan, 1986.

Chiu-chang suan-shu 九章算術. *Hsiang-chieh chiu-chang suan-fa* 詳解九章算法, ed. Yang Hui 楊輝. *Ts'ung-shu chi-ch'eng ch'u-pien* ed.

Ch'iu Hsi-kuei 裘錫圭. "Han-chien ling-shih" 漢簡零拾. *Wen-shih* 12 (1981): 1–37.

Chou Chen-ho 周振鶴 and Chou Hsiang-ho 周翔鶴. "Hsi-Han hsien-fei k'ao" 西漢獻費考. *Chung-hua wen-shih lun-ts'un* 4 (1981): 287–98.

Chou Chieh-cheng 周介正. "Wo-kuo hsiang-ma wai-hsing hsueh fa-chan shih lueh" 我國相馬外形學發展史略. In *Nung-shih yen-chiu chi-k'an*, 37–53. Peking, 1959.

Chou Chün-ch'i 周筠溪. "Hsi-Han ts'ai-cheng chih-tu chih i-pan" 西漢財政制度之一斑. *Shih-huo pan-yueh k'an* 3, no. 8 (March 1936): 8–36.

Chou Fa-kao 周法高. *Chin-wen ling-shih* 金文零釋. Taiwan, 1951.

Chou Fu-ch'eng 周輔成. *Lun Tung Chung-shu ssu-hsiang* 論董仲舒思想. Shanghai: Shanghai jen-min, 1961.

Chou Hung-hsiang 周鴻翔. *Shang-Yin ti-wang pen-chi* 商殷帝王本紀. Hong Kong: Wan-yu t'u-shu kung-ssu, 1958.

Chou K'un-t'ien 周昆田 et al. *Pien-chiang lun-wen chi* 邊疆論文集. Vol. 1. Taipei: Kuo-fang yen-chiu yüan, 1964.

Chou-li 周禮. (a) *Chou-li*. Taipei, 1956 ed.

———. (b) *Chou-li cheng-li* 周禮正義. Annotated by Sun I-jang 孫詒讓. *Wan-yu wen-k'u* ed. 24 vols.

———. (c) *Chou-li chin-chu chin-i* 周禮今註今譯. Trans. and annotated by Lin Yin. Taipei, 1972.

Chou Mi 周密. *Ch'i-tung yeh-yü* 齊東野語. Shanghai: Shang-wu yin-shu kuan, 1935.

Chou Tao-chi 周道濟. *Han-T'ang tsai-hsiang chih-tu* 漢唐宰相制度. Taipei, 1964.

Chou Ts'e-tsung [Chow Tse-tsung] 周策縱. *P'o-fu hsin-ku* 破斧新詁. Singapore: Hsin-she, 1969.
Chou Wei 周緯. *Chung-kuo ping-ch'i shih k'ao* 中國兵器史考. Peking, 1957.
Chu-chien ping-fa 竹簡兵法. Ed. Ho-Lo t'u-shu ch'u-pan she. Taipei, 1975.
Chu Fang-p'u 朱芳圃. *Yin-Chou wen-tzu shih-ts'ung* 殷周文字釋叢. Peking: Chung-hua, 1962.
Chu Hsieh 朱偰. *Chung-kuo yun-ho shih-liao hsuan-chi* 中國運河史料選輯. Peking: Chung-hua shu-chü, 1962.
Chu Shao-hou 朱紹侯. *Chün-kung chueh chih shih-t'an* 軍功爵制試探. Shanghai: Shanghai jen-min, 1980.
Ch'ü Chao-ch'i 瞿昭旂. "Liang-Han chih hsien-ling chih-tu" 兩漢之縣令制度. *Yü-kung* 6, no. 1 (September 1936): 1–12.
Ch'ü Hsuan-ying 瞿宣穎. *Han-tai feng-su chih-tu shih* 漢代風俗制度史. Peking, 1928.
———. *Chung-kuo she-hui shih-lueh ts'ung-ch'ao* 中國社會史略叢鈔. 3 vols. Changsha, 1938.
———. *Ch'in-Han shih tsuan* 秦漢史纂. Reprint. Hong Kong, 1967. Originally published in 1944.
Ch'ü Shou-yueh 曲守約. "Han-tai te t'ing" 漢代的亭. *Ta-lu tsa-chih* 10, no. 12 (June 1956): 17–19.
———. "Ku-tai chih kuan" 古代之關. In *Shih-hsueh t'ung-lun*, 161–65. Reprint. Taipei, 1960. Originally published in 1958.
Ch'ü Wan-li 屈萬里. "Shih-chi Yin pen-chi chi ch'i-t'a chi-lu chung so-tsai Yin-Chou shih-tai te shih-shih" 史記殷本紀及其他紀錄中所載殷周時代的史事. *Wen-shih-che hsueh-pao* (Taiwan Ta-hsueh) 14 (November 1965): 87–106.
———. *Shu-yung lun-hsueh chi* 書傭論學集. Taipei: Kai-ming shu-tien, 1969.
———. *Hsien-Ch'in wen-shih tzu-liao k'ao-pien* 先秦文史資料考辨. Taipei: Lien-ching, 1983.
Chuang-tzu 莊子. Taipei, 1968 ed.
Ch'un-ch'iu 春秋. 1. Taipei: *Wu-ching tu-pen*, 1952 ed. including *Tso-chuan* 左傳, *Kung-yang chuan* 公羊傳, and *Ku-liang chuan* 穀梁傳; 2. *Shih-san ching chu-shu* 十三經注疏 ed.; 3. in *Ch'un-ch'iu Tso-chuan chu* 春秋左傳注, ed. Yang Po-chün 楊伯峻. Peking: Chung-hua shu-chü, 1981.
Chung Shao-i 鐘少異. *Chung-kuo ku ping-ch'i t'u-chi* 中國古兵器圖集. Peking: Chieh-fang chün ch'u-pan she, 1990.
Chung-hua shu-chü pien-chi pu 中華書局編輯部. *Yun-meng Ch'in-chien yen-chiu* 雲夢秦簡研究. Peking: Chung-hua shu-chü, 1981.
Chung-kuo Ch'in-Han shih yen-chiu hui 中國秦漢史研究會. *Ch'in-Han shih lun-ts'ung* 秦漢史論叢. Sian, Shensi: Jen-min ch'u-pan she, 1981–.
Chung-kuo k'o-hsueh-yuan k'ao-ku yen-chiu so 中國科學院考古研究所. *K'ao-ku hsueh chi-ch'u* 考古學基礎. Peking, 1958.

———. *Hsin Chung-kuo te k'ao-ku shou-huo* 新中國的考古收穫. Peking, 1962.

Chung-kuo ku-tai ti-t'u chi 中國古代地圖集. Comp. Ts'ao Wan-ju et al. Peking: Wen-wu, 1990.

Chung-kuo shang-ku shih tai-ting kao 中國上古史待定稿. Comp. Chung-kuo shang-kuo shih pien-chi wei-yuan hui. 4 vols. Taipei: Chung-yang yen-chiu yuan, 1985.

Chung-kuo shih hsin-lun 中國史新論. Taipei: Hsueh-sheng shu-chü, 1985.

Chu-shu chi-nien 竹書紀年. 1. *Kuo-hsueh chi-pen ts'ung-shu* ed.; 2. *Ku-pen chu-shu chi-nien chi-chiao ting-pu* ed.; 3. *Chu-shu chi-nien pa-chung* ed.

Ch'u-t'u wen-hsien yen-chiu 出土文獻研究. Ed. Ku wen-hsien yen-chiu shih. Peking: Wen-wu, 1985.

Ch'u-tz'u 楚辭. Ch'ü Yuan 屈原, Sung Yü 宋玉, and others. 1. *Wan-yu wen-k'u* ed. (Wang I 王逸); 2. *Ch'u-tz'u chi-chu* ed.; 3. *Ch'u-fu hsien-pien* ed.

Fang Kuo-yü 方國瑜. *Chung-kuo hsi-nan li-shih ti-li k'ao-shih* 中國西南歷史地理考釋. 2 vols. Peking: Chung-hua shu-chü, 1987.

Fang Shih-ming 方詩銘. "Yü-men wei-chih pien" 玉門位置辨. *Hsi-pei t'ung-hsun* 西北通訊 1 (March 1947): 14–16.

———. "Ts'ung Hsü Sheng mai-ti ch'üan lun Han-tai 'ti-ch'üan' te chien-pieh" 從徐勝買地券論漢代地券的鑒別. *Wen-wu* 5 (1975): 52–55.

Fang Ying-k'ai 方英楷. *Hsin-chiang t'un-k'en shih* 新疆屯墾史. 2 vols. Urumuchi: Ch'ing-shao-nien ch'u-pan she, 1989.

Feng Ch'eng-chün 馮承鈞. *Hsi-yü ti-ming* 西域地名. Peking: Chung-hua shu-chü, 1955.

Feng-chien t'u-ti 封建土地. *Chung-kuo feng-chien she-hui t'u-ti so-yu-chih hsing-shih wen-t'i t'ao-lun chi* 中國封建社會土地所有制形式問題討論集. Ed. Department of History, Nank'ai University. 2 vols. Peking, 1962.

Fu Chen-lun 傅振倫. "Han-wu nien-hao Yen-ho shuo" 漢武年號延和說. *K'ao-ku hsueh-she she-k'an* 6 (June 1937a): 39–41.

———. "Chien-ts'e shuo" 簡策說. *K'ao-ku hsueh-she she-k'an* 考古學社社刊 6 (June 1937b): 1–38.

———. "Hsi-Han shih-yuan ch'i-nien ch'u-ju liu-ts'un fu-ch'üan" 西漢始元七年出入六寸符券. *Wen-shih* 10 (1980): 174.

Fu Ch'i-hsueh 傅啓學. "Ch'un-ch'iu shih-tai te wai-chiao" 春秋時代的外交. *She-hui k'o-hsueh lun-ts'ung* 10 (July 1960): 149–97.

———. "Chan-kuo shih-tai te wai-chiao" 戰國時代的外交. *She-hui k'o-hsueh lun-ts'ung* 11 (June 1961): 253–305.

Fu Heng 傅恆 et al. *Ch'in-ting Hsi-yü t'ung-wen chih* 欽定西域同文志. 3 vols. Taipei: Ssu-k'u ch'üan-shu chen-pen san-chi (Reprint, Taipei: Shang-wu, 1961–63).

———. *Ch'in-ting Huang-ch'ao Hsi-yü t'u-chih* 欽定皇朝西域圖志. Taipei: Wen-yu shu-tien, 1965. Originally published in 1756.

Fu Lo-ch'eng 傅樂成. *Han-T'ang shih lun-chi* 漢唐史論集. Taipei: Lien-ching, 1977.
Fu Ssu-nien 傅斯年. *Fu Meng-chen hsien-sheng chi* 傅孟真先生集. 6 vols. Taipei: T'ai-wan ta-hsueh, 1952.
———. *Fu Ssu-nien ch'üan-chi* 傅斯年全集. 7 vols. Rev. ed. Taipei: Lien-ching, 1977. Originally published in 1952.
Fu Wu-chi 伏無忌. *Fu Hou ku-chin chu* 伏侯古今注. *Ts'ung-shu chi-ch'eng ch'u-pien* ed. Fragments re-collected.
Han-chien [Kankan] 漢簡. 12 vols. Tokyo: Tōkyōdō, 1977.
Han Fei 韓非. *Han Fei tzu* 韓非子. 1. *Han Fei tzu chi-shih* 韓非子集釋, ed. Ch'en Ch'i-yu 陳奇猷. Peking: Chung-hua shu-chü, 1958; 2. *Han Fei tzu chi-chieh* 韓非子集解, by Wang Hsien-ch'ien. *Kuo-hsueh chi-pen ts'ung-shu* ed.
Han Fu-chih 韓復智. *Liang-Han te ching-chi ssu-hsiang* 兩漢的經濟思想. Taipei, 1969.
Han Ju-lin 韓儒林. "Han-tai hsi-pei t'un-t'ien yü Ch'e-shih I-wu te cheng-tuo" 漢代西北屯田與車師伊吾的爭奪. *Wen-shih tsa-chih* 2, no. 2 (1942): 25–34.
———. *Ch'iung-lu chi* 穹廬集. Shanghai: Shanghai jen-min, 1982.
Han K'ang-hsin 韓康信. *Ssu-ch'ou chih-lu ku-tai chü-min chung-tsu jen-lei hsueh yen-chiu* 絲綢之路古代居民種族人類學研究. Ürümqi: Hsin-chiang jen-min, 1994.
Han K'o-hsin 韓克信. "Liang-Han huo-pi chih-tu" 兩漢貨幣制度. *Shih-huo pan-yüeh k'an* 1, no. 12 (June 1935): 8–21.
Han-kuan 漢官. Anonymous. *Han-kuan ch'i-chung* 漢官七種 ed.
Han-kuan ch'i-chung 漢官七種. In *Han-kuan ch'i-chung t'ung-chien* 漢官七種通檢, ed. and comp. Chen Tsu-lung. Paris, 1961.
Han-min-tsu hsing-ch'eng wen-t'i t'ao-lun chi 漢民族形成問題討論集. Ed. Li-shih yen-chiu pien-chi-pu 歷史研究編輯部. Peking, 1957.
Han-T'ang ti-li shu ch'ao 漢唐地理書鈔. Collected by Wang Mo 王謨. Peking, 1961.
Han Yang-min 韓養民. *Ch'in-Han wen-hua shih* 秦漢文化史. Sian: Shensi jen-min chiao-yü ch'u-pan she, 1986.
Hao Ching 郝經. *Hsu Hou-Han shu* 續後漢書. 3 vols. *Kuo-hsueh chi-pen ts'ung-shu* ed. Shanghai, 1958. Originally published in 1937.
Ho Ch'ang-ch'ün 賀昌群. "'Liu-sha chui-chien' chiao-pu" 流沙墜簡校補. *T'u-shu chi-k'an* 2, no. 1 (1935): 1–18.
———. "Han-ch'u chih nan-pei-chün" 漢初之南北軍. *Chung-kuo she-hui ching-chi shih chi-k'an* 5, no. 1 (1937): 75–84.
———. "Feng-sui k'ao" 烽燧考. *Kuo-li Pei-ching ta-hsueh ssu-shih chou-nien chi-nien lun-wen* 國立北京大學四十周年紀念論文 2, no. 1 (1940): 77–102.
———. *Lun Liang-Han t'u-ti chan-yu hsing-t'ai te fa-chan* 論兩漢土地佔有型態的發展. Shanghai, 1956.
———. "Ch'in-Han chien ko-t'i hsiao-nung te hsing-ch'eng ho fa-chan" 秦漢間個體小農的形成和發展. *Li-shih yen-chiu*, no. 2 (1959).

———. "Tung-Han keng-i shu-i chih-tu te fei-chih" 東漢更役戍役制度的廢止. *Li-shih yen-chiu*, no. 5 (1962): 96–115.

Ho Chien-min 何建民. *Hsiung-nu min-tsu k'ao* 匈奴民族考. Shanghai: Chung-hua shu-chü, 1939.

Ho Ch'iu-t'ao 何秋濤. *So-fang pei-ch'eng* 朔方備乘. 2 vols. Reprint. Taipei: Wen-hai ch'u-pan she, 1966.

Ho Kuang-yueh 何光岳. *Pai-Yueh yuan-liu shih* 百越源流史. Nanchang: Chiang-hsi chiao-yü, 1989.

Ho-nan sheng wen-hua chü wen-wu kung-tso tui 河南省文化局文物工作隊. "Nan-yang Han-tai t'ieh-kung-ch'ang fa-chueh chien-pao" 南陽漢代鐵工廠發掘簡報. *Wen-wu* 1 (1960): 58–60.

———. "Ts'ung Nan-yang Wan-ch'eng i-chih ch'u-t'u Han-tai li-hua mo ho chu-fan k'an li-hua te chu-tso kung-i kuo-ch'eng" 從南陽宛城遺址出土漢代犁鏵和鑄範看犁鏵的鑄造工藝過程. *Wen-wu* 7 (1965): 1–11.

Ho Ping-ti 何炳棣. "Huang-t'u kao-yuan yü Chung-kuo nung-yeh teh ch'i-yuan" 黃土高原與中國農業的起源. Hong Kong: Chung-wen ta-hsueh ch'u-pan she, 1969.

———. "Chou ch'u nien-tai p'ing-i" 周初年代評議. *Hsiang-kang Chung-wen ta-hsueh hsueh-pao* 1 (1973): 17–35.

———. "Ssu-ma T'an: Ch'ien yü Lao-tzu nien-tai" 司馬談, 遷與老子年代. *Che-hsueh yen-chiu* 12 (1998): 1–18 (1999 revised copy used).

Ho Yu-ch'i 何幼琦. "Ti-i Ti-hsin chi-nien ho cheng I-fang te nien-tai" 帝乙帝辛紀年和征夷方的年代. *Yin-tu hsueh-k'an* 3 (1990): 1–9.

Hsia Nai 夏鼐. "Hsin-huo chih Tun-huang Han-chien" 新獲之敦煌漢簡 *Bulletin of the Institute of History and Philology, Academia Sinica* 19 (1948): 235–65.

———. "K'ao-ku-hsueh lun-wen-chi 考古學論文集. Peking, 1961.

Hsiang Ta 向達. "Yü-men-kuan Yang-kuan tsa-k'ao" 玉門官陽關雜考. *Chen-li tsa-chih* 1, no. 4 (1944): 389–98. Revised and included in Hsiang Ta, *T'ang-tai Ch'ang-an yü Hsi-yü wen-ming* 唐代長安與西域文明, 373–92. Peking, 1957.

Hsiang Ta 向達, trans. *Hsiung-nu shih* 匈奴史. Shanghai: Shang-wu yin-shu kuan, 1934. Translation of *The Empire of the Hiung-Nu*, by E. H. Parker.

Hsi-Han hui-yao 西漢會要. By Hsu T'ien-lin 徐天麟. Shanghai: Chung-hua shu-chü, 1955.

Hsi-Han Nan-yueh-wang mu 西漢南越王墓. Comp. Kuang-tung shen po-wu kuan et al. Peking: Wen-wu, 1991.

Hsi-ho chiu-shih 西河舊史. Author unknown, ed. Chang Shu 張澍. *Ts'ung-shu chi-ch'eng* ed. Shanghai, 1935.

Hsieh Ch'eng-hsia 謝成俠. *Chung-kuo yang-ma shih* 中國養馬史. Peking, 1959.

Hsieh I-cheng 謝詒徵. *Sung chih wai-chiao* 宋之外交. Shanghai, 1935.

Hsieh Kuei-hua 謝桂華 and Li Chün-ming 李均明. "Chü-yen Han-chien chia-i pien shih-wen pu-cheng chü-yü" 居延漢簡甲乙編釋文補正舉隅. *Li-shih yen-chiu* 5 (1982): 141–54.

———. "Yin-wan Han-mu hsin-ch'u *Chi-pu* k'ao-shu" 尹灣漢墓新出集簿考述. *Chung-kuo shih yen-chiu* 2 (1997): 29–37.

Hsin Shu-chih 辛樹幟. *Yü-kung hsin-chieh* 禹貢新解. Hong Kong: Chung-hua, 1973.

Hsin-chiang she-hui k'o-hsueh-yuan min-tsu yen-chiu so 新疆社會科學院民族研究所. *Hsin-chiang chien-shih* 新疆簡史. 2 vols. Ürümqi, Sinkiang: Jen-min ch'u-pan she, 1980.

Hsin-chiang Wei-wu erh tzu-chih ch'ü po-wu kuan 新疆維吾兒自治區博物館. *Hsin-chiang li-shih wen-wu* 新疆歷史文物. Peking: Wen-wu, 1972.

Hsin Chung-kuo ch'u-t'u wen-wu 新中國出土文物. Peking: Wai-wen ch'u-pan she, 1972.

Hsing I-t'ien 邢義田. *Ch'in-Han shih lun-kao* 秦漢史論稿. Taipei: Tung-ta t'u-shu kung-ssu, 1987.

Hsiung T'ieh-chi 熊鉄基. *Ch'in-Han hsin Tao-chia lueh-lun kao* 秦漢新道家略論稿. Shanghai: Shanghai jen-min, 1984. Rev. ed., 2001.

———. *Ch'in-Han chün-shih chih-tu shih* 秦漢軍事制度史. Nanchang: Chiang-hsi jen-min, 1990.

Hsu Chien 徐堅. *Ch'u-hsueh chi* 初學記. By Hsu Chien et al. 3 vols. Peking: Chung-hua shu-chü, 1962.

Hsu Cho-yun 許倬雲. "Hsi-Han cheng-ch'üan yü she-hui shih-li te chiao-hu tso-yung" 西漢政權與社會勢力的交互作用. *Bulletin of the Institute of History and Philology, Academia Sinica* 35 (September 1964): 261–81.

———. "Han-tai chia-t'ing chih ta-hsiao" 漢代家庭之大小. In *Symposium in Honor of Dr. Li Chi on His Seventieth Birthday*, vol. 2, Taipei, 1967.

———. *Ch'iu-ku pien* 求古編. Taipei: Lien-ching, 1981.

———. *Hsi-Chou shih* 西周史. Taipei: Lien-ching, 1984.

Hsu Chung-shu 徐中舒, "Yin-jen fu-hsiang chi hsiang chih nan-ch'ien" 殷人服象及象之南遷. *Bulletin of the Institute of History and Philology, Academia Sinica* 2, no. 2 (1930): 60–75.

———. "Ku-tai kuan-kai kung-ch'eng yuan-ch'i k'ao" 古代灌溉工程原起考. *Bulletin of the Institute of History and Philology, Academia Sinica* 5, no. 2 (1935): 255–69.

———. *Shang-ku shih-lun* 上古史論. Reprint. Taipei: T'ien-shan ch'u-pan she, 1986.

Hsu Fu-kuan 徐復觀. *Liang-Han ssu-hsiang shih* 兩漢思想史. Taipei, 1976.

Hsu Hung-chieh 徐宏杰. "Ch'in-Han she-hui chih t'u-ti chih-tu yü nung-yeh sheng-ch'an" 秦漢社會之土地制度與農業生產. *Shih-huo pan-yueh-k'an* 3, no. 7 (March 1936): 10–29.

Hsu Shen 許慎. (a) *Shuo-wen chieh-tzu* 說文解字. Annotated by Tuan Yü-ts'ai 段玉裁. *Wan-yu wen-k'u* ed. 18 vols. Shanghai: Shang-wu yin-shu kuan, 1930.

———. (b) *Shuo-wen chieh-tzu*. Shanghai: Shih-chieh shu-chü, 1963.

Hsu Sung 徐松. *Hsi-yü san-chung* 西域三種. Peiping, n.d.

———. *Han-shu Hsi-yü chuan pu-chu* 漢書西域傳補注. *Ch'ing-ch'ao fan-shu yü-ti ts'ung-shu* ed.

———. *Hsi-yü shui-tao chi* 西域水道記. *Ch'ing-ch'ao fan-shu yü-ti ts'ung-shu* ed.

Hsun-tzu 荀子. 1. *Hsun-tzu chi-chieh* 荀子集解. Ed. Wang Hsien-ch'ien. Reprint. Taipei: Shih-chieh shu-chü, 1952; 2. *Hsun-tzu ku-i*. Ed. Yang Liu-ch'iao. Chi-nan: Ch'i-lu shu-she, 1985.

Hsun Yueh 荀悅. *Ch'ien-Han chi* 前漢紀. *Kuo-hsueh chi-pen ts'ung-shu* ed.; *Ssu-pu ts'ung-k'an* ed.

Hu Chi-ch'uang 胡寄窗. *Chung-kuo ching-chi ssu-hsiang shih* 中國經濟思想史. 2 vols. Shanghai, 1962–63.

Hu Hou-hsuan 胡厚宣. *Chia-ku hsueh Shang-shih lun-ts'ung ch'u-chi* 甲骨學商史論叢初集. Chengtu: Ch'i-lu ta-hsueh, 1944; *Erh-chi* 二集, 1945. Reprint. Hong Kong: Wen-yu t'ang.

Hu Hou-hsuan et al. *Chia-ku wen yü yin-shang shih* 甲骨文與殷商史. Shanghai: Shanghai ku-chi, 1983.

Hu-nan sheng wen-wu kung-tso tui 湖南省文物工作隊. "Ch'ang-sha Heng-yang ch'u-t'u Chan-kuo shih-tai te t'ieh-ch'i" 長沙衡陽出土戰國時代的鐵器. *K'ao-ku t'ung-hsun* 1 (1956): 77–79.

Hu Nien-i 胡念詒. *Hsien-Ch'in wen-hsueh lun-chi* 先秦文學論集. Peking: Hsin-hua shu-tien, 1981.

Huai-nan tzu 淮南子. *Huai-nan tzu*. Comp. under the auspices of the prince of Huai-nan (Liu An 劉安). Liu Wen-tien 劉文典, *Huai-nan Hung-lieh chi-chieh* 淮南鴻烈集解 ed. 2 vols. Reprint. Taipei: Shang-wu yin-shu kuan, 1969.

Huan T'an 桓譚. *Hsin-lun* 新論. In CSK.

Huang Chang-chien 黃彰健. "Shih-lun 'Wu-ch'eng' yü chin-wen yueh-hsiang" 試論武成與金文月相. *Li-shih yen-chiu* 2 (1998): 1–24.

Huang Chin-yen 黃金言. *Ch'in-Han chün-chih shih lun* 秦漢軍制史論. Nan-chang: Chiang-hsi ch'u-pan she, 1993.

Huang Lieh 黃列. "Shih Han-chien chung yu-kuan Han-tai she-hui hsing-chih chu-li" 釋漢簡中有關漢代社會性質諸例. *Li-shih yen-chiu* 6 (1957): 65–78.

Huang Liu-chu 黃留珠. *Ch'in-Han shih-chin chih-tu* 秦漢仕進制度. Sian: Hsi-pei ta-hsueh, 1985.

Huang Wen-pi 黃文弼. *T'a-li-mu p'en-ti k'ao-ku chi* 塔里木盆地考古記. Peking: K'o-hsueh ch'u-pan she, 1958.

———. *Hsi-pei shih-ti lun-ts'un* 西北史地論叢. Shanghai: Jen-min ch'u-pan she, 1981.

Huang-fu Mi 皇甫謐. *Ti-wang shih-chi* 帝王世紀. *Ti-wang shih-chi chi-ts'un* 帝王世紀輯存 ed. Fragments re-collected and ed. by Hsu Tsung-yuan 徐宗元. Peking: Chung-hua shu-chü, 1964.

Hung Mai 洪邁. *Jung-chai sui-pi wu-chi* 容齋隨筆五集. 4 vols. *Kuo-hsueh chi-pen ts'ung-shu* ed.

I-ching 易經. 1. *Wu-ching tu-pen* ed.; 2. *Shih-san ching chu-shu* ed.; 3. *I-ching chu-i* ed.

I-li 儀禮. *I-li chu-shu chi pu-cheng* 儀禮注疏及補正 ed. Reprint. Taipei, 1963 (in *Shih san-ching chu-shu*).

Jao Tsung-i 饒宗頤. "Chü-yen Han-chien shu-shu 'erh-ming-mu-yun' chieh" 居延漢簡術數耳鳴目瞷解. *Ta-lu tsa-chih* 13, no. 12 (December 1956): 6–7.

Jen Chi-yü 任繼愈. "*Sun Tzu ping-fa* te che-hsueh ssu-hsiang" 孫子兵法的哲學思想. *Wen-wu* 3 (1974): 47–55.

———. *Chung-kuo Tao-chiao shih* 中國道教史. Shanghai: Shanghai Jen-min, 1990.

Jen Chi-yü, ed. *Chung-kuo Fo-chiao shih* 中國佛教史. Vol. 1. Peking: Hsin-hua, 1981.

Jen Nai-ch'iang 任乃強. *Ch'iang-tsu yuan-liu t'an-so* 羌族源流探索. Chungking: Hsin-hua, 1984.

Jen Yü-ts'ai 任育才. *T'u-fan [T'u-po] yü T'ang-ch'ao kuan-hsi chih yen-chiu* 吐蕃與唐朝關係之研究. Taichung: Tzu-li ch'u pan she, 1971.

Jui Ho-cheng 芮和笅. *Hsi-Han yü-shih chih-tu* 西漢御史制度. Taipei, 1964.

Jui I-fu [Ruey Yih-fu] 芮逸夫. "Chung-kuo min-tsu kou-ch'eng te ch'u-pu yen-chiu" 中國民族構成的初步研究. In *She-hui hsueh lun-chi*, 482–506. Taipei, 1977. Originally published in 1953.

———. *Chung-kuo min-tsu chi-ch'i wen-hua lun-kao* 中國民族及其文化論稿. 2d ed. 3 vols. Taipei: Taita, 1989. Originally published in 1972.

Jung Keng 容庚. *Chin-wen pien* 金文編. Peking: She-hui k'o-hsueh ch'u-pan she, 1959.

Kan Po-wen 甘博文. "Kan-su Wu-wei Lei-t'ai Tung-Han mu ch'ing-li chien-pao" 甘肅武威雷台東漢墓清理簡報. *Wen-wu* 2 (1972): 16–24. Eight plates.

Kan-su po-wu-kuan 甘肅博物館. "Kan-su Wu-wei Mo-tsui-tzu Han-mu fa-chueh" 甘肅武威磨咀子漢墓發掘. *K'ao-ku*, no. 9 (1960).

Kan-su sheng k'ao-ku yen-chiu so 甘肅省考古研究所, ed. *Ch'in-Han chien-tu lun-wen chi* 秦漢簡牘論文集. Lanchou, 1989.

Kan-su sheng po-wu kuan 甘肅省博物館. "Wu-wei Lei-t'ai Han-mu" 武威雷台漢墓. *K'ao-ku hsueh-pao* 2 (1974): 87–108. Eighteen plates.

Kan-su sheng t'u-shu kuan 甘肅省圖書館, comp. *Ssu-ch'ou chih-lu wen-hsien hsu-lu* 絲綢之路文獻敘錄. Lanchou, 1989.

Kan-su sheng wen-wu kung-tso tui 甘肅省文物工作隊 and Kan-su sheng po-wu kuan 甘肅省博物館, eds. *Han-chien yen-chiu wen-chi* 漢簡研究文集. Lanchou, 1984.

Kao Ch'eng 高承. *Shih-wu chi-yuan* 事物紀原. Reprint. Taipei: Hsin-hsing shu-chü, 1969. Originally published in 1447.

Kao Jui 高銳. *Chung-kuo shang-ku chün-shih shih-lueh* 中國上古軍事史略. 3 vols. Peking: Chün-shih k'o-hsueh ch'u-pan she, 1985.

———. *Ch'ung-kuo chün-shih shih-lueh* 中國軍事史略. 3 vols. Peking: Chün-shih k'o-hsueh, 1986.

Kao Min 高敏. "Lun Ch'in lü chung te 'se-fu' i-kuan" 論秦律中的嗇夫一官. *She-hui k'o-hsüeh chan-hsien* 1 (1979a): 135–41.

———. "'Yu-chih' fei 'se-fu' pien" 有秩非嗇夫辨. *Wen-wu* 3 (1979b): 70–72.

———. *Yun-meng Ch'in-chien ch'u-t'an* 雲夢秦簡初探. Chengchow: Ho-nan jen-min, 1979c.

———. *Ch'in-Han shih lun-chi* 秦漢史論集. Chengchow: Chung-chou shu-hua she, 1982.

Kao P'ing-tzu 高平子. "Han-li yin-ke i-t'ung chi ch'i wan-ch'eng shih-ch'i te hsin yen-chiu" 漢曆沿革異同及其完成時期的新研究. *Ta-lu tsa-chih* 7, no. 5 (September 1953a): 99, 143.

———. "Han-chien-shih jih-li shih-i" 漢簡式日曆釋義. *Ta-lu tsa-chih* 7, no. 12 (December 1953b): 28.

———. "Liu-sha chui-chien chung i-tsu Han-li nien-ch'i te k'ao-t'ing" 流沙墜簡中的一組漢歷年期的考訂. *Ta-lu tsa-chih* 8, no. 1 (January 1954): 14.

K'ao-ku Yen-chiu-so pien-chi-pu 考古研究所編輯部. "Wu-wei Mo-tsui-tzu Han-mu ch'u-t'u yü-chang shih-chien shih-wen" 武威磨咀子漢墓出土玉杖十簡釋文. *K'ao-ku*, no. 9 (1960).

Kao Tzu-ch'eng 高自試. "Han-tai ta-hsiao hu (shih) wen-t'i" 漢代大小斛（石）問題. *K'ao-ku*, no. 2 (1962): 92–94, 98.

Ko Chien-hsiung 葛劍雄. *Hsi-Han jen-k'ou ti-li* 西漢人口地理. Peking: Jen-min, 1986.

———. *I-chao ssu-min* 億兆斯民. Hong Kong: Chung-hua, 1989.

Ku Chi-kuang 谷霽光. "Chan-kuo Ch'in-Han chien chung-nung i-shang chih li-lun yu shih-chi" 戰國秦漢中間重農抑商之理論與實際. *Chung-kuo she-hui ching-chi shih chi-k'an* 7 (1944): 1–22.

———. *Fu-ping chih-tu k'ao-shih* 府兵制度考釋. Shanghai, 1962.

Ku Chieh-kang 顧頡剛. *Ch'in-Han fang-shih yü ju-sheng* 秦漢方士與儒生. Rev. ed. Shanghai: Shanghai ku-chi, 1954.

———. "Chou-kung she-cheng Ch'eng-wang" 周公攝政成王. *Wen-shih* 23 (1984): 1–30.

———. *Ku Chieh-kang ku-shih lun-wen chi* 顧頡剛古史論文集. 5 vols. Peking: Chung-hua, 1987–96.

———. "Shang-shu 'Wu-i' chiao-shih i-lun" 尚書無逸校釋譯論. *Wen-shih* 44 (1998): 1–11.

———. "Shang-shu li-tai chieh-shih hsuan-lu ho pu-ch'ung" 尚書歷代解釋選錄和補充. *Wen-shih* 49 (1999): 1–14.

Ku Chieh-kang et al. *Ku-shih pien* 古史辨. 7 vols. Reprint. Taipei: Ming-lun ch'u-pan she, 1970.

Ku Chieh-kang and Shih Nien-hai 史念海. *Chung-kuo chiang-yü yen-ko shih* 中國疆域沿革史. Changsha, 1938.

Ku T'ieh-fu 顧鉄符. *Ch'u-kuo min-tsu shih lueh* 楚國民族史略. Wuhan: Hupeh jen-min, 1984.

Ku Tsu-yü 顧祖禹. *Tu-shih fang-yü chi-yao* 讀史方輿紀要. 32 vols. T'u-shu chi-ch'eng chü, 1901.

Ku Tung-kao 顧棟高. *Ch'un-ch'iu ta-shih piao* 春秋大事表. 50 *chüan*. Wan-chüan lou ed.

Kua-ti chih 括地志. Comp. Li T'ai 李泰 et al. *Han-T'ang ti-li* ed.

Kuan-tzu 管子. 1. *Ssu-pu pei-yao* ed.; 2. *Kuo-hsueh chi-pen ts'ung-shu* ed.; 3. *Kuan-tzu chin-ch'üan* ed. Reprint. Taipei: Shang-wu, 1970; 4. *Kuan-tzu hsin-chiao* ed.

Kuan Tung-kuei 管東貴. "Han-tai te t'un t'ien yü k'ai-pien" 漢代的屯田與開邊. *Bulletin of the Institute of History and Philology, Academia Sinica* 45, no. 1 (1973): 75–77.

———. "Han-tai t'un-t'ien te tsu-chih yü kung-neng" 漢代屯田的組織與功能. *Bulletin of the Institute of History and Philology, Academia Sinica* 48, no. 4 (1977).

———. "Han-ch'u ching-chi fa-chan te li-shih pei-ching" 漢初經濟發展的歷史背景. In *Ch'ü Wan-li hsien-sheng ch'i-chih jung-ch'ing lun-wen chi*, 537–52. 1978.

———. "Ts'ung Han-chien k'an Han-tai pien-sai te feng-lin chih" 從漢簡看漢代邊塞的俸廩制. In *T'ao Hsi-sheng hsien-sheng pa-chih jung-ch'ing lun-wen chi*, 458–95. Taipei: Shih-huo, 1979.

———. "Feng-chien chih yü Han-ch'u tsung-fan wen-t'i" 封建制與漢初宗藩問題. In *Chung-yang yen-chiu yuan ti-erh chieh kuo-chi Han-hsueh hui-i*, 377–402. Taipei, 1989.

Kuo Hua-jo 郭化若. *Sun Tzu chin-i* 孫子今譯. Shanghai, 1977.

Kuo Ju-huai 郭汝瑰 et al. *Chung-kuo chün-shih shih* 中國軍事史. 5 vols. Peking: Chieh-fang chün ch'u-pan she, 1988.

Kuo Mo-jo 郭沫若. *Yin-Chou ch'ing-t'ung ch'i ming-wen* 殷周青銅器銘文. Peking: Jen-min ch'u-pan she, 1954.

———. *Liang-Chou chin-wen tz'u ta-hsi k'ao-shih* 兩周金文辭大系考釋. Reprint. Hong Kong, 1957a. Originally published in 1932.

———. *Ch'ing-t'ung shih-tai* 青銅時代. Peking: K'o-hsueh ch'u-pan she, 1957b.

———. *Shih p'i-p'an shu* 十批判書. Peking: K'o-hsueh, 1959.

———. *Yin-ch'i ts'ui-pien* 殷契粹編. Peking, 1965.

Kuo Pao-chün 郭寶鈞. *Chung-kuo ch'ing-t'ung shih-tai* 中國青銅時代. Peking: San-lien, 1963.

Kuo-yü 國語. *Kuo-hsueh chi-pen ts'ung-shu* ed. Shanghai: Ku-chi, 1978 ed.

Lao Kan 勞榦. "Han-tai nu-li chih-tu chi-lueh" 漢代奴隸制度紀略. *Bulletin of the Institute of History and Philology, Academia Sinica* 5, no. 1 (1935a): 1–11.

———. "Liang-Han hu-chi yü ti-li chih kuan-hsi" 兩漢戶籍與地理之關係. *Bul-*

letin of the Institute of History and Philology, Academia Sinica 5, no. 2 (1935b): 179–214.

———. "Liang-Han ko-chün jen-k'ou tseng-chien shu-mu chih t'ui-ts'e" 兩漢各郡人口增減數目之推測. *Bulletin of the Institute of History and Philology, Academia Sinica* 5, no. 2 (1935c): 215–40.

———. "Ts'ung Han-chien chung so-chien chih pien-chün chih-tu" 從漢簡中所見之邊郡制度. *Bulletin of the Institute of History and Philology, Academia Sinica* 8, no. 2 (1939): 159–80.

———. "Han-tai ping-chih chi Han-chien chung te ping-chih" 漢代兵制及漢簡中的兵制. *Bulletin of the Institute of History and Philology, Academia Sinica* 10 (1942a): 23–55.

———. "Chü-yen Han-chien k'ao-shih hsu-mu" 居延漢簡考釋序目. *Bulletin of the Institute of History and Philology, Academia Sinica* 10 (1942b): 647–58.

———. "Han-wu Hou-yuan pu-li nien-hao k'ao" 漢武後元不立年號考. *Bulletin of the Institute of History and Philology, Academia Sinica* 10 (1942c): 197–200.

———. "Han-chien chung te Ho-hsi ching-chi sheng-huo" 漢簡中的河西經濟生活. *Bulletin of the Institute of History and Philology, Academia Sinica* 11 (1943a): 61–75.

———. "Han-tai she-ssu te yuan-liu" 漢代社祀的源流. *Bulletin of the Institute of History and Philology, Academia Sinica* 11 (1943b): 49–60.

———. "Liang-kuan i-chih k'ao" 兩關遺址考. *Bulletin of the Institute of History and Philology, Academia Sinica* 11 (1943c): 287–96.

———. "Lun Han-tai chih lu-yun yü shui-yun" 論漢代之陸運與水運. *Bulletin of the Institute of History and Philology, Academia Sinica* 16 (1948a) [1947]: 69–91.

———. "Han-tai ch'a-chü chih-tu" 漢代察舉制度. *Bulletin of the Institute of History and Philology, Academia Sinica* 17 (1948b): 79–130.

———. "Shih Han-tai chih t'ing-chang yü feng-sui" 釋漢代之亭障與烽燧. *Bulletin of the Institute of History and Philology, Academia Sinica* 19 (1948c): 501–22.

———. "Chü-yen Han-chien k'ao-cheng pu-cheng" 居延漢簡考證補正. *Bulletin of the Institute of History and Philology, Academia Sinica* 14 (1948d): 229–42.

———. "Han-tai te t'ing-chih" 漢代的亭制. *Bulletin of the Institute of History and Philology, Academia Sinica* 22 (1950a): 129–38.

———. "Tun-huang chi Tun-huang te hsin shih-liao" 敦煌及敦煌的新史料. *Ta-lu tsa-chih* 1, no. 3 (August 1950b): 6–9.

———. "Ta-shih yü hsiao-shih" 大石與小石. *Ta-lu tsa-chih* 1, no. 11 (December 1950c): 21.

———. "Han-tai te ku-yung chih-tu" 漢代的顧傭制度. *Bulletin of the Institute of History and Philology, Academia Sinica* 23 (1951a): 77–87.

———. "Kuan-yü Han-tai kuan-feng te chi-ko t'ui-ts'e" 關於漢代官俸的幾個推測. *Wen-shih-che hsüeh-pao* 3 (1951b): 11–22.

———. "Chien-tu chung so-chien te pu-po" 簡牘中所見的布帛. *Academic Review* 1, no. 1 (September 1952a): 152–55.

———. *Ch'in-Han shih* 秦漢史. Taipei: Chung-hua wen-hua ch'u-pan shih-yeh wei-yüan-hui, 1952b.

———. "Han-tai chün-chih chi ch'i tui-yü chien-tu te ts'an-chao" 漢代郡制及其對於簡牘的參照. *Fu-ku-hsiao-chang Ssu-nien chi-nien lun-wen-chi*, December 1952c, 29–61.

———. "Han-tai ch'ang-fu shu-lueh" 漢代常服述略. *Bulletin of the Institute of History and Philology, Academia Sinica* 24 (1953): 177–83.

———. "Han-tai te hsien-chih" 漢代的縣制. *Annals of Academia Sinica* 1 (1954): 69–81.

———. "Yü-p'ei yü kang-mao" 玉佩與剛卯. *Bulletin of the Institute of History and Philology, Academia Sinica* 27 (1956a): 183–96.

———. "Han-tai te Hsi-yü tu-hu yü Wu-chi chiao-wei" 漢代的西域都護與戊己校尉. *Bulletin of the Institute of History and Philology, Academia Sinica* 28 (1956b): 485–96.

———. "*Shih-chi Hsiang yü pen-chi* chung 'hsueh-shu' ho 'hsueh-chien' te chieh-shih" 史記項羽本紀中學書和學劍的解釋. *Bulletin of the Institute of History and Philology, Academia Sinica* 30 (October 1959): 499–510.

———. "Lun Han-tai Yü-men-kuan te ch'ien-hsi wen-t'i" 論漢代玉門關的遷從問題. *Tsing Hua Journal of Chinese Studies*, n.s. 2, no. 1 (May 1960): 40–52.

———. "Han-tai cheng-chih tsu-chih te t'e-chih chi ch'i kung-neng" 漢代政治組織的特質及其功能. *Tsing Hua Journal of Chinese Studies*, n.s. 8, nos. 1–2 (August 1970): 228–45.

———. "Han-tai huang-chin chi t'ung-ch'ien te shih-yung wen-t'i" 漢代黃金及銅錢的使用問題. *Bulletin of the Institute of History and Philology, Academia Sinica* 42, no. 3 (1971): 341–90.

———. *Lao Kan hsueh-shu lun-wen chi* 勞榦學術論文集. 2 vols. Taipei: I-wen, 1976.

———. "Kuan-yü Kuan-tung chi Kuan-hsi te t'ao-lun" 關於關東及關西的討論. *Shih-huo*, n.s. 13, nos. 3–4 (July 1983): 142–46 (Hsing I-t'ien).

Lei Hai-tsung 雷海宗. "Chung-kuo te ping" 中國的兵. *She-hui k'o hsueh* 1, no. 1 (October 1935): 1–47.

———. "Tung-Chou Ch'in-Han chien chung-nung i-shang te li-lun yü cheng-ts'e" 東周秦漢間重農抑商的理論與政策. *She-hui k'o-hsueh* 5, no. 1 (October 1948): 79–89.

———. *Chung-kuo wen-hua yü Chung-kuo te ping* 中國文化與中國的兵. Reprint. Hong Kong, 1968. Originally published in 1940.

Li-chi 禮記. 2 vols. Taipei: Shang-wu yin-shu kuan, 1970 ed.; *Wu-ching tu-pen* ed.

Li Chieh-min 李解民. "Min yü Ch'ien-shou" 民與黔首. *Wen-shih* 23 (1984): 55–72.

Li Chien-nung 李劍農. *Hsien-Ch'in Liang-Han ching-chi shih kao* 先秦兩漢經濟史稿. Peking: Chung-hua, 1957.

Li Chih 李贄. *T'sang-shu* 藏書. 2 vols. Peking: Chung-hua shu-chü, 1959.

———. *Shih-kang p'ing-yao* 史綱評要. 3 vols. Peking: Chung-hua, 1974.

Li Chün-ming 李均明. "Liu-sha chui-chien shih-wen chiao-cheng" 流沙墜簡釋文校正. *Wen-shih* 12 (1981): 53–62.

Li Chung-ts'ao 李仲操. *Hsi-Chou nien-tai* 西周年代. Peking: Wen-wu, 1991.

Li Hsiao-ting 李孝定. *Chia-ku wen-tzu chi-shih* 甲骨文字集釋. 16 vols. Taipei: Chung-yang yen-chiu yuan, 1965.

Li Hsueh-ch'in 李學勤. *Tung-Chou yü Ch'in-tai wen-ming* 東周與秦代文明. 2d ed., Peking: Wen-wu, 1991. Originally published in 1984.

———. *Chien-po i-chi yü hsueh-shu shih* 簡帛佚籍與學術史. Taipei: Shih-pao wen-hua, 1994.

———. *Ku wen-hsien ts'ung-lun* 古文獻叢論. Shanghai: Yuan-tung, 1996.

———. *Hsia-Shang-Chou nien-tai hsueh cha-chi* 夏商周年代學札記. Shenyang: Liao-ning ta-hsueh, 1999.

Li Kuang-pi 李光璧 and Ch'ien Chün-yeh 錢君曄, eds. *Chung-kuo k'o-hsueh chi-shui fa-ming ho k'o-hsueh chi-shu jen-wu lun-chi* 中國科學技術發明和科學技術人物論集. Peking, 1955.

Li Kuang-t'ing 李光廷. *Han Hsi-yü t'u-k'ao* 漢西域圖考. Prefaced 1869. 4 vols. N.p. 19–.

Li Ku-yin 李古寅. *Han-tai Hsi-pei t'un-t'ien chieh-ku ch'u-t'an* 漢代西北屯田解構初探. Lanchow: Lanchow ta-hsueh, 1982.

Li Ling 李零. "Hsi-Chou chin-wen chung te chih-kuan hsi-t'ung" 西周金文中的職官系統. In *Chin-hsin chi*, ed. Wu Jung-tseng, 202–14.

Li Min 李民 and Chang Kuo-shuo 張國碩. *Hsia Shang Chou san-tsu yuan-liu t'an-so* 夏商周三族源流探索. Chengchow: Honan jen-min, 1998.

Li Shu-t'ung 李樹桐. "T'ang-tai ti ma-cheng yü chiao-t'ung" 唐代的馬政與交通. In *Li-shih hsueh-pao*, 183–228. Taipei: Kuo-li shih-fan ta-hsüeh, 5 (1977).

———. *T'ang-shih lun-ts'ung* 唐史論叢. Taipei: Chung-hua shu-chu, 1979.

Li-tai ko-tsu chuan-chi hui-pien 歷代各族傳記會編. Ed. Chien Po-tsan 翦伯贊 et al. Vol. 1. Peking: Chung-hua shu-chü, 1958.

Li T'ang 禮堂 [pseud.]. "Yü-chang shih-chien pu-shih" 玉杖十簡補述. *K'ao-ku*, no. 5 (1961): 259–60.

Li Tao-yuan 酈道元. *Shui-ching chu* 水經注. 1. *Kuo-hsueh chi-pen ts'ung-shu* ed.; 2. Wang Kuo-wei 王國維 ed. Shanghai: Jen-min, 1984; 3. Ch'en Ch'iao-i 陳橋驛 ed. Shanghai: Ku-chi, 1990.

Li Tsu-teh 李祖德. "Lun Hsi-Han te huo-pi kai-chih" 論西漢貨幣改制. *Li-shih yen-chiu*, no. 3 (1965): 83–98.

Li Tsung-t'ung 李宗侗 (Hsuan-po 玄伯). *Chung-kuo ku-tai she-hui hsin-yen ch'u-kao* 中國古代社會新研初稿. Peking: Lai-hsun ko shu-tien, 1930.

———. *Chung-kuo ku-tai she-hui shih* 中國古代社會史. 2 vols. Taipei: Chung-hua wen-hua, 1954.

Li Ya-nung 李亞農. *Hsi-Chou yü Tung-Chou* 西周與東周. Shanghai: Jen-min, 1956.

———. *Hsin-jan-chai shih-lun chi* 欣然齋史論集. Shanghai: Jen-min ch'u-pan she, 1962.

Li Yuan-ch'eng 李源澄. "Han-tai fu-i k'ao" 漢代賦役考. *Kuo-li Che-chiang ta-hsueh wen-hsüeh yüan chi-k'an* 1 (1941): 25–37.

Liang Ch'i-ch'ao 梁啟超. *Yin-ping shih wen-chi* 飲冰室文集. 48 vols. Shanghai: Chung-hua shu-chü, 1916. Ho-chi ed., 40 vols., 1932.

———. *Yin-ping shih ch'üan-chi* 飲冰室全集. Reprint. Tainan: Tsung-ho, 1975.

———. *Yen-chiu kuo-shih chi ch'i-t'a* 研究國史及其他. Reprint. Hong Kong, n.d.

Liang Yü-sheng 梁玉繩. *Shih-chi chih-i* 史記志異. *Hsu-hsiu ssu-k'u ch'üan-shu* ed. Peking: Chung-hua, 1981.

Liao Pai-yüan 廖伯源. "Han-tai chueh-wei chih-tu shih-shih" 漢代爵位制度試釋. *Hsin-ya hsueh-pao* 10, no. 1, pt. 2 (July 1973): 93–184.

———. "Han-tai chien-chün chih-tu shih-shih" 漢代監軍制度試釋. *Ta-lu tsa-chih* 70, no. 3 (March 1985): 1–6.

———. *Li-shih yü chih-tu* 歷史與制度. Hong Kong: Chiao-yü t'u-su kung-ssu, 1997.

Lieh-nü chuan 列女傳. Attributed to Liu Hsiang 劉向. *Ssu-pu pei-yao* ed.

Lin Chien-ming 林劍明. *Ch'in-kuo fa-chan shih* 秦國發展史. Sian: Shensi jen-min ch'u-pan she, 1981a.

———. *Ch'in-shih kao* 秦史稿. Shanghai: Shanghai jen-min, 1981b. Shanghai ed. of *Ch'in-kuo fa-chan shih*.

Lin Chien-ming et al. *Ch'in-Han she-hui wen-ming* 秦漢社會文明. Sian: Hsi-pei ta-hsueh ch'u-pan she, 1985.

Lin Kan 林幹. *Hsiung-nu shih* 匈奴史. Huhehot, Inner Mongolia: Jen-min ch'u-pan she, 1979.

Lin Kan, comp. *Hsiung-nu li-shih nien-piao* 匈奴歷史年表. Peking: Chung-hua shu-chü, 1984.

———. *Hsiung-nu shih-liao hui-pien* 匈奴史料彙編. 2 vols. Peking: Chung-hua shu-chü, 1988.

Lin Lü-chih 林旅芝. *Hsiung-nu shih* 匈奴史. Hong Kong: Chung-hua wen-hua shih-yeh kung-ssu, 1963.

Ling Shun-sheng 凌純聲. *Sung-hua chiang hsia-yu te Ho-che-tsu* 松花江下游的赫哲族. 2 vols. Peiping: Chung-yang yen-chiu yuan, 1934.

Liu Chieh 劉節. *Chung-kuo ku-tai tsung-tsu I-ch'ih shih lun* 中國古代宗族移殖試論. Reprint. Taipei: Cheng-chung, 1957.

———. *Ku-shih k'ao-ts'un* 古史考存. Hong Kong: T'ai-p'ing shu-chü, 1968.

Liu Ch'un-fan 柳春藩. *Ch'in-Han feng-kuo shih-i ssu-chueh chih* 秦漢封國食邑賜爵制. Shengyang, 1984.

Liu Hai-nien 劉海年. "Ch'in Han 'shih-wu' te shen-fen yü chieh-chi ti wei" 秦漢士伍的身份與階級地位. *Wen-wu* 2 (1978): 58–62.

Liu Hsi 劉熙. *Shih-ming* 釋名. Taipei: Kuo-min ch'u-pan she, 1959.

Liu Hsien-chou 劉仙洲. *Chung-kuo ku-tai nung-yeh chi-chieh fa-ming shih* 中國古代農業機械發明史. Peking: K'o-hsüeh ch'u-pan she, 1963.

Liu Hsing-t'ang 劉興唐. "Li-lu k'ao" 里廬考. *Shih-huo* 3, no. 12 (May 1936): 8–20.

Liu Kuang-hua 劉光華. "Chien-chün hou te Ho-hsi" 建郡後的河西. *Tun-huang hsueh chi-k'an* 2 (1982): 87–99.

———. *Han-tai Hsi-pei t'un-t'ien yen-chiu* 漢代西北屯田研究. Lanchou, 1988a.

Liu Kuang-hua, comp. *Chung-kuo ku-tai Hsi-pei li-shih tzu-liao hsuan-lu* 中國古代西北歷史資料選錄. Lanchou, 1988b.

Liu Po-chi 劉伯驥. *Ch'un-ch'iu hui-meng cheng-chih* 春秋會盟政治. Taipei: T'aiwan shu-chü, 1962.

Liu Shu 劉恕. *Tzu-chih t'ung-chien wai-chi* 資治通鑑外紀. Shanghai: Han-fen lou ed.

Lo Chen-yü 羅振玉. *Tseng-ting Yin-hsu shu-ch'i k'ao-shih* 增訂殷墟書契考釋. Tung-fang hsueh-hui, 1927.

———. *Ti-ch'üan cheng-ts'un* 地券徵存. N.p., n.d.

Lou Tsu-i 樓祖詒. *Chung-kuo yu-i fa-ta shih* 中國郵驛發達史. Chungking, 1939.

———. "Han-chien yu-i tzu-liao shih-li" 漢簡郵驛資料釋例. *Wen-shih* 3 (1963): 123–43.

Lü-shih ch'un-ch'iu 呂氏春秋. 1. *Lü-shih ch'un-ch'iu chiao-shih* 呂氏春秋校釋, comp. Yin Chung-jung 尹仲容. Taipei, 1952; 2. Ch'en Ch'i-yu ed. Shanghai: Hsueh-lin ch'u-pan she, 1984.

Lü Ssu-mien 呂思勉. *Yen-shih cha-chi* 燕石札記. Shanghai: Shang-wu yin-shu kuan, 1937.

———. *Hsien-Ch'in shih* 先秦史. Shanghai: K'ai-ming, 1941.

———. *Lü Ssu-mien tu-shu cha chi* 呂思勉讀書札記. 2 vols. Shanghai: Shanghai ku-chi, 1982.

———. *Ch'in Han shih* 秦漢史. 2 vols. Reprint. Hong Kong: T'ai-p'ing shu-chü. Reprint. Shanghai: Ku-chi, 1983.

Lu Wen-ch'ao 盧文弨. *Ch'ün-shu shih-pu* 群書拾補, collected and ed. Lu Wen-ch'ao. *Kuo-hsueh chi-pen ts'ung-shu* ed. 2 vols.

Ma Ch'ang-shou 馬長壽. *Pei-Ti yü Hsiung-nu* 北狄與匈奴. Peking: San-lieu, 1962.

Ma Fei-pai 馬非百 [Ma Yuan-ts'ai 馬元材]. "Ch'in-Han ching-chi shih-liao" 秦漢經濟史料. *Shih-huo pan-yueh k'an* 2, no. 8 (September 1935); 2, no. 10 (October 1935); 3, no. 1 (December 1935); 3, no. 2 (December 1935); 3, no. 3 (January 1936); 3, no. 8 (March 1936); 3, no. 9 (April 1936).

———. *Sang Hung-yang chuan* 桑弘羊傳. Chengchow: Chung-chou shu-hua she, 1981a.

———. "Yun-meng Ch'in-chien *Ta-shih chi* chi-chuan" 雲夢秦簡大事記集傳. *Chung-kuo li-shih wen-hsien yen-chiu chi-k'an* 2 (1981b): 66–92.

———. *Sang Hung-yang nien-p'u ting-pu* 桑弘羊年譜訂補. Chenchow: Chung-chou shu-hua she, 1982a.

———. *Ch'in Chi shih* 秦集史. 2 vols. Peking: Chung-hua, 1982b.

———. *Ch'in Shih-huang chuan* 秦始皇傳. Kiangsu: Kiangsu ku-chi ch'u-pan she, 1985. Rev. ed. of *Ch'in Shih-huang ti chuan*. 2 vols. Shanghai: Shang-wu, 1941.

Ma Heng 馬衡. "Chi Han Chü-yen pi" 記漢居延筆. *Kuo-hsüeh chi-k'an* 3, 1 (March 1932): 67–72.

———. "Chü-yen Han-chien k'ao-shih liang-chung" 居延漢簡考釋兩種. *K'ao-ku t'ung-hsun* 1 (January 1957): 107–11.

Ma Ta-ying 馬大英. *Han-tai ts'ai-cheng shih* 漢代財政史. Peking: Chung-kuo ts'ai-cheng ching-chi ch'u-pan she, 1983.

Ma Tuan-lin 馬端臨. *Wen-hsien t'ung-k'ao* 文獻通考. *Shih-t'ung* ed.

Ma-wang-tui Han-mu po-shu cheng-li hsiao-tsu 馬王堆漢墓帛書整理小組. *Ching-fa* 經法. Peking: Wen-wu ch'u-pan she, 1979.

Meng Fan-jen 孟凡人. *Lou-lan Shan-shan chien-tu nien-tai hsueh yen-chiu* 樓蘭鄯善簡牘年代學研究. Ürümqi: Hsin-chiang jen-min, 1995.

Meng Wen-t'ung 蒙文通. *Chou-Ch'in shao-shu ming-tsu yen-chiu* 周秦少數民族研究. Shanghai: Lung-men lien-ho shu-tien, 1958.

———. *Yueh-shih ts'ung-kao* 越史叢稿. Peking: Jen-min, 1983.

Mo Tung-yin 莫東寅. *Man-tsu shih-lun* 滿族史論. Shanghai: San-lien, 1979. Originally published in 1958.

Mo-tzu 墨子. 1. *Mo-tzu hsien-ku* 墨子閒詁, ed. and annotated by Sun I-jang 孫詒讓. 4 vols.; 2. *Wan-yu wen-k'u* ed.

Ning K'o 寧可. "Han-tai te she" 漢代的社. *Wen-shih* 7 (1980): 7–13.

Ou-yang Hsun 歐陽詢 et al. *I-wen lei-chü* 藝文類聚. 2 vols. Peking: Chung-hua shu-chü, 1965.

Pai Shou-i 白壽彝. *Chung-kuo chiao-t'ung shih* 中國交通史. Reprint. Taipei, 1965.

P'an Yin-ko 潘吟閣. *Shih-chi huo-chih chuan hsin-ch'üan* 史記貨殖傳新詮. Shanghai, 1931.

P'eng Hsin-wei 彭信威. *Chung-kuo huo-pi shih* 中國貨幣史. 3d ed. Shanghai, 1965.

P'eng Lin 彭林. *Chou-li chu-t'i ssu-hsiang yü ch'eng-shu nien-tai ti yen-chiu* 周禮主題思想與成書年代的研究. Peking: Chung-kuo she-hui k'o-hsueh, 1991.

P'u Mou-chou 蒲慕州. *Mu-tsang yü sheng-ssu* 墓葬與生死. Taipei: Lien-ching, 1993.

———. *Chui-hsun i-chi chih-fu* 追尋一己之福. Taipei: Yun-ch'en, 1995.

Sa Meng-wu 薩孟武. *Chung-kuo she-hui cheng-chih shih* 中國社會政治史. 4 vols. Taipei, 1975.

San-chün ta-hsueh 三軍大學, comp. *Chung-kuo li-tai chan-cheng shih* 中國歷代戰爭史. Taipei: Kuo-fang yen-chiu yuan, 1963. Rev. and enlarged ed. 18 vols. Taipei: Li-ming wen-hua shih-yeh ch'u-pan kung-ssu, 1980.

Sang Hsiu-yun 桑秀雲. "Shu-pu Ch'iung-chu ch'uan-chih Ta-hsia k'ao" 蜀部邛竹傳至大夏考 *Bulletin of the Institute of History and Philology, Academia Sinica* 41, no. 1 (1969): 67–86.

Shang-Chou k'ao-ku 商周考古. Comp. Li-shih hsi k'ao-ku chiao-yen shih of Peking University. Peking: Wen-wu, 1979.

Shao Yu-ch'eng 邵友誠. "Chü-yen Han-chien cha-chi" 居延漢簡札記. *K'ao-ku*, no. 1 (1962): 45.

Shen Chia-pen 沈家本. *Shen Chi-i hsien-sheng i-shu* 沈寄簃先生遺書. 32 vols. N.p., 1929.

Shen-hsi sheng po-wu kuan, Wen-wu kuan-li wei-yüan-hui 陝西省博物館, 文物管理委員會. "Shen-hsi sheng fa-hsien te Han-tai t'ieh-hua ho pi-t'u" 陝西省發現的漢代鐵鏵和鐴土. *Wen-wu* 1 (1966): 19–24.

Shen Yuan 沈元. "Chü-yen Han-chien niu-chi chiao-shih" 居延漢簡牛籍校釋. *K'ao-ku*, no. 8 (1962): 426–28.

Shih Chih-mien 施之勉. *Han-shih pien-i* 漢史辨疑. Taipei, 1954. Includes his "Ho-hsi ssu-chün chien-chih k'ao" 河西四郡建置考, originally published in the *Ta-lu tsa-chih* 3, no. 5 (September 1951): 20–21.

———. "Ch'in chih ch'ien-jen shuo" 秦之遷人說. In Sun K'ai, *Ch'in hui-yao*, 454–56. Rev. ed. Peking, 1959.

Shih-ching 詩經. 1. *Wu-ching tu-pen*, 1952 ed.; 2. *Mao-shih cheng-i* 毛詩正義. 6 vols. Hong Kong, 1964. Reprint from the *Shih-san ching chu-shu*; 3. Ch'ü Wan-li, *Shih-ching chu-shih* ed. 2 vols.

Shih-k'o tzu-liao chia-i pien 石刻資料甲乙編. Ed. Yen Keng-wang 嚴耕望. 420 vols. Taipei: Yi-wen, 1966.

Shih Nien-hai 史念海. "Han-tai tui hsi-pei pien chün te ching-ying" 漢代對西北邊郡的經營. *Wen-shih tsa-chih* 2, no. 2 (March 1942): 35–42.

———. *Ho-shan chi* 河山集. Hong Kong: Kuang ching chueh ch'u-pan she, 1977.

Shih-pen 世本. 1. *Ts'ung-shu chi-ch'eng ch'u-pien* ed.; 2. *Shih-pen pa-chung* ed.

Shih-san ching chu-shu 十三經注疏. 1. *Shih-san ching chu-shu*. *Ssu-pu pei-yao* ed.; 2. Reprint. Taipei: Shih-chieh shu-chü, 1963; 3. Reprint. Taipei: I-wen ed.

Shih Sheng-han 石聲漢. *Ts'ung Ch'i-ming yao-shu k'an Chung-kuo ku-tai te nung-yeh k'o-hsueh chih-shih* 從齊民要術看中國古代的農業科學知識. Peking, 1957.

Shih-t'ung 十通. 20 vols. Shanghai: Shang-wu yin-shu kuan, 1936.

Shu-ching 書經. 1. *Wu-ching tu-pen* ed.; 2. *Shih-san ching chu-shu* ed.; 3. *Shang-shu chin-chu chin-i* ed.; 4. *Shang-shu I-chu* ed., 5. *Shang-shu cheng-tu* ed.

Shui-hu ti Ch'in-mu chu-chien cheng-li hsiao-tsu 睡虎地秦墓竹簡整理小組. *Shui-hu ti Ch'in-mu chu-chien* 睡虎地秦墓竹簡. Peking: Wen-wu ch'u-pan she, 1978.

Ssu-shu 四書. *Ssu-shu chang-chü chi-chu* ed. Peking: Chung-hua shu-chü, 1983. Includes *Lun-yü* 論語, *Meng-tzu* 孟子, *Ta-hsueh* 大學, and *Chung-yung* 中庸, with Chu Hsi's commentary.

Su Ying-hui 蘇瑩輝. "Chung-yang t'u-shu-kuan so-ts'ang Han-chien te hsin-shih-liao" 中央圖書館所藏漢簡的新史料. *Ta-lu tsa-chih* 3, 1 (1951): 23–25.

———. *Tun-huang hsueh kai-yao* 敦煌學概要. Taipei: Chung-hua ts'ung-shu, 1964.

Su Yü 蘇輿. *Ch'un-ch'iu fan-lu i-cheng* 春秋繁露義證. Reprint. Taipei: Ho-Lo t'u-shu ch'u-pan she, 1974.

Suan-ching shih-shu 算經十書. Collated by Tai Chen 戴震. 4 vols. *Wan-yu wen-k'u* ed. Reprint. Taipei: Shang-wu yin-shu kuan, 1964.

Sun Hsiu-shen 孫修身. "Ts'ung 'Chang Ch'ien ch'u-shih Hsi-yü t'u' t'an Fo-chiao te tung-chien" 從張騫出使西域圖談佛教的東漸. *Tun-huang hsueh chi-k'an* 2 (1982): 128–31.

Sun K'ai 孫楷. *Ch'in hui-yao* 秦會要. Rev. ed., with corrections, additions, and supplements by Hsu Fu 徐復. Peking: Chung-hua shu-chü, 1959.

Sun Miao 孫淼. *Hsia-Shang shih kao* 夏商史稿. Peking: Wen-wu, 1987.

Sun-tzu ping-fa 孫子兵法. Ed. Yin-ch'ueh-shan Han-mu chu-chien cheng-li hsiao-tsu. Peking, 1976.

Sun Yü-t'ang 孫毓堂. "Hsi-Han te ping-chih" 西漢的兵制. *Chung-kuo she-hui ching-chi-shih chi-k'an* 5, no. 1 (March 1937): 1–74.

———. "Han-tai te chiao-t'ung" 漢代的交通. *Chung-kuo she-hui ching-chi-shih chi-k'an* 7, no. 1 (1944): 23–40.

Sung Chen-hao 宋鎮豪. *Hsia-Shang she-hui sheng-huo shih* 夏商社會生活史. Peking: She-hui k'o-hsueh, 1994.

Sung Hsu-wu 宋敘五. *Hsi-Han huo-pi shih ch'u-kao* 西漢貨幣史初稿. Hong Kong: Chung-wen ta-hsueh, 1975.

Ta-T'ang Liu-tien 大唐六典. Reprint. Taipei: Wen-hai, 1962.

T'ai Ching-nung 臺靜農. "Liang-Han yueh-wu k'ao" 兩漢樂舞考. *Wen-shih-che hsueh-pao* 1 (1950): 253–308.

Tai Chün-jen 戴君仁. *Mei-yuan lun-hsueh chi* 梅園論學集. 2 vols.. Taipei, 1970–73.

T'an Ch'i-hsiang 譚其驤 et al. *Chung-kuo li-shih ti-t'u chi* 中國歷史地圖集. 8 vols. Shanghai: Ti-t'u ch'u-pan she, 1982.

T'ang Ch'ang-ju 唐長孺. *T'ang-shu ping-chih chien-cheng* 唐書兵志箋正. Peking: Chung-hua, 1962.

T'ang Lan 唐蘭. *Hsi-chou ch'ing-t'ung ch'i min-wen fen-tai shih-cheng* 西周青銅器銘文分代史徵. Peking: Chung-hua, 1986.

T'ang Yung-t'ung 湯用彤. *Han-Wei Liang-Chin Nan-pei Ch'ao fo-chiao shih* 漢魏兩晉南北朝佛教史. 2 vols. Peking, 1955–63.

T'ao Hsi-sheng 陶希聖. *Hsi-Han ching-chi shih* 西漢經濟史. Shanghai, 1934.

———. *Chung-kuo cheng-chih ssu-hsiang shih* 中國政治思想史. 4 vols. Reprint. Taipei, 1954.

———. *Ch'in-Han cheng-chih chih-tu* 秦漢政治制度. Originally by T'ao Hsi-sheng and Tseng Ch'ien 曾謇. Reprint. Taipei: Shang-wu yin-shu kuan, 1964.

T'ao Pao-lien 陶保廉. *Hsin-mao shih-hsing chi* 辛卯侍行記. Reprint. Taipei: Chung-hua ts'ung-shu, 1957. Originally published in 1897.

T'ien Ch'ang-wu 田昌五. *Chung-kuo ku-tai nung-min ko-ming shih* 中國古代農民革命史. Shanghai: Jen-min ch'u-pan she, 1979.

T'ien Shih 天石. "Hsi-Han Tu-liang-heng lueh-shuo" 西漢度量衡略說. *Wen-wu* 12 (1975): 79–89.

Ting Ch'ien 丁謙. *Hsi-yü chuan k'ao-cheng* 西域傳考証. Taipei: I-wen yin-shu kuan, 1972. Reprint of the *Che-chiang t'u-shu kuan ts'ung-shu* ed.

Ting Shan 丁山. *Chia-ku wen so-chien shih-tsu chi-ch'i chih-tu* 甲骨文所見氏族及其制度. Peking: K'o-hsueh, 1956a.

———. *Yin-Shang shih-tsu pang-kuo k'ao* 殷商氏族邦國考. In Ch'en Meng-chia 1956b, part 2, pp. 1–159.

Ting Wen-chiang 丁文江 et al. *Chung-hua Min-kuo hsin ti-t'u* 中華民國新地圖. Shanghai: Shen-pao kuan, 1934.

Ts'ai Hsing-an 蔡興安. "Ch'in-tai chün-hsien shou-ling chih-tu k'ao" 秦代郡縣守令制度考. *Ta-lu tsa-chih* 31, no. 12 (December 1965): 30–33.

Ts'en Chung-mien 岑仲勉. *Liang-Chou wen-shih lun-ts'ung* 兩周文史論叢. Shanghai: Shang-wu, 1958.

———. *Han-shu Hsi-yü chuan ti-li chih chiao-shih* 漢書西域傳地理志校釋. 2 vols. Peking: Chung-hua shu-chü, 1981.

Tseng Tzu-sheng 曾資生 [Tseng Ch'ien 曾騫]. "Ch'in-Han te shui-li kuan-kai yü t'un-t'ien k'en-t'ien" 秦漢的水利灌溉與屯田墾田. *Shih-huo pan-yueh-k'an* 5, no. 5 (March 1937): 26–34.

———. *(Chung-kuo) Ch'in-Han cheng-chih chih-tu shih* 秦漢政治制度史. Reprint. Taipei: Ch'i-yeh, 1969. Originally published in 1942 under the title *Chung-kuo cheng-chih chih-tu shih*, vol. 2; vol. 1: *Hsin-Ch'in cheng-chih chih-tu shih* (先秦).

Tseng Wen-wu 曾問吾. *Chung-kuo ching-ying Hsi-yü shih* 中國經營西域史. Shanghai: Shang-wu yin-shu kuan, 1936.

Tseng Wu-hsiu 曾武秀. "Chung-kuo li-tai ch'ih-tu kai-shu" 中國歷代尺度概述. *Li-shih yen-chiu* 3 (1964): 163–82.

Tseng Yung 曾傭. "Han-tai te t'ieh-chih kung-chü" 漢代的鉄制工具. *Wen-wu* 1 (1959): 16–19.

Tso-chuan 左傳. 1. *Wu-ching tu-pen* ed.; 2. *Shih-san ching chu-shu* ed.; 3. Li Tsung-t'ung, *Chin-chu chin-i* ed. Taipei: Shang-wu; 4. Yang Po-chün, *Ch'un-ch'iu Tso-chuan chu* ed. 4 vols. Peking: Chung-hua, 1980.

Tsou Heng 鄒衡. *Hsia-Shang-Chou k'ao-ku hsueh lun-wen chi* 夏商周考古學論文集. Peking: Wen-wu, 1980.

Ts'ui Shih 崔寔. *Ssu-min yueh-ling* 四民月令. Shih Sheng-han 石聲漢, *chiao-chu* 校注 ed. Peking: Chung-hua, 1965.

Ts'ui Shu 崔述. *Ts'ui Tung-pi i-shu* 崔東壁遺書. Shanghai: Ya-tung t'u-shu kuan, 1936. New ed. Shanghai: Ku-chi, 1983.

Tsun Hsin 遵信. "*Sun Tzu ping-fa* te tso-che ch'i shih-tai" 孫子兵法的作者及其時代. *Wen-wu* 12 (1974): 20–24.

Tu Cheng-sheng 杜正勝. "Ch'eng-pang kuo-chia shih-tai te she-hui chi-ch'u" 城邦國家時代社會基礎. M.A. thesis, National Taiwan University, 1973a.

———. "Shih-lun Hsien-Ch'in shih-tai te Ch'eng T'ang ch'uan-shuo" 試論先秦時代的成湯傳說. *Ta-lu tsa-chih* 47, no. 2 (August 1973b): 1–16.

———. *Chou-tai ch'eng-pang* 周代城邦. Taipei: Lien-ching, 1979. Rev. ed. of his 1973 M.A. thesis.

———. "Ts'ung k'ao-ku tzu-liao lun Chung-yuan kuo-chia te ch'i-yuan chi-ch'i tsao-ch'i te fa-chan" 從考古資料論中原國家的起源及其早期的發展. *Bulletin of the Institute of History and Philology, Academia Sinica* 58, no. 1 (1987).

———. "Chou-li shen-fen te hsiang-cheng" 周禮身份的象徵. In *Chung-yang yen-chiu yuan ti-erh chieh kuo-chi Han-hsueh hui-i lun-wen chi*, 295–306. Taipei, 1989.

———. *Pien-hu ch'i-min: Ch'uan-t'ung cheng-chih she-hui chieh-kou chih hsing-ch'eng* 編戶齊民：傳統政治社會結構之形成. Taipei: Lien-ching, 1990a.

———. "Hsia-tai k'ao-ku chi-ch'i kuo-chia fa-chan te t'an-so" 夏代考古及其國家發展的探索. *K'ao-ku*, no. 1 (1990b): 1–45.

Tu Hsueh-chih 杜學知. "Ku-tai Chung-yuan i-hsiang k'ao" 古代中原役象考. In *Hsien-Ch'in shih yen-chiu lun-chi* 先秦史研究論集, vol. 2, 247–48. Taipei, 1960.

Tu Yu 杜佑. *T'ung-tien* 通典. *Shih-t'ung* ed.

T'u-ching 圖經. *Sha-chou t'u-ching* 沙州圖經. In *Ming-sha shih-shih i-shu* 鳴沙石室遺書, vol. 3. Shanghai: Tung-fang hsueh-hui, n.d.

T'u-ti chih-tu 土地制度. *Chung-kuo li-tai t'u-ti chih-tu wen-t'i t'ao-lun chi* 中國歷代土地制度問題討論集. Ed. Li-shih yen-chiu pien-chi-pu. Peking, 1957.

Tung-Han hui-yao 東漢會要. By Hsu T'ien-lin 徐天麟. Chung-hua shu-chü ed. Shanghai, 1955.

Tung Tso-pin 董作賓. *Yin-li p'u* 殷曆譜. 14 chüan. Li-chuang Nan-hsi: Chung-yang yen-chiu yuan, 1945.

———. *Chia-ku hsueh wu-shih nien* 甲骨學五十年. Taipei: I-wen, 1955.

Tung Yueh 董說. *Ch'i-kuo k'ao* 七國考. Taipei: Shih-chieh shu-chü, 1960.

T'ung-chien 通鑑. *Tzu-chih t'ung-chien* 資治通鑑. By Ssu-ma Kuang 司馬光. Ku-chi ch'u-pan she ed., 6 vols. Shanghai, 1957.

T'ung-chien k'ao-i 通鑑考異. *Tzu-chih t'ung-chien k'ao-i*. By Ssu-ma Kuang. *Ssu-pu ts'ung-k'an* ed.

T'ung Shu-yeh 童書業. "Ts'ung Chung-kuo k'ai-shih yung-t'ieh te shih-tai p'ing Hu Shih p'ai te shih-hsueh fang-fa" 從中國開始用鉄的時代評胡適派的史學方法. *Wen-shih-che* 2 (1955): 30–33.

———. *Ch'un-ch'iu shih* 春秋史. Reprint. Hong Kong: Tai-p'ing shu-chü, 1964. Originally published in 1941.

———. *Ch'un-ch'iu Tso-chuan yen-chiu* 春秋左傳研究. Shanghai: Jen-min, 1980.

Wan Kuo-ting 萬國鼎. *Chung-kuo t'ien-chih shih* 中國田制史. Nanking, 1933.

———. "Ch'in-Han tu-liang-heng mu k'ao" 秦漢度量衡畝考. *Nung-yeh i-ch'an yen-chiu chi-k'an* 2 (1958): 141–55.

Wan Ssu-nien 萬斯年. *T'ang-tai wen-hsien ts'ung-k'ao* 唐代文獻叢考. Trans. Wan-Ssu-nien. Shanghai, 1957.

Wang Chen 王楨. *Nung-shu* 農書. 3 vols. Wan-yu wen-k'u ed. Reprint. Taipei, 1965.

Wang Chia-wu 王家梧. *Ch'in-Han hsiang-t'ing-li chih chih yen-chiu* 秦漢鄉亭里制之研究. Taichung, 1954.

Wang Chuang-hung 王壯弘. *Tseng-pu chiao-pei sui-pi* 增補校碑隨筆. By Fang Jo 方若. Shanghai: Shanghai shu-hua ch'u-pan she, 1981.

Wang Ch'ung 王充. *Lun-heng* 論衡. *Lun-heng chi-chieh* 論衡集解 ed. by Liu P'an-sui 劉盼遂. Shanghai, 1957.

Wang Chung-lo 王仲犖. "Shih-shih T'u-lu-fan ch'u-t'u te chi-chien yu-kuan kuo-so te T'ang-tai wen-shu" 試釋吐魯番出土的幾件有關過所的唐代文書. *Wen-wu* 7 (1975): 35–42.

Wang Chung-shu 王仲殊. "Han-tai wu-chih wen-hua lueh-shuo" 漢代物質文化略說. *K'ao-ku t'ung-hsun* 1 (1956): 57–76.

———. *Han-tai k'ao-ku hsueh kai-shuo* 漢代考古學概述. Peking: Chung-hua, 1984.

Wang Hsien-t'ang 王獻唐. *Shan-tung ku-kuo k'ao* 山東古國考. Chinan: Ch'i-Lu shu-she, 1983.

Wang Kuei-min 王貴民. "Shang kuan-chih chi ch'i li-shih t'e-tien" 商官制及其歷史特點. *Li-shih yen-chiu* 4 (1986): 107–19.

Wang Kuo-wei 王國維. *Wang Chung-ch'ueh-kung i-shu* 王忠慤公遺書. Shanghai, 1927.

———. *Kuan-t'ang chi-lin* 觀堂集林. 4 vols. Peking: Chung-hua shu-chü, 1959.

———. *Wang Kuan-t'ang hsien-sheng Ch'üan-chi* 王觀堂先生全集. 16 vols. Reprint. Taipei: Wen-hua, 1968.

Wang Meng-ou 王夢鷗. "Tu 'chien' chih-i suo-chui" 讀簡志疑瑣綴. *Kuo-li cheng-chih ta-hsueh hsueh-pao* 13 (May 1966): 1–15.

Wang Ming 王明. "Chien yü po" 簡與帛. *K'ao-ku t'ung-tsuan* 2 (March 1955): 55–59.

Wang Ming-che 王明哲 and Wang Ping-hua 王炳華. *Wu-sun yen-chiu* 烏孫研究. Ürümqi: Hsin-chiang jen-min ch'u-pan she, 1983.

Wang Ming-sheng 王鳴盛. *Shih-ch'i-shih shang-chueh* 十七史商榷. 2 vols. Shanghai: Shang-wu yin-shu kuan, 1959.

Wang Nien-sun 王念孫. *Tu-shu tsa-chih* 讀書雜誌. 3 vols. Reprint. Taipei: Kuang-wen shu-chü, 1963.

Wang Ping-hua. *Ssu-ch'ou chih-lu k'ao-ku yen-chiu* 絲綢之路考古研究. Ürümqi: Hsin-chiang jen-min, 1993.

Wang Shu-nan 王樹枏 et al, comp. *Hsin-chiang t'u-chih* 新疆圖志. 6 vols. Reprint. Taipei: Wen-hai ch'u-pan she, 1965. Originally published in 1923.

Wang Ying-lin 王應麟. *Han-chih k'ao* 漢制考. N.p., 1881.

———. *K'un-hsueh chi-wen* 困學紀聞. *Kuo-hsueh chi-pen ts'ung-shu* ed.

Wang Yü-ch'üan 王毓銓. "Han-tai t'ing yü hsiang li pu-t'ung hsing-chih pu-t'ung hsing-cheng hsi-t'ung shuo" 漢代亭與鄉里不同性質不同行政系統說. *Li-shih yen-chiu*, no. 2 (1954): 127–35.

———. *Lai-wu chi* 萊蕪集. Peking: Chung-hua shu-chü, 1983.

Wang Yun-tu 王云度. *Ch'in-shih pien-nien* 秦史編年. Sian: Shensi jen-min, 1986.

Wei Chien-kung 魏建功 et al. "Kuan-yü Chia I *Hsin-shu* chen-wei wen-t'i te t'an-so" 關於賈誼新書真偽問題的探索. In *Pei-ching ta-hsüeh hsueh-pao, jen-wu p'ien*, 3d *chi*, 307–14. Reprint. Nagoya, Japan, 1967. Originally published in 1961.

Wei Hung 衛宏. *Han-chiu-i* 漢舊儀. In *Han-kuan ch'i-chung* ed.

Wen-hsuan 文選. Comp. Hsiao T'ung 蕭統, with commentary by Li Shan 李善 et al. *Wan-yu wen-k'u* ed.

Wen-hua ta-ko-ming ch'i-chien ch'u-t'u wen-wu 文化大革命期間出土文物. Peking, 1972.

Wen Shao-feng 溫少峰 and Yuan T'ing-tung 袁庭棟. *Yin-Hsu pu-tz'u yen-chiu* 殷墟卜辭研究. Chengtu: Ssu-ch'uan sheng she-hui k'o-hsueh yuan, 1983.

Wu Ch'e 吳車. *Tzu-ch'an te ssu-hsiang yü chih-chi chih yen-chiu* 子產的思想與治績之研究. Taipei: Kuo-chang ch'u-pan she, 1979.

Wu Ch'eng-lo 吳承洛. *Chung-kuo tu-liang-heng shih* 中國度量衡史. Reprint. Taipei, 1966.

Wu Ch'ien-fu 吳潛甫. *Feng-ni hui-pien* 封泥匯編. Shanghai: Shanghai shu-tien, 1984.

Wu Chiu-lung 吳九龍. *Yin-ch'üeh-shan Han-chien shih-wen* 銀雀山漢簡釋文. Peking: Wen-wu ch'u-pan she, 1985.

Wu Hui 吳慧. *Sang Hung-yang yen-chiu* 桑弘羊研究. Chinan: Ch'i-Lu shu-she, 1981.

Wu Jung-tseng 吳榮曾. "Han hsing-t'u chuan shih tsa-shih" 漢刑徒磚志雜釋. *K'ao-ku* 3 (1977): 193–96.

Wu Jung-tseng, ed. *Chin-hsin chi: Chang Cheng-lang hsien-sheng pa-shih ch'ing-shou lun-wen chi* 盡心集: 張政烺先生八十慶壽論文集. Peking: Chung-kuo she-hui k'o-hsueh, 1996.

Wu Po-lun 吳伯倫. "Kuan-yü ma-teng wen-t'i chi Wu-wei Han-tai chiu-chang chao-ling mu-chien" 關於馬鐙問題及武威漢代鳩杖詔令木簡. *K'ao-ku*, no. 3 (1961): 163–65.

Yanai Wataru 箭内瓦. *Yuan-ch'ao chih-tu shih* 元朝制度史. Trans. Ch'en Ch'ing-ch'üan 陳清泉 and Ch'en Chieh 陳捷. Reprint. Taipei, 1952.

Yang Chao-ming 楊朝明. "Lu-kuo li-yueh ch'uan-t'ung yen-chiu" 魯國禮樂傳統研究. *Li-shih yen-chiu* 3 (1995).

Yang Chien-hsin 楊建新 and Lu Wei 魯葦. *Ssu-ch'ou chih-lu* 絲綢之路. Lanchou: Jen-min ch'u-pan she, 1981.

Yang Chung-chien 楊鍾健 and Liu Tung-sheng 劉東生. "An-yang Yin-hsu chih p'u-ju tung-wu ch'ün pu-i" 安陽殷墟之哺乳動物群補遺. *Chung-kuo k'ao-ku hsueh-pao* 4 (1949): 145–52.

Yang Hsi-mei 楊希枚. "Lun Han-chien chi ch'i-t'a Han wen-hsien so-chien te hei-jen wen-t'i" 論漢簡及其他漢文獻所見的黑人問題. *Bulletin of the Institute of History and Philology, Academia Sinica* 39 (1969): 309–24.

———. *Hsien-Ch'in wen-hua shih lun-chi* 先秦文化史論集. Peking: She-hui k'o-hsueh ch'u-pan she, 1995.

Yang Hsiang-k'uei 楊向奎. *Hsi-Han ching-hsueh yü cheng-chih* 西漢經學與政治. Chungking: Tu-li, 1945.

———. *Chung-kuo ku-tai she-hui yü ku-tai ssu-hsiang yen-chiu* 中國古代社會與古代思想研究. 2 vols. Shanghai: Shanghai jen-min, 1964.

———. *Yang Hsiang-k'uei hsueh-shu wen-hsuan* 楊向奎學術文選. Peking: Jen-min, 2000.

Yang Hung 楊泓. *Chung-kuo ku ping-ch'i lun-ts'ung* 中國古兵器論叢. Peking: Wen-wu, 1985.

———. *Chung-kuo ku-tai ping-ch'i yü ping-shu* 中國古代兵器與兵書. Peking: Hsin-hua, 1993.

Yang K'an 楊侃. *Liang-Han po-wen* 兩漢博聞. *Ts'ung-shu chi-ch'eng ch'u-pien* ed.

Yang K'uan 楊寬. "Chan-kuo shih-tai te yeh-t'ieh shou-kung yeh" 戰國時代的冶鐵手工業. *Hsin chien-she* 6 (1954): 32–37.

———. "Chan-kuo shih-tai shui-li kung-ch'eng te ch'eng-chiu" 戰國時代水利工程的成就. In *Chung-kuo k'o-hsueh chi-shu fa-ming ho k'o-hsueh chi-shu jen-wu lun-chi*, 99–119. Peking, 1955a.

———. *Chung-kuo li-tai ch'ih-tu k'ao* 中國歷代尺度考. Shanghai, 1955b.

———. *Lun Chung-kuo ku-tai yeh-t'ieh chi-shu te fa-ming ho fa-chan* 論中國古代冶鐵技術的發明和發展. Shanghai: Jen-min ch'u-pan she, 1956.

———. *Ku-shih hsin-t'an* 古史新探. Peking: Chung-hua, 1965.

———. "Lun Ch'in-Han te fen-feng" 論秦漢的分封. *Chung-hua wen-shih lun-ts'ung* 1 (1980): 23–38.

———. *Chan-kuo shih* 戰國史. 3d ed. Shanghai: Shanghai jen-min, 1981.

———. *Hsi-Chou shih* 西周史. Shanghai: Shanghai jen-min, 1999.

Yang Lien 楊鍊, trans. *Hsi-pei ku-ti yen-chiu* 西北古地研究. By Fujita Tōyōhachi. Reprint. Taipei: Shang-wu yin-shu kuan, 1963a.

———. *Chang Ch'ien hsi-cheng k'ao* 張騫西征考. By Kuwabara Jitsuzō. Reprint. Taipei: Shang-wu yin-shu kuan, 1963b.

Yang Lien-sheng 楊聯陞. "Ts'ung *Ssu-min yueh-ling* so-chien Han-tai chia-tsu te sheng-ch'an" 從四民月令所見漢代家族的生產. *Shih-huo pan-yueh k'an* 1, no. 6 (February 1935): 8–11.

———. "Han-tai ting-chung lin-chi mi-su ta-hsiao shih chih-chih" 漢代丁中廩給米粟大小石刻. *Kuo-hsueh chi-k'an* 7, no. 1 (1950): 99–104.

———. "Lun Tung-Chin nan-ch'ao hsien-ling feng-lu te piao-chun" 論東晉南朝縣令俸祿的標準. *Tōyōshi kenkyū* 21, no. 2 (1962): 98–102.

———. *Yang Lien-sheng lun-wen chi* 楊聯陞論文集. Peking: Chung-kuo she-hui k'o-hsueh, 1992.

Yang Shen 楊慎. *Ch'ien-tan hsu-lu* 鉛丹續錄. *Kuo-hsueh chi-pen ts'ung-shu* ed.

Yang Shou-ching 楊守敬. *Li-tai yü-ti t'u* 歷代輿地圖. 42 *ts'e*. Shanghai, 1906–11.

Yang Shu-fan 楊樹藩. "Han-ch'ao hsiang-t'ing chih-tu te yen-chiu" 漢朝鄉亭制度的研究. *Ta-lu tsa-chih* 11, no. 10 (November 1955): 14–17.

Yang Shu-ta 楊樹達. *Han-shu pu-chu pu-cheng* 漢書補注補正. Shanghai: Shang-wu, 1925.

———. *Han-tai hun-sang li-su k'ao* 漢代婚喪禮俗考. Shanghai, 1933.

———. *Han-shu k'uei-kuan* 漢書窺管. Reprint. Taipei: Shih-chieh. 1960. Also included in Yang Shu-ta 1986.

———. *Chi-wei-chü ts'ung-shu* 積微居叢書. 3 vols. Reprint. Taipei: Ta-t'ung shu-chü, 1971.

———. *Yang Shu-ta wen-chi* 楊樹達文集. Shanghai: Shanghai ku-chi, 1986.

Yang Yuan 楊遠. "Hsi-Han te jen-k'ou" 西漢的人口. In *Kuo-shih shih-lun* 國史釋論, 375–88. Taipei: Shih-huo, 1988.

Yao Shun-ch'in 姚舜欽. *Ch'in-Han che-hsueh shih* 秦漢哲學史. Shanghai, 1936.

Yen I-p'ing 嚴一萍. *Yin-Shang shih-chi* 殷商史記. 3 vols. Taipei: I-wen, 1985.

Yen Keng-wang 嚴耕望. *Liang-Han t'ai-shou tz'u-shih piao* 兩漢太守刺史表. Shanghai: 1948.

———. *Ch'in-Han ti-fang hsing-cheng chih-tu* 秦漢地方行政制度. Taipei: Chung-yang yen-chiu yuan, 1961.

———. *T'ang-shih yen-chiu ts'ung-kao* 唐史研究叢稿. Hong Kong: Hsin-ya, 1969.

———. *T'ang-tai chiao-t'ung t'u-k'ao* 唐代交通圖考. Taipei: Chung-yang yen-chiu yuan, 1985.

Yen Tun-chieh 嚴敦傑. "Chü-yen Han-chien suan-shu" 居延漢簡算書. *Chen-li tsa-chih* 1 (1943): 315.

Yen Wen-ju 嚴文儒. "Ho-hsi k'ao-ku chien-pao" 河西考古簡報. *K'ao-ku hsueh-pao* 7, no. 1 (1950): 115–40.

———. "Ho-hsi k'ao-ku tsa-chi" 河西考古雜記. *Wen-wu ts'an-k'ao tzu-liao* 12 (1953): 53–57.

Yin Ta 尹達 et al. *Chi-nien Ku Chieh-kang hsueh-shu lun-wen chi* 紀念顧頡剛學術論文集. Chengtu: Pa-Shu shu-she, 1990.

Ying Shao 應劭. *Feng-su t'ung-i* 風俗通義. 1. Lu Wen-ch'ao 盧文弨 ed. *Ssu-pu pei-yao* (including *I-wen*); 2. Wu Shu-p'ing 吳樹平, *Feng-su t'ung-i chiao-shih* 風俗通義校釋 ed. Tientsin: Jen-min ch'u-pan she, 1980.

———. *Han Kuan-i* 漢官儀. *Han-kuan ch'i-chung* ed.

Yü Hao-liang 于豪亮. "Chü-yen Han-chien chia-pien pu-shih" 居延漢簡甲編補釋. *K'ao-ku*, no. 8 (1961): 451–55.

———. "Chü-yen Han-chien chung te sheng-tsu" 居延漢簡中的省卒. *Wen-wu* 11 (1963a): 44–46.

———. "Chü-yen Han-chien chiao-shih" 居延漢簡校釋. *K'ao-ku*, no. 3 (1963b): 156–58.

———. "Chü-yen Han-chien shih-ts'ung" 居延漢簡釋叢. *Wen-shih* 12 (1981): 39–52.

———. *Yü Hao-liang hsueh-shu wen-ts'ung* 于豪亮學術文叢. Peking: Chung-hua, 1985.

Yü Ho-nien 于鶴年. "Han-tai Hsi-yü hsing-cheng chih-tu yen-ko shu-lueh" 漢代西域行政制度沿革述略 (Chung-shan ta-hsueh). *Wen-shih hsueh yen-chiu so yueh-k'an* 2, no. 5 (February 1934): 157–63.

Yü Hsing-wu 于省吾. *Shuang-chien i chi-chin wen-hsuan* 雙劍誃吉金文選. 2 vols. Preface dated 1932. N.p.

———. "Lueh-lun Hsi-chou chin-wen chung te 'Liu-shih' ho 'Pa-k'u' chi ch'i t'un-t'ien chih" 略論西周金文中的六𠂤和八𠂤及其屯田制. *K'ao-ku*, no. 3 (1964): 152–55.

Yü T'ai-shan 余太山. *Sai-chung shih yen-chiu* 塞種史研究. Peking: Chung-kuo she-hui k'o-hsueh, 1992.

Yü Wei-ch'ao 俞偉超. *Hsien-Ch'in Liang-Han k'ao-ku hsueh lun-chi* 先秦兩漢考古學論集. Peking: Wen-wu, 1985.

Yuan Tsu-liang 袁祖亮. *Chung-kuo ku-tai jen-k'ou shih chuan-t'i yen-chiu* 中國古代人口史專題研究. Chengchow: Chung-chou ku-chi, 1994.

Index

This index is highly selective. It includes only a limited number of key terms, phrases, names, institutions, and major historical events in the text and notes but omits names of persons and terms of no major historical significance as well as names of modern authorities quoted and referenced.

Afghanistan (Ta-Hsia, Bactria), 2 map 1, 4
age and marriage, 207n
age and the military service, 70–73, 196n
amnesties, 133, 193–94n
An-kuei (Lou-lan king), 158
aristocratic rank
   and age, 63–65
   Chou structure, 69
   in Chü-yen, 59, 60, 61, 194–95n
   effect on migration, 69–70
   Han structure, 59–70, 195n
   property qualification, 62
   shih-wu status, 195n

balance between control and communication, 172
black people in China, 48
border
   border expansion and empire, 22
   control policy, 131
branding (*chan, p'iao, ch'ieh*)
   of Emperor Wu-ti, 131
   of oxen, donkeys, horses, 213–14n
calamities
   on Central Plain, 56
   population density and, 56

cart drivers (*chü-fu, chü-tsu, chü-nu*), 212n, plate 3
carts (*chü*), 212n
   in Chü-yen, 144–48
   organization of, 146
   origins of, 145
cattle herders (*mu-shih*), 41–42
   geographical origin of, 42
cavalrymen (*ch'i-shih*)
   in Chü-yen, 34, 73–77, 132
   and military regionalism, 73–78
   regional distribution, 74
   special status, 34, 73–74, 203n
Central Plain region, 53, 56
   population density in, 53–56
chang (fortress), 91–92
Chang Ch'ien (Chang Kien), 4–5
Chang Yen, 137
Ch'ang-an (Han capital), 45, 56, 76, 157, 158, 160
Ch'ang-i *kuo*, change of status and names, 192n
Chang-yeh (Chang-i), 3, 7 map 2, 8, passim
   chün in 111 B.C., 8
Chao Ch'ung-kuo (general), 203n
Chao Kuo, 40–41
Chao P'o-nu (general), 8

293

Ch'ao Ts'o, 18–20
    and Han frontier policy, 18–20
Ch'ao-hsien (Korea), 121, 174
Chavannes, Edward, 38
ch'eng (walls, walled city). See *ch'eng, chang, and sui*
ch'eng, chang, and *sui,* 91–92, 95 fig. 1
    as fortresses of various sizes, 80–81, 103–4
    as headquarters of garrison uints, 80–89
Cheng, Hsuan, 222n
Cheng Chi, 157, 216n
ch'i-shih (horsemen). See cavalrymen
Ch'iang, 4–5, 8, 158, 173
    Han conquest of, 8–9, 203n
    in Ho-hsi, 4–5
    population of, 8
Ch'ien Wen-tzu, xxxiii
Ch'in empire, xxxiii, 130, 176–77
Ch'in from state to empire, xxxiii, 4, 15, 22
    border expansion and forced population removal 639 B.C., 16
    later, 359–223 B.C., 16–17
    after 221 B.C. (to Vietnam, Mongolia), 17–18
    dynasty founded by Ying Cheng (Ch'in Shih huang-ti), xxxiii
Ch'in unification of China (conquest of six warring states: Han, Chao, Wei, Yen, Ch'u, and Ch'i), 16
Chinese in Han times
    height differentials between interior and Ho-hsi, 51
    skin color of, 48, 192n
    stature of adults, 50
Chiu-ch'üan, 3, 8, 9, 13, 57, 137
    dating of (111 B.C.), 13
    development of, 9–13
Chiu-yuan (in modern Suiyuan), 2 map 1, 8
Chou dynasty, 15, 16, 176
Chü-shih (Ku-shih, in modern Turfan area), 158
Chü-yen region
    defined, 183–84n
    developmental stages, from watch stations (*ting-sui*) to chief commandant (*tu-wei*) unit and administrative area (region) to district (*hsien*), 9–13, 23, 29–32
    garrison units in (7 *hou-kuan,* 40 *hou,* 260 *t'ing/sui*), 11

geographic distribution of colonists in, 53–56
geography and area size of, 3, 7 map 2, 80, 82 map 3
Han colonists in, 32–61
Han conquest of, 12–13
height of Han colonists in, 48–51
non-Han peoples in, 47–48
skin color of Han colonists in, 51–53
Chuan (travel document), interpretation of, 137–38
Chung Chün, 209–10n
Chung-yuan. See Central Plain region
civil administration and channels of authority in developing frontier region, 29–33
civilian establishment
    hsiang (county), 31, 33
    hsien (district), 29–31, 33
    li (ward), 31, 33, 89–91
civilians, 33–34
    in Chü-yen, 33–34, 42–48, 113–14, 116–17
    geographic origin of, 53–56
    height of, 48–51
    skin color of, 51–53
    settlements on frontier, 89–91, 102
class, 60, 64, 69
    nan-tzu, 67–68
    shih-wu, 65–68
    See also aristocratic rank
class, society, and the frontier, 59–70
colonists, 32–61
colonization, Han system of, 9–11
    administrative units
        hou (*pu;* subcommandant area), 10, 33
        hou-kuan/hou (commandant area), 10, 33
        sui/t'ing (commander area), 9–10, 25
        tu-wei (chief commandant area), 10, 33
    garrison units
        hou-chang (subcommandant), 10, 24, 27, 33
        hou-kuan/hou (commandant), 10, 24, 27, 33
        sui-chang/t'ing-chang (commander), 9–10, 23–25
        tu-wei (chief commandant), 10, 24, 27, 33
t'un-t'ien organization, *nung tu-wei, t'ien-kuan, chang-kuan, ts'ang-chang,* 28–29

INDEX • 295

command structure of colonial/frontier establishment
  Han system, 26–27
  of Ho-hsi, 1, 6–8, 9, 174
  implications of, 175–76
  model of, 15–16
  pattern of, 9–12
  Shang-Chou practices, 16, 21
  t'un-t'ien system, 8, 28, 147, 175
communication on the frontier, 155 fig. 7, 159 map 4
  cattle, oxen, elephants, horses, 144–53
  within Chü-yen, 154–56
  from Chü-yen to the Western Regions (Hsi-yü), 158–60
  conveyance of message, 160–68
  express post
    li-ma ch'ih-hsing, 164, 219–20n
    wang-jen ch'ih-piao han, ch'ih-piao han, 164
  roadway transport, and communication, 153
  by signals (*feng-huo*), 169–72
  time limits of transmission of correspondence, 165–69
  use of waybill (*p'ai-tan*), 164, 216–18n
construction and structure of the Han settlements in a frontier region, 91–99, plates 1, 2, 3, 11
constructions on the frontiers, 93–99
  in Chü-yen settlements, 91–92
  names of, 93
control
  of border, 130
  of border markets, foreign trade, 130
  changes of with different reigns, 131
  checkpoints, passes, stations, 130–35
  of foreigners, visitors, residents, and immigrants, 130
  of materials of strategic importance, such as weapons, horses, metal, tools, vehicles, livestock, 130
  registration of local population in different classes and forms, 132
  use of passports and travel documents, 131
conveyance of messages, 160–69
convicts (*t'u, ch'ih-hsing*) and slaves, in Chü-yen, 44–45, 56, 134–35, 148, 150

defense policy, 18–20, 21, 61, 130
demographic characteristics of the Han frontier, 123–28
documentary style in bureaucratic operation (Ch'in and Han administrations)
  ch'eng-shu ts'ung-shih hsia tang-yung che, chu-che hsing-shih, shu-tao yen, pieh-shu hsiang-pao, shu-ta ming-pai pu, hsia tang-yung che, 218–19n
  kan yen chih, 187n
Documents on Wood, Bamboo, and Silk (*chien-tu, chien-po*), xxxv–vi, 18
  Chiu-ch'üan documents, xxxvi–viii, 182n, passim
  Chü-yen documents, xxxvi, 181n, passim, plates 5, 6, 7, 8, 10, 11
  Hsuan-ch'üan documents, xxxviii, 182n, plate 5
  Lop-nor documents, xxxvii, 182n, passim
  Ma-wang-tui documents, 205n, 214n
  Ta-t'ung documents, xxxvii, 182n
  Tung-huang documents, xxxvi, 181–82n, passim
  Yin-ch'üeh-shan documents, 182n, 205–6n
  Yin-wan documents, 205–6n, 207n
  Yun-meng document, 214n

economy, of Central Plain, 57
Edsen-gol, 3, 13, 23, 80, 100, 143, 154
elephants in China, 147, 211–12n
Emperor Chao, xxxv, 41, 83, 140
Emperor Ch'eng, 131, 138, 143
Emperor Ching, 75, 131
Emperor Hsuan, xxxv, 71, 76, 84, 119, 131, 176
Emperor Hui, 68
Emperor Kao-ti, 18
Emperor Kuang-wu, xxxv
Emperor Lü, 131
Emperor Wen, 18–20, 131
Emperor Wu-ti, xxxiv
  T'ai-ch'u period, 12
  Yuan-feng period, 23
  See also border: control policy; frontier and frontier system: and empire; frontier and frontier system: under Han Wu-ti; rank holders; social stratification: and Emperor Wu-ti; Ta-yuan Expedition; territorial expansion, of Wu-ti

Emperor Yuan, 62, 139
Empress Lü, 131

family members of servicemen, 42–44
Fan Yeh, 9, passim
  and *Hou-Han shu*, 9
farming house, 96, 98
farming soldiers, 34
farming stations, 96, 98
feng-huo (signals), 169–72
fortresses. *See* watch stations
frontier and frontier system
  ancient origins (Shang, Chou), 16
  Ch'ao Tso's frontier scheme (16 articles), 18–20
  Ch'in system (state and dynasty), 16–18
  civil administrative structure on frontier, 29–33
  and colonization, 22
  control and categories of frontier, 21, 130–31
  education in frontier region, 124–25
  and empire, 21–22, 177
  Han frontier practices, 9, 15–16, 20–21, 23, 41, 119, 130–31
  Han model, 15–16
  under Han Wu-ti, 9, 15–16, 21, 23, 117, 119
  and immigration, 6, 16–17
  religion in frontier region, 125
  t'un-t'ien (military-agricultural colonization) systems on the frontier, 8, 147, 175

garrison settlements, *tu-wei*, *hou-kuan*, *hou*, and *sui* or *t'ing*, 80–89
garrison soldiers, 34–35
garrison system
  common structure of, 27
  distribution of aristocratic rank among garrison personnel, 60
  Han garrison settlements in Chü-yen, 81–86
  horses, oxen, donkeys, elephants, and other animals in Han garrison in Chü-yen, 149–54
  rank and pay scale of personnel, 30
  regional background of personnel, in Chü-yen, 54
  skin color, height, and other physical characteristics of personnel, 48–53, 191–92n
General Huo Ch'u-ping. *See* Huo Ch'ü-ping
General Meng T'ien, 17–18
general pattern of Han colonization, 9–14
granary, 28–29

Han colonial empire, 173–75
  See also colonization, Han system of; frontier and frontier system; immigration
Han dynasty and Han colonial empire
  the Han expansion
    from Ho-hsi (Kansu west of the Yellow River) to Hsi-yü (the Western Regions in Central Asia) including Ta-yuan (Ferghana in eastern Uzbekistan) and K'ang-chü (Sogdiana in central Uzbekistan), xxxiv, 5–14, 174
    to Korea (4 *chün* established), 20, 174
    to Mongolia, xxxiv, 9, 173
    to Vietnam (4 *chün* established), 21, 173
  Liu Ch'e (Wu-ti), the empire builder, xxxiii
  Liu Pang (Kao-ti), the founder of, xxxiii
  under other rulers before Han Wu-ti (Hui, Wen, Ching, Empress Lü), 18–20, 68, 75, 131
Han frontiersmen and colonists, 32–48
Han military, 23–78
  cavalry force, 73–75
  classification of personnel, 27–78
  command structure, 23–27
  strength in Chü-yen, 107–18
Han pattern of frontier control, 130–31
Han society, 60–64, 69, 118–28
  immigration, frontier, colonization, 9–14
  under later emperors (Chao, Hsuan, Yuan, Ch'eng, P'in), 41, 62, 71, 83–84, 131, 138–40, 176
hierarchy of garrison settlements, 80, 99
hired soldiers, 37
ho-ch'in, 18
Ho-hsi
  before 121 B.C., 3–5
  colonization of, 6, 9–14
  end of Hsiung-nu rule, 6, 23
  four *chün*, Wu-wei, Chang-yeh, Chiu-ch'üan, Tun-huang, 8–9, 13–14

INDEX • 297

geography and landscape of, 3–4, 7 map 2
Han acquisition and development of, 5–9
Han immigration into, 6
Hsiung-nu in, 4–5
Kansu (Ho hsi) Corridor, 3
original residents in (Yueh-chih, Wu-sun, Ch'iang), 4–6
Honan, 16, 53, 56, 144
Hopei, 144
horse-breeding, 76–77
horses
    characteristics of, 150
    in Chü-yen, 148–52
    private, 149
    provision for, 151
hou, interpretation of, 81–84, 85, 88–89
    See also *sui*, interpretation of
Hsi-yü (Western Regions), Han conquest and development of, 9
Hsia-hou Sheng, 176
hsiang (county), 80, passim
hsien (district), 11, 80, passim
hsien government, 24, 29–32
Hsin-ch'in chung (region), 6
Hsiu-ch'u city, 12
Hsiu-ch'u king (Hsiung-nu), 5–6
Hsiung-nu, 4, 5, passim
    control of eastern Hsi-yü (Western Regions), 4
    control of Ho-hsi, 4–5
    end of rule in Ho-hsi, 6
    Hsiu-ch'u wang, 5–6
    Hun-yeh Wang, 5–6
    population of, 4
    Yu-hsien Wang, 5
Hsu Shen, 196n
Hunan, 119
Huo Ch'ü-ping, 5–6
    conquest of Hsiung-nu in Ho-hsi, 6
    expedition to Ho-hsi, 5

Ili Valley, 158
immigration
    Ch'in border expansion and, 16–18
    earlier origins, 16, 176
    empire building and, 16, 176–77
    Han, 6, 23–78, 107–28
    legacy, 173–77
Inner Mongolia, 20, 173
interpreters, 157

Jade Gate Pass. See Yü-men *kuan*
Jou-chih. See Yueh-chih
Ju Shun, 65, 76, 137

K'ang-chü (in Uzbekistan), xxxiv, 2 map 1
Kansu, 3, 5, passim
Kansu Corridor. See *under* Ho-hsi.
King-sun Ho (general), 8
ko. See storehouses
k'o-tzu, 45–47
Korea, 20, 174
k'un-mo, title of Wu-sun king, 4
kuo-so, interpretation of, 137–38

La-chiao-mi (Wu-sun king), 4–5
Lebanon, xxxiv
li. See ward
Li Ch'i, 44, 65, 137
Li Tao-yuan, 12
    and *Shui-ching chu*, 12
Lien-sheng Yang, 41
Ling-chü (in Yung-teng, P'ing-fan, Kansu), 6
    and Han westward expansion, 8
link between frontier and empire, 48–78
Liu Ching (Lou Ching). See *ho-ch'in*
Liu Hsi, 137
logistical units. See granary; transportation; treasury
Lop-nor, 2 map 1, 174
Lop-nor (Salt Lake), 11
Lou-lan (in Lop-nor), 174
Lu Po-te (Han general), 23
    in Che-lu Fortress, 23
Lu-chü (in Outer Mongolia), 9
Lun-t'ai, 9, 174
Lung-hsi (*chün*), 6
Lung-le, 9

Mao-mu (Ting-hsin, in Kansu), 11
measures of control on the Chü-yen frontier, 132–43
migration, forced
    Chin practice, 16–18
    Han policy, 18–20
    Shang-Chou practice, 16
    and social change, 69–70
military draft age, 70–73, 196n
    different views on Han, 70–73
    of Emperor Chao's reign, 70–71
military highway, in Chü-yen, 143

military regionalism, of Central Plain, 77–78
Mongolia, xxxiv, 9
mu-shih. See cattle herders
mu-tsu. See hired soldiers

Nan-tou-mi (Wu-sun king), 4
Nan-tzu (commoner), 67–68, 195n
Ninghsia, 3, 5, 20, 41
nomads. See Ch'iang; Hsiung-nu; Wu-sun; Yueh-chih
non-Chinese, 47–48
  See also Ch'iang; Hsiung-nu; Wu-sun; Yueh-chih

offensive strategy, 22
organizational hierarchy, in Chü-yen, 11, 24–32, 80, 99, 103–4
oxen
  characteristics of, 153
  in Chü-yen, 152–53

pa-tsu. See retired servicemen
Pan Ku, 1, 176, passim
passes and control points (*kuan*), 135–37
passports and travel documents (*kuo-so, chuan, fu-chuan*), 52, 137
  forms of, 137–43
  system and use of, 138–42
  See also travel documents
Pei-ti (*chün*), 6
physical characteristics of the Han colonists, height, skin color, 48–53
pi. See t'ing-pu
population
  in Chang-yeh, 121
  in Chü-yen region
    civilian (6,016 persons), 118–22
    density of, 123
    military (4,066 persons), 107–18
    demographic characteristics as seen in Chü-yen documents
      age, 126–27
      age and marriage, 126–27, 207n
      age and draft, 196n
      sex ratio, 126, 206–7n
    density and calamities, 56
    density of, 123
    family size and types, 119–28, 207n
    of a *hsiang* (500–10,000 households), 119–20
  of a *hsien* (200/300–20,000 households), 119
  of a *li* (about 50 households), 121
  national census in 1–2 A.D., 119, 191n
  physical characteristics (height and skin color), 48–53, 192n
  and social stratification, 69
postal system (*chuan, chuan-she, yu, t'ing, chih*)
  in Chü-yen, 160–67
  speed of transmission, 167–69, 170
  See also communication on the frontier: express post; communication on the frontier: use of waybill
protection of individual rights and privacy and property, 172, 222n

rank holders, Wu-ti's expansion of, 61–62, 68, 69, 75
registers
  border, 143
  carts, 147
  garrison personnel, 52, 66
  horses, 149
  oxen, 152
registration
  height and skin color in, 133–35
  civilians, 133–35
  servicemen, 132–33
residents and population in Chü-yen
  civilians, 113–14, 116–17
  economic conditions/agricultural development, 101
  hierarchy, 103–5
  patterns of, 100, 103–5
  servicemen, 108–13, 114–16, 117, 118
retired servicemen, 35–36
roadways, transport and communication, 153–60
  external, 156
  internal, 154–56

Sai (tribes), Sakās, in I-li and Lake Balkhash, 4
Sang Hung-yang (Sang Hung-hsiang), 9
  colonization and *t'un-t'ien* proposal by, 9
security system, and Chü-yen garrison command, 29
servicemen
  age of, 70–71, 72

in Chü-yen, 34–42, 108–13, 114–16, 117, 118
tenure and promotion of, 71
settlement and colonization, 100–105
settlement density, in Chü-yen, 102
settlements in Chü-yen
   civilian, 89–91
   garrison, 80–89, 93–94
sex ratio in Han times, 126–27
   discussion and comparison, 206–7n
Shang (*chün*), 6
Shang dynasty, 15, 16, 22, 176
Shansi, 18
Shantung, 53, 56, 119, 144
Shen Chia-pen, 65
Shen Ch'in-han, 65
sheng-tsu, interpretation of, 38–41
Shensi, 6, 16
Shih huang-ti (Ch'in), 18, 177
shih-wu, interpretation of, 65–68, 195n
shu-kuo (dependent state) system, 191n
shu-tsu. See garrison soldiers
Silk Road, xxxiv, 158–59
   in Ho-hsi, 160, 174
Sinkiang, 1, 3, 4, 20, 157, 173
Six Dynasties period, 174
skin color of Han Chinese, 48, 192n
slaves, in Chü-yen, 43, 44–45
So-fang (*chün*), 6
social stratification
   103 B.C.–A.D. 9, 69
   and Emperor Kao-ti, 59
   and Emperor Wu-ti, 68
socioeconomic characteristics, of Chü-yen settlers, 124–25
soldiers. See cavalrymen; farming soldiers; garrison soldiers; hired soldiers; retired servicemen; servicemen
Sommarström, Bo, 84, 98, 135, 154
Southern and Northern Dynasties period, 91
Ssu-ma Ch'ien, xxxviii, 1, 176, passim
Statute on Arresting, 172, 222n
storehouses (*ti, ko, t'ing-pu, t'ien-ts'ang*), 97–98
   in Chü-yen, 38, 98–99, 154
Su Lin, 137
sui, interpretation of, 84, 86–88
sui, t'ing-sui, watch station. See *sui*, interpretation of
   See also *hou*, interpretation of

systems of transportation and communication, 153–72
Szechwan Basin, 57, 77, 78

Ta-Ch'in (the Roman Empire), xxxiv
Ta-hsia (Bactria), 2 map 1, 4
Ta-yuan Expedition, 12
t'ai-shou (governor), 11, passim
tai-t'ien (field method), 41, 188n
temporary visitors, in Chü-yen, 45–47
territorial expansion, of Emperor Wu-ti, 1, 5, 20, 77, 173, 176
Three Kingdoms period, 137
ti. See storehouses
T'ien-hsia (All under Heaven), 177
T'ien-pei (in Chü-yen), 13, 82 map 3
t'ien-sai. See farming stations
t'ien-she. See farming house
t'ien-ts'ang. See storehouses
t'ien-tsu. See farming soldiers
time, measure and marking of, 220n
t'ing. See watch stations
t'ing-pu. See storehouses
t'ing-pu, residential sections outside a city or within a military garrison unit, in garrison settlements (also called *pi* or *wu-pi*), 11
transportation, and Chü-yen garrison command, 28–29
travel documents (*fu, chuan, fu-chuan, kuo-so*), 208–9n
   See also passports
treasury, and Chü-yen garrison command, 28–29
Tsinghai, 3, 5, 20, 173
Tun-huang (*chün*), 3, 7 map 2, 8, 9–12, passim
Tun-huang (*hsien*), 7 map 2, 9–12
Tun-huang region, developmental stages from border barrier (*sai*) to walled city (*ch'eng*) to *hsien* (district) to *chün* (98 B.C.), 8–12
t'un-t'ien (military-agricultural colonization), 8, 117, 174, 175
   chün-t'un ("land cultivation by troops stationed"), 16, 21
   in Chü-yen, 24, 26–28, 29, 35–36, 174–75
   command structure of *t'un-t'ien* organization, 28, 117–18

t'un-t'ien (*continued*)
   farming houses and farming stations, 96–98
   in Ho-hsi, 8
   min-t'un ("land cultivation by migrant civilians"), 16
Tung Yueh, 65
Tyre (in Lebanon), xxxiv

volunteers as colonists, 43

wall in Chü-yen garrison settlements, 93–94
Wang Kuo-wei, 25, 38
Wang Mang (Hsin dynasty founder), 71
Wang Ming-sheng, 65
Wang Ying-lin, xxxviii
ward (*li*, residential unit), 11
   in Chü-yen, 94–96, 97
   organization and naming of, 89–91
   size of, 200n
watch stations (*sui*, *t'ing-sui*, *t'ing*)
   construction of, 91–92
   formation of, 6, 9, 13
   residents of (*see* Chü-yen region; garrison settlements; residents and population in Chü-yen; settlements in Chü-yen)
   as types of settlements, 80

weapons, plate 9, passim
Wei Ch'ing (Han general), 6
Wei Hung, 44, 65, 67
Western Regions (Hsi-yü), 9
wu, *wu-pi*, *pi* (walls, residences in garrison fortresses), 93–94, 95 fig. 1
Wu-sun, 4–5, 6–7, 158
   in Ho-hsi, 4
   in the I-li Valley, 5–6
   population of, 4
Wu-wei, 3, 8, 12, 13, 14, 47, 57, 133
   chün in 72 B.C., 8
Wu-yuan (*chün*), 2 map 1, 9

Yellow River, 3, 5, 6, 17, 18, 20
Yen Shih-ku, 36, 65
Ying Shao, 41, 89, 118, 121
Yü-lin barrier (*sai*), 9
Yü-men *kuan* (Jade Gate Pass), 2 map 1, 7 map 2, 9
Yü-men tu-wei, organization of (2 *hou-kuan*, 3 *hou*, 15 *sui/t'ing*), 10–11
Yueh-chih, 4–5
   in Central Asia, 4–5
   in Ho-hsi, 4
   Minor (Little) Yueh-chih, 4
   population of, 4
   See also Ta-hsia

About the Author

CHUN-SHU CHANG is Professor of History at the University of Michigan and Honorary Professor of Chinese History, People's Republic of China. He served as Chair of History and Head of the Department of History at the Chinese University of Hong Kong in 1984–85 and lectured in Taiwan as Distinguished Visiting Professor of Chinese History. He is the author of a number of books and monographs in both English and Chinese, including *The God of Soil in Ancient China*, *Studies in Han Frontier History*, *South China in the Twelfth Century*, *The World of Han China in the Han Wooden and Bamboo Documents*, *The Intellectuals and Their Cultural World in Early Modern China*, *Crisis and Transformation in Seventeenth-Century China: Society, Culture, and Modernity* (with Shelley Hsueh-lun Chang), *Redefining History* (with Shelley Hsueh-lun Chang), and *Theatre and State in Seventeenth-Century China*. He also compiled *Premodern China: A Bibliographical Introduction* and *The Making of China: Main Themes in Premodern Chinese History*.